W9-AZS-681

A CENTURY OF
COUNTRY

A CENTURY OF COUNTRY

An Illustrated History
of Country Music

Robert K. Oermann

TV Books

NEW YORK

Copyright © 1999 by Robert K. Oermann
Introduction copyright © 1999 by Chet Flippo

Library of Congress Cataloging-in-Publication Data
Oermann, Robert K.
A century of country : an illustrated history of country music / Robert K. Oermann
p. cm.
Includes index.
ISBN 1-57500-083-0 (hardcover)
1. Country music—history and criticism.   I. Title.
ML3524.O34 1999
781.642'09—dc   2199-33596
CIP

AUTHOR'S NOTE:
Except where indicated in the text, all quotes are from the TNN cable series
"Century of Country" or from the author's interviews. Research for the early
chapters was partially provided by Douglas B. Green. Grateful acknowledgment
also goes to historians Bill C. Malone, Paul Kingsbury, John Lomax III, Barry
McCloud, Ronnie Pugh, and, especially, Bob Pinson and Charles Wolfe.
Dedicated with a century's worth of love to Mary A. Bufwack.

All photographs courtesy of the Robert K. Oermann Collection except those on pages:
15 (Charles Wolfe), 20, 21 (Gene Wiggins), 22 (Bear Family Records), 24 (Miller),
25, 28, 46, 47 (Bailey), 50 (Stone), 59, 60 (Satherley), 64, 70, 71 (Duncan), 99,
124 (Parker), 27 (Owen Bradley), 128, 177, 182, 183 (Walker), 191, 196, and
234 (Street), courtesy of Country Music Hall of Fame; and page 290, courtesy of
Front Page Publicity. Author's portrait, page 320 and back jacket flap, by Kay Williams.

The publisher has made every effort to secure permission to reproduce copyrighted material and would like to apologize should there have been any errors or omissions.

TV Books, L.L.C.
1619 Broadway, Ninth Floor
New York, NY 10019
www.tvbooks.com

Interior design by Tim Shaner, Night and Day Design
Manufactured in the United States of America

Contents

Introduction

by Chet Flippo

In calendar years, Uncle Jimmy Thompson and the Dixie Chicks are about one hundred years apart, but musically, they are very close neighbors. The late storyteller and eccentric fiddler Thompson began playing music around 1860, dividing his time between the Dallas, Texas, area and Nashville, Tennessee, and later galvanized *Grand Ole Opry* audiences in its inaugural days in the late 1920s with his folksiness and musical immediacy; the Dixie Chicks, with their flamboyant, fiddle-based, modern interpretations of the classic country style, burst onto the national country scene in the late 1990s as the standard bearers of contemporary country music at the end of the century.

Uncle Jimmy Thompson was one of the first country music street-corner buskers, playing and passing the hat throughout the South. The Dixie Chicks followed that classic tradition in their early years in Dallas, literally playing on the pavement for listener contributions and later graduating to the Texas State Fair in Dallas before landing on a Nashville music label. Both Uncle Jimmy Thompson and the Dixie Chicks were initially considered a little too strong for supposedly placid country tastes. Each proved to be exactly what the country wanted. The same can be said of countless country performers over the music's colorful history. And each has shown that country music, despite its many commercial spikes, fluctuations, and all-too-human deviations, invariably returns to being just country music—music that, at its perfect core, represents the heart and soul of its listeners.

The first hundred years of country music as a definable art form incorporates influences as diverse as the lingering legacy of the Civil

War and the Dust Bowl, the industrialization and population shifts wrought by two World Wars, and displacements ranging from wars and a workforce emigration north to Detroit and Chicago to the disappearance of the family farm and the malling of the South. The music both defines and reflects a culture, spanning the panorama of the last century. Country songs have lingering lavender-suffused melancholy overtones from the Anglo-Celtic immigrants to the American South, who settled especially in the Appalachian Mountains.

That exquisitely homesick music of lamentation and celebration—early-on dubbed "hillbilly"—combined with the South's blues and gospel traditions, and to some extent the traditions of Louisiana's Cajun music, the Southwest's rich Mexican music, the West's cowboy trail tales and songs, and the jazz heritage that informed Western Swing music, to form a rich and ever-changing music that exists under the umbrella shelter of country music.

As country historian Robert K. Oermann recounts in these pages, country music's sagas and stories have paralleled the country's own emerging mass culture. The music began as an immediate, tribal, live presentation, first for family and friends and then for a slowly enlarging outer shell of curious onlookers. Live shows slowly gave way to more organized, live barn dances and concerts. The emergence of radio in the 1920s suddenly catapulted country's appeal far beyond its previously small circumference of the live audience into homes across the country. As sheet music slowly gave way to the phonograph record, country's most immediate performers became music stars. The barn dances, thanks to powerful clear-channel radio stations such as Nashville's WSM and Chicago's WLS, became coast-to-coast musical and cultural influences. Barnstorming musical shows growing out of those barn dances replaced local talent shows with an organized national circuit of live country shows. As radio stations multiplied, country music became a staple of the form, and as of the end of the twentieth century was represented by more full-time stations—just under twenty-five hundred—than those of any other musical or talk format. Country was quickly adopted by music purchasers, whether of sheet music or of recorded cylinders or later of 78rpms, 45rpms, LPs, 8-track tapes, cassettes, and CDs. Both the Carter Family and Jimmie Rodgers sold millions of recordings early on. A wartime song such as Elton Britt's "There's A Star-Spangled Banner Waving Somewhere" could sell three-million-plus copies of recordings and sheet music in 1942. Today, Garth Brooks is the best-selling solo recording artist of all time.

Country rapidly adapted to the television in the infancy of the new medium, as it did later to specialized cable and video outlets, and to movies as well. It traveled into space with the astronauts; now, it's entrenched on the Internet and will obviously attach itself to whatever means of cultural transference will emerge in the future, in this or any other universe.

Country's history is ever-fascinating. Its main wellsprings continue today, in constantly varying degrees. The official birth of country music goes back to the famous field recordings in Bristol, Virginia, in 1927, with The Carter Family and Jimmie Rodgers. The former perfectly captured the Americanization of the Scottish-Irish ballads that had immigrated to the United States. Rodgers eloquently melded the blues and folk music and early jazz into a free-wheeling form of country music that influenced modern cowboy songs as well as honky-tonk music.

Country both gave rise to and was declared dead because of rock 'n' roll: Elvis Presley and any number of aspiring rockabilly and rocking-country artists in his wake were born of country's dedication to roots music and its inherent love of free-form music. When country's children formed rock 'n' roll and tried to kill their parent, the resilient parent country music turned to a smooth country pop that it would later renounce in favor of the honky-tonk influence that never quite goes away. In many ways, country is an ever-fascinating Ferris wheel of styles and performers that never seem to change and yet always do change.

What country music has always done best is be the barometer—for better or for worse—of its attendant culture. That it continues to do, for better or for worse, and—one is certain—it always will.

One

The Century Begins

On April 23, 1900, the *New York Journal* offered what is believed to be the first use of the word "hillbilly" in print.

The word would come to define a new branch of the music business. It would be embraced as a description of a style, then rejected as an insult, then embraced again as America rounded the corner of another century.

The *New York Journal* described the people who were frolicking to square-dance tunes and singing folk songs in these terms: "A Hill-Billie is a free and untrammeled white citizen of Alabama, who lives in the hills, has no means to speak of, dresses as he can, talks as he pleases, drinks whiskey when he gets it, and fires off his revolver as the fancy takes him."

That 1900 stereotype would linger throughout the century to come. And yet the hillbilly and his music would rise to become one of the most durable and significant elements in American popular culture.

The term "country music" wasn't in the vocabulary in 1900, but the music itself certainly was. In fact, it is as old as the nation. Thomas Jefferson and Davy Crockett were both country fiddlers. Confederate soldiers took their fiddles to campgrounds and were often photographed with them.

11

LEFT: *In 1900 the banjo was in vogue as a ladies' parlor instrument.*
ABOVE: *College music clubs also popularized the banjo.*

Bob Taylor

In the 1880s Tennessee voters were courted by brothers Bob and Alf Taylor. Both were accomplished fiddlers, and they staged musical contests at campaign stops as they vied to be elected governor. In 1899 Bob wrote a public letter in defense of his fiddling. Addressed "To the Fiddlers," it read, "Politicians sneered at me as a fiddler, but the girls said it was no harm, and the boys voted while I fiddled, and the fiddle won." When he began publishing *Bob Taylor's Magazine* in Nashville in 1904, he pictured a fiddle on its cover and included country songs in a series of reminiscences titled "The Fiddle and the Bow."

By the early 1890s Knoxville, Tennessee, was having fiddle contests at its annual Labor Day festivities that drew contestants from the nearby Appalachian Mountains. In Texas, future hillbilly recording pioneer Eck Robertson became a professional musician in 1903; and in 1907 he triumphed over eighty-six other performers at an eight-day fiddling contest in Dallas. Atlanta was the site of a particularly important annual fiddling contest. It hosted one as early as 1885, and by the early years of the twentieth century these annual events were being publicized by newspaper reporters fascinated by the rowdy, colorful old-time geezers who competed and by the thousands of shouting, stomping fans who attended. A Fourth of July fiddle contest in 1912 in nearby Lawrenceville, Georgia, drew a reported six thousand fans. Future hill-

billy stars Gid Tanner and Fate Norris both competed. Many southern communities offered similar amusements, often in conjunction with Confederate-soldier reunions.

In 1909 folklorist Louise Rand Bascom described a small Appalachian fiddle contest in the pages of the *Journal of American Folklore.* "The convention is essentially an affair of the people, and is usually held in a stuffy little schoolhouse…with a rude, temporary stage," she wrote. "On this, the fifteen fiddlers and 'follerers of banjo pickin' sit, their coats and hats hung conveniently above their heads…until…each contestant has finished his allotted three pieces.

"To one unused to mountain tunes, the business of selecting the best players would not be unlike telling which snail had eaten the rhododendron leaf, for execution and technique differ little with the individual performer, and the tune, no matter what it may be called, always sounds the same.… The tunes are played at all the dances, whistled and sung by men and boys everywhere. The mountaineer who cannot draw music from the violin, the banjo, or the 'French harp' [harmonica] is probably non-existent."

By 1900, all of the fiddlers who became country's pioneering recording artists were reaching maturity. Uncle Jimmy Thompson (born 1848), Eck Robertson (1887), Fiddlin' John Carson (1868), Blind Joe Mangrum (1853), Fiddlin' Powers (1870), Uncle Am Stuart (1856), and their peers were all active as hillbilly musicians by the turn of the century.

They were "stars" long before there was such a thing as commercial country music, for the fiddle was unquestionably the dominant instrument in rural culture in 1900.

Country's other corner-stone instruments were all coming into vogue as the century began. The banjo came to America with African slaves and was initially popularized in minstrel shows of the 1840s. By the 1890s it had been elevated to parlor-instrument status. Banjo clubs were all the rage on college campuses in 1900, as were similar societies popularizing the Italian mandolin.

The steel guitar created a sensation when it was brought to the mainland by touring Hawaiian musicians. Frank Ferrara and Joseph Kekuku popularized it on national tours in 1902 and 1904, respectively, and the instrument's emotional, sliding-steel tones fired the imaginations of rural musicians everywhere.

What would come to be known as "country music" was also onstage by this time. Powder River Jack and Kitty Lee, for instance, were cowboy singers with Buffalo Bill's Wild West Show from 1895 on. By 1900 they were spreading the lyrics to "Red River Valley" throughout the United States. The Oklahoma oil boom of 1903 was the backdrop for country singers George Hall and Margaret Lillie, who raked in thousands of dollars entertaining the roughnecks. Missouri's Leon "Abner" Weaver liked to bill himself as

"vaudeville's first rube," for he began treading the boards as a musical hayseed in 1902. In addition to playing mandolin, guitar, and fiddle, he claimed to have invented the musical saw.

In 1910 Marion Try Slaughter II packed up his possessions and moved with his wife and two children from Dallas to New York City. He was in search of a career in music and would find it in years to come as "Vernon Dalhart." In 1912, blind singer Riley Puckett became a street singer in Atlanta. He, too, would become one of country's greatest early artists. Laid off by a strike at the Fulton Bag and Cotton Mill, Fiddlin' John Carson turned to full-time music making in Atlanta in 1913. The following year he won the Atlanta fiddlers contest and was written up in *Musical America* magazine. Ten-year-old Bob Wills played his first square dance in 1915.

While country's future recording artists were evolving, so was their song repertoire.

On April 29, 1900, a thirty-six-year-old engineer from Jackson, Tennessee, was at the throttle of the Cannonball Express as it sped through Mississippi in the dead of night. A stalled train appeared around a bend. He shouted for his fireman to jump for safety, stayed at his post, and managed to slow his train enough to save his passengers in the crash that took his life. He was immortalized by the song "Casey Jones."

On September 27, 1903, the Southern Railroad's Fast Mail Express from

ABOVE: *The fiddlers of Ireland contributed their tunes to the early country-music repertoire.*

Washington to Atlanta was running behind schedule. Racing at top speed through the mountains of Virginia, the locomotive hit the curve on the high trestle near Danville and plunged into the ravine below, inspiring the song "The Wreck of the Old 97."

In the wee hours of the night on April 14, 1912, on her maiden voyage, the *Titanic* struck an iceberg in the North Atlantic. More than fifteen hundred lost their lives. This event, too, spawned the creation of a country classic, "The Sinking of the Titanic."

Tin Pan Alley's songwriters were creating many other songs that would become hillbilly-music staples in the decades to come. Between 1900 and 1915 came such country chestnuts as "In the Sweet Bye and Bye," "Red Wing," "Daisies Won't Tell," "When the Bees Are in the Hive," "Bake Dat Chicken Pie," "Bill Bailey," "Are You from Dixie," "Alabama Jubilee," and "Will the Circle Be Unbroken."

Pop songs of an even earlier vintage were already in the hands of the string bands, songsters, and comics who would comprise country's first generation of stars. "The Little Old Log Cabin in the Lane" (1871), "Listen to the Mockingbird" (1855), "Wildwood Flower" (1860 as "I'll Twine Mid the Ringlets"), "Mollie Darling" (1871), "In the Baggage Coach Ahead" (1895), "Old Dan Tucker" (1843), "Buffalo Gals" (1844), "Arkansas Traveler" (1851), "Maple on the Hill" (1880), "Lightning Express" (1898), and dozens of other country standards have nineteenth-century show-biz roots.

Another sizable part of the early country repertoire came from gospel songbooks that were distributed throughout the land by traveling "singing school" teachers. Around the turn of the century they were teaching the rudiments of reading music and singing harmony to thousands of rural dwellers. Singing evangelist Ira Sankey, for instance, had sold a reputed fifty million gospel songbooks by the time of his death in 1908. He and his peers left behind such enduring titles as "When the Roll Is Called up Yonder," "Leaning on the Everlasting Arms," "Life's Railway to Heaven," and "Amazing Grace."

The rustic folks who were singing such "golden oldies" were gradually coming to the notice of the media. In 1900 the *Journal of American Folklore* published the first article ever written about mountaineers and their songs. Emma Bell Miles waded in deeper in her *Harper's Monthly* article of 1904. Titled "Some Real American Music," this was probably the first appreciation of Appalachian music ever published in a popular magazine.

"Here among the mountains of Kentucky, Tennessee and the Carolinas, is a people of whose inner nature and its musical expression almost nothing has been said," wrote Miles. "The music of the Southern mountaineer is not only peculiar, but, like himself, peculiarly American.

"Nearly all mountaineers are singers. Their untrained voices are of good timbre, the women's being sweet and high and tremulous, and their sense of pitch and tone and rhythm remarkably true. The fiddler and the banjo player are well treated and beloved among them, like the minstrels of feudal days.

15

"Surely this is folk-song of the highest order. May it not one day give birth to a music that shall take a high place among the world's great schools of expression?" Indeed it did.

As a result of folklorists' interest from 1905 to 1920, such gems of Americana as "Barbara Allen," "Tom Dooley," "Black Jack Davey," "Silver Dagger," "Frankie and Johnny," and "On Top of Old Smoky" were collected and preserved. At this same time, westerners were beginning to catalog the rich musical heritage of the cowboy. Doubtless fueled by the enormously popular Wild West shows, songs such as "Streets of Laredo," "Clementine," "Sweet Betsy from Pike," "The Colorado Trail," "Bury Me Not on the Lone Prairie," "The Yellow Rose of Texas," "Git Along, Little Dogies," "The Old Chisholm Trail," "Home on the Range," and "Shenandoah" were published and popularized. Tin Pan Alley responded with a flood of cowboy and western-themed titles of its own in 1905–19.

At the turn of the twentieth century, songs were being spread farther and faster than ever before. A hit sheet-music title would sell in the millions in those days. In 1910 a staggering two billion copies of sheet music were sold. Three years later, *Billboard* inaugurated its first music popularity charts, ranking the best-selling sheet-music titles. And with the dawn of the new century, songs were also getting to the mass audience's ears via recordings.

In 1900 the most popular home entertainment phenomenon was the phonograph. Thomas Edison had invented the phonograph in 1877, but it was initially perceived as

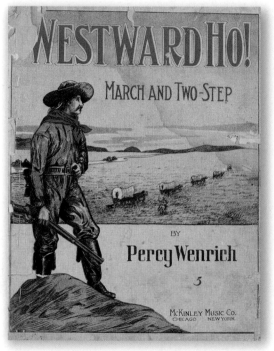

an office machine. Columbia Records didn't print the first catalog offering musical selections on disc until 1891. The foil and wax cylinders of the early days of recording technology had been replaced by 78-rpm flat discs by the turn of the century. After the 1895 recession, prices for wind-up Victrolas dropped so that everyday citizens could afford them. As the record player left the penny arcade and invaded living rooms, record companies were beginning to realize that the opera singers, marching bands, and classical ensembles they had been marketing to the wealthy should be supplemented by vaudevillians and other vernacular stylists. By 1905 three-quarters of the Victor label's offerings were discs by popular musicians rather than classical ones.

Significantly, 1900 was the year that Victor adopted one of the most famous logos in marketing history. A French artist, Francois Barraud, painted the little dog Nipper listening to a gramophone and titled the result *His Master's Voice*. Record executive Emile Berliner bought the painting from a gallery, and on July 10, 1900, he registered both the painting and the slogan as a trademark in the U.S. Patent Office. Nipper and the gramophone have been on Victor and RCA discs ever since.

As the popularity of records increased, labels recorded increasingly diverse stylists. Whistlers, barbershop quartets, spiritual singers, Hawaiian acts, preachers, and storytellers were all put on disc. So were the precursors of country music.

From 1904 to 1912 Cal Stewart, Billy Golden, Len Spencer, Ada Jones, and Billy Murray

ABOVE: *Tin Pan Alley became fascinated with Western themes during the teens.*
RIGHT: *"My Pony Boy" was enormously popular as a commercial cowboy tune in 1909.*

MY PONY BOY

SONG

Giddy Up Giddy Up Giddy Up Whoa

LYRIC BY
BOBBIE HEATH **CHARLIE O'DONNELL**

MUSIC BY

As Sung by Miss LILLIAN LORRAINE
in F. ZIEGFELD Jr's Latest Triumph
ANNA HELD
IN
"MISS INNOCENCE"

JEROME H. REMICK & CO. NEW YORK DETROIT

Will Rogers

recorded as musical bumpkin/rube characters. A few classical violinists recorded fiddle tunes. Ethnic dialect records became popular. Columbia, the first record company to specialize in low-brow music, featured a version of "Arkansas Traveler" in its 1901 catalog, describing the recording as "a native sitting in front of his hut scraping his fiddle, and answering the interruptions of the stranger with witty sallies." Victor's 1903 catalog offered "The Little Old Log Cabin in the Lane" and "Turkey in de Straw," both of which would become hillbilly standards.

By 1913 Columbia was advertising "barn dances" as a category of records for sale. Vernon Dalhart's disc debut occurred in 1916–17 with "Can't Yo' Heah Me Callin', Caroline" and "Just a Word of Sympathy." During the same period Charles Ross Taggart had a series of popular discs as "The Old Country Fiddler."

In 1900 there were approximately 150 medicine shows touring rural America, providing proving grounds for dozens of future hillbilly stars.

In 1915 former Wild West show cowboy Will Rogers (1879–1935) created a sensation on Broadway in the *Ziegfield Follies*. He then shot to fame as America's "poet lariat." Rogers toured as a humorist onstage, wrote wry newspaper columns as the voice of country people, became a movie star, and triumphed on radio when that medium came into existence in the '20s. In 1914 the hillbilly act The Weaver Brothers and Elviry debuted in vaudeville. Another Broadway event of note in these precountry days was the 1904 production of *The Virginian*, complete with singing cowboys. This was the entertainment climate when country music's pioneer

artists were first drawing breath. Ralph Peer was born in 1892, Jimmie Rodgers in 1897, Sara Carter in 1899, Jimmie Davis in 1899, Roy Acuff in 1903, Bob Wills in 1905, Gene Autry in 1907, Maybelle Carter in 1909, Red Foley in 1910, Bill Monroe and Roy Rogers in 1911, Minnie Pearl in 1912, Grandpa Jones in 1913, Hank Snow in 1914, Owen Bradley in 1915, Eddy Arnold in 1918, and Kitty Wells in 1919. And such figures as Uncle Dave Macon (1870), Vernon Dalhart (1883), and A.P. Carter (1891) were already making music themselves.

Disc sales soared as the nation emerged from World War I. That all of these humbly born talents found a worldwide audience was due to the marketing of a new genre of music by the record companies. The labels had stumbled upon the blues music market in 1920 when vaudeville belter Sophie Tucker failed to show up for a recording session and Mamie Smith stepped up to the microphone instead. The birth of the country industry was similarly "accidental."

Eck Robertson (1887–1975) was a brash thirty-five-year-old fiddler when he marched into the Victor Records office in New York in June 1922. With him was Henry Gilliland, seventy-four, a Civil War veteran who played second fiddle to Robertson. The two Texans had been performing at a Confederate Veterans Reunion in Richmond, Virginia, turning the lobby of the Jefferson Hotel into a "barn dance," as a newspaper reported. When they presented themselves for a Victor audition, Robertson's cowboy outfit and forthright manner impressed the record executives.

A 1924 Victor catalog blurb described the scene like this: "When we first saw these two artists, it

ABOVE AND RIGHT: *Souvenir plates and commemorative joke books suggest the superstardom of Will Rogers, who was featured on radio, in newspapers, in films, and on stage as a country humorist.*

OVER 1,000 JOKES

10,000 LAUGHS

WILL ROGERS

Greatest Exponent of Simple Homely Truths-That Will Endure Forever

JOKES

WIT

WISDOM

RADIO

SCREEN

STAGE

World Beloved Humorist and Philosopher

PRICE—PAY WHAT YOU PLEASE

Eck

John Carson

was at our own Victor door in the garb of Western plainsmen. They told us they could play the fiddle and asked for a hearing. As we knew several thousand persons who could play the fiddle, more or less, we were not especially impressed, but we asked them to begin. After the second number or so, we engaged them to make records of the old American country dances."

Robertson's own account of that day is in the pages of Charles Wolfe's book *The Devil's Box*: "You couldn't fool that man that was running the shop...in the Victor office....He just come into the room just in a hurry with a long piece of paper with names on it. He done that on purpose, you see. Thought he'd get rid of me just like he had all the rest of them. He said, 'Young man, get your fiddle out and start with a tune....I can tell right quick whether I can use you or not.' Well, I just said right back to him, just as honest as I could, 'Mister, I've come a long way to get an audition with you. Maybe I better wait and come back some other time.'...I didn't get to play half of 'Sallie Gooden'; he just threw up his hands and stopped me. Said, 'By Ned, that's fine! Come back in the morning at nine o'clock and we'll make a test record.'"

On September 1, 1922, Victor issued "Sallie Gooden"/"Arkansas Traveler" as Robertson's disc debut. The first "Hill-Billie" was officially on records.

"You will notice their fine, instinctive timing," instructed the Victor catalog, "and, if you are a musician, the difference in the quality of their tone from a concert violinist....They are played in the traditional fashion of the American country fiddler, without accompaniment."

All kinds of musical experimentation was occurring when the country-music industry was being born. Country was just one of many styles that were introduced. The 1920–1935 era also saw the emergence of blues, jazz, torch singing, crooning, and early swing. It was the period when the Hollywood musical flowered. It was the time of the Harlem Renaissance and of all-black shows

coming to Broadway for the first time. The first folk festivals were staged.

We think of this era as the Jazz Age. America was leaving its rural past behind and coming out of World War I rushing headlong into modernity. In 1920 we had our first commercial airline service and first telephone dial service. Women got the right to vote in 1920. The eight-hour workday

came in at U.S. Steel (1922) and Ford (1926). There were 14,500 movie theaters in the country by 1925. Tennessee banned "flappers" from public schools in 1923 unless they rolled their hosiery above their knees.

As a reaction to this environment, there was a powerful nostalgia for the old-fashioned rural life and a widespread resistance to modernism. Prohibition went into effect in 1920. In 1923 roughly forty thousand

21

Robertson

Riley

Henry Whitter

Ku Klux Klan members marched on Washington, D.C. In Nashville, the Agrarians emerged as a literary movement. Their "I'll Take My Stand" manifesto stated that they preferred to stand for southern culture, rather than mass culture. When industrialist Henry Ford sponsored fiddle contests in the mid-1920s, thousands attended.

The record business was booming like never before. In 1920 Sears marketed a phonograph player for $115, and within a few short years prices were half that. In 1921 record sales soared to $105.6 million. *Billboard* magazine reflected the disc's new importance by inaugurating record popularity charts in 1922. The jukebox came on the scene in 1927. The popularization of records went hand in hand with the recording of increasingly vernacular music, including hillbilly tunes.

The biggest star of prewar recordings, opera tenor Enrico Caruso, died in 1921. The record industry introduced scores of less refined celebrities to take his place. Paul Whiteman, "The King of Jazz," debuted in 1920. Al Jolson, Gene Austin, Fanny Brice, and Eddie Cantor all scored massive hits in 1921–26. Bessie Smith's "Downhearted Blues" sold a reported two million copies in 1923. Louis Armstrong and Duke Ellington made their disc debuts in 1925. Rudy Vallee arrived in 1929. Bing Crosby and Kate Smith, "The Songbird of the South," first topped the charts in 1931.

Little by little, country music was finding its niche in this exciting cultural era. In 1921, Uncle Dave Macon, age fifty-one, put on his first show. "The Methodist Church needed a new door," he later recalled. "I gave a show, then passed the hat and collected the money, seventeen dollars." In 1922, Gene Autry, age fifteen, began singing for fifty cents a night in a Tioga, Texas, club, and

then hit the road with The Fields Brothers Marvelous Medicine Show. "I earned fifteen dollars a week," he recalled in his autobiography. "For a teen-aged boy in the 1920s, this was more than money. It was the riches of Arabia." Nashville fiddler Uncle Jimmy Thompson outfitted his Model-T truck with a camper on the back and began driving around to Tennessee communities to put on shows in 1922. Down in Alabama, future Delmore Brothers star Alton Delmore wrote his first song.

That was the same year that hillbilly music hit the infant radio airwaves for the first time—in Dallas, WFAA began to broadcast fiddlers; in Kansas City, WDAF put Carson Robison on the air; in Atlanta, WSB aired Fiddlin' John Carson and Blind Andy Jenkins. Gennett Records entered the infant hillbilly recording field in 1922 by issuing some fiddle performances.

In Atlanta, furniture dealer Polk Brockman sensed that there was money to be made from the city's phenomenally successful annual fiddle contests. Brockman was selling phonographs in one of his stores, as well as records to play on them. On a business trip to New York he saw a newsreel of a Virginia fiddling contest and recalled how popular his hometown's Fiddlin' John Carson was. He badgered a reluctant Ralph Peer into recording Carson for OKeh Records. Although Peer pronounced the music "pluperfect awful," the initial pressings sold out. So Peer recorded Carson some more.

John Carson (1868–1949), whose colorful life is chronicled in the book *Fiddlin' Georgia Crazy*, became country music's first recording "star." His initial record, "Little Old Log Cabin in the Lane" backed with "The Old Hen Cackled and the Rooster's Going to Crow," was issued in the summer of 1923. Carson sold copies

23

Puckett

LEFT: *Blind singer Riley Puckett recorded some of the most charming vocal hillbilly discs of the 1920s.*
ABOVE: *Henry Whitter's success led record companies to expand their country-music activities.*

at the Atlanta fiddlers' contest that year and created country's first "hit." Its success led OKeh Records to enter the hillbilly recording field whole hog. Earlier that year, Virginia millhand Henry Whitter (1892–1941) had made a pilgrimage to OKeh's New York studios. Impressed by Carson's sales, Peer issued Whitter's "Wreck on the Southern Old 97." It sold, but the disc phenomenon of 1923 was Wendell Hall's hayseed tune "It Ain't Gonna Rain No Mo'," which sold two million copies for Victor Records and took the nation by storm.

Somewhat to the surprise of New York's record executives, the "novelty" of recording folk songs and old-time fiddle tunes was a runaway success. Enthused by the successful 1923 sales of Carson and Whitter, the next year Peer recorded Blind Andrew Jenkins, Land Norris, Bascom Lamar Lunsford, Al Hopkins, and others.

Jealous of OKeh's success with Fiddlin' John Carson, Columbia Records went to Atlanta to find its own fiddle star. It found him in Gid Tanner (1885–1960) and got his hugely popular Skillet Lickers band in the bargain. The hard-drinking band's "Down Yonder" would become one of the biggest-selling tunes of the era. "Bully of the Town"/"Pass around the Bottle and We'll All Take a Drink" sold two hundred thousand copies for The Skillet Lickers in 1926; and 1927's playlet "A Corn Licker Still in Georgia" sold more than 250,000 and spawned thirteen sequels.

"The fiddle and guitar craze is sweeping northward!" proclaimed a Columbia ad in *Talking Machine World* in June 1924. Skillet Lickers member Riley Puckett (1894–1946) recorded "Sleep Baby Sleep" as the first recorded yodel; and Emmett Miller (1900–1962), whose "Lovesick Blues" would make a star of Hank Williams, also made his disc debut in 1924. So did Uncle Dave

Macon. Ernest Thompson's "Little Rosewood Casket," the Fiddlin' Powers Family's "Old Joe Clark," and Charlie Poole's "Don't Let Your Deal Go Down" were other country successes of 1924–25. In Chicago, the infant WLS radio station launched a live Saturday-night hoedown broadcast in 1924 that would serve as the template for dozens of such programs for decades to come. Dubbed *The National Barn Dance,* it became country music's first coast-to-coast showcase. Union Grove, North Carolina, launched the

most famous and enduring of all fiddle contests in that same year.

Texas-bred tenor Vernon Dalhart (1883–1948) eyed this emerging hillbilly fad and recorded Whitter's "Wreck of the Old 97" for Edison Records. When he went to Victor to do the same, the firm was issuing two-sided discs and asked for a second performance. Dalhart sang "The Prisoner's Song" and created a multimillion-selling 1924 phenomenon. The record's sales have been estimated at twenty million copies; "The Prisoner's Song" was so pervasive a hit that it was sung by street urchins in Humphrey Bogart's 1937 film classic of New York slum life, *Dead End.*

Dalhart would go on to immortalize "The Letter Edged in Black," "Little Rosewood Casket," the topical "Lindbergh (The Eagle of the U.S.A.)," the 1925 event ballad "The Death of Floyd Collins," and dozens of other titles. Whitter, the man whose song launched Dalhart's career, was destined for comparative obscurity.

TOP: *Vernon Dalhart, shown here with collaborator Carson Robison, recorded country's first million-seller.*
ABOVE: *Emmett Miller originated "Lovesick Blues."*
RIGHT: *Carl T. Sprague became the first singing-cowboy star.*

Emmett

Miller

Ernest "Pop" Stoneman

Down in West Virginia, carpenter Ernest V. "Pop" Stoneman (1893–1968) heard Henry Whitter's record, too. He told his wife he could do better. She suggested that he prove it, so he bought a train ticket to New York and knocked on Ralph Peer's OKeh Records door. Stoneman's 1925 recording of "The Titanic" became a smash hit and launched a career that would take him through five decades of country-music history.

In pursuit of the market uncovered by Victor and OKeh, other labels recorded Samantha Bumgarner, Carson Robison, Kelly Harrell, The Leake County Revelers, The Carolina Tar Heels, The East Texas Serenaders, and other pioneers. Dr. Humphrey Bate became Nashville's first country radio performer when he broadcast over WDAD in 1925. Later that year, on November 28, Uncle Jimmy Thompson went on the air on WSM, inaugurating a Saturday-night Nashville tradition that became known as *The Grand Ole Opry*.

Ranch hand Carl T. Sprague (1895–1979) noted the recording success of fellow Texan Vernon Dalhart and approached Victor for an audition. Among the ten tunes he recorded for the company in 1925 was "When the Work's All Done This Fall." It sold an amazing nine hundred thousand copies. As the first successful singing cowboy, Sprague founded an entire country-music genre.

OKeh recorded the first Cajun record, sung by New Orleans amateur Dr. James F. Roach. That 1925 event gave birth to another of country's vibrant substyles.

Influenced by the boom in fiddle music, poet Stephen Vincent Benet published "The Mountain Whippoorwill" in 1925. This tale of a showdown between a boy fiddler and a champion inspired Charlie Daniels to create "The Devil Went Down to Georgia" fifty years later.

Wheeling's WWVA staged its first barn-dance radio show in 1926. Will Rogers was among the stars of NBC's first national network broadcast that year. Columbia issued "Pictures from Life's Other Side"/"Where We'll Never Grow Old" by the Georgia act Smith's Sacred Singers, and was surprised when the rustic harmonizers had its best-selling gospel disc. The group was rushed back into the studio to record sixty-six more performances. Henry Ford's deliberately "retro" 1926 fiddle contest crowned the 5-foot, 120-pound Uncle Bunt Stephens as its champion. Uncle Bunt promptly entered the recording studio in New York and the radio studio in Nashville. He also traded in the Lincoln he'd won for a Ford and put the $1,000 difference in cash toward a new suit and some dental work.

A 1926 edition of *Radio Digest* reported, "A few weeks ago, radio station WRC at Washington, D.C., broadcast a concert by an organization called 'The Hill Billies.' The response was astounding. Letters and postcards arrived from the mountains of Tennessee, from the hills of Kentucky and the Carolinas and the Blue Ridge counties of Maryland and Virginia. Phone calls, local and long distance, demanded favorite numbers, and repeats, and whatnot." *Variety* magazine complained about the 1926 hillbilly fad, describing the music as "sing-song, nasal-twanging vocalizing" and its fans as having "the intelligence of morons." In 1927, Brunswick joined Columbia, Victor, Vocalion, Gennett, and OKeh in the hillbilly field by inaugurating its "Songs from Dixie" series with DeFord Bailey, Mac & Bob, Frankie Marvin, Buell Kazee, and others. The billing is significant, because nobody really knew what to call this emerging style yet. OKeh's country records were listed as "Old-Time Tunes." Columbia

27

Maybelle Carter

Al Hopkins   The

Folksinger Bradley Kincaid began his rise to superstardom on WLS. And there was more.

Ralph Peer (1892–1960) had left OKeh and approached Victor about becoming its talent scout in 1926. He offered to hit the road on the label's behalf to discover new artists throughout the South in return for the publishing rights to their songs. Victor took Peer up on the offer and he scheduled his first road trip for Bristol, Virginia, in the summer of 1927. There he hit the proverbial paydirt.

Would-be Dalhart mountaineers poured into Bristol after the newspaper published an article about Peer's presence and purpose there. Gospel singers, vaudevillians, old-time string bands, traditional folk balladeers, family groups, and Appalachian instrumentalists were all milling around during his twelve-day recording marathon. Among those who had read the article was Alvin Pleasant "A.P." Carter (1891–1960), who brought his wife Sara Dougherty Carter (1899–1979) and sister-in-law Maybelle Addington Carter (1909–1978) to town.

"He said, 'We're going to Bristol tomorrow to make a record,'" Maybelle recalled years later. "I just fluffed him off. I didn't

offered "Familiar Tunes—Old and New." Vocalion billed them as "Old Southern Tunes." The Sears catalog listed them as "Southern Fiddling and Song Records," "Mountain Ballads," and "Old Time Southern Songs." Montgomery Ward came up with "Hill Country Melodies."

The name that stuck was provided by Al Hopkins (1889–1932). After recording for Peer in 1925, the question of his band's name came up. "Call the band anything you want," said Hopkins. "We are nothing but a bunch of hillbillies from North Carolina and Virginia anyway." Peer instructed his secretary to list the records as by "The Hill Billies." At the same time, George Daniell's Hill Billies were performing on Atlanta's powerful WSB. The term that both of these bands used would soon apply to the whole field of country music.

If there was a pivotal year for the development of country music, 1927 was surely it. The Gibson banjo catalog pictured country musicians for the first time—Dave Macon, Charlie Poole, and Sam McGee.

28

TOP: *The band that named the sound was Al Hopkins and his Hill Billies.*
ABOVE: *Ralph Peer next to the building where he discovered The Carter Family and Jimmie Rodgers.*

Ralph Peer

Carter Family

think about makin' a record. The next morning he said, 'Y'all get ready. We're goin' to Bristol.' And I said, 'Well, should I take my guitar?' He said, 'How are you gonna make a record if you don't take your guitar?' I said, 'Well, okay.' And we all got ready and took off."

"'Course we didn't think anything about it," recalled Sara. "Just thought it was more or less a trip. We made it home. Never thought no more about it, never dreamed of the record business turning out like it did."

"As soon as I heard Sara's voice, that was it," Peer remembered. "I knew that it was going to be wonderful." On August 1, 1927, he made the first records of The Carter Family.

The Carters' debut discs appeared in November. "I had the surprise of my life when we went into Bristol one day and saw a crowd of people gathered around listening to . . . Carter Family records that were being played over the loudspeakers," Maybelle reported. "This was something new and caught on like wildfire."

The Carter Family's importance to the history of popular music is incalculable. The act is simply unmatched as a preserver and popularizer of folk songs and Victorian-era compositions. Maybelle's then-revolutionary "drop thumb" guitar style helped to transform the instrument from serving as a background rhythm provider to being the lead sound in pop music. Sara and Maybelle's vocals defined country harmony singing for generations.

From the Carters came Roy Acuff's "Wabash Cannonball," Emmylou Harris's "Come in Stranger," The Kingston Trio's "Worried Man," Elvis Presley's "Are You Lonesome Tonight," and Linda Ronstadt's "I Never Will Marry." The trio's "I'm Thinking Tonight of My Blue Eyes" provided the melody for three future blockbusters—Acuff's "Great Speckled Bird," Hank Thompson's "Wild Side of Life," and Kitty Wells's "It Wasn't God Who Made Honky-Tonk Angels." The melody of the Carters' "Little Darling Pal of Mine" was borrowed by Jimmie Davis for his immortal "You Are My Sunshine." Woody Guthrie used the Carters'

"When the World's on Fire" as the basis of "This Land Is Your Land." Joan Baez launched her career with Carter favorites such as "Engine 143." Maybelle's picking on "Wildwood Flower" still sets a standard for young guitarists. Bluegrass musicians everywhere know "Keep on the Sunny Side," "Foggy Mountain Top," "Gold Watch and Chain," and dozens of other Carter songs. And the

entire world sings The Carter Family's "Will the Circle Be Unbroken."

Sara sang lead; Maybelle harmonized with her and provided the lead guitar accompaniment. A.P. found or wrote the songs and occasionally sang bass. When the royalty checks started coming in, he pushed the women to record more and to increase their

29

ABOVE: *From left are Maybelle, A.P., and Sara Carter, whose impact on American music was enormous.*

Jimmie

performance schedule. The shows were nothing fancy, usually schoolhouse bookings on crude stages lit by kerosene lamps. By the early '30s the three were touring weekly to communities in West Virginia, North Carolina, Tennessee, Virginia, and occasionally Maryland, Pennsylvania, and New England.

The hits that emerged from the 1927 session were "Single Girl, Married Girl" and "Bury Me under the Weeping Willow." Succeeding records sold so well that the act was one of the few in country music that was in the studio every year throughout the Depression, when the rest of the record business nearly died. "Anchored in Love," for instance, sold more than one hundred thousand copies in 1928. "Little Moses"/"God Gave Noah the Rainbow Sign" managed to sell sixty thousand even though the stock market was crashing in 1929 and nobody had any money. "The Storms Are on the Ocean," "Diamonds in the Rough," and "John Hardy Was a Desperate Little Man" were also healthy sellers for the homespun trio. During one two-year period, sales of The Carter Family's discs totaled seven hundred thousand. A giant country hit in 1930 would sell perhaps fifty thousand copies—million sellers were extremely rare in any field of music until after the United States emerged from World War II.

In 1938–39 the trio broadcast over the Mexican megawatt border-radio station XERA, spreading their music to millions. And after the original Carter Family broke up in 1943, Maybelle carried its music forward into the modern era in a new group with her daughters Helen, June, and Anita.

"The Carters really were reporters," says Marty Stuart. "Take 'Cyclone of Rye Cove' or 'Wabash Cannonball.' They were reporters of what was going on every day. That's where country music came to life; it simply reported the truth—good, bad, ugly, pretty—and handed it back to its people."

Among the other acts milling around Bristol in the hot summer of 1927 were the Jimmie Rodgers

Entertainers. The little combo was in the mountains getting occasional show dates at theaters, dances, and schoolhouses, as well as some appearances on WWNC radio in Asheville, North Carolina. But after a band squabble about billing, Jimmie Rodgers walked into Ralph Peer's makeshift studio in Bristol as a solo on August 4, 1927, and made country-music history.

A native of Meridian, Mississippi, Rodgers incorporated the blues songs of black railyard workers, the yodels of the Alpine Swiss, and the syncopations of 1920s pop into his style. Within two years of his discovery by Peer, he was a hillbilly superstar as "The Singing Brakeman."

In 1928 his sales exploded—Rodgers pulled alongside pop tenor Gene Austin as Victor's biggest-selling disc maker. He toured on the Loew's Circuit. He

ABOVE: *An ad in Talking Machine World predicted the country craze in 1924.*
LEFT: *The superstardom of Jimmie Rodgers made the prediction come true.*

recorded "T for Texas," "Daddy and Home," "Waiting for a Train," and "In the Jailhouse Now" that year, and took in more than $200,000 in royalties. In 1929 he headlined on an R-K-O theater tour, filmed his *Singing Brakeman* movie short, and recorded "Any Old Time," "Hobo Bill's Last Ride," "Frankie and Johnny," and other classics at sessions in New York, Dallas, New Orleans, and Atlanta.

By 1930 he'd sold more than six million records. He toured with Swain's Hollywood Follies tent company in 1930. Victor recorded fourteen sides by him in Los Angeles, including "Moonlight and Skies," "Pistol Packin' Papa," and "Muleskinner Blues." On "Blue Yodel No. 9" Rodgers was accompanied by jazz great Louis Armstrong. "When the Cactus Is in Bloom," "T.B. Blues," and "Travellin' Blues" were among the songs he recorded in 1931. That was also the year he toured with Will Rogers and recorded with The Carter Family, Cliff Carlisle, and the Louisville Jug Band.

In the studio in 1932, Rodgers teamed up with star fiddler Clayton McMichen on "Peach Pickin' Time down in Georgia." That was also the year he immortalized "Mother the Queen of My Heart," "Roll along Kentucky Moon," and "Miss the Mississippi and You."

Jimmie Rodgers (1897–1933) became the role model for a generation of performers. Gene Autry began his career by singing exactly like "America's Blue Yodeler." Before he created "You Are My Sunshine" (1940), "Nobody's Darling but Mine" (1934), and the rest of the classics that led to his election as the governor of Louisiana, Jimmie Davis was a Jimmie Rodgers disciple, too. Hank Snow, Lefty Frizzell, and Ernest Tubb all began as Rodgers imitators.

"My dad thought he was God; he idolized the man," recalled Justin Tubb shortly before his death. When Hall of Famer Ernest Tubb began his career, "he patterned his style after Jimmie. Every song he sang, he sang just like Jimmie. He wrote songs

about Jimmie. Mrs. Rodgers took him under her wing. She gave him Jimmie's guitar to use. And she would go out on the road and introduce him on the show, saying, 'I'm Mrs. Jimmie Rodgers and this young man I have found, I picked to carry on my husband's singing and his musical career.'"

Recalls Hank Thompson, "I used to go around singin' his songs—well before I went to school—three, four, five years old. I'd sing his songs and I'd try to yodel." Says Ray Price, "The first country music I ever heard was Jimmie Rodgers."

"Jimmie was a total influence," concurs David Frizzell. "My mom had an old Victrola where the doors opened up and the sound came out. Lefty would lay there with his head inside that Victrola listening to Jimmie Rodgers. He was heavily influenced by Jimmie. He could sound just like him. He had the yodel down."

"Jimmie Rodgers is where I learned to yodel," said Hall of Famer Patsy Montana before her 1997 death. "I don't remember how old I was, except I had to stand on a box to wind up the old Victrola," back home on the family farm in Arkansas. Patsy launched her career by singing Jimmie's "Whisper Your Mother's Name" and "Yodeling Cowboy" in amateur contests.

"So many credit him with their beginning," says *Grand Ole Opry* star Jean Shepard. "I credit him with my beginning. Because I learned to yodel off the old Jimmie Rodgers records. I used to sit out on my mother's bench where she washed the clothes on the rub board. And I would entertain the whole 'holler,' as we call it. The whole valley could hear me singing Jimmie Rodgers and yodeling."

"Jimmie Rodgers was a special artist," says Jimmie Davis. "He opened the world up with yodeling and singing. He was the greatest artist I've ever heard, because his diction was so good. And his records usually told a story. 'Course that's what country music does.

"If I had to pick a favorite of all the country music singers, I would pick Jimmie Rodgers. No-

Stoneman

body can really replace him. I think he was the most complete artist of his kind."

During Jimmie Rodgers' recording career, 1927–1933, he sold more than ten million singles. He knew that career would be brief from the start. Throughout his stardom he was afflicted with tuberculosis, and that is what killed him when he was in New York for recording sessions in 1933. He was thirty-five years old.

Grandpa Jones all issued collections of Rodgers songs in the 1950s and 1960s. One of the landmark tributes was Merle Haggard's 1969 album *Same Train, Different Time.*

Dolly Parton scored her first top-ten hit in 1970 with Rodgers' "Muleskinner Blues." "In the Jailhouse Now" was revived by Johnny Cash (1962), Sonny James (1977), and Willie Nelson (1982). "T for Texas" has versions by acts as diverse as

"When the train left New York City bringin' his body back to Meridian, the engineer tied the whistle open in a low moan," said Boxcar Willie. "And people lined the railroad all the way from New York clear to Meridian. He was such a legend. We think about Elvis and the thousands of people that would mob Elvis. But back in 1933, it was like that with Jimmie Rodgers."

Bill Monroe's 1940 revival of "Muleskinner Blues" is one of the hundreds of records that have kept Rodgers' legacy alive. Webb Pierce topped the charts with "In the Jailhouse Now" in 1955. Hank Snow, Elton Britt, Lefty Frizzell, and

Grandpa Jones (1963), Tompall Glaser (1976), and Lynyrd Skynyrd (1976).

As recently as 1989, Tanya Tucker hit the charts with "Daddy and Home." "Miss the Mississippi and You" has been revived by Crystal Gayle (1979) and K.T. Oslin (1996). The last song recorded by The Grateful Dead's Jerry Garcia before his death in 1995 was "Blue Yodel No. 9." That was for the 1997 Jimmie Rodgers tribute album spearheaded by Bob Dylan.

Nolan Porterfield's 1979 biography *America's Blue Yodeler* captured Rodgers' spirit and his times. Clint

33

ABOVE: *Virginia's Ernest V. "Pop" Stoneman, center, poses with family members and friends as the "Blue Ridge Corn Shuckers" in 1926.*

Old-Time
SOUTHERN
TUNES

VICTOR
RECORDS
Orthophonic Recording

Eastwood's 1982 film *Honky Tonk Man* co-opted part of his story.

In the sixty-five years since his death, Jimmie Rodgers records have never gone out of print. Rounder Records put every one of his performances on a series of CDs in 1990–91.

"Rodgers was popular enough that at one point they said the miners in the coal fields in West Virginia would go into the company store at the end of the week and say, 'Give me a pound of baloney, a loaf of bread, and the latest Jimmie Rodgers record,'" reports historian Charles K. Wolfe.

The discovery of Jimmie Rodgers and The Carter Family within the same week was a watershed for the young country industry. These two became the first nationally popular hillbilly recording stars.

"Those two weeks in Bristol in the summer of 1927, in a nutshell, it was the 'Big Bang' of country music," says Wolfe. "Ralph Peer learned at that point that there was not only a market, but a ravenous market for this kind of music. He was not a folklore collector; he was a hard-headed, pragmatic business man. And even though he really did in many ways invent the country-music industry, he was paid handsomely for it" through a publishing company that owned the rights to the treasure-trove catalogs of both of his major discoveries.

The rise to stardom of Rodgers and the Carters in 1928–29 coincided with increasing enthusiasm about the hillbilly field by the record companies—country and southern-gospel recordings reportedly were accounting for 27 percent of Victor's sales and for 40 percent of Gennett's. The 1929 National String Instruments catalog pictured popular silent-screen cowboy Hoot Gibson with a trio of guitar-picking cowboys. The hugely successful "Birmingham Jail" and "Columbus Stockade Blues" made disc stars of the duo Darby & Tarlton in 1928. The Allen Brothers ("New Salty Dog") and The Beverly Hillbillies ("Strawberry Roan") would soon follow as hit makers.

The media began to take notice—*Collier's* magazine discussed the growing hillbilly trend in a 1929 feature story that mentioned the astonishingly large sales of event songs and murder ballads and took note of such figures as Carson Robison, Frank Luther, and Andy Jenkins.

The article stated, "The phonograph companies found they had opened a new market, one that they had not dreamed existed; a wide market among the folk of the mountains, of the mining districts and the timberlands. Plain folk to whom the story is the important part of any song; who like the accompaniment simple and the words understandable."

And so it was that Victor made its 1928 pilgrimage to Nashville to record the *Opry's* old-time string bands, that Cajuns Joseph Falcon and Amede Ardoin were recorded, and that Gene Autry made his disc debut. So did Cliff Edwards, the genial "Ukulele Ike." The Rex Cole Mountaineers began broadcasting on NBC from New York in 1928. In Tennessee, WSM began to pay its radio rustics for the first time, $5 a show. Bradley Kincaid published the first country-music songbook in 1928. In North Carolina, Bascom Lamar Lunsford launched the Mountain Dance and Folk Festival in 1928. In Texas, Bob Wills moved to Fort Worth and joined a medicine show in 1929. Jimmie Davis began to record for Victor.

Better Homes and Gardens picked up on the country-music phenomenon in 1931. A piece titled "Cowboy Ballads at Our Own Firesides" offered the observation: "The reason is radio. Turn the dial this way or that, before long you are perfectly sure to hear some songs that are as wholly American as cornbread. . . . No program of oldtime tunes is without a sprinkle of genuine folk music."

The emphasis on radio is significant. By this time the Depression had hit, and record sales were in a free fall, dropping from $46.2 million in 1930 to $17.6 million in 1931. They would continue to drop precipitously throughout the next two years. Radio, on the other hand, was booming. And with it boomed country music.

Two

The Radio Barn Dance

Even during the height of the Great Depression, people wouldn't part with their radios. Social workers of the day found that destitute Americans would part with their refrigerators, telephones, or beds to pay the rent rather than give up the magic box that brought the world to their doorsteps. You might not be able to afford to go to the movies, buy records, subscribe to magazines, or acquire board games, but you could afford the free hours of amusement the radio offered.

"We were sharecroppers; we didn't have any money," recalls Jimmie Davis. "But they give us thirty days to pay for the radio. We put it up in the house, and people would come and stay all night lookin' at it, just listenin'. All night long."

"That first radio was like heaven broadcasting into my house," recalls Johnny Cash. "It was like there was a world out there of space and mystery and beauty that I couldn't have ever imagined."

"The radio was my only way of finding out what was out there beyond the cotton fields of home," says Charley Pride.

"It was this wonderful thing," says Dolly Parton, "a world beyond the Smokey Mountains. And boy, I lived inside that radio. You know that song [Lionel

37

LEFT: *Louise Massey and The Westerners brought the cowboy songs of New Mexico to the radio in 1933.*
ABOVE: *The* Grand Ole Opry *comedy team Sarie and Sallie on the cover of a 1938 issue of* Rural Radio *magazine.*

Cartwright] wrote called "I Watched It All on My Radio"? We did! We used to sit and watch the radio. I have never yet seen a movie or a television show that could compare with my imagination of listenin' to the radio and all those great old shows."

"In my childhood, radio was just about the most important entertainment that we knew about—in fact, it was the only entertainment we knew about except what we created ourselves on the back porches after work, after supper in the evening," relates *Renfro Valley Barn Dance* announcer Jim Gaskin. "I think the secret of radio was that it called on our imaginations. We didn't have to see everything; it was what was created in our minds by what was coming out of the speaker of that radio."

"It was 'theater of the mind,'" agrees Bill Anderson.

It was also the thing that turned hillbilly music into an entertainment industry.

America's radio craze had begun in the teens with the manufacturing of kits for building crystal receiving sets for home hobbyists. In 1920 KDKA in Pittsburgh became the first commercial broadcasting station in the United States. A year later there were

8 stations. By 1922 there were 30. By 1923 there were 556. There were more than 600 commercial stations on the air by the dawn of the 1930s.

Sales of receivers skyrocketed in corresponding fashion. In 1933 more than three million sets were produced. By 1938 approximately 82 percent of U.S. households had a radio. National radio networks were created in 1926 (NBC) and 1928 (CBS). Their ad revenues soared from $3 million in 1927 to $75 million in 1929. Small wonder that they were joined by Mutual in 1935 and ABC in 1945. By the dawn of the television era in the early 1950s, more than twenty-five hundred radio stations were broadcasting into the nation's homes.

And at one time or another, nearly all of them featured country music. Country music and radio grew side by side. Almost from the moment commercial radio began in 1920, there were country musicians on the airwaves. Fort Worth's WBAP and Atlanta's WSB, as well as Pittsburgh's groundbreaking KDKA, had all presented country performers by 1924.

But it was Chicago's WLS that provided the template for country radio entertainment. It created the prototype of the Saturday-night "barn-dance" show—square dancers, homey announcers, sentimental "heart" singers, string bands, barbershop

ABOVE: *The cast of* The National Barn Dance, *America's most popular country radio show, poses proudly on the stage of Chicago's Eighth Street Theater in 1944.*

George

Grace Wilson

quartets, rube comics, cowboy crooners, and the like, knit together in a weekly repertory company. WLS also inaugurated road shows for its ensemble cast and was the first to develop a public-relations "image" for its variety show.

The station dubbed its weekly country showcase *The National Barn Dance*. Here is how it came to be: The Sears & Roebuck company put a little five-hundred-watt station on the air on March 21, 1924, in order to broadcast a one-hour show about agriculture that would promote the retailer's products. On April 9 the station assumed the call letters WES (for "World's Economy Store") and aired a test program featuring singer Grace Wilson and the folksy musical-comedy team Ford & Glenn. Wilson sang "Bringing Home the Bacon," which would become her lifelong *National Barn Dance* theme song. Response to the broadcast was so strong that listeners telephoned Sears all night long.

Convinced it had a winner on its hands, Sears put the station on the air for keeps as WLS ("World's Largest Store") on April 12. Ford & Glenn member Glenn Rowell wrote later, "How well I remember that opening night with Ethel Barrymore and [silent-movie cowboy star] William S. Hart. How I worried about what Bill Hart would do on radio. How confident I felt that Ethel Barrymore would 'carry' the show with her tremendous dramatic experience.

"Then I'll never forget Miss Barrymore, after her flowery introduction, freezing and staring into the little round mike and finally saying those never-to-be-forgotten words: 'Turn the damned thing off!'"

The cowboy was rushed to the mike, despite misgivings about his ability to perform. Hart re-cited a poem in a deep, rich voice, charming everyone. A week later, WLS inaugurated a show that would feature exclusively cowboys and other rural types. Grace Wilson, Ford & Glenn, and a square-dance band were put on the air from the mezzanine of Chicago's Sherman Hotel on April 19, 1924.

That night, a Sears executive was reportedly throwing an elaborate dinner party in Chicago to show off the radio as the store's marvelous new advertising tool. He turned on his set and heard the square-dance band ripping into "Turkey in the Straw." Outraged, he demanded that the hillbilly show be cancelled at once. But the ensuing deluge of letters and telegrams from listeners soon changed his mind.

A few weeks later, *The National Barn Dance* became truly professional. Historian James F. Evans reports that gangster Al Capone's girlfriend was a singer in The College Inn at the Sherman Hotel. "She appeared one night on the Barn Dance at the request of the station. Capone watched the performance with smiling approval which later turned to suggestive firmness when he asked the producer, 'Well, don't she get paid?' She was. Grace Wilson took this as a cue for demanding equal courtesy, whereupon WLS . . . set up a full payroll for talent."

For the next four decades, *The National Barn Dance* would define and shape country entertainment like no other show. As the announcer put it, "This program is to be sincere, friendly, and informal, planned to remind you folks of the good fun and fellowship of the barn warmings, the husking bees, and the square dances in our farm communities of yesteryear and even today."

39

D. Hay

ABOVE: *Both "Bringing Home the Bacon" singer Grace Wilson and announcer George D. Hay, "The Solemn Ol' Judge," began their radio careers at WLS in Chicago.*

Bradley Kincaid

In late 1924 the first nationwide radio popularity poll was conducted. The winner as America's Favorite Announcer was none other than the Barn Dance's George D. Hay (1895–1968). He and Grace Wilson (1890–1962) were just the beginning of a parade of stars that the show would introduce.

In 1926 The Maple City Four quartet arrived at WLS for a long, long tenure. Two years later, the show's first superstar arrived. Kentucky native Bradley Kincaid (1895–1989) was in college at the YMCA's school in Chicago when he was spotted by the WLS music director at a student show. Kincaid knew and sang mountain folk songs, so the executive figured, correctly, that he would be an ideal addition to *The National Barn Dance* cast.

"They thought I was going to be popular," Kincaid recalled in Loyal Jones's biography *Radio's Kentucky Mountain Boy*. "And they wanted to get a catchy name. They said, 'How'd you get started in this?' And I told them about my father trading a foxhound for the guitar. They said, 'That's it, Bradley Kincaid and his Houn' Dog guitar.'"

By the time Kincaid graduated four years later, the formerly penniless student was the owner of a brand-new Packard and had $15,000 in the bank as a result of his singing. Bradley Kincaid published the first country-music songbook (1928), discovered Grandpa Jones (1935), became a major force in popularizing country in the urban Northeast (1934–42), starred on *The Grand Ole Opry* (1944–49), and had a recording career that stretched into the 1970s. Sears marketed a replica of his "hound dog" guitar in its catalogs for years, and sales of his songbooks reportedly topped three hundred thousand.

Kincaid discovered the power of radio the day he scheduled his first concert. He arrived in Peoria, Illinois, and headed for his engagement. "When I walked up to the theater, there was a line several blocks long and people were being turned away. I walked across the street and asked a fellow what was going on. He said, 'Why, that radio singer from WLS is going to be here.'...I'd never made a public appearance in my life."

Among the songs that became nationally popular thanks to Bradley Kincaid are "The Letter Edged in Black," "The Legend of the Robin's Red Breast," and the immortal "Barbara Allen," the most collected Appalachian folk song of all. Kincaid hated the term "hillbilly" and referred to himself as a folksinger and by the nickname he kept throughout his career, "The Kentucky Mountain Boy."

In 1928 Sears sold WLS to *Prairie Farmer* magazine for $250,000. The publication's chief, Burridge Butler, poured enormous resources into *The National Barn Dance*. Evocative photo portraits of its stars were distributed, along with highly embellished biographies designed to endear them further to listeners. WLS began publishing beautiful annual souvenir *Family Albums* promoting its stars, as well as a weekly with similar aims, *Stand By*.

Butler had definite ideas about what the country-music image should be. Liquor and cigarette advertising were banned on WLS, as were any song lyrics that were even remotely suggestive. Chicago torch singer Ruth Etting ("Love Me or Leave Me," "Ten Cents a Dance," etc.) was barred from appearing because of her stormy, mobster-dominated personal life. "Her voice is too sexy for our type stations," sniffed a WLS executive. *The National Barn Dance* cast members were expected to conduct themselves like sweet, innocent country folk at all times.

ABOVE: *Bradley Kincaid was the first country star to publish a songbook.*
RIGHT: *When LuluBelle and Scotty published this songbook in 1937, she was the most popular woman on U.S. radio.*

Lulu Belle's & Skyland Scotty's Home Folk SONGS

We gratefully dedicate this collection of our songs to our many Friends of the Airways, to the loyal listeners of WLS, and to Radio Station WLS itself, all of whom have made this book possible.

Lulu Belle + Skyland Scotty

Price 50 Cents

The Happy Radio Home

Butler installed a bronze plaque on the *Prairie Farmer* building. Titled "The WLS Creed," it read: "To me radio is far more than a mere medium of entertainment. It is a God-given instrument which makes possible vital economic, educational and inspirational service to the home-loving men, women and children of America. As long as it is our privilege to direct the destinies of WLS, we will hold sacred this trust that has been placed in our hands. No medium developed by mankind is doing more to broaden the lives of rich and poor alike than radio.

"When you step up to the microphone never forget this responsibility, and that you are walking as a guest into all those homes beyond the microphone."

All that morally upright, folksy business worked. By 1932, at the height of the Depression, reservations for *National Barn Dance* tickets were made seven months in advance. The show moved to downtown Chicago's Eighth Street Theater and started charging for admission. At a time when a movie ticket cost a dime, *The National Barn Dance* charged ninety cents a seat and still had to turn people away.

For twenty-five consecutive years *The National Barn Dance* performed two sold-out shows weekly for twelve hundred paying customers per show in the theater. On the road the troupe drew ten to twenty thousand people to outdoor venues, often at midwestern state fairs.

On July 30, 1939, the WLS road show came to Forest Park in Noblesville, Indiana. Traffic jammed for seven miles in all directions out of the town, and an estimated sixty thousand people sat on blankets on the hillsides surrounding the amphitheater. "The progression of songs, laughter and encores engulfed both viewers and performers," reported *Prairie Farmer*, "until a program planned for one hour extended nearly three, ended only by the need to get about fifty thousand cows milked on time."

During its nearly forty years as a country-music institution, more than three million people saw *National Barn Dance* shows.

Countless more heard them. In 1931 WLS became a fifty-thousand-watt radio behemoth, blasting its signal throughout the populous Midwest. In 1933, *The National Barn Dance* became a Saturday-night feature on the NBC radio network, making it the first nationally broadcast country radio show. A new product

ABOVE: *WLS's annual* Family Album *helped give country music its identity as wholesome, downhome entertainment.* RIGHT: *Arkie the Arkansas Woodchopper's songbooks sold millions and his radio stardom lasted more than 30 years.*

John Lair

called Alka Seltzer became its sponsor, and within a decade it was a household word.

The program's cast members became country's earliest national radio idols. Arkie the Arkansas Woodchopper (Luther Ossenbrink, 1907–1981), who had arrived in 1929, was a major WLS star for the next thirty years. George Gobel, Red Foley, Linda Parker, The Hoosier Hot Shots, the blind duo Mac & Bob, Pat Buttram, The Three Little Maids, Karl & Harty, The Cumberland Ridge Runners, and dozens of others became coast-to-coast favorites during the 1930s.

Their styles and repertoires were largely molded at WLS by John Lair, who had been impressed by Bradley Kincaid's mountain sincerity. Lair (1894–1985) would go on to make country-music history as a promoter, music scholar, writer, and founder of the still-thriving *Renfro Valley Barn Dance*.

Several in *The National Barn Dance* cast left lasting legacies. Singer-comic LuluBelle (Myrtle Cooper Wiseman, 1913–1999) was voted the most popular woman on U.S. radio in 1936, ahead of pop-music stars, Hollywood actresses, and political celebrities. She and her husband Scotty Wiseman (1909–1981) created the country standard "Have I Told You Lately That I Love You" and popularized such tunes as "Turn Your Radio On," "Mountain Dew," "Does the Spearmint Lose Its Flavor on the Bedpost Overnight," "This Train," and "Remember Me (When the Candle Lights Are Gleaming)." LuluBelle eventually parlayed her radio fame into a seat in the North Carolina House of Representatives.

The cast's Louise Massey (1908–1983) had one of country's first pop-crossover hits, 1941's "My Adobe Hacienda." She and her family band The Westerners also were among the earliest country acts to popularize Spanish-language material. The act graduated from WLS to its own NBC shows *The Log Cabin Dude Ranch* and *Plantation Party,* where a young Mike Wallace was their announcer. Band member Curt Massey later became the musical director and songwriter for

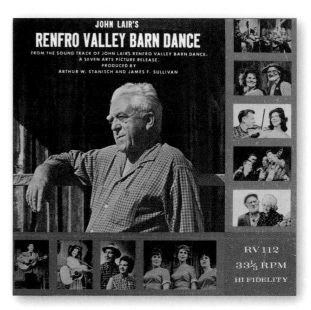

the TV series *The Beverly Hillbillies* and *Petticoat Junction.*

National Barn Dance cowgirl Patsy Montana created what is said to be country's first million seller by a woman, 1935's "I Want to Be a Cowboy's Sweetheart." Gene Autry parlayed his 1931–34 *National Barn Dance* tenure into Hollywood superstardom. The show's Girls of the Golden West became the most successful sister duo in country-music history.

Bob Atcher, Rex Allen, Dolph Hewitt, Doc Hopkins, Homer & Jethro, Smiley Burnette, The DeZurick Sisters, Hugh Cross, Red Blanchard, Cristy Lane, Les Paul, and even Andy Williams are all part of *The National Barn Dance* saga. So are the enduring images it helped to mold—the hayseed comic, the sunbonnet country sweetheart, the singing cowboy, the sentimental crooner, brother acts, sister duos, and the rest of the stereotypes that populated the country-radio community.

By 1932 thirteen million people were unemployed and Bing Crosby was singing "Brother Can You Spare a Dime." The record business hit bottom a year later. Sales were a dismal $5.5 million worth of discs ($104 million had been sold in 1927). One out of four U.S. households was on relief by 1935, and the Midwest was becoming a Dust Bowl. The old Columbia, Paramount, and Gennett labels went under, and recording opportunities for coun-

43

ABOVE: *John Lair's* Renfro Valley Barn Dance *is still going strong in central Kentucky. In 1966 he made a movie and this soundtrack album with the show's cast.*

try acts withered. "By January 1933 the record business in America was practically extinct," wrote phonograph historian Roland Gellatt. "You did not buy luxuries when banks were foundering on all sides." Radio, on the other hand, was a fertile field.

By that time, *The National Barn Dance* had spawned dozens of imitators. Within a few years, barn-dance programs would be a staple of radio stations everywhere. KMOX started its radio barn dance in St. Louis in 1930. Country radio expanded further with the 1932 additions of WHO's *Barn Dance Frolic* in Des Moines and WOWO's *Hoosier Hop* in Fort Wayne. In 1934 WBT in Charlotte, North Carolina, launched its *Crazy Barn Dance* as yet another weekly hillbilly radio show. Kansas City launched its *Brush Creek Follies* on KMBC in 1935 and Cincinnati would have its *Midwestern Hayride* on WLW within a year. Virginia's *Old Dominion Barn Dance*

WLW BOONE COUNTY JAMBOREE

(WRVA) and Kentucky's *Renfro Valley Barn Dance* (WHAS) were close behind.

"The old time barn dances on the radio were kind of ironic," observes historian Charles Wolfe. "In one sense they were utilizing the newest of these brash new media to send out their message. On the other hand, they were pretending that here we are at the old farm house. And here are our friends and neighbors who have dropped by to play a few tunes for us."

Dr. J.L. Brinkley was the epitome of "brash." There was no ceiling on the amount of power a radio station could have in Mexico, so the quack set up a number of stations just across the Texas border that broadcast at strengths up to five hundred thousand watts. Along with hawking his goat-gland

operation designed to restore sexual potency in men, his stations advertised nostrums ranging from laxatives to hair coloring, as well as Bibles, baby chicks, and seeds. They also featured lots of country music.

The Pickard Family, The Delmore Brothers, Roy Faulkner, Cowboy Slim Rinehart, W. Lee O'Daniel, Patsy Montana, Little Jimmie Sizemore, and others reached vast audiences thanks to their border-radio broadcasts. The Carter Family began introducing Sara's children Janette and Joe and Maybelle's daughters Helen, June, and Anita during their border-radio stint in 1938–42.

June remembers well the impact that radio had on her as a little girl. "The room was full of bushel baskets of mail and I thought, 'These are an awful lot of letters somebody's got to answer,'" she recalls. "And I looked and they were all to The Carter Family!"

WWVA decided to join the barn-dance craze in Wheeling, West Virginia. On January 7, 1933, it broadcast its first *Jamboree*. On April 1 the show moved to Wheeling's thirty-six-hundred-seat Capitol Theater, where it has remained ever since, as one of the longest tenured of all radio barn-dance shows.

In Shreveport, Louisiana, KWKH launched its barn dance in 1936, but the World War II draft siphoned off its original talent pool by 1941. The show rose again as *The Louisiana Hayride* in 1948, made it onto network radio, and became known as "The Cradle of the Stars" because of the extraordinary number of *Hayride* performers who went on to become headliners in Nashville.

By the mid-1940s, country's six hundred radio programs were playing to a combined audience of forty million. Atlanta's *WSB Barn Dance, The*

ABOVE: *Saturday night in Cincinnati in 1940 meant another broadcast by the cast of the* Boone County Jamboree.
RIGHT: *In Wheeling, station WWVA still beams its* Jamboree *each weekend. This tour book dates from 1941.*

Jimmy Thompson

Big D Jamboree in Dallas, Boston's *Hayloft Jamboree,* Philadelphia's *Sleepy Hollow Ranch,* and the *Hometown Jamboree* in Los Angeles had all entered the radio barn-dance sweepstakes by then.

The longest-lasting of all the radio barn dances is the one that made Nashville the world headquarters for country music. WSM's *Grand Ole Opry* is not only a country-music institution; it is the longest-lasting radio show in the world.

WSM wasn't Nashville's first radio station. In 1922 Boy Scout Jack DeWitt (1906–1999) began broadcasting Enrico Caruso records on WDAA, a station he constructed on the Ward-Belmont school campus, at the head of where Music Row is today. The first commercial radio application in the state was filed for WOAN, south of Nashville in Lawrenceburg. It promoted the gospel records and songbooks of its owner, the James D. Vaughan Publishing Company. When WOAN upgraded its equipment in 1925 from 150 watts to 500 watts, a radio supply store in Nashville bought the old gear and launched WDAD, the city's first commercial broadcaster. The station immediately began airing the hillbilly sounds of Sid Harkreader, Humphrey Bate, Herman Crook, and DeFord Bailey, all of whom would soon become *Opry* stars.

The Nashville-based National Life

and Accident Insurance Company was eyeing this radio trend with interest. Founder Cornelius Craig's son Edwin Craig was fascinated by the new phenomenon and urged the company to build a station in its new downtown office building in 1925. Once it made the commitment, National Life decided to go "first class" by investing $50,000 in the facility.

The station was named WSM, which stood for the company slogan "We Shield Millions." When it went on the air on October 5, 1925, it had one thousand watts of power, making it one of the two most powerful stations below the Mason-Dixon line (the other being Atlanta's WSB, "Welcome South Brother"). From the outset, WSM was more powerful than 85 percent of all stations then broadcasting in America. Nashville radio pioneer Jack DeWitt was hired as the station's engineer—he would eventually become WSM's president. After George D. Hay was named the nation's favorite announcer, WSM lured him away from WLS. Hay immediately began forging a barn-dance show in imitation of his alma mater.

On November 28, 1925, he put seventy-seven-year-old fiddler Uncle Jimmy Thompson on WSM. Thompson (1848–1931), backed by his niece Eva Thompson Jones on piano, romped through one hoedown melody after another. Concerned about the old man's stamina, Hay asked Uncle Jimmy if he was getting tired after an hour's worth of energetic bowing. "An hour?" the fiddler replied. "Fiddlesticks! A man can't get warmed up in an hour. This program's got to be longer." Telegrams and telephone calls poured in. Hay and Thompson repeated the next week. And the next. The *Tennessean* newspaper then announced, "Because of this recent revival in the

Herman

ABOVE: *The first sounds of* The Grand Ole Opry *in 1925 were announcer George D. Hay and Uncle Jimmy Thompson.*
RIGHT: *Dressed in farmers' clothes to look more "country," harmonica player Herman Crook is at upper left.*

DeFord Bailey

popularity of the old familiar tunes, WSM has arranged to have an hour or two every Saturday night, starting Saturday, December 26." *The Grand Ole Opry* was officially on the air.

It got its name when Hay ad-libbed some remarks after an NBC network classical-music show aired on WSM in 1927. Conductor Walter Damrosch had concluded his broadcast by saying that there was little room for realism in classical music; then he conducted a short orchestral piece imitating a train ride. Switching to WSM's local programming, Hay proclaimed, "From here on out for the next three hours we will present nothing but realism. It will be down to earth for the earthy." The black harmonica stylist DeFord Bailey (1899–1982) then performed his train-imitation instrumental "Pan American Blues." Said Hay, "For the past hour we have been listening to the music taken largely from the Grand Opera, but from now on we will present *The Grand Ole Opry*."

Harmonica stylists were characteristic of the show in its early days. In addition to Bailey, they included Herman Crook (1898–1988), who would back the *Opry*'s square-dance troupes for an incredible sixty-two years, from 1926 until his death in 1988.

In the early days of the *Opry*, Kitty Cora Cline brought her hammered dulcimer to the WSM studios. Theron Hale and His Daughters played twin fiddles on "Listen to the Mockingbird." The Pickard Family came down the Cumberland River to Nashville from nearby Ashland City to sing old-time tunes like "She'll Be Comin' 'Round the Mountain," "Buffalo Gals," "Kitty Wells," "The Old Gray Goose Is Dead," and "Little Red Caboose behind the Train." Blind Uncle Joe Mangrum brought a storehouse of fiddle tunes he'd learned during the Civil War. The harmony trio The Vagabonds offered Victorian parlor songs. Asher Sizemore (1906–1975) brought his four-year-old son Little Jimmy (born 1928) to the show and began publishing a series of songbooks that would spread their fame nationwide.

By 1933 Hay had begun costuming the *Opry*'s acts in overalls or farmer outfits and giving them colorful rustic names. The Fruit Jar Drinkers, The Binkley Brothers Dixie Clodhoppers, Paul Warmack and His Gully Jumpers, Ed Poplin's Barn Dance Orchestra, and Dr. Humphrey Bate's Possum Hunters all became early favorites on WSM. The finest of the early *Opry*'s hoedown bands was comprised of the dazzling fiddler Arthur Smith (1898–1971), the dexterous guitarist Sam McGee (1894–1975), and his banjo-playing brother Kirk McGee (1899–1983), who were dubbed The Dixieliners.

The blackface duo Lasses and Honey, "Talking Blues Man" Robert Lunn, and the hilarious sister team Sarie and Sallie provided the show's comedic moments. Bate's daughter Alcyone Bate Beasley was billed as "the little girl with the great big voice." DeFord Bailey became "The Harmonica Wizard." Hay introduced the *Opry* shows by blowing on a steamboat whistle he called "Hushpuckena." He dubbed himself "The Solemn Old Judge" and dressed in a long-tailed black coat and bowler hat.

These trappings followed the example of the *National Barn Dance* cast—who were variously cowboys/cowgirls, sunbonnet sweethearts, overalled rustics, and gingham-dressed warblers—in the development of visual "signatures" for the emerging style. It was a recognition of the commercial value of having an image to go

47

Crook

TOP: *Country music's first black star was* The Grand Ole Opry's *"Harmonica Wizard" DeFord Bailey.*
ABOVE: *Asher Sizemore and his son Little Jimmie did a whopping business with songbooks and autographed photos.*

with the music. It was a statement that country music was being marketed.

One of *The Grand Ole Opry*'s performers needed no image making, nicknaming, or down-home hucksterism. Uncle Dave Macon (1870–1952) was a one-of-a-kind phenomenon. As Hay, himself, remarked, "Here's the one who wears no man's collar but his own." "The Dixie Dewdrop," as Macon was known, was part medicine-show barker, part minstrel, part comic, part evangelist, and all ham. A virtual walking museum of nineteenth-century show-biz and early hillbilly culture, Uncle Dave became the *Opry*'s first superstar.

Uncle Dave played tunes that ranged from minstrel songs to folk ballads. He was a wagon driver with his own delivery company, and folks who lived along his route used to see him riding by, playing the banjo as he went along. He started his career professionally in 1918 when a theatrical agent heard him and booked him on the vaudeville circuit.

"His parents had run a theatrical hotel on Broadway in Nashville [in the 1880s]," recounts folk musician John Hartford. "He was very much entranced by the minstrel shows and wanted to go into vaudeville. At first, he did it on a very part time basis, which I think is pretty traditional to a lot of country musicians. Because country musicians basically don't think of themselves as being professionals. They think of themselves as farming, or working on the railroad, or doing something like that, and this entertainment's something you do on the side.

"Anyhow, Uncle Dave learned that he could make a good living playing music, which he really did dearly love to do. Then he wound up being, I would say, country music's first really potent singer/songwriter/performer/instrumentalist."

Dave Macon was fifty-three years old when he began touring on the vaudeville circuit in 1923. But his vigor was ageless. With his gold teeth, whiskers, twirling banjo, cigar stub, gates-ajar collar, and ready stash of country witticisms, Macon was an instant smash. He began recording in 1924. So Uncle Dave was already a professional when he joined the *Opry* cast in 1926. And he remained an undisputed headliner there until his death in 1952. His onstage ebullience and capti-

48

TOP: *Arthur Smith with Dixieliners Sam and Kirk McGee.*
LEFT: *Uncle Dave Macon became the* Opry's *first superstar.*
RIGHT: *"Blues Stay Away From Me" became a massive hit for the Delmore Brothers.*

ndpa Jones

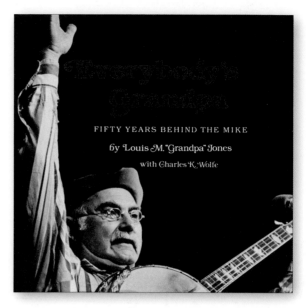

vating skills as a raconteur have been reported by virtually everyone who ever saw him live.

"He was the funniest man in the world," says Brother Oswald. "He beat anything I had ever seen. He was the best one-man showman I had ever seen in my life. I watched every show that he done when he was in the [traveling] tent show with us. I'd watch him every night. Everything I do, I copied from him. Jokes, banjo playing, and all."

As the funny man in Roy Acuff's Smoky Mountain Boys band, Oswald would bring Uncle Dave's style into the modern era. Macon, himself, continues to charm admirers today, thanks to his appearance in the 1940 film *Grand Ole Opry* and to a series of albums that have reissued some of the more than two hundred recordings he left behind. His memory is also recalled via Uncle Dave Macon Days, an annual old-time music festival in Murfreesboro, Tennessee.

Macon is the only one of the early *Opry* stars who is enshrined in the Country Music Hall of Fame. There is a strong push in Nashville, however, to induct the show's sweet-singing duo The Delmore Brothers. Rabon (1916–1952) and Alton Delmore (1908–1964) practically breathed in harmony. Country historian Charles Wolfe calls them "the most musically sophisticated, most creative, and most technically proficient of all the duo acts."

They grew up in northern Alabama and derived their style from old-time gospel harmonizing. They joined the *Opry* in 1933 and by 1936 were the most popular act on the show. Alton's song-

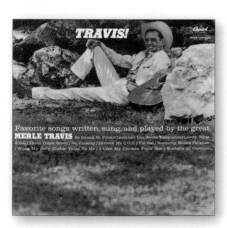

writing and Rabon's fluid guitar work blossomed, as did the Delmores' recording career. "Brown's Ferry Blues" (1933), "Gonna Lay down My Old Guitar" (1933), and "Til the Roses Bloom Again" (1937) typify the gentle, fireside warmth of their early performances.

After a career lull, the brothers reinvented themselves in the mid-1940s. They upped the tempo and the blues content of their performances to specialize in country-boogie tunes such as "Blues Stay Away from Me" (1949), "Midnight Special" (1945), and "Freight Train Boogie" (1946). Alton's posthumously published autobiography *Truth Is Stranger Than Publicity* remains one of the remarkable documents of early country-music history.

It was during the second phase of their career that the Delmores also formed that definitive country gospel quartet The Browns Ferry Four. Recording in Cincinnati for King Records with radio barn-dance stars Merle Travis and Grandpa Jones, they turned in classic performances such as 1946's "Just a Little Talk with Jesus," "Over in Glory Land," and "Salvation Has Been Brought Down." Along with The Chuck Wagon Gang, the Browns Ferry Four defined gospel quartet harmonies for a generation of performers to come, such as The Statesmen and The Blackwood Brothers.

Browns Ferry Four member Merle Travis (1917–1983) would go on to be-

49

ABOVE: *Old-time music star Grandpa Jones published his memoirs via the University of Tennessee in 1984.*
LEFT: *Merle Travis left a lasting legacy as a guitarist, songwriter, and recording star. This LP appeared in 1962.*

come one of country's most revered guitarists, a hit recording artist ("Divorce Me C.O.D.," "So Round So Firm So Fully Packed," "No Vacancy," etc.), and the composer of such classics as "16 Tons," "Smoke! Smoke! Smoke! (That Cigarette)," and "Dark as a Dungeon." Based on the West Coast, he became a regular on such TV shows as *Town Hall Party* and *Hometown Jamboree* and was featured in the 1953 film *From Here To Eternity*.

The fourth member of the quartet, Grandpa Jones (Louis Marshall Jones, 1913–1998), eventually became a pillar of *The Grand Ole Opry* cast. But his résumé is much longer than that. The Kentucky native was initially a Jimmie Rodgers imitator who began his radio career in Akron, Ohio, as "The Young Singer of Old Songs." Bradley Kincaid took him to Boston and dubbed him "Grandpa" because of his grumpy temperment on early-morning broadcasts. At age twenty-two, Jones adopted the persona and costume that would remain with him throughout his career.

By 1937 Jones was working in West Virginia, where he was taught his "clawhammer" banjo style by entertainer Cousin Emmy. After teaming up with Travis and the Delmores at WLW in Cincinnati, he headed for Nashville and the *Opry* in 1946. There, Grandpa Jones would become one of country's most dedicated champions of old-time hillbilly music. With the rise of television, he became familiar to millions on *Hee Haw*.

Hillbilly entertainers like Jones and The Delmore Brothers were gypsies during radio's golden age. They would work at a barn dance, advertising their concerts in the listening area over the air. After several seasons, they'd generally move on to another radio barn dance and another territory.

There were plenty to choose from: *The Saddle Mountain Round-Up* in Tulsa (KVOO), *The Tennessee Barn Dance* in Knoxville (KNOX), *The Sunset Valley Barn Dance* in Minneapolis (KSTP), *The Bluff Creek Round-Up* in Oklahoma City (KOMA), *The Ozark Jubilee* in Springfield, Missouri (KWTO), *The WHN Barn Dance* in New York City, *The Dinner Bell Roundup* in Pasadena, California (KXLA), and hundreds of smaller shows were on the air in towns throughout the United States in the 1930s and 1940s.

During World War II, *The Grand Ole Opry* took steps to ensure that it would become preeminent among them. Although George D. Hay continued as an announcer, his influence diminished as David Stone (1898–1968) took over the show's reins in the 1930s. This meant less emphasis on old-time string-band music and an increasing concentration on singing stars. The *Opry* moved out of the insurance company's building and began hosting paying audiences in the Hillsboro Theater in 1934. Two years later it moved to the larger Dixie Tabernacle in East Nashville. After a 1939–43 stint at the prestigious War Memorial Auditorium, the *Opry* settled at The Ryman Auditorium, "The Mother Church of Country Music."

WSM had become a fifty-thousand-watt giant with the world's tallest radio tower in 1932. NBC began carrying half-hour *Opry* shows in 1939 and went weekly with nationwide Saturday-night broadcasts in 1943. Republic Pictures

ABOVE: *Roy Acuff Flour sacks were printed with a doll pattern.*
RIGHT: *David Stone made* The Opry *a country-music showcase.*
OPPOSITE: *Bob Miller was one of the first songwriters to make a living penning country tunes.*

Pee Wee King

released *Grand Ole Opry* as a feature in 1940. Paramount countered with *The National Barn Dance* in 1944, but by then Chicago's show was waning—it lost its NBC spot in 1946, and although it was picked up by ABC, things were never the same again.

Meanwhile, Stone went on a talent drive to attract major acts to the *Opry*. In 1938 an East Tennessee singer stepped up to WSM's microphone to sing "The Great Speckled Bird" and walked away from it a star. Roy Acuff (1903–1992) would become a living symbol of *The Grand Ole Opry* to millions for fifty years to come. Baseball great Dizzy Dean dubbed him "The King of Country Music."

"I had wanted for a long, long time to come to Nashville and try to get on the *Opry*," Acuff recalled. "I realized I had to do something to get the attention of the people. I didn't have any idea when I sang 'The Great Speckled Bird' that I'd get the response that I did. But I sang differently from anybody back then. There were crooners back then that'd get up close to the microphone, but I rared back like I was going after the cows, the same way when I used to drive cows out to pasture on the farm. In them hills up there in Union County I sang loud. I've knocked a lot of small stations off of the air. They wasn't expecting a voice with a lot of force and a lot of feeling.

"I took four or five encores that first night. It never happened on *The Grand Ole Opry* before. And my mail came in in bushel baskets, hundreds of letters, hundreds. Then WSM called and asked me if I'd take a regular job. I was real happy that I had impressed the station here with my type of entertainment."

Acuff's full-throttle mountain delivery cut through the airwaves like a knife. It electrified listeners. Within two years

he was the *Opry*'s biggest star and the headliner on the nationally broadcast portion of the show sponsored by Prince Albert Tobacco. In rapid succession in 1938–48 came "Wabash Cannonball," "Wreck on the Highway," "Fireball Mail," "Night Train to Memphis," "Blue Eyes Crying in the Rain," "The Precious Jewel," "Waltz of the Wind," and the rest of the classic records by Roy Acuff and His Smoky Mountain Boys. His songbooks sold like crazy; his gate receipts on the road mushroomed. By 1942 he was making $200,000 a year.

"Roy was 'Mr. Personality,'" says longtime Smoky Mountain Boys guitarist Charlie Collins. "He was an entertainer. He put everything he could into a song. When Roy would sing a song that was sad, I've seen him cry. He wanted to give them everything that he could."

52

LEFT: *Bob Miller managed the hillbilly-music divisions of the Columbia and OKeh labels.*
ABOVE: *Pee Wee King is at lower left as he gathers his Golden West Cowboys around the WSM microphone in 1937.*

Bob Miller

Jimmie Davis

"If ever there was a great country show on the road it was Roy Acuff and the Smoky Mountain Boys," says *Opry* star Jimmy C. Newman. "There was never a dull moment. Every member of the band was featured. I remember on my first tour with them, one of the guys came up and said, 'How about doing the "Baby Buggy" song?' And I said, 'I don't know how it goes.' He said, 'It don't go, you gotta push it!' These guys would take you off guard; and they gave me good training."

Acuff's arrival coincided exactly with the *Opry*'s rise to the front ranks of the radio barn dances. The show recruited Bill Monroe (1939), Ernest Tubb (1942), Eddy Arnold (1943), Red Foley (1946), Hank Williams (1949), and Hank Snow (1950), giving it an unparalleled cast of stars. All of these men left indelible marks on the subsequent history of country music.

Pee Wee King and his Golden West Cowboys auditioned at WSM in the spring of 1937. This was the act that taught the rest of the cast true professionalism. The band was dressed to kill in silk western attire. Years of radio work in Kentucky had polished its presentation to a sheen.

"We knew what we were doing," King recalled. "We were organized." The band came to the *Opry* with a complete variety show—a comic, a "girl singer," an emcee, and a hot fiddler. The package even included a promoter/booking agent, the innovative J.L. Frank. Within a year of the act's arrival at the *Opry* he had King in Hollywood making a movie with Gene Autry.

King (Frank Kuczynski, born 1914) was a diminutive accordion player who'd backed Autry on *The National Barn Dance*. After rising to stardom on radio in Louisville, he brought his

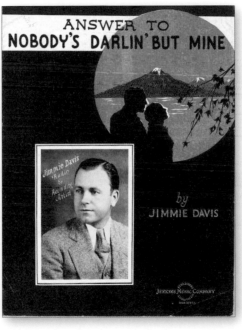

waltzes, polkas, and western songs to the *Opry* stage. During his ten years as an *Opry* star, he introduced drums, the trumpet, and the electric guitar to the barn dance. With band member Redd Stewart he wrote the classics "Slow Poke," "You Belong to Me," "Bonaparte's Retreat," and "The Tennessee Waltz." At various times his troupe included future stars Eddy Arnold, Ernest Tubb, and Cowboy Copas.

King's band also included Minnie Pearl (Sarah Ophelia Colley Cannon, 1912–1996), the beloved comic who joined the *Opry* cast in 1940. On the road with King during the war years, she developed her stage character, the quintessential hillbilly spinster who tells funny stories about her neighbors and relations in mythical "Grinders Switch." In years to come she would become the *Opry* stars' "mother confessor" as well as the show's leading ambassador to the world at large.

"I have never gotten over the debt that I owe the *Opry*," she said. "The *Opry* was a marvelous break for me that I will always remember. When I came in 1940, most of the people who listened to the *Opry* were considered hillbillies. Nowadays, you don't know where you're going to find a country fan. I see people coming to my museum from all walks of life. Those of us who have lived this long in show business cannot explain to you who haven't how much this has changed. Every time I go to the *CMA Awards Show* I think about how far we've come."

The radio barn-dance era was a time of tremendous growth for the country-music industry. The radio stars showed amateurs that it was possible to make a living playing hillbilly music.

53

ABOVE: *Jimmie Davis was a 37-year-old radio and records sensation when pictured on this sheet music in 1936. In 1999 he celebrated his 100th birthday.*

Farm and Ranch

SOUTHERN AGRICULTURIST

JANUARY 1955

Howw...deee!

Minnie Pearl

Carson J. Robison

In 1932, for instance, radio entertainers Carson J. Robison and His Buckaroos became the first country act to tour internationally—to England, Scotland, Australia, New Zealand, and Canada. Robison (1890–1957) was also one of country's first songwriting professionals, contributing "My Blue Ridge Mountain Home," "Barnacle Bill the Sailor," "Life Gets Tee-Jus, Don't It," and a number of other classics to the genre during his thirty-year career.

As the record business rebounded in the mid-1930s, many of the radio rubes found themselves with nationally popular hits. The prolific Bob Miller (1895–1955) joined Robison as one of country's earliest professional songwriters by coming up with two of the earliest hits, 1933's "Twenty-One Years" and "Seven Beers with the Wrong Woman." Gene Autry's "That Silver Haired Daddy of Mine," Tex Owens's "Cattle Call," and Karl & Harty's "I'm Here to Get My Baby out of Jail" were disc successes of 1934. The following year, Dallas radio stars Bill Boyd's Cowboy Ramblers had a smash with their instrumental "Under the Double Eagle." North Carolina's *Crazy Barn Dance* radio act J.E. Mainer's Mountaineers scored with "Maple on the Hill" in 1936.

When Decca Records was formed in 1934, it made an immediate commitment to country music. The label signed Jimmie Davis (born 1899), whose "Nobody's Darling but Mine" (1934) was one of the biggest hits of the Depression. Davis would go on to have hits with "There's a New Moon over My Shoulder" (1945), "Supper Time" (1950), and "You Are My Sunshine" (1940), and translated his country stardom into the governorship of Louisiana in 1944. His 1947 movie *Louisiana* was the first biographical film made about a country star.

"I'll never forget when I was elected Governor, *Life* magazine carried a two-page spread that said, 'Hillbilly elected Governor of Louisiana,'" Davis recalled. "I guess they thought Louisiana was ruined. I don't know. But anyway, that's what they said.

"*Louisiana* was made while I was still Governor. It was the story of my life, from the ground on up. I didn't know anything about acting, but all I had to do was be myself.

"I was known as The Singin' Governor. That's what they'd call me. Sometimes they might call you somethin' else. But one thing about it, it sold a lot of records for me."

In 1936 *Radio Guide* magazine estimated that country's barn-dance performers were a $25 million business, stating that five thousand radio programs had featured hillbilly music in 1935. *Collier's* checked in with a 1938 piece prophetically titled "There's Gold in Them Hillbillies."

Thanks to radio, country music had become a permanent part of the American cultural landscape.

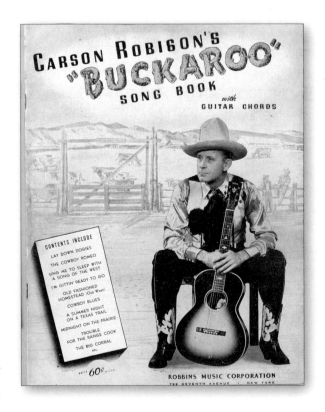

55

Three

Sons of the Pioneers
A REPUBLIC PICTURE

Singing Cowboys

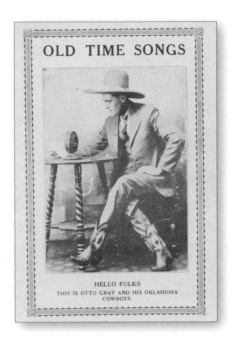

Our early folk heroes were frontiersmen, the brave explorers of a vast and unknown continent. Men like buckskin-clad Daniel Boone and Davy Crockett captured the public's imagination in the early 1800s. The true and mythic deeds of Natty Bumppo ("The Deerslayer"), Lewis and Clark, Johnny Appleseed (John Chapman), Paul Bunyan, Mike Fink, Jim Bowie, Old Stormalong, "Squawman" Jim Beckwourth, and the like, paraded across the cultural landscape. But around the time of the Civil War, another kind of frontier hero supplanted them.

The California Gold Rush of 1848 was followed by the western migration of "sodbusters" who staked their claims to the western prairies. Soon after the Civil War it became feasible for Texas ranchers to drive their vast herds of cattle to midwestern railroad hubs where they could fetch top dollar. The men who drove them became known as "cowboys."

A typical cattle drive might consist of twenty-five hundred longhorns attended by perhaps a dozen cowboys. They slept outdoors, sang around campfires at night, and rode for hundreds of miles at the rate of ten or twenty miles a day.

Almost at once, the image of the workingman out in nature captured

57

LEFT: *The Sons of the Pioneers surround bearded cowboy sidekick Gabby Hayes in 1942.*
ABOVE: *The most important early popularizer of cowboy songs was Otto Gray.*

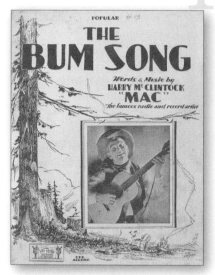

the imagination of easterners. Dime novels of the 1870s and 1880s romanticized the cowboy's life. Rustlers, sharpshooters, frontier marshals, gunslingers, outlaws, and the rest of the west's mythic population was set in place in these little books. And although the era of the long cattle drive was over by 1895, the cowboy image took permanent hold on the American imagination.

"Europe had knights in shining armor, Robin Hood, King Arthur and all that; and we didn't," explains singing cowboy Don Edwards. "But along came the cowboy. It was a lot more romantic than the farmer or the clerk in the store or anything like that. They would send these stories back East, just as fast as they could write them, romanticizing this lifestyle."

Owen Wister's 1902 novel *The Virginian* sold more than two million copies and inspired a long-running play and four movies. Calamity Jane's highly embellished "autobiography" was a top seller in 1896. Wyatt Earp, Billy the Kid, Bat Masterson, Kit Carson, Belle Starr, Jesse James, and Wild Bill Hickok all paraded to fame.

In 1910 John Lomax (1875–1948) published *Cowboy Songs and Other Frontier Ballads*, the most popular and influential collection of authentic cowboy folk music. Expanded and reissued in 1916 and 1938, it remains in print to this day. In its pages are the definitive versions of such standards as "Git along Little Dogies," "The Old Chisolm Trail," "Goodbye Old Paint," "The Colorado Trail," and "Sweet Betsy from Pike."

Like the Appalachian songs of The Carter Family, some of these cowboy folk tunes have their roots in the British Isles. Says Michael Martin Murphey, "Irish music was phenomenally popular in the west. 'Streets of Loredo' is based on a song that was originally called 'The Unfortunate Rake.' 'Streets of Loredo'

depicts the same thing that the old Irish ballad depicts, the rake who regrets his life and warns the others not to go this way.

"Another example would be 'Oh Bury Me Not on the Lone Prairie,' originally called 'Bury Me Not in the Deep Deep Sea.' It was used as an Irish sailors' burial song."

"The Yellow Rose of Texas," on the other hand, is American folk music all the way. The song commemorates a mulatto servant named Emily D. West, who worked on a plantation south of present-day Houston. When the Mexican dictator/general Santa Anna came calling in 1836, Emily's beauty and wiles kept him occupied while Sam Houston's Texas revolutionaries launched the Battle of San Jacinto, defeating a force twice their size and freeing the Lone Star State from Mexico.

These folk songs were soon joined by commercially written western material. Tin Pan Alley's sheet-music composers did their part in popularizing the "Golden West" by turning out a number of songs with Indian characters in 1903–10, followed by a rash of western titles between 1905 and 1919.

William F. "Buffalo Bill" Cody (1846–1917) put together his Wild West Show in 1883 as a dramatic spectacle that showed audiences reenactments of Indian battles and the Pony Express, bronco busting, roping demonstrations, displays of marksmanship, and equestrian derring-do. Annie Oakley, Chief Sitting Bull, and the rest of the cast played to millions during the next twenty years.

Powder River Jack and Kitty Lee joined the troupe in 1895 and formed one of the pioneering western-music acts. "Red River Valley" and several of the other singing-cowboy standards were in their repertoire. Billy McGinty was another of Buffalo Bill's singing cowboys. He eventually

ABOVE: *Singing cowboy "Mac" McClintock was also among the foremost popularizers of hobo songs, as this sheet music attests.*

ac" McClintock

formed his own traveling cowboy band in vaudeville.

Otto Gray and His Oklahoma Cowboy Band was the most popular and widely traveled of all the early singing-cowboy units. Formed in 1918, Gray's troupe merged with McGinty's and became a major vaudeville attraction. The act made a fortune by taking the exotic image of the rope-twirling cowboy to eastern cities. Otto Gray and His Oklahoma Cowboy Band eventually graduated to records and film shorts before retiring in 1936.

Gray (1890–1967) promoted the act in large *Billboard* magazine ads that pictured the band's customized travel vehicles and flashy white ten-gallon hats. "They can broadcast for eighteen hours without repeating and without looking at a sheet of music or referring to memoranda for their radio program dialogue," boasted one piece of publicity.

The record industry made hay with singing cowboys beginning with Carl T. Sprague's 1925 hit "When the Work's All Done This Fall," followed closely by Jules Verne Allen, who recorded such classics as "Home on the Range" and "Little Joe the Wrangler" for Victor in 1928–29.

Harry "Mac" McClintock (1882–1957) was one of early country music's most colorful characters. The former cowboy, railroad worker, and hobo became a radio entertainer in 1925 on KFRC in San Francisco. Between 1928 and 1931 "Hay-wire Mac" recorded a number of his cowboy tunes for Victor. His ultimate legacy, however, was popularizing hobo songs and lore including "Big Rock Candy Mountain," "Hallelujah I'm a Bum," and "The Bum Song."

Jimmie Rodgers popularized a number of cowboy tunes, as did Vernon Dalhart. Kansas native Carson Robison adopted the image completely, took it overseas with his Buckaroos, and con-

tributed "Carry Me Back to the Lone Prairie" to the cowboy song repertoire. In 1929 Billie Maxwell became the record industry's first singing cowgirl. Marc Williams, "The Singing Texan," was another western-music pioneer, recording for Brunswick in 1928 and 1934.

The emerging movie industry was also quick to capitalize on the cowboy image. Buffalo Bill's troupe was filmed by Thomas Edison in 1894, and the resulting shorts were widely popular in penny arcades in the hand-cranked Kinetoscope "peep show" machines. After the development of projected films around the turn of the century, the first "feature film" was a western, 1903's ten-minute-long *The Great Train Robbery*. One of its cast members, Bronco Billy Anderson, became the very first person you could call a "movie star."

Bronco Billy was succeeded by silent stars William S. Hart, Tom Mix, Buck Jones, Hoot Gibson, and others as the emerging movie studios began to create the first generation of cinema idols. Wild West show veteran Will Rogers made an easy transition from the vaudeville stage to the silver screen.

The coming of sound meant the coming of music to the movies. In late 1929 Universal Pictures filmed *The Wagon Master*, which featured Ken Maynard singing two cowboy tunes. Maynard recorded them for Columbia Records after the film was released the following year. His *In Old Santa Fe* film in 1934 had a musical segment in the middle that featured a better singer, newcomer Gene Autry.

"Autry's magnetism was really obvious," says western-music historian Charlie Seemann. "*In Old Santa Fe* was ostensibly a Ken Maynard movie; he was the star. But Gene Autry comes cruising through, singing a song, and you can just feel everybody's at-

Bill

ABOVE: *The Wild West shows of Buffalo Bill Cody were seen by millions and were the launchpad for several western-music performers.*

Art Satherley

tention shift from Maynard to Autry."

Gene Autry (1907–1998) was already a well-known country-music personality by then. Born and raised in Tioga, Texas, he'd begun his musical career in that town's clubs and on the road entertaining in The Fields Brothers Marvelous Medicine Show. He was nineteen and working as a telegraph operator when a visiting Will Rogers swapped songs with him and urged him to become a music professional. Autry was a Jimmie Rodgers imitator, so in 1927 he went to New York to audition for Rodgers' label, Victor Records.

Told he wasn't yet ready to record, Autry began singing on KVOO in Tulsa, Oklahoma. He finally made his disc debut in 1929. According to David Rothel's *The Gene Autry Book*, record producer "Uncle" Art Satherley (1889–1986) advised the would-be recording star, "I'm just starting and if you'll sign with me, I'll do everything in the world I can to promote you. You'd be my first artist. Victor is a big company and they have several big artists that they have to concentrate on. I don't think you'll get the promotion that I can give you."

Satherley was an executive with the newly formed American Record Corporation (ARC). Autry had his sights set on Victor. But he signed with Satherley and struck paydirt when he recorded the million-selling "That Silver Haired Daddy of Mine" for ARC in 1931.

ARC marketed its music on customized labels for various department stores, including Banner (sold by W.T. Grant stores), Oriole (McCrory's), Romeo (S.H. Kress), and Conqueror (Sears). The Sears connection was ideal for Autry's next move. In late 1931 he was hired to entertain on Chicago's mighty WLS and its *National Barn Dance*. His own program was called "Conqueror Record Time,"

sponsored by Sears. The Chicago-based retailer capitalized on the tie-in by prominently featuring Autry's records in its catalogs, then Gene Autry songbooks, guitar instruction manuals, and a Gene Autry "Round-Up" guitar.

Satherley urged Autry to focus on western songs and to build up his cowboy image. Autry obliged with the 1933 hits "The Last Roundup" and "Cowboy's Heaven." NBC began carrying *The National Barn Dance* on network radio in 1933; meanwhile, Autry was badgering Hollywood for an audition. ARC executive Herbert Yates had film business interests and pressured Republic Pictures into giving the singing cowboy a try. In 1934 Autry headed for California.

"I only had the one scene to do in Maynard's picture, the barn dance scene, and I was nervous about it," he recalled in his autobiography *Back in the Saddle Again*. "My hands worried me. I didn't know what to do with them. So it occurred to me to wear gloves. Then, when I had nothing else to do, I could tug on them. It became my most identifiable screen habit."

After *In Old Santa Fe*, Autry was cast in a Maynard serial called *Mystery Mountain*. His own twelve-chapter serial, *Phantom Empire*, and his first starring feature, *Tumbling Tumbleweeds*, made him a star in 1935. By 1939 he was one of the biggest box-office attractions in Hollywood.

"This was the heart of the Depression," comments Ranger Doug Green of *The Grand Ole Opry*'s western trio Riders In the Sky. "People looked for an escape or something wonderful and romantic, away from the pressure. Free life. Fresh air. Gene Autry on his horse just took the nation by storm. He was

ABOVE: *British Art Satherley loved singing cowboy music.*
RIGHT: *Gene Autry's face appeared on the sheet music of dozens of classic cowboy songs.*
OPPOSITE: *All major singing cowboys starred in comic books.*

BIG 52 PAGES OF EXCITING ADVENTURES IN FULL COLOR

A Fawcett Publication

Monte Hale
WESTERN

NOV.
10¢
NO. 54

THRILL TO
MONTE HALE'S
ADVENTURES IN
FRONTIER DANGER!

PLUS **GABBY HAYES**

sort of Everyman. He was your uncle. And he solved problems not with his fists, but with his beautiful smile and a song."

Adds the trio's Fred LaBour, "Gene Autry's code was be nice to old people and women and treat 'em with respect, and be nice and gentle with kids. And kids sense that. This is a grown-up who also has a bit of a kid in him. This is someone that a kid can really relate to. He's dressing in these outlandish clothes and lives this life of going camping with his friends and singing songs.

"He just has this likable, American sort of flat midwestern voice that's very accessible. It's a comforting kind of voice. It's pleasant, you know?"

"I personally never considered myself a great actor, a great singer or anything of that sort," said Autry. "But what the hell is my opinion against that of 250 million other people?

"I didn't deserve it, but I've had lumbago a few times and I didn't deserve that either."

Unquestionably one of the greatest American superstars of all time, Autry made 90 films, sold more than 40 million records, recorded more than 635 selections, and wrote some 200 songs. Among his many classics are "Mexicali Rose" (1936), "South of the Border" (1939), "Be Honest with Me" (1941), "Jingle Jangle Jingle" (1942), "Don't Fence Me In" (1945), and "Buttons and Bows" (1948), as well as the holiday standards "Here Comes Santa Claus" (1948), "Rudolph the Red Nosed Reindeer" (1949), "Peter Cottontail" (1950), and "Frosty the Snowman" (1950).

His *Melody Ranch* was a nationwide radio show from 1939 to 1955. In 1950 he became the first movie star with his own TV series. By the 1980s he owned radio and TV stations, a luxury hotel, three song-publishing companies, a record label, considerable California real estate, oil interests, and the California Angels baseball team.

"It's a mom-and-pop operation worth $450 million," observed country star Cliffie Stone wryly.

"We only go through this life once," Autry said. "I don't know anybody that's come back. There's only two things you have to worry about—if you're happy or unhappy. I've had an awful lot of fun.

"I have always wanted to perpetuate for future generations the glorious history of the West and relate how it has influenced America and the world. I wanted to record the history of the West, so that people would remember how this nation was built."

To that end, he endowed the magnificent Gene Autry Western Heritage Museum as "my gift to posterity and the city of Los Angeles."

Autry's silver-screen popularity ignited a craze for singing cowboys in Hollywood in the 1930s and 1940s. Dick Foran, who was the Warner Bros. entry in the sweepstakes, introduced the pop standard "I'll Remember April." Opera-trained Fred Scott was at Spectrum Pictures. Monogram had Jack Randall, who died in a horseback riding accident while filming in 1945. Bob Baker was at Universal. Smith Ballew was at Twentieth Century Fox. Ken Curtis was at Columbia.

Ray Whitley (1901–1979) was RKO's cowpoke—he wrote Gene Autry's theme song, "Back in the Saddle Again," and developed Gibson's J-200 deluxe acoustic guitar, which became the instrument of choice for all singing cowboys. Easygoing Monte Hale (born 1921) made Republic's first color film, *Home On the Range*, and sold more than two million comic books per month during his heyday in the late 1940s. Eddie Dean (Edgar Dean Glosup, 1907–1999) and Jimmy Wakely (1914–1982) gained fame in the 1940s by introducing the landmark "cheating" songs "One

Ray Whitley

ABOVE: *Ray Whitley's singing-cowboy contributions include songwriting and guitar innovations.*

Jimmy Wakely

Has My Name (The Other Has My Heart)" (1948, Dean) and "Slipping Around" (1949, Wakely in a duet with Margaret Whiting).

Tex Ritter (Woodward Maurice Ritter, 1905–1974) came to Monogram Pictures by way of the Great White Way. A true scholar of western music, Ritter had learned from John Lomax at the University of Texas. After appearing as a singing cowboy on Houston radio, Ritter went to New York, where he was cast to sing four songs in the 1930 Broadway production *Green Grow the Lilacs*, the play that would later become the celebrated 1943 cowboy musical *Oklahoma!* While in New York he became a singing cowboy on radio and starred at the Madison Square Garden Rodeo.

In the wake of Autry's spectacular success, Ritter headed for Hollywood and made his singing-cowboy debut in 1936's *Song of the Gringo*. His disc career caught fire when he signed with the new Capitol Records label in 1942.

Ritter's highly distinctive Texas drawl created such hits for the company as "Jealous Heart," "Rye Whiskey," "Deck of Cards," "Pecos Bill," and "You Two Timed Me One Time Too Often" in 1944–48. He reemerged as a musical force with 1952's Oscar-winning theme song from *High Noon* ("Do Not Forsake Me O My Darling") and in 1961 with his hit recitation of Eddie Dean's "I Dreamed of a Hillbilly Heaven."

In 1965 "America's Most Beloved Cowboy" moved to Nashville, joined the cast of *The Grand Ole Opry*, became a radio personality with WSM's Ralph Emery, and ran unsuccessfully for political office.

"I was just that much richer by being around Tex Ritter," says Hank Thompson, who was

brought to Capitol Records by the singing cowboy. "Tex knew all kinds of things. He was a student of not only Texas history, but of American history, world history. He had studied law in college. He was well versed.

"He had a great sense of humor—he never told jokes; he told stories. And what a performer on the stage! He was a fellow that if I could just be around him, I felt like some of this was rubbin' off on me."

"He was pretty much imitated," says son John Ritter, who is now a popular TV actor. "A lot of the country artists, while he was living and after he died, took great joy in imitating his distinctive tear in his voice, where he'd break a note up."

Most of the movie cowboys' songs were quite different from the traditional tunes sung by real range riders. They were melodic, pastoral odes to the great outdoors, the glories of the western landscape, and the ideals of cowboy life. Their finest composers were unquestionably the members of The Sons of the Pioneers.

The group was formed when Ohio-bred Leonard Slye (soon to become Roy Rogers) teamed up with Oklahoman Tim Spencer and Canadian Bob Nolan as The Pioneer Trio in 1933. The Los Angeles radio station KFWB took them on and provided valuable exposure. The trio's stunning three-part harmony yodeling and strikingly handsome looks began drawing bigger and bigger crowds to its personal appearances in southern California. In 1934 fiddler Hugh Farr joined the act, which then became The Sons of the Pioneers. A year later the Sons joined the roster of the new label Decca Records and added Hugh's gifted guitarist brother Karl Farr to the act.

The Farrs were sensational instru-

63

ABOVE: *Sheet music printers were glad to boost sales with the smiling faces of singing cowboys like Tex Ritter and Jimmy Wakely.*

Sons of the Pioneers

mentalists. Spencer and Nolan were both superb songwriters. The latter contributed "Cool Water," "Tumbling Tumbleweeds," "Chant of the Wanderer," "One More Ride," "Way out There," "When Pay Day Rolls Around," and more than a hundred other western classics. Spencer's songs include "Cigareetes, Whusky and Wild Women," "Moonlight on the Trail," and "Room Full of Roses."

"Tumbling Tumbleweeds" became a top pop hit in 1934, launching a string of successes on Decca that included "Cool Water" (1941), "Cielito Lindo" (1941), and "Private Buckaroo" (1942). The Sons switched to RCA Victor in 1945, scoring major hits with "Stars and Stripes on Iwo Jima" (1945), "Baby Doll" (1947), "Blue Shadows on the Trail" (1948), and others.

The group's undeniable talent inevitably led to its discovery by the moviemakers. Within a few short years of banding together they were penning songs "on demand" for westerns. In 1935–37 they became film stars, themselves, when Columbia tapped The Sons of the Pioneers to appear in a series of Charles Starrett westerns.

In 1937 group member Leonard Slye was in a hat shop to pick up the white Stetson he'd left there for cleaning. An actor rushed in, apparently in a hurry to buy a cowboy hat. Slye asked him what all the excitement was about.

"He said that Republic Pictures was holding auditions the next day for a new singing cowboy, and he needed a hat fast so he could look the part," recalled Roy Rogers in his book *Happy Trails*. "Republic already had Gene Autry, but Gene's contract was up for renewal and the word around town was that he was hoping for the big raise he thought he deserved. To put the pressure on Gene to keep his contract demands in line, Republic had set up these auditions to find another singing cowboy.

"I didn't have an appointment, but I went anyway. On Oct. 13, 1937, I became a contract player at Republic Pictures."

At the time, Slye was billing himself as "Dick Weston." In 1938 the studio dubbed him "Roy Rogers." Autry did what he had been threatening

to do. He quit, and Rogers was rushed into the lead role of what was to be Autry's next Republic western, *Washington Cowboy*. Retitled *Under Western Stars*, it launched the cinema stardom of "The King of the Cowboys." Gene Autry rejoined the studio, but when he enlisted in World War II, Rogers was given Republic's big publicity buildup. Blessed with a glorious, sunny yodel, a trim physique, natural horsemanship, and drop-dead handsome, dimpled looks, Roy Rogers (1911–1998) became one of the most beloved entertainment figures in history. He starred in ninety-one feature films, and then moved on to a

wildly successful career as a Saturday-morning kiddie-TV star. His old friends The Sons of the Pioneers quickly switched from appearing in Starrett's westerns to joining Rogers' casts.

So did Trigger. Virtually all of the movie cowboys had showy trademark horses, including Champion (Autry), White Dust (Fred Scott), Apache (Bob Baker), Sunset (Jimmy Wakely), Pardner (Monte Hale), Tony (Tom Mix), Tarzan (Ken Maynard), and Eddie Dean's steeds Copper, Flash, and White Cloud. But Trigger lived up to his billing as "The Smartest Horse in the Movies."

"They threw away the pattern when they made Trigger," said Rogers fondly. "He was just the greatest horse that ever came along. The studio said, 'We gotta have a horse

65

LEFT: *Eddie Dean's career began in 1926 and his singing voice was still powerful well into the 1990s.*
ABOVE: *Roy Rogers, third from left, fronts his beloved Sons of the Pioneers.*

Dale

for ya,' when I first signed up out there. They called all the stables and said, 'Bring your real pretty stock.' Trigger was about the third one I looked at. I just can't say enough for Trigger. He could do anything. He could go anywhere. I got a picture of him with seven of my kids on him, from his ears back to his tail. And he'd just never get mad or never had a mean thought in his mind."

Roy Rogers is the only person who has been enshrined twice in the Country Music Hall of Fame, once as a member of The Sons of the Pioneers and once as a solo star. Although he was probably the best vocalist of all the singing cowboys, he ironically was never the record star that Autry, Wakely, and Ritter were.

Still, singing cowboy Rex Allen was in awe of his rival. "When I first saw Roy Rogers and heard him sing and with those great Sons of the Pioneers behind him, I thought, 'My Lord, that's the greatest guy I've ever heard in my life.' And I still feel the same way.

"God, he had merchandise of everything. Anything he could put Roy and Trigger on, he had it. And Roy made a lot of money in the merchandise business, more than any of them."

"Roy Rogers was second only to Walt Disney," says record producer and western memorabilia collector Snuff Garrett. "He had so many products out. Merchandising was always an important part to Roy Rogers' career. Autry missed some of it because he was away in the service for over four years. The Lone Ranger had a few items. Hopalong Cassidy, in the early days of television, had many products. They had a Range Rider cowboy set. In Annie Oakley's day, they had the Annie Oakley talking whip. That's why I always wanted to know Annie well. She had a talking whip."

Oakley was portrayed on TV by Gail

Davis, who also attempted a recording career. *Annie Get Your Gun,* the 1946 musical about Oakley's life, starred Ethel Merman on Broadway, and Betty Hutton got the part in the movie after Judy Garland fell ill.

Singing cowgirls rode alongside singing cowboys. Grand National Pictures promoted Dorothy Page in the 1939 features *Ride 'Em Cowgirl, Water Rustlers,* and, appropriately, *The Singing Cowgirl.* The WLS *National Barn Dance* had Louise Massey & The Westerners, The Girls of the Golden West, cowgirl-garbed Jenny Lou Carson, and Patsy Montana.

The last-named got her moniker when she made movie shorts as a member of Montie Montana's trio The Montana Cowgirls. After rising to stardom at WLS, Montana (Rubye Blevins, 1912–1996) returned to Hollywood to appear in Autry's 1939 feature *Colorado Sunset.* In it, she performed her cowgirl anthem "I Want to Be a Cowboy's Sweetheart."

"The first time I was on the Barn Dance, I had to do a song about Montana," she recalled. "So I took [Stuart Hamblen's] 'Texas Plains' and just changed states to make it 'Montana Plains.' That sort of set my style. In fact, 'Cowboy's Sweetheart' is written almost like 'Texas Plains' on purpose. 'Cause I've always had to do little peppy, western-swing type tunes. Still my favorites."

Montana had her own network radio show in 1946–47, starred on *The Louisiana Hayride* in 1948, and continued to perform concerts well into the 1990s.

"I've never done anything else," she said shortly before

ABOVE: *Roy Rogers waves from Trigger.*
RIGHT: *Singing cowgirl Patsy Montana is credited as the first female country artist to record a million-seller.*
OPPOSITE: *Dale Evans poses as "The Queen of the West."*

Evans

her death. "If I had to get a job now, it'd be baby sittin' or washin' dishes or somethin'. It's so nice to do somethin' you like to do. I get fan letters from people that's been writin' for fifty years. I've watched them grow old along with me."

The most famous singing cowgirl was yet another member of the Roy Rogers troupe, Dale Evans, "The Queen of the West." Born Frances Octavia Smith in 1912, she was a radio singer who was cast opposite Roy Rogers in 1944's *The Cowboy and the Senorita*. The team clicked with audiences as well as with one another. They married in 1947 and became national radio costars the following year.

The media became fascinated with the couple's Christian lifestyle and the children they adopted. To deal with a series of tragedies associated with her family, Evans wrote twenty-five inspirational books. She was also a major songwriter, creating "Aha San Antone," "I Wish I Had Never Met Sunshine," "The Bible Tells Me So," and their immortal TV theme song "Happy Trails."

The Roy Rogers/Dale Evans TV series of 1951–64 featured her as the owner of the Eureka Cafe in mythical Mineral City. Her horse Buttermilk, the "wonder dog" Bullet, and Pat Brady's jeep Nellybelle were all part of the action.

By the time that Rogers, Evans, and Autry were on TV, the classic era of the Hollywood singing cowboy was ending. The last major star was Rex Allen, another graduate of *The National Barn Dance*. Born in Arizona in 1920, Allen was one of the few of his ilk who actually grew up as a cowboy.

"They were looking for another idiot in a white hat and I was there," he says with a chuckle. "They billed me at

68

Barn Dance [1945–49] as The Arizona Cowboy. And we had a national following, so it just became the title of my first movie because Republic wanted to capitalize on that.

"Roy Rogers was leaving Republic and going out on his own and he wanted to do a television series. I said, 'Roy, there's so many cowboys out there now doin' movies and things. Isn't there enough of 'em?' He said, 'There's room for fifty more of us. Just come and get it.' Republic thought television was a thing that was a little baby that would just go away, that the picture business was still where it should be. But Roy and Gene both went into television immediately. Republic—would you believe?—wouldn't even let me do an interview on television.

"You work exclusively for that one studio and you eat what they tell you to eat and you wear what they tell you to wear. You belong to 'em, lock, stock, and barrel. There was a morals clause in the contract—never smoke in public; never be seen with a drink in your hand. I was never to walk out my front door unless I had western attire on. You had to play the same character in real life that you played on the screen. And it was not a hard way to live. I kinda enjoyed it. Still do.

"My movies were made for a young audience, from five years old to twelve. Our movies were good babysitters for moms and dads who wanted to get rid of the kids for a couple of hours while they did some shopping or something.

"But people quit going to the theaters. They wouldn't go see hardly anything because they had the little boob tube in the corner of the room. And it hurt the motion picture business terribly."

On his famous horse Koko, golden-voiced Rex Allen became the last of the great singing cowboys. From his radio, movie, and TV fame he built a recording career that included the hits "Crying in the Chapel" (1953) and "Don't Go Near the Indians" (1962). In the 1960s he became the narrator of more than eighty Walt Disney films, notably the "True Life Adventure" series.

ABOVE: *Golden-voiced Rex Allen appeared on the cover of country music's most enduring fan magazine in 1954.*

Rex Allen

Jeffries

At one time, the country-music world was full of western stars—Foy Willing & The Riders of the Purple Sage, Johnny Bond, Bill Boyd, Jack Guthrie, and dozens of others were nationally known. The genre was even called "country and western" in the late 1940s and early 1950s. The popularity of the romanticized West lifted country music to previously undreamed of popularity.

Children everywhere played cowboys, as black singer Herb Jeffries discovered when he was relaxing behind a Columbus, Ohio, nightclub one evening in 1935.

"There were about eight or nine kids running up the alley," Jeffries recalls. "And a little black child was falling behind and crying. So the boys in the band called him over and said, 'What happened? Did those boys hit you?' And he said, 'No, they're my friends. But they don't want to let me play cowboy with them. I want to be Tom Mix and they won't let me be, because Tom Mix is not a negro.' That really got to me."

And so smooth baritone Herb Jeffries became *The Bronze Buckaroo*, a black singing cowboy. Mantan Moreland and The Four Tones were other rhythm-and-blues (r&b) acts that transformed themselves into African American singing cowboys in low-budget features. Jeffries (born 1912) would go on to perform in Duke Ellington's band (1940–42) and have pop hits such as 1947's "When I Write My Song" and 1949's "The Four Winds and the Seven Seas" before returning to western music with a Warner Bros. Records album in 1995 at the age of eighty-three.

The singing cowboy left a number of permanent marks on country music. Not the least of these is image. To this day, cowboy boots, rodeo belt buckles, blue jeans, and cowboy hats are the uniform of male country artists. And there are acts that take cowboy couture to even more elaborate lengths—rhinestone-bedecked jackets that evolved from rodeo costume attire and Mexican Mariachi-band costumes.

Roy Rogers recalled how these were introduced: "I got to playin' these big, Madison Square Garden auditoriums. When they introduced you, you'd come out, and you'd look like a little doll, you're so far away. So I thought, 'I've gotta figure out some way where the people can at least see me.' So I started with 'Nudie' Cohen, talked him into makin' me those real flashy things. So when I come through the gates and the spots hit us, we lit up like a Christmas tree. That's basically what caused all of the flashy stuff."

Rogers wore vivid embroidered cowboy shirts, dripping with inches of silver fringe that danced in the spotlights. Little Jimmy Dickens introduced this flashy attire to the stage of *The Grand Ole Opry* in 1949, and thereafter virtually all of the show's classic stylists of the 1950s were resplendent in rhinestoned and appliquéd creations, including Faron Young, Webb Pierce, Carl Smith, Porter Wagoner, and Ray Price.

"Those costumes, I understand, evolved from parade outfits," says Marty Stuart. "If you'll watch the Rose Bowl Parade or whatever, you'll see these elaborate saddles and rhinestone costumes. Country singers, by way of the singing cowboys, just bought those costumes. And it made perfect sense—western wear and country music.

"The first band that really deserves the credit is The Maddox Brothers and Rose. Right at the end of the Depression, they would arrive in town in five identical

ABOVE: *Herb Jeffries was "The Bronze Buckaroo." He returned on disc as a singing cowboy at age 83.*

Milton Bro

sive it even penetrated country's jazzy substyle western swing. This style was the merger of hot hillbilly fiddle music with big-band oomph. Milton Brown (1903–1936) was one of its earliest proponents. In 1930 he joined Bob Wills and guitarist Herman Arnspiger in The Light Crust Doughboys.

In 1932 Milton Brown formed his influential Musical Brownies. They held Saturday-night dances in Fort Worth, Texas, that were promoted via their broadcasts on the city's powerful WBAP. Brown's 1934–36 recordings established the early western-swing repertoire with "Right or Wrong," "Corinne Corinna," "Sitting on top of the World," and the like. But the bandleader died at age thirty-two on April 18, 1936, as a result of injuries in a car crash. An estimated thirty-five hundred music lovers attended his funeral.

That left Bob Wills (1905–1975) to carry the torch. Raised as a Texas country fiddler, he left the Doughboys a year after Brown's death. With vocalist Tommy Duncan (1911–1967), Wills headed for Oklahoma City and KVOO radio. His Texas Playboys organization prospered there in 1934–40 and grew to sixteen players.

Recording success with producer Art Satherley on the ARC labels led to Wills's joining the Hollywood singing-cowboy brigade in 1940. During the next five years he made thirteen films. Cindy Walker provided songs for many of these, including such Wills classics as "Dusty Skies," "Blue Bonnet Lane," "Hubbin' It," "Miss Molly," and "You're from Texas."

Wills reformed the big-band Texas Playboys after World War II and rose to even greater fame. Huge crowds in California attended dance halls to hear his twenty-two-piece group, making him one of the highest-paid bandleaders in America. "Cherokee Maiden" (1941), "New San Antonio Rose" (1943), "Texas Playboy Rag" (1945), "Stay a Little Longer" (1946), "New Spanish Two Step" (1946), "Roly Poly" (1946), "Bubbles in My Beer" (1948), "Faded Love" (1950), and other hits made him an even bigger recording star than before.

Cadillacs, jump out of these cars in these elaborate costumes, heavily embroidered with rhinestones, hit the stage with a high energy show, and leave people wonderin' what happened. Now that's what it's all about to me to this day. Those costumes just made the music sound better, as far as I was concerned."

"There came a time when it became very unhip and very uncool to wear these kinds of clothes," observes Bill Anderson, "but I never felt as much like a star on the stage dressed any other way."

The music as well as the visual style of the singing cowboys has undergone a resurgence. Michael Martin Murphey's West Fest celebrations, launched in 1986, have western art, gun and rope-twirling exhibitions, Indian and mountain-man exhibits, campfire food, and showcases of pottery, jewelry, and other western-style crafts, as well as plenty of cowboy music. The annual cowboy poetry conventions in Elko, Nevada (begun in 1985), have encouraged a flowering of western vernacular verse making. Baxter Black and Waddie Mitchell are just two of the many cowboy poets on today's scene.

In Nashville, the cowboy "look" has never disappeared. And in the 1990s Warner Bros. Records launched its Warner Western division to distribute the singing-cowboy works of latter-day practitioners such as The Sons of the San Joaquin, Red Steagall, Michael Martin Murphey, Tim Ryan, and Don Edwards.

During its heyday in the 1930s and 1940s, cowboy music was so perva-

ABOVE: *Milton Brown and his Musical Brownies were the pioneering western-swing band and the superstars of Fort Worth, Texas.*

Tommy

Tex Williams

Several of the hits crossed over from country to the mainstream pop charts.

Duncan left to form his own band in 1948. Leon Rausch (born 1927) stepped in as the new Playboys vocalist in the 1950s, and after Wills gave up bandleading, Rausch became the new leader of The Texas Playboys.

Following his West Coast sojourn, Wills had stints in Las Vegas, Sacramento, Oklahoma City, and Dallas. He suffered his first heart attack in 1962, but lived long enough to enjoy his 1968 induction into the Country Music Hall of Fame and the 1970s revival of western swing.

Wills's style became institutionalized in the country sound. Patsy Cline brought back "Faded Love"; Floyd Cramer revived "San Antonio Rose"; Barbara Mandrell picked the "Steel Guitar Rag." In 1962 Ray Price issued a tribute album of Wills favorites, and in 1967 Mel Tillis recorded with the legend himself. Merle Haggard launched a major Wills revival with the 1970 LP *A Tribute To the Best Damn Fiddle Player in the World*. Today, western swing resonates through the work of such diverse acts as Shelby Lynne, Commander Cody, Riders in the Sky, George Strait, and, unmistakably, Asleep at the Wheel.

"Western swing would have just been a footnote in American music if it weren't for Bob Wills," observes Ray Benson of Asleep at the Wheel. "Because Bob Wills was the Elvis Presley of his day. He was charismatic; he was funny; he was innovative; and he brought a style that was beyond the music. People who didn't really even realize what Bob was doing musically came to see this guy who would holler 'Ah-Haaa!' in between songs, strut around the stage like a game cock and had just an incredible aura about him. He had black eyes that just pierced. The

people loved him, and that's really why we have this legacy."

"He was quite a performer," agrees Patti Page. "Bob Wills and his little fiddle would go all over the stage. It was natural to him and I think that was the charm about Bob. Everything was natural.

"When I joined Al Clauser and His Oklahomans we did country swing, the 'San Antonio Rose' and all. But when I did start recording for Mercury, I don't know whether they were interested in my doing any western swing. They put me in the pop field. I did do the first country album that a pop star had done with Mercury Records. That was in 1948."

Oklahoma native Patti Page (Clara Ann Fowler, born 1927) graduated from western swing to mainstream-pop success. But the biggest-selling female vocalist of the 1950s had many of her biggest successes with country songs, including 1949's "Money Marbles and Chalk," 1951's "Mockin' Bird Hill" and "Detour," 1961's "Mom and Dad's Waltz," and the immortal 1950 blockbuster "Tennessee Waltz," which became one of the biggest-selling records in the history of show business.

In addition to being the first pop star to devote an album to country tunes, Page was the pioneer of "double-track" recording, singing harmony with herself. She graduated to TV stardom with three variety series in the 1950s, performed as a

71

TOP: *Tex Williams graduated from Spade Cooley's band to solo singing success.*
LEFT: *Tommy Duncan and Laura Lee McBride as two Texas Playboys vocalists.*

Duncan

Spade Cooley

singing evangelist in the Oscar-winning 1960 movie *Elmer Gantry*, returned to country recording in Nashville in the 1970s, earned the Pioneer Award in 1979 from the Academy of Country Music, presided at the launch of the Nashville Network cable TV channel in 1983, and won a long overdue Grammy Award for a CD she recorded in 1998.

Hers wasn't the only career launched in western swing. Fiddler Spade Cooley (1910–1969) led a California band whose popularity rivaled The Texas Playboys'. Patti Page's pop version of "Detour" derived from Cooley's 1946 western-swing hit of the song. Cooley also hit the top of the charts with 1945's "Shame on You." And his vocalist Tex Williams (1917–1985) scored a major solo hit with 1947's western swinger "Smoke! Smoke! Smoke! (That Cigarette)."

But Spade Cooley murdered his singing wife Ella Mae Evans in 1961 and was sentenced to life imprisonment. He died of a heart attack while performing at a policemen's benefit show two months before he was scheduled to be paroled in 1969.

Bob Wills's brother Johnnie Lee Wills was another western-swing vet who found chart success, notably with 1950's novelty "Rag Mop." Hank Penny, Carolina Cotton, Deuce Spriggins, Laura Lee McBride, Bill Boyd, Hank Thompson, and Paul Howard are just a few of the other country graduates from western swing's ballrooms.

"Western swing is primarily dance music," summarizes Benson. "And dancing is the original interactive form of entertainment. You interact with the band—you are a part of the experience.

"In Texas they do a number of dances derived from the German/Bohemian/Czechoslovakian tradition—schottis-

ches, the cotton-eyed joe. The other thing about Texas is there are a lot of polkas. You go up to Wisconsin and polkas are big there, too. These are partner and line dances that go around in a circle, folk dances. People danced from Thursday 'til Sunday and brought the family."

Country music embraced Cleveland, Ohio, polka king Frank Yankovic (1915–1998), whose "Just Because" (1948) and "Blue Skirt Waltz"/"Charlie Was a Boxer" (1949) became top-ten hits on the hillbilly hit parade. In later years, Yankovic was a regular visitor to Nashville's recording studios, and most of the albums of polka's Grammy-winning champion Jimmy Sturr are recorded in Music City. All of which is a reminder that Patsy Montana's "I Want to Be a Cowboy's Sweetheart" was, after all, a polka.

A dance tradition is also a big factor in the indigenous music of southern Louisiana. That region's Cajun music was another substyle that was incorporated into country music.

"The Cajun people came from France to Nova Scotia," says Jo-El Sonnier, explaining the roots of this culture. "They were deported from Nova Scotia in 1755, and went to different areas, Mississippi, New Orleans, and part of Louisiana, and that's where the story starts." Classic Cajun country hits have included "Jole Blon" (Harry Choates, 1947), "Jole Blon's Sister" (Moon Mullican, 1947), "Jambalaya" (Hank Williams, 1952), "Alligator Man" (Jimmy C. Newman, 1961), and "Louisiana Man" (Rusty & Doug, 1961). The style entered the modern country era with "Diggy Diggy Lo" (Doug Kershaw, 1969), "Cajun Baby" (Hank Williams Jr., 1969), "Big Mamou" (Fiddlin' Frenchie Burke, 1974), "Marie Laveau" (Bobby Bare, 1974), and "Louisiana Saturday Night" (Mel McDaniel, 1981)

As recently as 1991, Mary Chapin Carpenter's "Down at the Twist and Shout" featured the Cajun act Beausoleil; George Strait's "Adalida" (1995) had Cajun rhythm, as did Mark Chesnutt's "Gonna Get a Life" (1995).

Cajun's r&b cousin, zydeco music, popped up

ABOVE: *The dark good looks of Spade Cooley, "The King of Western Swing," stemmed from his Cherokee ancestry.*
RIGHT: *Western-swing superstar Bob Wills on the cover of* The Mountain Broadcast and Prairie Recorder.

Bob Wills

The Mountain Broadcast
and Prairie Recorder

1947
JANUARY
25¢

BOB WILLS

with a big country hit when Rockin' Sidney's "My Toot Toot" became a 1985 phenomenon. Joseph Falcon, D.L. Menard, Vin Bruce, The Balfa Brothers, Nathan Abshire, and Iry LeJeune are just a few of the Cajun acts that have marched through country music's history. And the style is represented on the country scene of the twentieth-century millennium by energetic performers such as Zachary Richard, Wayne Toups, and Jo-El Sonnier, the last of whom enjoyed a string of hit RCA singles in 1987–90.

Interestingly, the longest-tenured country string band of all time is Louisiana's Hackberry Ramblers (founded in 1933), which mixes Cajun tunes with western-swing numbers. The band began recording in 1935 and was nominated for a Grammy Award as recently as 1997 for its CD *Deep Water*.

"Combining Cajun and country music was one of the secrets of our success," says the group's Glen Croker. "Another secret of our success is the simplicity. We use the 'kiss' principle, K-I-S-S: 'Keep It Simple, Stupid.' We relate to The People. You can't play music to impress other musicians in the audience. You have to play music for the people dancin' out there."

The regional styles with the closest ties to western music are the border sounds of conjunto, ranchera, mariachi, norteno, Tex-Mex, and Tejano stylists. Despite Hollywood's portrayals, one out of every four working cowboys prior to 1900 was either Mex-

ican or black. And much of cowboy culture reflects a south-of-the-border influence. Terms such as "lariat," "chaps," "ranch," and "buckaroo" derive from Spanish-language cowboy lingo. "El Rancho Grande," "Ceilito Lindo," "La Cucaracha," and "The Gay Cabellero" were traditional cowboy favorites that further illustrate the strong ties.

In addition to Cowboy Slim Rinehart, the biggest stars of the Mexican border-radio-station broadcasts of the 1930s and 1940s included Lydia Mendoza, known as "The Lark of the Border," and Rosa Dominguez, "Mexico's Nightingale." New Mexico's bilingual Louise Massey & The Westerners recorded a great deal of Spanish-language material for the country market in the 1940s.

Just as was the case with western swing, singing-cowboy music, and the Cajun/zydeco styles, Tex-Mex material has displayed a remarkable longevity in the country sound. Modern star Linda Ronstadt is of Mexican descent. She "connected the dots" between western music and ranchera melodies with her *Canciones* and *Mas Canciones* albums of 1987 and 1991.

And such entertainers as Johnny Rodriguez (born 1951) have made the connection between the cultures equally explicit: "I grew up close to the border, a little bitty town down there close to San Antonio and Del Rio," Rodriguez begins. "And growin' up down there, a lot of Mexican-American people like myself grew up listenin' to country music. But we didn't have anybody to identify with, I guess. And that was part of

ABOVE: *Frank Yankovic toured far with polkas that were accepted on both pop and country charts in the late 1940s.*
RIGHT: *Louisiana's Hackberry Ramblers perform both Cajun tunes and western-swing numbers.*

what I wanted to do, go in there and sing country music and keep my last name. Thank God I got that accomplished.

"The traditional Mexican music, it's related closely to country music because of the way the lyrics are written. It's about drinkin' or mom and stuff like that and the songs are put together in very similar ways."

Rodriguez broke into Spanish on such big country hits as 1975's "Love Put a Song in My Heart," 1977's "Eres Tu," and 1978's "Love Me with All Your Heart."

He was joined on the charts by Freddy Fender (Baldemar Huerta, born 1937), who scored even bigger dual-language hits with "Before the Next Teardrop Falls" and "Secret Love" in 1975 and "Vaya con Dios" in 1976.

Texan Rick Trevino picked up the tradition in the 1990s. "My father was a professional musician for many years and he played Tex-Mex music," he recalls. "I think that's why I started at such a young age. Those nightclubs remind me of a big family function—there's a lot of Hispanics, a lot of tamales, a lot of just great food and a lot of music. And it's a very ethnic celebration. I grew up listening to Tejano music. My friends would come over and my dad would have this Mexican music blarin' full blast and I'd say, 'Dad turn that stuff down.' Like, 'Sssshh: I don't want my friends to hear that Mexican music.' It was like an immature thought to have.

"My dad was a big Bob Wills fan, and that was pretty much it when I was a kid. I saw Johnny Rodriguez early on in my career. It's kinda neat 'cause him and Freddy Fender kind of came out first with putting the Spanish lyrics in, and people began to realize how beautiful the Spanish language is. It kind of gives me a boost of confidence to know, 'Hey those guys did it, I can do it.'"

Even more recently, Tejano superstar Emilio began building bridges to the country community. The San Antonio native (Emilio Navaira III, born 1963) was the male parallel of Selena (Selena Quintanilla Perez), whose tragically short life was made into a major Hollywood film. The two sang award-winning duets together when both were Spanish-only performers. Emilio had been including cowboy classics like "South of the Border" in his live shows for five years before he approached Nashville in 1994. His seven non-English albums were million sellers and he'd been performing for Hispanic crowds of fifty-thousand at a time, but he wanted something more.

"God gave me this career that I love so much that it puts a smile on my face everyday," he said. "But this is a challenge and I love a challenge."

Between 1991 and 1995 Tejano music sales quadrupled to a $120-million-a-year business. The style's awards show was broadcast to more than twenty countries in 1996. Hispanic Americans became the U.S.A.'s largest ethnic minority at the end of the decade.

Clearly, the most important chapters about country's connections to its Latin substyles have yet to be written.

"There's something about roots music," says Ricky Skaggs, "whether it be rock 'n' roll, whether it be blues, whether it be Cajun or western swing. There's still something about the roots music that will always have a place in America."

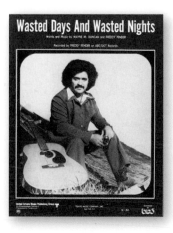

75

TOP: *Tex-Mex star Johnny Rodriguez gazes from the jacket of a 1984 LP.*
ABOVE: *Bilingual Freddy Fender is pictured on the cover of the sheet music for one of his biggest hits.*

Four

Bluegrass Is Born

The country substyle that has survived and prospered best is bluegrass music. With little support from mainstream radio, scarcely any television outlets, and no access to major urban performance venues, country's back-to-basics acoustic style has blossomed for fifty-five years.

Bluegrass has its roots in the old-time string-band tradition, where greased-lightning fiddling was so paramount. Thus its emphasis on instrumental brilliance. It draws the sentiments in its songs from the popular mandolin-guitar brother-duet teams of the 1930s and 1940s. These acts were inspired by such pioneers as Darby & Tarleton ("Birmingham Jail"/"Columbus Stockade Blues") and the *National Barn Dance* teams Mac & Bob ("When the Roses Bloom Again") and Karl & Harty ("Kentucky"), none of whom were brothers.

One of the earliest true brother duets with a hit was The Allen Brothers, who hailed from the Chattanooga area. Austin and Lee Allen's "Salty Dog Blues" of 1927 (originally recorded as "Bow Wow Blues") eventually became a bluegrass standard.

The much-recorded Shelton Brothers (Bob Attlesey and Joe Attlesey) from

77

LEFT: *Lester Flatt sings for Martha White flour on the Opry stage while Earl Scruggs tickles the banjo strings.*
ABOVE: *The Osborne Brothers originated "Rocky Top," now the University of Tennessee's football rallying song.*

Blue Sky Boys

Texas created such 1935 classics as "Just Because" and "Deep Elem Blues." These, too, became perennially popular.

The Callahan Brothers struck gold with "She's My Curly Headed Baby" (1936), one of the biggest country hits of the Depression. Walter Callahan adopted the folksy "Joe" as his stage name. Brother Homer became "Bill." Their career took them from North Carolina to Hollywood before settling into radio stardom in Texas.

The Dixon Brothers were South Carolina cotton mill workers who are remembered as the originators of Roy Acuff's hit "Wreck on the Highway." Dorsey and Howard Dixon also recorded one of country music's better-known *Titanic* songs, "Down with the Old Canoe," during their 1936–38 stint on Victor's Bluebird label.

North Carolina's Blue Sky Boys were perhaps the most enchanting of all the brother-duet teams. Bill Bolick (born 1917) and his younger brother Earl (1919–1998) sang with sweet, soft harmony precision. They did exquisitely tasteful instrumental work and had a beautiful repertoire of gospel and folk material. Their 1949 version of "The Sweetest Gift (A Mother's Smile)" is the one that has been copied by Hazel & Alice, The Judds, and many other contemporary acts.

"Dust on the Bible," "As Long as I Live," and "I Want to Be Loved" (1945), plus "Whiskey Is the Devil" and "Oh So Many Years" (1947), are part of the recorded legacy of The Bailes Brothers. Walter Bailes and his brother Johnny came from West Virginia for a two-year stint at *The Grand Ole Opry* beginning in 1944. Later, brothers Homer and Kyle joined them on fiddle and bass, respectively.

These teams and others inspired generations of country performers. Encouraged by the outstanding popularity of its Delmore Brothers, the *Opry* brought two more brother duets to its cast in the 1950s, The Louvin Brothers and The Wilburn Brothers.

The Louvins' spine-tingling harmonies are thrilling listening experiences. Ira Loudermilk (1924–1965) was the mandolinist, high harmony singer, and songwriter of the pair. Brother Charlie (born 1927) sang lead and played guitar. Raised in Alabama, they arrived at the *Opry* in 1955, well past the heyday of brother duets. Nevertheless, they managed to score big hits in 1955–58 with "When I Stop Dreaming," "I Don't Believe You've Met My Baby," "Hoping That You're Hoping," and "My Baby's Gone" in an increasingly electrified country climate.

Ira died in a car crash in 1965. Charlie fashioned a successful solo career and remained in the *Opry* cast. The Louvin Brothers became the subjects of the 1996 biography *In Close Harmony*, and their unearthly sound has continued to inspire younger musicians. Emmylou Harris scored her first country hit with her 1975 single of the Louvins' "If I Could Only Win Your Love." Nicolette Larson revived the Louvins' "You're Running Wild" in 1986.

The Wilburn Brothers enjoyed a longer tenure on the *Opry* than the ill-fated Louvin team. Doyle

ABOVE: *The intimate, close-harmony sound of The Blue Sky Boys made them one of the most revered brother-duet acts.*

The Louvin Brothers

(1930–1982) and Teddy (born 1931) Wilburn took the brother-duet tradition into the Nashville Sound era with such hits as "The Knoxville Girl" (1959), "Trouble's Back in Town" (1962), "It's Another World" (1965), and "Hurt Her Once for Me" (1966). The duo is also notable for its successful syndicated TV series, its Wil-Helm Talent Agency, and its Sure-Fire Music. The last named published the career-making hits of Loretta Lynn and provided a teenage Patty Loveless with her earliest show-business break.

One of the biggest hits of the classic brother-duet era was "What Would You Give in Exchange for Your Soul" sung by The Monroe Brothers in 1936. The Kentucky siblings had begun their country careers as part of a *National Barn Dance* square-dance group in Chicago. They then landed a recording contract with Bluebird and became big radio favorites in the Carolinas. After their breakup in 1938 older brother Charlie Monroe formed his own band, The Kentucky Pardners.

High harmony vocalist and mandolinist Bill Monroe (1911–1996) also formed his own band. But by the late 1930s the old string-band tradition was being supplanted by the more modern sounds of the western-swing groups and the cowboy vocalists. Monroe began experimenting with the instrumental lineup of his Blue Grass Boys, trying to find something ear catching and new. His unique voice and dazzling instrumental skills needed the right showcase.

"I wanted the sound to go like I wanted it," Monroe recalled, "like putting some of the blues in there. I wanted to keep the timing of the music right, to have a good drive to it, because it was good for the fiddle and good for the banjo, mandolin. A lot of my songs has got the old-time Methodist, Baptist, and Holiness singing in it, the touch and the feeling of the way the songs used to be. I put that in this music."

Son James Monroe adds, "His mother could play fiddle and sing, so he learned some things from her, I think. He had an Uncle Pen that played fiddle that he learned a lot from—Pendleton Vandiver. He later wrote a song about him called 'Uncle Pen.' He heard of a black man who came through that country called Arnold Schultz who played blues guitar, and that really enthused my father.

"He sang tenor over my Uncle Charlie. And Charlie had a high lead voice. To sing tenor over that man, well, you had to have a high-pitched voice. Most men don't have that kind of a voice. So when Bill Monroe sang, that's where your 'high lonesome sound' came from."

In 1939 Monroe and his new band auditioned at *The Grand Ole Opry*. "I come there on a Monday—I went to the *Opry*, and I seen Harry Stone, David Stone, and the Solemn Old Judge," Monroe reported. "They was all going out, I believe, to eat. They said they'd be back in just a little bit and they'd listen to me. Well they come back pretty soon, and I played about three or four numbers. And they told me, 'You can go to work here any time. You can start here this Saturday night.' But they thought I wanted

ABOVE: *Charlie Louvin recites at the WSM mike while brother Ira looks on during a broadcast of* The Midnight Jamboree.

Jimmy Ma

to check some other radio stations where I might make bigger money. I told 'em no, that I wanted to make my home right here in Nashville at *The Grand Ole Opry*. They said, 'Well, if you ever leave here, you'll have to fire yourself.' So I've been there ever since."

He debuted on the show with his arrangement of Jimmie Rodgers' "Muleskinner Blues." On October 28, 1939, Bill Monroe received three standing ovations, a first in *Opry* history.

After several editions of The Blue Grass Boys, Monroe hired guitarist/singer Lester Flatt and banjo player Earl Scruggs in 1945. This version of his band defined the emerging style. In fact, its name comes from the name of Monroe's group, where dozens of bluegrass music's most important figures have subsequently been trained.

"I would say bluegrass is the coming together of Bill Monroe and Earl Scruggs, and their musical styles," says John Hartford. "These were guys who were old-time musicians, but they were so individualistic. It was hard to say, 'That's old-time music.' It wasn't. It was the music of Bill Monroe and Earl Scruggs. But because it was in the Bill Monroe Blue Grass Boys band that that transformation first took place, the music was called bluegrass music.

"Bluegrass music had a passion and

80

a ferociousness that really got you excited. When Earl Scruggs stepped up to the microphone and picked that banjo, man, every note was just as clear as crystal."

Ricky Skaggs knows The Blue Grass Boys story inside out. He recites, "It was five members—Chubby Wise on fiddle, Bill Monroe on the mandolin, Earl Scruggs on the banjo, Lester Flatt with his wonderful lead singing and guitar playing and a guy named Howard Watts, Cedric Rainwater was his stage name, played the bass. Those five people created what we now know as bluegrass music.

"When they were on stage it sounded like The Beatles were on stage. I mean, I've heard live shows that they did and I hear these country people screaming at the top of their voice hearing this new music that no one had ever heard before. It was a new sound, a new day."

Ronnie McCoury concurs: "You listen to the live broadcasts that they taped. Earl Scruggs steps up to the mike and women are screaming and they're just fallin' apart out there in that audience. It was Bill Monroe and The Blue Grass Boys and every time Bill stepped up to the mike, well, he was Big Daddy."

Bill Monroe and his Blue Grass Boys would provide much of the classic bluegrass repertoire.

ABOVE: *The Wilburn Brothers on the cover of their debut LP.*
RIGHT: *Bill Monroe clutches his legendary Gibson mandolin on a 1965 LP jacket.*
OPPOSITE: *Jimmy Martin, "The King of Bluegrass."*

Mac Wisem

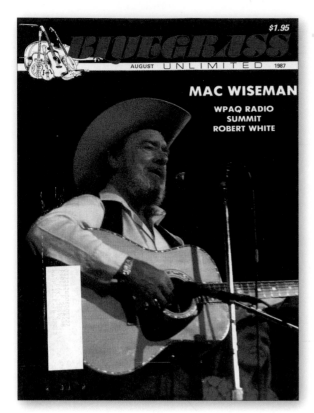

In addition to "Uncle Pen," that songbook would include "Blue Moon of Kentucky," the instrumental "Raw Hide," "Walk Softly on This Heart of Mine," "Molly and Tenbrooks," "Will You Be Loving Another Man," "My Little Georgia Rose," "In the Pines," "Christmas Time's A-Comin'," and "Footprints in the Snow."

Future bluegrass headliners Sonny Osborne, Bill Keith, Vassar Clements, Don Reno, Carter Stanley, Clyde Moody, Byron Berline, Peter Rowan, Jimmy Martin, and Mac Wiseman were all trained in Monroe's band.

"Bill Monroe came through on tour working some theaters and he did a promotional spot on our noon-time radio show," recalls Virginia's Mac Wiseman. "Right on the air he said 'If you ever want a job, just come on down to Nashville. I'll give you a job.' About six to eight months later I went to WSB in Atlanta, on my own again. That barn dance closed in the spring of 1949. I got in touch with Bill and went to the *Opry*, Easter weekend.

"It was through my association with him that I did what is called 'blue-

grass' today. My music was more 'country' before the bluegrass terminology came along. It was basically the same music with a different tag."

Wiseman (born 1925) graduated from The Blue Grass Boys to have his own bluegrass hits, notably with revivals of Mac & Bob's "Tis Sweet to Be Remembered," The Carter Family's "Jimmy Brown the Newsboy," and the pop chestnut "Love Letters in the Sand" in the late 1950s and early 1960s.

East Tennessean Jimmy Martin recalls his training at the feet of the Master as well. "I never had been in a town as big as Nashville," Martin recalls. "I got on the bus and came myself. When I got to the Greyhound bus station in Nashville, I asked the people there, 'Where's *The Grand Ole Opry*?' I went down there and got me a ticket. That night I went and I seen Bill Monroe. He had a red shirt on, and white pants and a white hat. When he got off the program I went around the back and asked them where did the *Opry* stars come out. They said, 'Right there.'

"So I stood there and leaned up against a light pole until Bill come out with his red shirt on. Told him who I was, and what I did. I said, 'I've listened to you all my life on radio stations, and I've always wanted to come and meet you and sing one with you.' And he said, 'Well, I'd like to hear you sing. What do you want to sing?' I said, 'Well, I heard a record of you and Lester Flatt, "Old Crossroads."' So we cut loose on it and sung it. My knees was shaking, being a little ole farm boy getting a chance to sing with my idol, Bill Monroe.

"After we got through a-singing that he said, 'Can you sing a solo?' And I said, '"Poor Ellen Smith."' After that Bill called me off to the side. I told him, 'I ain't got no clothes.' He said, 'Anything you need, you just ask.' Bill give me twenty dollars. Our first show date was Fort Smith, Arkansas. I worked with him for five years."

Martin, born in 1927, joined The Blue Grass Boys in 1949. His powerful lead voice led to recording his own set of bluegrass classics, including "Widow Maker," "Hold Whatcha Got," "Sophronie," and "Sunny Side of the Mountain."

82

ABOVE: *The magazine* Bluegrass Unlimited *is vital in the bluegrass world. Mac Wiseman has been on its cover many times.*

Reno

An outgoing, natural showman, Martin spread the bluegrass gospel to a number of barn-dance stages in the 1950s and 1960s.

"They told me in Detroit, 'You can't bring bluegrass music up here and sell it.' We proved we could. So the manager of *The Louisiana Hayride* called me and wanted me to come down there and try out. The first thing I heard around the stage was, 'Boys, that style of music's been starved out. You better get you an electric guitar.' I said, 'Don't tell me that. Let's just see how we do.' We tore the house down and took two and three encores every time we was out on stage.

"I left there and went to Wheeling, West Virginia. When I went up there, I heard the same thing: 'Son, you've come up here where you're gonna starve to death.' I said, 'That's what I heard down at *Louisiana Hayride*. Please don't tell me that.' On the *Wheeling Jamboree,* we took the house down ever time we's on the stage. When I picked my mail up, there was a basket full of mail that I had to answer. We'd set up 'til eleven, twelve o'clock at night with postcards answering the mail."

Former Blue Grass Boy Peter Rowan went on to have a career that encompassed folk, rock, and country as well as bluegrass. He recalls his Monroe training sessions: "Bill would meet us down at WSM, go to his post office box, bring out all his latest mail, and say, 'Okay, you boys now go ahead and pick,' while he looked at his mail. That was our rehearsal. After we had played our few tunes that we were so proud of having learned, he would take out his mandolin and teach, set up in the little studio in WSM. He'd take out his mandolin and lead us into other realms of old-time music, the roots of old-time music. Mostly

he was insisting that we learn all the dance beats, like a waltz, two steps, the backstep."

Don Reno (1927–1984) and Red Smiley (1925–1972) developed one of the most entertaining bluegrass road shows with their band The Tennessee Cut-Ups. They took brother-duet harmonies, bluegrass instrumental flash, and unbridled energy to forge a highly distinctive career in the late 1950s and early 1960s. Among the most memorable of the Reno & Smiley hits are "I'm Using My Bible for a Road Map," "I Know You're Married (But I Love You Still)," "Love Oh Love, Oh Please Come Home," "Don't Let Your Sweet Love Die," and "Money Marbles and Chalk," all of which are now bluegrass standards.

In conjunction with another partner, Arthur "Guitar Boogie" Smith, banjoist Reno also helped write and record the original version of "Feuding Banjos," the instrumental that became nationally popular as "Dueling Banjos" on the soundtrack of the 1973 hit movie *Deliverance.* Don Reno served his tenure as a Blue Grass Boy in 1948–49.

Despite the celebrities involved, none of Monroe's band lineups had quite the impact or the historical significance as The Blue Grass Boys of 1945–48 did.

"That was the zenith," says Ricky Skaggs. "That was everything he had ever wanted, musically. There was such an exchange of creativity. I mean, the well was open. Then all of a sudden it stops when Earl Scruggs decides to leave and Lester Flatt decides to leave."

In early 1948 Flatt, Scruggs, and Cedric Rainwater left to form a band of their own. The Foggy Mountain Boys became the second branch of the bluegrass family tree. This was the group that truly popu-

ABOVE: *Don Reno and Red Smiley had a wildly entertaining bluegrass road show with their Tennessee Cut-Ups.*

larized bluegrass on a national level. Monroe felt so betrayed that he wouldn't speak to Flatt or Scruggs for twenty years.

Lester Flatt (1914–1979) and Earl Scruggs (born 1924) had a couple of aces that their former boss lacked. One was congeniality, which was in marked contrast to Monroe's temper and stubbornness. The other was Earl's wife Louise Scruggs, a self-trained promoter/manager who perceived that bluegrass could succeed at folk festivals, on college campuses, in movie soundtracks, and on national television. Bill Monroe may have defined it, but Flatt & Scruggs made bluegrass popular.

"I always loved the five string banjo," says John Hartford. "We had a disc jockey up there in St. Louis named Roy Queen, and Roy Queen came on the radio one morning and said, 'Here's a brand new record by a group called Lester Flatt and Earl Scruggs.' He put that record on the radio, and at first I thought it was electric guitar. Then I said, 'Wait a minute, that's a banjo!' I come piling out of that bed, and it just nailed me to the wall. I'd never heard anything like it. I would sit for days by the radio listening to everything, just in hopes that another one of those records would be played.

"That summer he had a hillbilly

park at Chain of Rocks, up on the Mississippi River, and he announced that Lester Flatt and Earl Scruggs and the Foggy Mountain Boys will be at Chain of Rocks this Sunday. So we all piled in the car and we went up there. It was Lester and Earl and Benny Martin and Curly Seckler and Kentucky Slim on the bass. They had on those two-tone shoes and they walked out on the stage and I've never been the same since. It just transported me. I never saw or heard anything like it before, or since. It was just amazing. Even today, when I listen to those old tapes, that's the best band that ever was, period, to my ear."

"I heard Flatt & Scruggs on an album, the Newport Folk Festival album, and it just knocked me out," recalls Chris Hillman. "I loved the three-part harmony singing, duet and trio singing, this improvisational playing and this high energy. It was just wonderful. And I had to learn how to do that."

Flatt & Scruggs hit the charts with "The Ballad of Jed Clampett" (1962), "Petticoat Junction" (1964), and "Foggy Mountain Breakdown (The Theme from *Bonnie & Clyde*)" (1968). They became regulars on *The Beverly Hillbillies*, America's most popular TV series at the time. They took bluegrass to college campuses, became spokesmen for Martha White Flour, and starred in their own TV series.

Their Foggy Mountain Boys band helped to introduce another instrument to the bluegrass arsenal. When Josh Graves joined the band in 1955, he brought the mournful, sliding sound of the dobro to the style.

"I come from East Tennessee in the mountains," says Graves (born 1928). "We grew up on this stuff and one day somebody come up and called it bluegrass music. They used to call it hillbilly music and mountain music. I can't see no difference.

"Back when I started out, like in '42, they'd say, 'Stay out of a college town; they won't come out to see you.' But it all changed around and the kids picked it up. For years there we played every

ABOVE: *The classic Stanley Brothers albums on King Records are, sadly, out of print today. This one appeared around 1961.*

Jim & Jesse

major college or university there was. It amazed me to see that happen. There was doctors and lawyers and everything there studying and you'd think they'd want something different, but they wanted the old-time stuff that we'd been playing for years. You felt right at home with the kids. I'd go to their parties and everything."

Flatt & Scruggs broke up in 1969. Flatt stayed in bluegrass as the leader of Nashville Grass. Future country star Marty Stuart got his start in country music as a teenage mandolinist in that band.

Scruggs formed a group with his sons that explored country's connections to rock, jazz, folk, and pop. The Earl Scruggs Revue toured and recorded with everyone from Bob Dylan and Joan Baez to The Byrds and Dan Fogelberg. In 1971 Scruggs was instrumental in wedding the folk-rock of The Nitty Gritty Dirt Band with a who's who of old-time country music on the band's landmark *Will the Circle Be Unbroken* collection. Among the participants were Roy Acuff, Maybelle Carter, Merle Travis, Doc Watson, Brother Oswald, and Norman Blake. Blue Grass Boys alumni Jimmy Martin and Vassar Clements "stole the show."

There was one more early Blue Grass Boy who would become a bluegrass legend in his own right. Carter Stanley (1925–1966) was Monroe's lead singer in 1951. But he and his banjo-playing brother Ralph (born 1927) were forging their bluegrass style earlier than that.

The Stanley Brothers, like any good brother duet, had an emotion-charged singing style that evolved when they were teenagers in the mountains of Virginia. They recorded as early as 1947, scoring a regional success with "Little Glass of Wine" which led to a Columbia Records contract. Monroe was reportedly so upset that The Stanley Brothers were "stealing" his sound that he left Columbia and signed with Decca.

The subsequent Stanley recordings are considered bluegrass classics. By adding a sky-high third harmony part by Pee Wee Lambert, Carter

and Ralph created such unforgettable 1950s discs as "The Fields Have Turned Brown," "The White Dove," and "The Lonesome River." They even made the mainstream country charts with 1960's "How Far to Little Rock."

"Flatt & Scruggs' music was more polished than ours was," says Ralph Stanley. "We brought it right out of the mountains and the hollers. We didn't try to put any extra things in it. We sung it just the way it was wrote." After Carter's death, Ralph went on to have a successful solo bluegrass career and enjoy status as a living legend.

Two other star bluegrass acts with direct links to the brother-duet tradition are The Osborne Brothers and Jim & Jesse. Banjo virtuoso Sonny Osborne (born 1937) served his bluegrass apprenticeship—where else?—in the ranks of Monroe's Blue Grass Boys. Brother Bobby (born 1931) is a guitarist and mandolinist who was seasoned in the bands of Jimmy Martin and The Stanley Brothers.

The Kentucky natives formed The Osborne Brothers in 1953. A tape found its way to Nashville, where the act was signed to MGM Records. "Ruby," one of their trademark tunes, became a regional favorite and led to national breakthroughs with "Once More" (1958) and "Rocky Top" (1968). The

85

ABOVE: *Jim and Jesse have been recording since 1951. This LP compiled some of their many Epic Records performances.*

The Stonemans

Osborne Brothers became *Grand Ole Opry* members in 1964. They won the Country Music Association's Vocal Group of the Year Award in 1971, and two years later they became the first bluegrass band to play the White House.

The Jim & Jesse sound is characterized by brother harmonies as well as Jesse's innovative, complex "cross-picking" mandolin style. Jim McReynolds (born 1927) and Jesse McReynolds (born 1929) are natives of the Virginia Appalachians who began recording in 1951. In 1964, Jim & Jesse issued the first of their classics, "Cotton Mill Man," followed three years later by the hit "Diesel on My Tail." In 1965, the year after they joined the *Opry*, they recorded a bluegrass tribute to Chuck Berry titled *Berry Pickin' in the Country*.

"We did a few 'different' things," Jesse admits. "First thing we did different, I guess, was some Chuck Berry songs. I never worked so hard on a project, 'cause it was new for us. We didn't put the rhythm into it like Chuck would; we did it bluegrass style, the way we felt it. I have also done some recording with a lot of non-bluegrass groups. In fact, I did one session with The Doors on *The Soft Parade* album. We have got a little criticism for some of the things we've done from a few people. But not enough to hurt.

"One thing that's the big appeal to bluegrass music is that it's live music. It really has to be seen to be appreciated. And that's one thing that keeps the festivals goin' so well. They've been goin' on about thirty years now. We thought when they started, 'Well how long will this last?' They're still goin' strong; and when one shuts down, why, they's three more opens up somewhere."

The key to bluegrass music's survival has, indeed, been the creation of its annual outdoor festivals. More than five hundred of these events take place each year in various states throughout the country. They grew out of the folk-music boom of the late 1950s and early 1960s. Bluegrass bands, notably Flatt & Scruggs and The Foggy Mountain Boys, were welcomed on folk-festival stages as "authentic" folk musicians.

In 1961 musician Bill Clifton adapted the folk-festival concept by staging an all-bluegrass program on the Fourth of July at Luray, Virginia. But it was the three-day gathering staged by promoter Carlton Haney at Fincastle, Virginia, on September 3–5, 1965, that set the pattern of the true bluegrass festival.

As the festivals proliferated during the next thirty years, they gave the bluegrass performers a sense of community, provided rallying points for the style's fans, offered increased booking opportunities for bands, acted as recruiting events for new bluegrass converts, and were a training ground for aspiring pickers. *Bluegrass Unlimited* magazine, founded in 1966, further strengthened the bonds between festival goers.

"A bluegrass festival more so than anything else is just a big get together for people to have fun and listen to some good music," says Clinton Gregory. "The majority of the people that come to 'em I think go for the 'jam sessions' that they have after the show is over. Some of the better music is when everybody's out around a bonfire playing, drinking, having fun. It's a great experience. Everybody needs to experience that at least once in their life."

"Bluegrass is one of the few musics left where they can bring the families," adds Wilma Lee Cooper. "Most of the festivals are family oriented."

"One thing about bluegrass festivals, it's brought more people together and made more friends than any music in the

LEFT: *From left are Roni, Van, Patsy, Jimmy, and Donna Stoneman, who were among the first to popularize bluegrass with urban and collegiate audiences.*
ABOVE: *This 1981 LP turned Ricky Skaggs into a country star.*

world," said Bill Monroe. "They all plan on how we'll be back there next year, and we'll visit each other and we'll hear the music."

Carlton Haney was aided by folklorist Ralph Rinzler when he staged that first bluegrass festival. And it was Rinzler who brought Monroe back to center stage as a bluegrass attraction. The patriarch initially wanted nothing to do with long-haired college kids and seethed in resentment as Flatt & Scruggs, The Stanley Brothers, and The Osborne Brothers attracted wider and wider audiences. Rinzler broke through Monroe's resistance and made him the centerpiece of that first festival. In 1967 the legend launched his own annual event at Bean Blossom, Indiana. As the years went by, he took his place alongside the other bluegrass legends on noncountry stages.

"We started playing a lot of colleges, the folk concerts, the coffee houses," recalls James Monroe. "We'd work at a place called The Gaslight in Greenwich Village. We worked Carnegie Hall and just all the big places. Those were good times, I thought. In the '60s we had a lot of fun. It was like a revival for him.

"He just kept on keepin' on. He kept on writing right up until the last year of his life. Music was in him. Just came out of him all the time."

By the time Bill Monroe died in 1996, the music he had once been so jealous and personal about was in many, many good hands. New Grass Revival had taken bluegrass into experimental "newgrass" stylings. Mandolinist Chris Thile developed "grassical" music. The Dillards and The Country Gentlemen helped modernize the style. Yet The Johnson Mountain Boys and Del McCoury became popular by clinging hard to the old bluegrass traditions.

Joe Diffie, Vince Gill, Travis Tritt, Kathy Mattea, Kenny Chesney, Keith Whitley, Marty Stuart, and the members of Shenandoah, Diamond Rio, and The Dixie Chicks are just a handful of the contemporary country stars who received their musical training in blue-

grass bands. The one who championed the music more than any other was Ricky Skaggs.

Born in eastern Kentucky in 1954, Skaggs was a mandolin prodigy who sang The Osborne Brothers' "Ruby" onstage with Bill Monroe at age five. Two years later he appeared on the Flatt & Scruggs TV show in Nashville. At age fifteen he and Keith Whitley formed a band that performed note-perfect imitations of Stanley Brothers songs. When Ralph Stanley heard them, he hired them both to become members of his band in 1970.

Stints with The Country Gentlemen and Boone Creek ensued. Skaggs rose to national fame after he was hired by Emmylou Harris in 1977. He helped her create her bluegrass homage LP of 1980, *Roses in the Snow*. Then, in the midst of Nashville's pop-country era, he was signed to a major-label recording contract by Epic Records.

Critics and hard-core country lovers hailed his advent. *The Grand Ole Opry* enthusiastically recruited him for its cast in 1982. More surprising was the fact that country radio embraced his revivals of Flatt & Scruggs's "Crying My Heart Out over You" and "Don't Get above Your Raisin,'" Jim Eanes's "I Wouldn't Change You if I Could," Carter Stanley's "I'll Take the Blame," and Bill Monroe's "Uncle Pen." Skaggs won the country music world's highest awards in 1982–87, including the Country Music Association's 1985 Entertainer of the Year trophy.

He began heading back toward his roots with the 1989 album *Kentucky Thunder*. By the mid-1990s he was leaving the country concert trail behind and playing bluegrass festivals again. During the last few years of Monroe's life, Skaggs and Monroe had drawn closer and closer together. They played mandolins together; they ate lunch together; they hunted together; they went to church together. But after Monroe suffered a stroke in 1996, Skaggs saw the spark of life dimming in the old man's eyes.

"The last few weeks that I saw him, he looked very depressed," Skaggs recalls. "He was worried about his horses and his chickens and his cattle.

RIGHT: *Fiddler Stoney Cooper was adept on dobro, as this 1945 publicity shot from West Virginia's WMMN radio indicates. Wilma Lee, his wife, set a pattern for bluegrass female vocalists with her passionate mountain style.*

& Stoney Cooper

Alison Krauss

He was worried about his dogs. He was lonely. And he was worried about the music."

Skaggs told the dying legend, "Bill, I want to make you a promise right now. I promise you that I will play this music as long as I live. I'll tell people about you and how you started this music and gave it life. Don't worry about it. I promise you it's in good hands."

The repertoire on Skaggs's 1997 *Bluegrass Rules!* album was drawn strictly from the works of Monroe, Stanley, Flatt, and Scruggs. Skaggs says that was intentional. He wants young country and bluegrass fans to become acquainted with the classic bluegrass repertoire. *Ancient Tones*, his 1999 CD, intensified his bluegrass commitment.

"I just wanted Mr. Monroe to know, 'Look, this music is going to survive. I'm going to play it. Others will. Don't worry about it. Have peace.'"

Perhaps the most surprising trend as the twentieth-century millennium turned was the emergence of women as bluegrass stars. The field was almost completely male-dominated during the first forty years of its commercial development. Without warning, the *Bluegrass Unlimited* charts seemed to be flooded with female voices—Rhonda Vincent, Dale Ann Bradley, Claire Lynch, Lynn Morris, and the like.

Actually, there was some "warning." These women have a few ancestors in bluegrass. In the string-band era there were all-female groups such as The Amburgey Sisters and The Coon Creek Girls. And although women were in the distinct minority, some did play a role in bluegrass history.

The folk-revival collegiates rediscovered country-music pioneer Pop Stoneman. He assembled a family band that included sons Jimmy, Van, and champion fiddler Scott as well as daughters Patsy on guitar, Donna on mandolin, and Roni on banjo. The Stonemans won on *Arthur Godfrey's Talent Scouts* CBS TV show in 1956 and became coffeehouse favorites in the Washington, D.C., area.

"We passed the hat after every set," recalls Patsy. "Every time Jimmy passes the hat he says, 'Put some money in,' and they said, 'I just put some in a while ago.' Jimmy said, 'Well, you're still listening, ain't ya?'

"There's very little difference, if any, between what's called bluegrass music and the old-time music. It's the same instruments. If you're happy, they get loud and they get fast. The Stonemans always played fast. We're pretty happy people. Later on they referred to it as 'bluegrass.' What we played was referred to as old-time country music. But it sounded the same to me."

In 1957 Patsy Stoneman left the family group to become the first woman to lead her own bluegrass band. Little sister Donna became one of country's most admired mandolinists. Roni took her banjo to TV's *Hee Haw* and gained national fame as a comic.

The Stonemans starred in their own syndicated TV series in 1966. In 1967 the act won the CMA's first Vocal Group of the Year Award. After Pop Stoneman's death in 1968, Patsy assumed leadership of the family band, and this increased in the wake of Scott's death. Often cited as the finest fiddler in bluegrass history, Scotty Stoneman died of alcohol poisoning in 1973.

Patsy kept the group together as long as she could, but by the time Ivan Tribe's biography *The Stonemans* appeared in 1993, the family band was largely inactive.

Pennsylvania's Gloria Belle (Flickinger) was another female bluegrass pioneer. She was singing as early as 1957 and eventually became part of Jimmy Martin's troupe. Ohio's Lillimae (Haney) began recording bluegrass in 1959. The bluegrass-gospel family acts The Lewis Family and The Sullivan Family also featured female lead vocals.

Most of these women patterned their styles after mountaineer stylists such as Molly O'Day and Wilma Lee Cooper, who was once billed as "the she-Roy Acuff."

Born Wilma Lee Leary in 1921, the powerhouse

vocalist initially performed with sisters Gerry and Peggy in their West Virginia family band. The act was chosen to represent the state at the 1938 National Folk Festival in Washington and was recorded there by the Library of Congress. Later that year the family hired fiddler Dale Troy "Stoney" Cooper (1918–1977). He and Wilma Lee married in 1939.

Wilma Lee and Stoney Cooper took their new band to radio jobs in Nebraska, Indiana, and Illinois as they honed their hard-driving sound. The comparison between their Clinch Mountain Clan and Acuff's Smoky Mountain Boys is apt, for both acts specialized in Appalachian fervor and both featured the dobro.

"My music is accepted in the bluegrass field," says Wilma Lee Cooper. "Now, to have good bluegrass, I think you've got to have a banjo and a mandolin and a fiddle. I don't use a mandolin. The fiddle, of course, Stoney always played it. And Stoney was our first dobro player. But then when we formed the band, and he was the MC and everything, it was too much for him to jump from one instrument to the other and try to talk and run a show, too. So he quit playing the dobro, and Bill Carver played our dobro."

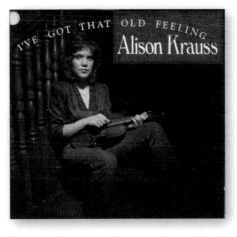

The Coopers rose to stardom at WWVA's fifty-thousand-watt *Wheeling Jamboree* in 1947–57. *The Grand Ole Opry* and a recording contract lured them to Nashville, where they scored hits with "Come Walk with Me" (1958), "Big Midnight Special" (1959), and "There's a Big Wheel" (1959). Wilma Lee continued to lead the band following Stoney's death, and today she is the *Opry*'s lone mountain-music matriarch.

Women such as North Carolina's Betty Fisher, Oklahoma's Delia Bell, Alabama's Ginger Boatwright, Maryland's Cathy Fink, West Virginia's Hazel Dickens, and sisters Sharon and Cheryl White in the *Opry*'s family band The Whites kept a female presence on the bluegrass circuit through the 1970s and 1980s. Then the floodgates opened as Laurie Lewis, Suzanne Thomas, Wanda Vick, Jeanette Williams, Sonya Isaacs, Valerie Smith, Pam Gadd, Sharon Cort, Tina Adair, The Cox Family, The New Coon Creek Girls, and others stepped into the spotlight with acclaimed bluegrass albums and shows.

Unquestionably the most important of these women is Alison Krauss. She is arguably the brightest young star in contemporary bluegrass, male or female. Born in Illinois in 1971 Krauss was winning fiddle contests by age twelve. Signed to Rounder Records at age fourteen, she delivered her first album in 1987. With her band Union Station, she instantly became the sensation of the bluegrass world. Succeeding albums showcased her aching, high-soprano voice as well as her deft fiddling.

Krauss was twenty-one when she was inducted into the *Grand Ole Opry* cast in 1993. Two years later the bluegrass wonder achieved the unthinkable when her CD *Now That I've Found You* sold two million copies and led to four Country Music Association awards. Backstage at the CMA gala, the reporters for *Bluegrass Unlimited* wept for joy.

"The only reason bluegrass isn't this big, huge thing is that people haven't heard it," Krauss said to reporter Jack Hurst in 1992. "I think it should be mixed in with country on the radio.

"Bluegrass is a killer. It's acoustic rock 'n' roll."

"Bluegrass is what it is," adds Ricky Skaggs. "It's heart. It's soul. It's spirit music. It's earth music. It's the music of the people."

91

ABOVE: *Fiddler/singer Alison Krauss was still a teenager when she issued this CD in 1990. By the end of the decade she was modern bluegrass music's biggest star.*

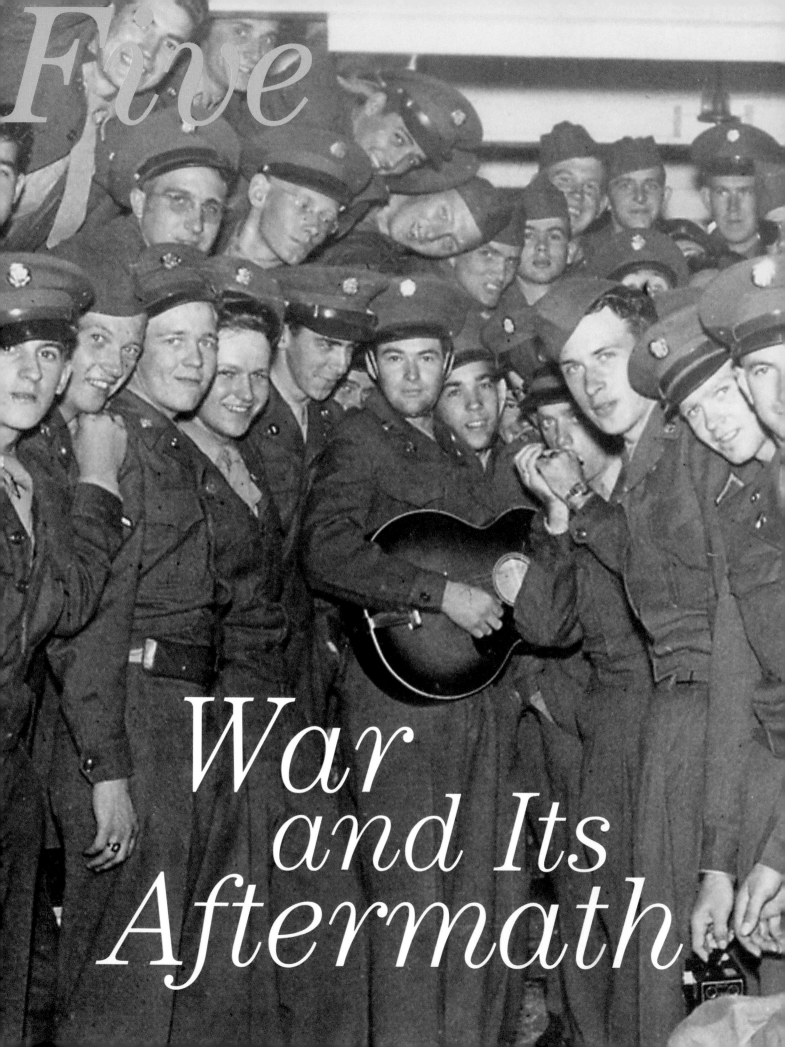

Five

War
and Its
Aftermath

America grew up during World War II. The war touched and defined all aspects of the nation's life. Rationing, travel restrictions, women entering the workforce, victory gardens, war-bond drives, and population shifts all characterized the era. The United States became an industrial giant during World War II and emerged from the conflict as the most powerful country on earth.

For hillbilly musicians the war brought about profound changes. The vinyl shortage meant that recording restrictions had to be imposed by the record companies. Rubber and gasoline rationing curtailed concert touring. Patriotism ran high, which meant single young musicians volunteered to fight or went willingly when drafted.

On the day after Pearl Harbor, singer Tommy Duncan arrived at the KVOO radio studios in Tulsa and announced to the rest of The Texas Playboys, "I don't know about you guys, but I'm going to join 'this man's army' and fight those sons-of-bitches!" He was joined in the service by the band's leader, Bob Wills, and its steel player, Leon McAuliffe. In 1942 Gene Autry was sworn in as a sergeant in the Army Air Corps during one of his *Melody Ranch* radio broadcasts. Merle

LEFT: *G.I.s around a country boy with his guitar. Such encounters during WWII spread the popularity of country music.*
ABOVE: *Covers of the* WLS Family Album *during the war years reflected the mood of the nation.*

Judy Canova

Travis, The Blue Sky Boys, and Grandpa Jones enlisted as well.

By 1944 a total of forty-nine staffers at *The National Barn Dance* were in the service, including singing star Bob Atcher. WWVA's Doc Williams, members of The Sons of the Pioneers, George Gobel, Buck Nation, Pee Wee King's singer San Antonio Rose (Eva Nichols), Joe Maphis, the Maddox Brothers, and Hank Thompson all went into the armed forces.

"In World War II, there was a mixture of people of different cultures and people from different parts of the country," says Thompson. "And I think this is how country music and baseball and things like that were spread around the world. I know that when I was in boot camp and on board ship, I was among fellow sailors who came from all over America. And many of them had never heard the kind of music that I was singing. And they liked it."

When southern soldiers came in contact with northern troops, they introduced many of them to the country sound. The same thing happened when workers from various geographic regions were thrown together in defense plants. Troupes of country entertainers performed hundreds of USO shows to G.I. audiences, further spreading the music's popularity.

"When Marty Robbins first started singing was when he was in the service," reports son Ronnie Robbins. "He learned to play guitar while he was on ship. He was in the South Pacific during World War II. And they were out for many months at a time, with nothin' to do other than maybe play guitar or play cards or whatever. Being in the South Pacific, he learned a lot of the Hawaiian songs and taught himself how to yodel."

"Being in the Marine Corps, the Japanese used Roy Acuff's name to try to get us to charge at night," recalls Ray Price. To

rile the soldiers, the Japanese troops would yell, "To hell with Roosevelt! To hell with Babe Ruth! To hell with Roy Acuff!" The anecdote demonstrates both the extent of Acuff's stardom and what powerfully "American" feelings country music stirred.

In occupied Germany the G.I.s were polled in 1945 via the Armed Forces Radio Network (AFRN) about their musical preferences. As historian Bill C. Malone reports, out of thirty-seven hundred votes cast, Acuff placed first with six hundred more votes than Frank Sinatra. The AFRN launched its *Hillbilly Jamboree* program from Munich as a result.

Like many, Acuff sang topical material about the conflict, notably 1943's "Cowards over Pearl Harbor" and "Searching for a Soldier's Grave." Acuff, Bob Wills, Red Foley, and songwriter Zeke Clements all sang 1944's "Smoke on the Water," which described what the scene would look like "when our army and our navy overtake the enemy." Bob Wills and The Sons of the Pioneers both charted with 1945's "Stars and Stripes on Iwo Jima." *Billboard* magazine reported that the most popular hillbilly number during the first year of the war was Carson Robison's topical "1942 Turkey in the Straw."

Judy Canova (1916–1983) and Patsy Montana both closed their wartime radio broadcasts with "Good Night Soldier." Hillbilly comic Canova made a number of hugely popular Republic films with World War II plots, notably *Joan of Ozark* (1942), *True To the Army* (1942), and *Sleepy Lagoon* (1943). Throughout 1943 she toured army camps and entertained on war-bond selling drives. Her weekly radio listening audience swelled to more than eighteen million. By 1946 she was getting 250,000 fan letters a week and earning $8,500 per broadcast.

Gene Autry ("At Mail Call Today"), Ernest

ABOVE: *Judy Canova was country music's most popular comic in the '40s, appearing in Hollywood films, newspaper columns, war-bond drives, and network radio shows.*

Tubb ("Soldier's Last Letter"), Tex Ritter ("Gold Star in the Window"), Molly O'Day ("Teardrops Falling in the Snow"), and many others issued war-themed songs. Tokyo Rose tried to use Floyd Tillman's wistful "Each Night at Nine" during her Japanese radio broadcasts to lower American enlisted men's morale.

The biggest of all the war-era hits belonged to Elton Britt (James Eldon Baker, 1913–1972). Initially a Jimmie Rodgers disciple, he was billed as "the highest yodeler in the world." Britt's sentimental, straightforward reading of "There's a Star Spangled Banner Waving Somewhere" made him a World War II sensation. The 1942 disc sold a reported four million copies and was an authentic "crossover" phenomenon into the pop-music marketplace. At President Roosevelt's request, Britt traveled to the White House to sing the song.

The Arkansas native would have other hits, notably his yodel showpiece "Chime Bells" (1948) and his Rosalie Allen duet "Quicksilver" (1950), but nothing approaching the phenomenon that "There's a Star Spangled Banner Waving Somewhere" became. In 1951 the singer was honored by the Defense Department for his war-era contribution.

In Nashville WSM launched its "Camel Caravan" in the summer of 1941. Sponsored by R.J. Reynolds Tobacco, the touring show for servicemen featured Pee Wee King, Eddy Arnold, and Minnie Pearl. Lovely young "Camelettes" tossed free cigarettes to the soldiers while boosting morale. By December 1942 the Camel Caravan had visited hundreds of military installations in thirty-two states, the Canal Zone, Panama, and Guatemala. And in the process it significantly popularized country music.

Polly Jenkins and Her Plow Boys performed

nearly nine hundred USO and military-base shows during World War II. In 1944 she took out a full-page ad in *Billboard* stating that she was "now booking dates to follow Hitler's funeral." Dorothy Shay, "The Park Avenue Hillbillie," broke into show business on the wartime USO circuit, as did the future *Grand Ole Opry* duet The Poe Sisters.

Country-music parks in New England, Pennsylvania, and New York proliferated as country became a national phenomenon. A square-dancing fad erupted. Between 1939 and 1942 *The National Barn Dance*'s road shows grossed more than $500,000. WLW's *Boone County Jamboree* grossed as much as $12,000 a day on its road shows.

The ballroom on the Venice Pier was converted into "The Los Angeles County Barn Dance" in 1942. Bob Wills drew 8,600 when he appeared. Roy Acuff's appearance drew 11,130—a crowd so large that organizers feared the pier would collapse from the weight. Within months, six more large country ballrooms were active in southern California.

"On the road, hillbilly troupes will consistently outdraw legitimate Broadway plays, symphony concerts, sophisticated comedians and beautiful dancing girls," stated the "Hillbilly Boom" article in the *Saturday Evening Post* in February 1944. "This is a great mystery to the clever strategists of show business who plan projects on Broadway and in Hollywood."

On August 23, 1941, *Billboard* magazine decreed that Jimmie Davis's "You Are My Sunshine" was "the taproom and tavern classic of the year." The following year the publication inaugurated its "Western and Race" column to cover the rapidly developing country and r&b fields and then a separate column devoted to the topic "American Folk

95

ABOVE: *Yodeler Elton Britt is pictured on the cover of his 1943 songbook. He was in high demand for USO shows during World War II.*

Records." It officially began tracking country records' popularity in 1944 with a chart titled "Juke Box Folk Records," which was followed in 1948 by a chart that reflected the biggest-selling country records in stores.

To cash in, a number of new labels sprang up that were eager to record the suddenly booming country sound. Capitol (1942), King (1943), 4-Star (1945), Mercury (1946), MGM (1947), Imperial (1947), and a number of smaller companies began snapping at the major labels' heels by introducing a new generation of country stars.

By 1943 the country-music phenomenon had grown to such proportions that even *Time* magazine was forced to acknowledge it. The magazine's October 4 issue contained a story titled "Bull Market in Corn."

"The dominant music of the U.S. today is hillbilly," it read. "By last week the flood of camp-meetin' melody had been rising steadily in juke joints. Big names in the drawling art of country and cowboy balladry were selling on discs as never before. An homely earful of the purest Texas corn, Al Dexter's 'Pistol Packin' Mama,' had edged its way to first place among the nation's jukebox favorites. All over the country were the Appalachian accents of the geetar and the country fiddle."

By 1949 at least 650 radio stations were featuring live country music. *Newsweek* checked in with its "Corn of Plenty" article on June 13, 1949. "The corn is as high as an elephant's eye, and so are the profits," the piece stated. "Hillbilly music is now such a

vogue that it is 'just about pushing popular tunes, jazz, swing, bebop and everything else right out of the picture,' noted *Downbeat* magazine. While the rest of the music industry remained in its chronic fluttery state, the hillbilly output remained fairly constant. But the demand for it has multiplied fivefold since the war."

Prewar country music had drawn its inspiration from Victorian culture. Sentiments of home, family, romance, and religion predominated as hillbilly-music themes. The aftermath of World War II changed all of that forever.

The postwar era was a time of tremendous social upheaval in the United States. The nation was "modern" and cosmopolitan like never before. More strikes racked the country in 1946 than in any year since the union-organizing days of 1916. Psychoanalysis became popular. Between 1948 and 1958, eleven million suburban homes were built, completely altering the geography of American life. *Playboy* hit the newsstands in 1953. A "Red Scare" stirred anti-Communist hysteria. Television ownership grew from one million sets to fifteen million sets in just one year, 1950–51. Marilyn Monroe, Jane Russell, Lana Turner, and Elizabeth Taylor were the voluptuous new movie goddesses. After the war, America became a much more mobile society and took on the rootless, restless quality it has retained ever since.

Country boys by the thousands had gone to war and seen the world. Country girls had left the home, gone into the wartime factories, and tasted social and financial independence. After the war,

romantic relationships became unstable; family life dwindled in importance, and the divorce rate soared. In 1946 a record-setting six hundred thousand marriages ended in court.

One of them was Bob Atcher's. Almost immediately after his return from the armed forces he divorced his *National Barn Dance* duet partner Bonnie Blue Eyes (Loeta Applegate). Atcher (1914–1993) then married Maggie Whitehall in 1947 and promptly began billing *her* as "Bonnie Blue Eyes" on his radio appearances. Later the mayor of Schaumburg, Illinois, Atcher bridged the gap musically between the old-time era and the rough-and-tumble scene of postwar country music.

Country music responded to the emotionally turbulent times by facing them head-on. Previously taboo subjects such as infidelity ("cheating"), alcohol, and divorce were addressed in country songs and soon came to dominate the style's themes. Things like drinking, sex, and "good times" no longer seemed so sinful— once you've smelled death on the battlefield, the neighborhood bar hardly seems like a den of iniquity.

Recalls Hank Thompson, "People had moved out of the country and into where the factories were, where the jobs were. That thrust people into different ways of life. Little by little people began to acknowledge, 'Yeah, these things happen. Let's admit it. Sure, they would slip around. Sure, somebody broke my heart. Sure, I went out and got drunk.' They

say that misery loves company. To realize, 'Well, I'm not the only one that's happened to' takes the burden off."

"During and after the war people left the farm," said fiddler Jerry Rivers. "They had heard about all they wanted to about the farm. They wanted to hear about the everyday life of love and cheating and gettin' in trouble and the wife puttin' you in the dog house, gettin' a little drunk and goin' out in the pickup truck."

Country music called its taverns "honky-tonks" and filled them with music that took the same name. This term was not originally connected with country music. Americans were using "honky-tonk" (or "honka-tonk") as early as the turn of the century. At that time it was associated with jazz and ragtime music and the whorehouses and bars where they were played. The 1910 song "Honka-Tonk Rag" bears this out.

Tin Pan Alley's "Everything Is Hunky Dory down in Honky-Tonk Town" (1918), jazz music's "Sister Honky-Tonk" (1924), the blues tune "Honky-Tonk Train Blues" (1927), and Mae West's Hollywood number "They Call Me Sister Honky-Tonk" (1933) illustrate how widespread the term was before country music adopted it in the 1940s.

97

Bob Atcher

TOP: *The postwar honky-tonk took many forms, as these four Tennessee examples demonstrate.*
ABOVE: *WLS star Bob Atcher, one of several country celebrities who enlisted during World War II.*

Floyd Tillman

The first use of "honky-tonk" in country music is believed to be Al Dexter's 1936 song "Honky Tonk Blues." But neither the term nor the style really took root until after the war. The shift appears to have begun in the postwar climate of the Texas oil fields and California farmlands populated by Okies. There, small clubs developed that catered to a rougher, less innocent country fan.

Oil-field laborers who had worked hard all week gravitated to these new social gathering places where they could raise hell on a Saturday night. In the postwar moral climate, women came to roadhouses, too; and the honky-tonk's atmosphere soon evolved into one of liquor drinking, sexual encounters, and the casual violence of fistfights and thrown beer bottles.

"Some of them would be just one square building," recalls Ray Price about these dingy dives. "No paint on the outside. And you'd go in and it would have a wooden dance floor, a long bar, tables, and a small bandstand. They fought an awful lot in those days. You'd sweep up earlobes and eyeballs every morning."

"A honky tonk is a place where working people hang out," says Mark Chesnutt. "You walk in there and it is filled with smoke. Kind of dusty. There'll be a jukebox in there somewhere. A lot of people dancing. But the main thing is you'll see mostly people in there that work hard. They come into there to dance, to listen to country music and drink a lot of beer. Maybe a fight every now and then."

"I always think of Saturday night as honky-tonk night," says Marty Stuart. "You're through workin,' you've been thinkin' about it all week long. You go find you a honky-tonk band that'll make you dance, forget about your troubles, have a good time."

"It's a beer-drinkin' church," offers Willie Nelson, "a place where they can

go and listen to what they want to hear, the sermons they want to listen to, something that applies to them personally, something they can relate to."

The musical accompaniment to a honky-tonk's raucous behavior was usually the jukebox. These electronic amplifiers of dance records achieved wide popularity in 1938–48. In fact, "juke joint" was a synonym for "honky-tonk." The glowing, multicolored jukebox had bass volume that cut through the crowd noise. When live country music was brought into the din of these smoke-filled barrooms, the bands had to adjust their style.

Western swing was country's dominant country dance style of the time. But a western-swing band was too large and too expensive for a roadside beer joint. A small combo would have to do. But a traditional country or bluegrass string band wouldn't fit the bill. Their sentimental, old-time repertoires were unsuited to the honky-tonk scene and their acoustic instruments were inaudible there in any case.

So country developed a new sound. More than ever before, rhythm was emphasized. The upright bass became an essential instrument, to be followed in the 1950s by the electric bass. Small drum kits were eventually introduced. Another development was the electric lead guitar. A honky-tonk singing style evolved as well. The homey delivery of acts like The Carter Family was replaced by histrionic wailing. Honky-tonk singers were unashamedly emotional—they moaned, shouted, whined, pleaded, and wept. Vocal breaks, hiccups, and note-rending "cries" became common effects. Honky-tonk singers slurred phrases, bent notes, and practically shed tears in tunes. This attention-getting showmanship transformed country music forever.

The sound that is most identified with honky-

ABOVE: *Floyd Tillman was a honky-tonk contributor as a vocal stylist, a composer and an electric guitarist.*
RIGHT: *Tillman's friend and bandmate in Houston was Ted Daffan, one of the major songwriters of the honky-tonk era.*

Ted Daffan

tonk music is that of the steel guitar. The whipped-dog whine of the instrument is what people think of when they think of country music to this day. Initially a lap-held instrument referred to as a "bisquit board," the steel guitar went electric in the mid-1930s. In Nashville in the 1950s, foot pedals were added to the board and it became a freestanding instrument. The steel guitar's notes could then be sustained and twisted in imaginative new ways. The instrument's piercing sound and wide emotional range cut through the thud and volume of the honky-tonk like nothing else.

Al Dexter's "Honky Tonk Blues" and "Pistol Packin' Mama" have both been mentioned as hallmark honky-tonk recordings. Along with Floyd Tillman and Ted Daffan, Dexter (1905–1984) was indisputably a pioneer of the style. Albert Clarence Poindexter began his career playing in the oil-field boomtowns of East Texas.

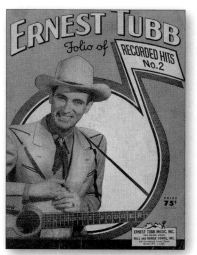

No one who was alive during World War II could fail to remember the impact of his "Pistol Packin' Mama." It was more than a hit record. It was a national catchphrase. Its instantly catchy, singalong melody and memorable chorus were on everyone's lips in those days. Al Dexter and his Troopers' hit version was picked up by Bing Crosby and The Andrews Sisters. Dexter's recording sold three million copies, and his sheet-music sales tallied two hundred thousand. Countless parodies of the tune were sung on army bases and in USO shows.

By 1944, Dexter was making $3,500 a week in bookings. The singer-songwriter would have several other hits, notably such quintessential honky-tonk titles as "Too Late to Worry, Too Blue to Cry" (1944), "Triflin' Gal" (1945), "Guitar Polka" (1946), and "Down at the Roadside Inn" (1947).

100

Ted Daffan (1912–1996) was a product of the Houston honky-tonks. He wrote country's first trucking song, 1939's "Truck Driver's Blues," but scored an even bigger hit with 1940's "Worried Mind." Then he topped that with the double-sided honky-tonk classic "Born to Lose"/"No Letter Today" of 1944. The unremittingly mournful "Born to Lose" has since been sung by everyone from Jerry Lee Lewis to Ray Charles, as well as hundreds of honky-tonk performers.

Ted Daffan and his Texans became headliners on the lucrative California ballroom scene of the postwar era. One of the finest songwriters of the honky-tonk pioneers, steel guitarist Daffan penned such hits as Hank Snow's "Tangled Mind" (1957), Faron Young's "I've Got Five Dollars and It's Saturday Night" (1957), and Les Paul & Mary Ford's "I'm a Fool to Care" (1954).

Daffan's career closely parallels that of Floyd Tillman. Both men, as well as honky-tonk piano player Moon Mullican, were band members in The Blue Ridge Playboys as youngsters in Houston in the 1930s. Both men were superb songwriters. Both men were interested in electronics and applied this to their instruments. Tillman (born 1914) was honky-tonk music's groundbreaking electric guitarist.

But it is his singing that has left the most lasting mark on country music. Tillman's eccentric drawling phrasing, which bends notes every which way and toys freely with meter, has influenced dozens of subsequent stylists, including Lefty Frizzell, Merle Haggard, and Willie Nelson.

His songs are lasting as well. Tillman's "It Makes No Difference Now" became a pop hit for Bing Crosby in 1941. His own recording of "G.I. Blues"/"Each Night at Nine" was a wartime hit; and Tillman's rendition of "They Took the Stars out of Heaven" was the first record to hit No. 1

ABOVE: *Ernest Tubb included such honky-tonk tunes as "Drivin' Nails in My Coffin" and "The Warm Red Wine" in his 1950 songbook.*

Ernest Tub

Al Dexter

when *Billboard* introduced its country popularity charts on January 8, 1944. His "Drivin' Nails in My Coffin" (1946) is a classic honky-tonk lyric. The composer's most recorded song is 1948's "I Love You So Much It Hurts Me," but his biggest hit was 1949's "Slippin' Around." Regarded as country's breakthrough infidelity song, it became a chart-topping hit in a duet by singing cowboy Jimmy Wakely and pop star Margaret Whiting.

Tillman, Daffan, and Dexter all based their careers in the Lone Star State. The man who took the honky-tonk style to Nashville was another Texan, Ernest Tubb (1914–1984). One of the most influential and important country stars of all time, Tubb became a country-music institution during his extraordinarily long career.

"He had a very rich, expressive voice," says Junior Brown. "Sincerity was the bottom line with Ernest Tubb."

In his heyday, Tubb "was on the cutting edge, bringing country music up to another level," believed son Justin Tubb. "I think he brought the blue-collar country song into existence. The war was a big part of his success. He cut a lot of war songs—'Soldier's Last Letter,' 'Seaman's Blues' and things like that. That helped spread the popularity of country music."

"He just had a special way of reading the lyric," producer Owen Bradley recalled. "It wasn't so much the way he sounded as the way he expressed himself. If you listen to him, it's the way he talks to you that he delivers the lyric. And after all, that's really the whole point about singing. Ernest was a true stylist. And he was a very handsome guy, carried himself beautifully."

Radio work in San Antonio led Tubb to a recording career that began in 1936. He patterned himself after his idol, Jimmie Rodgers, but by the 1940s had forged his own highly distinctive style. His first success was "Blue Eyed Elaine"/"I'll Get along Somehow" (1940), followed by the 1941 honky-tonk blockbuster "Walking the Floor over You." The hit took him to Hollywood, where Tubb

made several films, and then to Nashville, where he joined the cast of *The Grand Ole Opry* in 1943.

"Tomorrow Never Comes" (1945), "It's Been So Long Darling" (1945), "Rainbow at Midnight" (1946), and "Filipino Baby" (1946) cemented his postwar style, a spare approach that prominently featured the electric guitar. By now a superstar, Tubb began campaigning for the elimination of the term "hillbilly," which he found demeaning. He urged the music business to adopt the term "country music" instead. He headlined the troupe that sold out two shows and grossed $9,000 at Carnegie Hall in 1947, a milestone for the country industry.

Concerned that country records were often hard for fans to find, he founded The Ernest Tubb Record Shop in Nashville in 1947. It is now the largest mail-order supplier of country music in the world. An outgrowth of the store was its radio program, *The Midnight Jamboree*. Airing on WSM after the *Opry* on Saturday nights, this program has long been a launchpad for talent. Elvis Presley, Loretta Lynn, Patsy Cline, and dozens of other acts have been introduced on the show, which is still broadcasting weekly in Music City.

Tubb's drawling, half-spoken delivery of lyrics in his deep baritone remained one of the most recognizable sounds in country music throughout the 1950s and 1960s

101

ABOVE: *Al Dexter's "Pistol Packin' Mama" was a national disc sensation of 1943–44.*

Hank

Williams

on hits such as "Blue Christmas" (1950), "Goodnight Irene" (1950, with Red Foley), "The Yellow Rose of Texas" (1955), and "Waltz across Texas" (1965). His relentless, nonstop touring with his Texas Troubadours and his devotion to his fans both became legendary.

"Ernest worked constantly," says Jack Greene. "I remember one tour that was three and a half months long, and we had two nights off. And during that two nights off we had to jump from Seattle to Texas.

"He would spend hours and hours talking to his fans. We were always late getting out of the auditoriums. He'd sit on the bus for hours while we were rolling those miles through Texas, answering mail."

"The act that really changed my life was Ernest Tubb and the Texas Troubadours," says Marty Stuart. "They came rollin' into the fairgrounds on this big green bus painted with, 'Decca Records presents Ernest Tubb and the Texas Troubadours, Stars of *The Grand Ole Opry* and *The Ernest Tubb Record Shop Midnight Jamboree.*' It was a colorful bus. They all got out and they had on those matching cowboy hats and those suits, the ties hangin' off their necks, patent leather cowboy boots, the belts matched. The old man came out there and did his bit. Flipped that guitar over and on the back it said, 'Thanks.'"

"Ernest Tubb had a big soft spot in his heart for me because him and Daddy were big friends," recalls Hank Williams, Jr. "And sometimes when Daddy would have a binge going on, Ernest would come over and see him and say, 'Now Hank, I'm not sure about this.'"

Hank Williams (1923–1953) was honky-tonk music's tortured genius. Dead at age twenty-nine from drug and alcohol abuse, he originated the "live fast, love hard, die young" ethos that would permeate rock music for generations to come. Williams was probably an alcoholic before he left his teens. He rose to radio stardom in Montgomery, Alabama, and was pushed to greater ambitions by his wife Audrey. They came to Nashville in 1946 and auditioned for song publisher Fred Rose, who signed Williams as a songwriter and got him a recording contract.

"Move It on Over" became the first Hank Williams hit in 1947, followed by "Honky Tonkin'" (1948), "I'm a Long Gone Daddy" (1948), and "Mansion on the Hill" (1949). On June 11, 1949, Hank Williams debuted on the *The Grand Ole Opry* stage with "Lovesick Blues." Pandemonium erupted and he was brought back for an unprecedented six encores by the screaming audience. Overnight, he became the biggest star in country music. Rose's connections in New York led to big pop hits for several Hank Williams songs—including Tony Bennett's recording of "Cold Cold Heart," Rosemary Clooney's version of "Half As Much" and Jo Stafford's rendition of "Jambalaya"—while Williams's own versions became gigantic country hits.

"He came to Nashville to be a songwriter; and it just tickled him good when somebody else would record one of his songs, especially Tony Bennett," reports Don Helms.

"He was always nice to me, but he was pretty cruel to some of the people who turned down his songs," recalls Chet Atkins. "I remember he once played a song for Hank Snow and Hank didn't like it. He got very offended and told Mr. Snow he could do some impossible physical things to himself."

"He was a very moody person," says Jimmy Dickens. "I suppose I was as close to him as most people. You'd be talkin' to him once, he'd be laughin'. Then the next thing you'd know, Hank Williams would be in deep thought about something."

103

LEFT: *Hank Williams began recording in 1946. By 1953 he had risen to superstardom and died before reaching age 30.* ABOVE: *Hank Thompson has made the jukebox, radio, sales, and video charts in the '40s, '50s, '60s, '70s, '80s, and '90s.*

Between 1949 and his death just four years later, Williams poured out "Hey Good Lookin'," "Kaw-Liga," "Your Cheatin' Heart," "I Can't Help It (If I'm Still in Love with You)," "Take These Chains from My Heart," and the rest of his immortal songs. They defined an era and made Hank Williams the most influential singer-songwriter in country-music history.

"I don't guess anybody can define charisma," says steel guitarist Joe Talbot. "Whatever it was, he had it. I watched him work back in those days. He just absolutely laid the people out flat. The man just had something that all great stars have, the ability to connect with the emotions of the audience."

Says Horace Logan, "I've had him sing songs for me, just me in the studio, with himself and the guitar only. And tears would run down his cheeks and drop on the guitar. He emoted." Logan ran *The Louisiana Hayride,* to which Williams was exiled when his drinking escalated beyond the *Opry*'s tolerance.

"He didn't drink like anyone else," reports Ray Price, who roomed with Williams. "He'd get in a room and he'd pour himself a great big glass of whiskey and drink it straight down, just like that. Of course it would come straight back up. Then he'd pour another one down until it stayed down."

"I had no idea he was that far gone," says Logan, who was shocked by Williams's looks at *The Louisiana Hayride.* "His physical condition had deteriorated badly. He was bloating up and thinning down and bloating up. He was taking all sorts of pills. He got to the point where he couldn't control his bodily functions. He'd been known to wet his britches in public. And it was hard to watch.

"The day that I learned he died, I went home and sat on my bed and cried. That's how difficult it was."

"It was almost impossible for the funeral procession to get from Hank Williams' mother's home to the city auditorium in Montgomery where the service was," Jerry Rivers reported. "It took probably two hours and it was only five or six blocks. It was estimated that there were about twenty-five thousand people countable present for that funeral."

The power of Hank Williams has touched generations of country singers and continues to touch people today. A boxed set of his music on compact discs won two Grammy Awards in 1999.

Williams's own explanation of his success appeared in "Country Music Goes to Town," a 1953 article in *Nation's Business.* "It can be explained in just one word: sincerity," he was quoted as saying. "When a hillbilly sings a crazy song, he feels crazy. When he sings 'I Laid My Mother Away,' he sees her a-laying right there in the coffin. He sings more sincere than most entertainers because the hillbilly was raised rougher than most entertainers. You got to know a lot about hard work. You got to have smelt a lot of mule manure before you can sing like a hillbilly. The people who has been raised something like the way the hillbilly has, knows what he is singing about and appreciates it."

"He put his heart and soul and tears and everything into a song," said Faron Young. "He had such sincerity that poured out. I don't care who you were, you had to love what he was doing 'cause he opened up completely when he sang."

Alcohol, pep pills, and harder drugs were part of the honky-tonk lifestyle. Williams was only one of many whose careers would be touched by substance abuse.

"I was a problem drinker," confesses Wanda Jackson. "I was havin' to depend upon it. And it scared me. Drugs and alcohol can be devastating. This business will either keep you young or take you early."

"Drink has ruined some careers, and could have ruined mine if I hadn't got it under control," said Justin Tubb. "Any kind of drugs—uppers or downers or whatever—back in the old days they were so easy to get. Alcohol's still easy to get."

"Don Gibson would take those little pills and get out of his skull," says Chet Atkins. "Waylon

RIGHT: *Nashville native Kitty Wells, "The Queen of Country Music."*

Kitty Wells

DL 78293
enhanced for STEREO
Printed in U.S.A.
DECCA
RECORDS
HIGH FIDELITY
KITTY WELLS' Country Hit Parade
MAKIN' BELIEVE • RELEASE ME
CHEATIN'S A SIN • THERE'S POISON IN YOUR HEART
I'VE KISSED YOU MY LAST TIME
WHOSE SHOULDER WILL YOU CRY ON
IT WASN'T GOD WHO MADE HONKY TONK ANGELS
THE THINGS I MIGHT HAVE BEEN
PAYING FOR THAT BACK STREET AFFAIR
I DON'T CLAIM TO BE AN ANGEL
I'M TOO LONELY TO SMILE
SEARCHING FOR A SOLDIER'S GRAVE

Lefty Frizzell

Jennings had that problem too. The Everly Brothers had that problem. I think a lot of musicians are susceptible to drugs. But I'm such a square. When I had a lot of artists on that stuff, I didn't know it."

"We were a wild bunch," recalls Norma Jean. "It's widely known that we drank and took pills, and I did as well as anybody else. I'm not proud of it. I'm sorry that I did it. But I did. I didn't take as many as Johnny Cash."

"Definitely, it is an occupational hazard," adds Freddy Fender. "I got into a lot of trouble because I wanted to try everything from dried up orange peelings to marijuana and any kind of pills. A pill to wake up, a pill to go to sleep, cocaine. I didn't never take morphine that I know of. I took some crack one time. I wanted to experiment. If you told me that pigeon droppings would get me high, I would have to try it out. I've been sober more than ten years now."

"I drank as much as any of 'em," Hank Thompson chuckles; "I just didn't do it all at one time. Hank Williams would get so soused up they had to take him to the hospital to sober him up. Then he'd go for months and never touch a drop. Those guys would drink as much in two or three days as I would in two or three weeks. When they sobered up, I was still drinkin'. I just kinda spread mine out."

Several of Thompson's classics are drinking-song standards—1960's "A Six Pack to Go," 1968's "On Tap, in the Can or in the Bottle," 1961's "Hangover Tavern," and the like. His amber-brandy voice has a genial, homey-barroom tone that put seventy-nine singles on the hit parade between 1948 and 1982.

Born in 1925, Thompson got his first guitar as a result of his fascination with Gene Autry and Jimmie Rodgers. He was on local radio in Waco, Texas, before his high school graduation. He polished his singing and songwriting skills while he was in the navy during World War II.

In 1946, recalls Thompson, "I recorded 'Whoa Sailor' with 'Swing Wide Your Gates of Love' on a regional label. So we went to Columbia, RCA and Decca and they all said, 'Oh yeah, we'll take the songs, but we don't care for the kid who's singing.' Through Tex Ritter, we went to Capitol. Since it was a new label back then, they probably didn't know any better and signed me."

Thompson fused the jazzy, western-swing style of Bob Wills with a Texas-roadhouse thump to craft a string of massive honky-tonk hits. He created more than forty during his Capitol recording tenure.

By the time he left Capitol in 1965, Thompson had sold more than thirty million records. He was far from finished. He continued to make the charts in the 1970s and 1980s and in 1998 became the first country artist in history to make the charts in six successive decades.

Thompson brought true professionalism to the honky-tonk era. During his heyday, *Billboard* magazine named Hank Thompson & The Brazos Valley Boys country's No. 1 band for fourteen consecutive years. He was the first country star to record in stereo, the first to record a live album, and the first to headline in Las Vegas. Thompson was the first to build his own recording studio and the first on the road with his own sound and lighting equipment. He was also the first to do a musical show on color TV. He was the first to tour with corporate sponsorship, under the banner of Falstaff Beer.

Not the least of his many accomplishments is the fact that Hank Thompson was responsible for the honky-tonk era's major female stars. His 1952 hit "The Wild Side of Life" said, "I didn't know God made honky-tonk angels" and criticized a loose woman who "would never make a wife." In response, Kitty Wells fired back with "It Wasn't God Who Made Honky Tonk Angels."

Wells (Muriel Deason, born 1919) was a Nashville native who'd been kicking around on the country barn-dance circuit since 1939 as the "girl singer" on the Johnny & Jack show. She'd married Johnny Wright in 1937 and by 1952 was the mother of three and a little tired of show business.

LEFT: *The astonishing voice of Lefty Frizzell still inspires singers today. His mercurial phrasing set a honky-tonk benchmark.*

"We went to Shreveport to *The Louisiana Hayride* from '48 to '52, then we moved back to Nashville," Wells relates. "Johnny & Jack started working on *The Grand Ole Opry*. I was just gonna retire and stay at home. Decca Records executive Paul Cohen heard this song that he liked. So we got the song 'It Wasn't God Who Made Honky Tonk Angels.' I said, 'Well, at least we'll go in and get the session fee off of making the record,' never ever dreamin' it was gonna make a hit.

"I didn't know at the time it'd been released. Audrey Williams, Hank's wife, had been to Montgomery and driving back to Nashville she kept hearing the song on all the radio stations as she was driving along. When she got back home she said, 'Girl, you've got a hit on your hands.' She was the first one who told me.

"They said that I was the first woman libber with that song, but I never really even thought about that and I never really promoted women's lib. 'Course it's all right for those who like that. I never really felt like I was a victim or anything like that.

"I never was one to really go around honky tonks too much. It was all about the cheatin' and carryin' on, which I never did. But I had several 'answer' songs. 'Paying for That Back Street Affair' was the answer to Webb Pierce's song 'Back Street Affair.'"

Kitty Wells's "cheatin'" titles include her duets with Red Foley ("One by One") and Roy Acuff ("Goodbye Mr. Brown"), as well as such hits as 1953's "I Don't Claim to Be an Angel" and "Honky-Tonk Waltz." More often she portrayed the woman victimized by a honky-tonker's lifestyle, as in "I Heard the Jukebox Playing," "She's No Angel," and "Cheatin's a Sin."

Among Kitty Wells's eighty-one hits are such standards as "Release Me" (1954), "Makin' Believe" (1955), and "I Can't Stop Loving You" (1958), all of which she introduced. She was and remains "The Queen of Country Music."

"There's something so guileless about her singing, so restrained," comments Emmylou Harris. "I think that the passion that comes from country music is in the control and the restraint. It's that tightness, that intensity. With Kitty Wells, it was just kind of effortless. This lovely young woman singing about heartbreak. You could almost feel like she was in her living room. There was a 'non-performance' kind of performance about it. It was very natural."

Hank Thompson was indirectly responsible for Kitty Wells's stardom. For other female performers he took a more active role. On tour in California in 1951 Thompson heard an all-female band called The Melody Ranch Girls and invited its seventeen-year-old vocalist to share the bandstand with him.

"He asked me if I had a recording contract," remembers Jean Shepard. "And I said, 'No sir.' He said, 'Well you will have soon.' When Hank Thompson asked Ken Nelson about signing me to Capitol Records he said, 'Hank, there's just no place in country music for women.' We proved him wrong, and I'm so happy we did.

"*Songs of a Love Affair* was my first album. Ken Nelson hand picked the songs. He always wanted me to do songs where I was the woman that was being done wrong. I couldn't be on 'the wrong side of the fence,' because, he said, 'you're just a real sweet little country girl and we can't have you breaking up a marriage or doing anything.' He didn't know how mean I was."

Shepard was born in 1933, one of ten children in an Oklahoma sharecropping family. She would need all the true grit she could muster during her five decades as a country headliner. Known for her shoot-from-the-hip frankness, blunt honesty, and feisty, good-ol'-gal attitude, Shepard was the first unchaperoned female star of the honky-tonk era.

She also recorded some of the style's finest female performances of her day—"Crying Steel Guitar Waltz," "Seven Lonely Days," "Sad Singin' Slow Ridin'," "Girls in Disgrace," "Don't Fall in Love with a Married Man," and "I Want to Go Where No One Knows Me" among them. Shepard scored her first No. 1 by duetting with Ferlin Husky on the 1953 Korean War song "Dear

John Letter." After her husband Hawkshaw Hawkins was killed in the plane crash with Patsy Cline in 1963, Shepard rebounded with hits such as her yodel showcase "Second Fiddle" (1964) and the antialcohol "Many Happy Hangovers to You" (1966). She underwent a third career resurgence in the 1970s with clever discs like "Slippin' Away" and "At the Time," and continues to star on *The Grand Ole Opry* today.

The sublime vocal technique of Lefty Frizzell (William Orville Frizzell, 1928–1975) made him the most imitated of all the honky-tonk stars. His behind-the-beat phrasing, throaty curlicues, note-bending slips, and slurs into tones led Merle Haggard to call him "the most unique thing that ever happened to country music." Haggard, Dwight Yoakam, Johnny Rodriguez, John Anderson, Keith Whitley, Stoney Edwards, John Conlee, George Jones, Willie Nelson, Randy Travis, George Strait, and hundreds of others have been influenced by the peerless Frizzell.

"He was what I call a master phraser," says brother David Frizzell. "He'd take a word and just run that thing around and milk the emotion out of it. Then he'd go on to the next word. He would hold it right in there and expect the microphone to come in and get it. He was original. He still is today. He's still the boss."

The son of an itinerant Texas oil driller, Frizzell was in beer joints by age seventeen. Like most of his honky-tonk contemporaries, the boozy, brawling boxer served his musical apprenticeship in the school of hard knocks. By the mid-1940s Frizzell was a regular on the honky-tonk circuit, performing in the mode of Ernest Tubb and Ted Daffan. But his career was interrupted when he was jailed for statutory rape in 1947.

While behind bars Frizzell wrote "I Love You a Thousand Ways" to woo back his wife. After his release he recorded it with "If You've Got the Money I've Got the Time" and scored a double-sided No. 1 hit in 1950. By 1951 he was as hot as Hank Williams, with whom he toured.

"Lefty was one who didn't know if it was day or night, didn't care," says brother David. "Couldn't tell you how much money he had in the bank or anywhere else. He just was not into that. He was into his songs, singing. That was it. There was nothing else."

On October 27, 1951, Frizzell's "Always Late" was No. 1 on the country hit parade; "Mom and Dad's Waltz" sat at No. 2; "I Love You a Thousand Ways" was No. 6; and "Travelling Blues" was No. 8. Never before or since has a performer placed four songs in the top-ten simultaneously. By the dawn of 1954 he had racked up fourteen consecutive top-ten successes.

He moved to California, became a regular on TV's *Town Hall Party*, starred at the first country concert ever staged at the Hollywood Bowl (1955), and was given a star in the Hollywood Walk of Fame. Frizzell drank prodigiously throughout his life, and his boozing and poor business sense led to a decline in his recording career.

He staged a major comeback in 1959 with the stark, haunting, folk-styled "The Long Black Veil." A second comeback occurred with 1964's "Saginaw Michigan." He had begun a third with performances like "I Never Go around Mirrors" and "That's the Way Love Goes" when he was felled by a stroke in 1975 at age forty-seven.

"There's no doubt at all in my mind that the drinking caused him to be taken away from us way prematurely," says David Frizzell. "There was pills, uppers, 'bennies' they called them; but mostly it was booze. There was a lot of drinking going on."

There would be more, as a second generation of honky-tonkers arrived who were every bit the founding fathers' equals as hell-raisers.

109

ABOVE: *Honky-tonk trailblazer Jean Shepard recorded country's first female concept album, 1954's* Songs of a Love Affair.

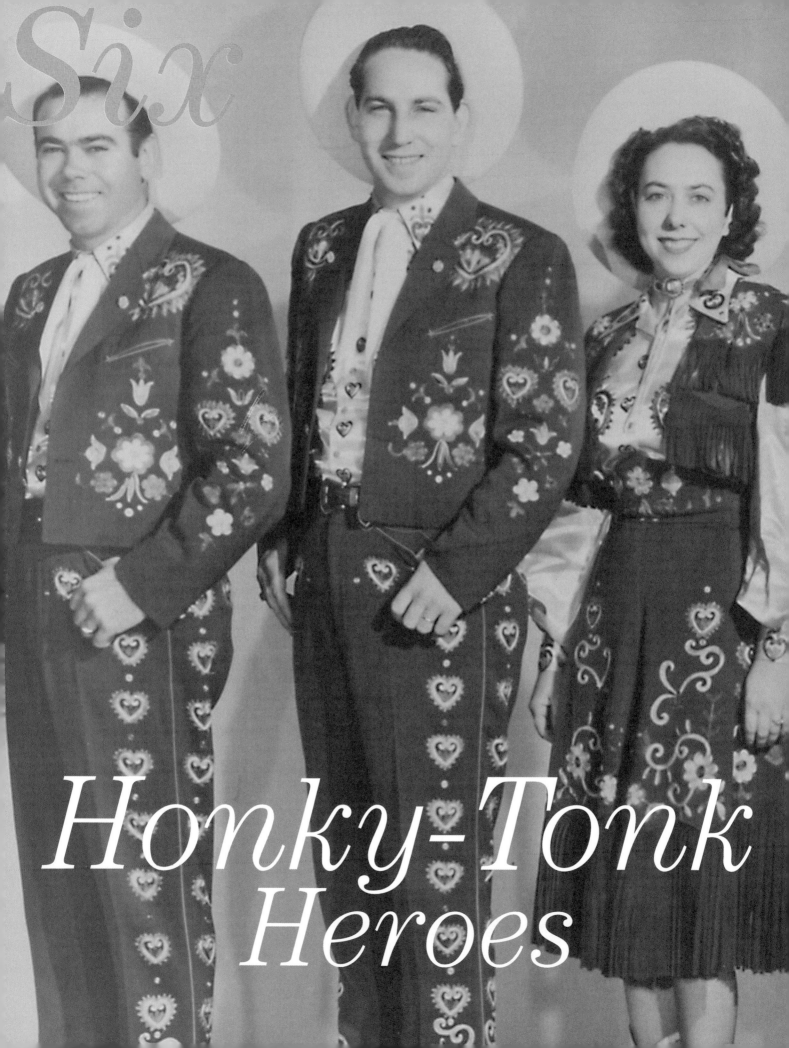

Six

Honky-Tonk Heroes

The immediate successor to the throne of Hank Williams was his former roommate, Ray Price. After the superstar's death, Price inherited his Drifting Cowboys band.

"I got into country music by accident," says Price (born 1926). "When I was in college, we had a little group that we'd play music on the side. I sang some songs to a publisher and I wound up with a contract. Hadn't planned that at all. But then after I got into it, I discovered that's really what I wanted to do."

The former World War II marine began singing in Dallas-area clubs around 1949. Lefty Frizzell wrote Price's first Columbia Records single, and Hank Williams wrote his first radio success. Then Price struck paydirt with a series of instant honky-tonk classics, 1952's "Don't Let the Stars Get in Your Eyes," 1954's "I'll Be There (If You Ever Want Me)" and "Release Me," 1958's "City Lights," and 1959's "Heartaches by the Number."

During his honky-tonk heyday, Price aided many up-and-comers. Willie Nelson, Roger Miller, and Johnny Paycheck are among his former band members. And Nelson, Harlan Howard, and Hank Cochran were all discovered as songwriters by his Pamper Music publishing company.

111

LEFT: *The Maddox Brothers and Rose were among the first to wear country's flashy "uniform" in the '50s and '60s.*
ABOVE: *Ray Price, "The Cherokee Cowboy," roomed with Hank Williams and inherited his band.*

In the 1960s Price embraced the softer style of the Nashville Sound and reinvented himself as the tuxedo-clad balladeer of "Danny Boy," "For the Good Times," and the like.

His Columbia Records label-mate Jimmy Dickens is generally given the credit for introducing the electric bass to *Grand Ole Opry* audiences. Dickens is also the artist who first dazzled in the show's spotlights wearing the sequined cowboy suits that became the standard uniform for all of the honky-tonkers of the 1950s.

"I thought he had the best band in Nashville," says steel guitarist Buddy Emmons. "Meeting Jimmy Dickens was probably one of the most pleasurable moments of my life, because he had a band that was so much farther ahead than most of the bands at that time. It was electric bass, the first electric bass in town. He used drums and twin guitars in harmony. I felt very fortunate to be able to jump right in the middle of that."

Dickens was born in West Virginia in 1920 to a musical family. After achieving prominence on radio in the Mountain State, he hit the road in the 1940s. He was discovered and brought to the *Opry* by Roy Acuff in 1948.

Backed by the propulsive sound he developed at the *Opry*, Dickens hit the popularity charts with "Take an Old Cold Tater and Wait," "Country Boy," and "My Heart's Bouquet," all of which became top-ten hits in 1949. "Hillbilly Fever" and "A-Sleeping at the Foot of the Bed" confirmed his record stardom in 1950, as did such other 1950s performances as "Pennies for Papa" and "Out behind the Barn." Many of his songs have become evergreens—Charley Pride ("We Could"), Gene Watson ("Farewell Party"), Ricky Van Shelton ("Life Turned Her That Way" and "Hole in My Pocket"), and Martina McBride ("I'm Little but I'm Loud") have all repopularized numbers that Dickens originated.

Dickens is only four feet, eleven inches tall and many of his best-loved songs have been high-energy novelty num-

RIGHT: *Jimmy Dickens was the first country star to circle the globe on tour.*

Little Jimr

Carl Smith

bers. This includes his most famous hit, 1965's "May the Bird of Paradise Fly up Your Nose."

"Boy, I have never been so surprised by a hit record," he says. "I just thought it would be a good piece for my stage show. Hap Wilson had put a melody to an old comic poem. He brought the tape to the studio and asked me to take five minutes to listen to it. We went back in the studio and ran it down. On the first 'take,' we got it. Johnny Carson had been kicking that phrase around on *The Tonight Show*. So I wound up singing 'May the Bird of Paradise Fly up Your Nose' on the Carson show."

The last jewel in Columbia's 1950s honky-tonk crown was Carl Smith. The handsome native Tennessean (born 1927) placed records on the popularity charts for the label for twenty-three consecutive years.

"When it comes to 'honkin',' Carl Smith invented it," says his daughter Carlene Carter. "My dad wrote the honky-tonk book. He gave me some of his albums awhile back and the first one I put on, I went, 'God! I want to do this. This is really cool.' He has so much pizzazz. He's still got it. He opens his mouth and it sounds perfect."

Possessed of a supple, expressive tenor, Smith ruled the charts with "If Teardrops Were Pennies," "Are You Teasing Me," "It's a Lovely Lovely World," "Hey Joe," "Cut across Shorty," and more than thirty other hits in 1951–60. In the 1970s the feisty, independent personality left the music business without so much as a backward glance.

"My daddy had so much integrity and I think he got a lot of respect by stopping when he did," Carter comments. "He stopped at the height of his career, 'cause I guess he was sick of it. He wanted to stay home, raise a family, and ride horses. So that's what he did."

Columbia's longtime country-music rival, RCA, signed one of the honky-tonk era's most distinctive stylists, Canadian-born Hank Snow. His clipped diction, back-of-the-palate phrasing, superb song taste, and deft acoustic guitar playing made Snow stand out any time he performed.

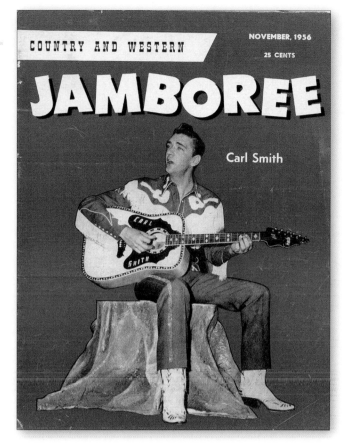

"I think that what made Hank Snow a star was, first of all, he was different," offers Joe Talbot. "He wrote quite a few of his own songs and even at the time when I was playing steel guitar for him I realized that a lot of his stuff wasn't just hillbilly country. I don't know if you'd say he was ahead of his time, or if he just had a little bit different twist. But I think that's what made him so outstanding."

"Hank worked very hard at the craft," adds Chet Atkins. "He'd come in with his guitar all in tune, his capo placed in the right place, his music with the words typed up. He had already rehearsed. And he was very easy to record because he had that great voice with the edge to it; and he sang on pitch. He would look hard for great songs."

Snow was no overnight success. Born in Nova Scotia in poverty in 1914 and raised as an abused child, he began singing on local radio in 1933. His first recording session was in 1936. He struggled as an artist

113

y Dickens

ABOVE: *Handsome, charismatic Carl Smith is pictured here on the cover of a 1956 country fan magazine.*

Hank Snow

for years before Ernest Tubb pestered the *Opry* into hiring Snow in 1950. Later that year, Hank Snow finally got a No. 1 record, the railroad classic "I'm Movin' On."

After that, Snow was an unstoppable force. He placed eighty-five titles on the country charts during the next thirty years, including such huge hits as "A Fool Such as I" (1952), "I Don't Hurt Anymore" (1954), "Let Me Go Lover" (1955), "Miller's Cave" (1960), "I've Been Everywhere" (1962), and "Hello Love" (1974). He published his autobiography in 1994 and went into semi-retirement in 1998.

"I made entertainment money the hard way," he says, summing up his long struggle to the top. "Back then, we didn't get what they get now. It was five-hundred-dollar shows and thousands of miles with a car and trailer."

As big as he was, Hank Snow was not the biggest hit maker of the honky-tonkers. That distinction belongs to Louisiana's Webb Pierce (1921–1991), who placed ninety-six titles on the charts, including more than a dozen No. 1 hits.

"Webb was about as pure as you can get, certainly as pure vocal-wise as a Hank Williams, as an Ernest Tubb," says songwriter Harlan Howard. "I think Webb Pierce influenced me more than anybody else," says singer Gail Davies. "There was just this heartfelt crying to his music, you know, 'There Stands the Glass.' It caught your attention and held your attention. It was real emotional."

"There Stands the Glass" was a hit of 1953, one of a string of barroom anthems that Pierce's nasal, sharp-edged tenor made memorable. "Wondering," "Missing You," "Fallen Angel," and others were radio staples in 1952–62. "More and More" launched the songwriting career of Merle Kilgore. "I'm Tired" was Mel Tillis's first hit as a writer. Working for Pierce's Cedarwood publishing company, Tillis also provided the star with "Honky Tonk Song" (1957), "Tupelo County Jail" (1958), "I Ain't Never" (1959), "No Love Have I" (1959), and "Crazy Wild De-

sire" (1962). "Slowly," a Webb Pierce classic of 1954, is the recording that introduced the sound of the pedal steel guitar.

"When that sound starting hitting, everybody went crazy trying to figure out what was happening," recalls Buddy Emmons. "I had already ordered a pedal steel guitar before 'Slowly' ever came out. I don't know why, but after Bud Isaacs, who played on the record, got everything stirred up he left town and started panning for gold or something out in some western state. Fortunately, the timing was right for me." Emmons would become the instrument's sonic architect and create the Sho-Bud steel guitar company with fellow player Shot Jackson.

The flamboyant Webb Pierce is often remembered for his colorful stage attire, his guitar-shaped swimming pool, and his convertible studded with silver dollars, upholstered in tooled leather, and sporting six-shooters as door handles. But he was also a shrewd businessman and an astute judge of talent. In addition to Tillis, he aided

the Nashville careers of The Wilburn Brothers, Floyd Cramer, and his honky-tonk rival, Faron Young (1932–1996).

The day that Pierce heard Don Gibson's song "Sweet Dreams" in 1956, he telephoned Young and summoned him to his house. "You need to record this song; it's a hit," Pierce said. Young obeyed the older and more established star and introduced one of country music's greatest standards.

Faron Young had many more great performances, including the honky-tonking "Live Fast, Love Hard, Die Young" of 1955, "Goin' Steady" of 1953, "If You Ain't Lovin' (You Ain't Livin')" of 1954, and "Hello Walls" of 1961.

The hell-raising stylist attributed his music success to laziness: "My desire was to get off of a farm," he said. "I was raised on a dairy farm and milked the cattle two times a day, got up at four o'clock in the morning for ten years. I developed my voice by calling the cows. That's what I tell everybody. They say, 'It still sounds like what you should be doing.' I was just wanting to get away from that farm; I didn't care how—I might of went into bank robbery, whatever was more convenient.

"I really had to learn how to sing country music, how to break my voice and do different things to sing it. I wanted to sing smooth like Eddy Arnold with that big round voice. But with Hank Williams and Webb Pierce having that whiney style, I knew that's what I'd have to learn to do."

Young invested in a Music Row office building and founded the popular country consumer monthly *Music City News* in 1966. Although he was always a salty, outgoing, and controversial personality, Faron Young still shocked Nashville when he committed suicide with a self-inflicted gunshot wound in 1996.

The last of the major honky-tonk figures to emerge in Nashville was—like Floyd Tillman, Ernest Tubb, Ray Price, and many other honky-tonkers before and since—a Texan. And, like

Hank Williams, Faron Young, and Lefty Frizzell, George Jones would live the honky-tonk life as well as sing its songs. His divorces, outbursts of violence, drinking, drug taking, financial problems, and wild mood swings have made him an almost mythic figure in the modern country pantheon. Perhaps the most surprising thing about his honky-tonking is revealed in the title of his 1996 autobiography, *I Lived to Tell It All*.

George Jones was born in East Texas in 1931. As a child he sang on the streets of Beaumont for spare change. By 1950 he was performing professionally on local radio. He was also already drinking heavily. He first recorded in 1954 and struck paydirt a year later with the hit "Why Baby Why." Jones moaned classic honky-tonk ballads such as "Color of the Blues" (1958), "The Window up Above" (1960), "Tender Years" (1961), "She Thinks I Still Care" (1962), "Walk through This World with Me" (1967), "If My Heart Had Windows" (1967), and "A Good Year for the Roses" (1970). But like his idol Hank Williams, he could kick up his heels with up-tempo romps like "White Lightning" (1959), "The Race Is On" (1964), and "Love Bug" (1965).

"George sings with emotion, very much in the same way that mountain people sing from their heart, from their gut,

115

Webb Pierce

ABOVE: *Webb Pierce dressed the part of a honky-tonk hero. He had a convertible that was decorated with tooled leather, silver dollars, steer horns on the grill, and pistols for door handles.*

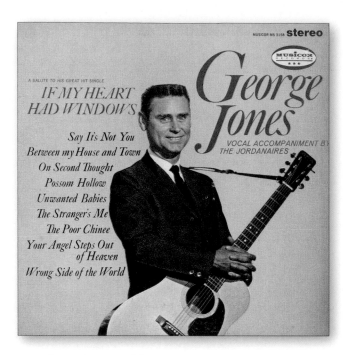

from their soul," says Dolly Parton. "He's a true stylist. He's like nobody else. And he's very versatile. George can sing the saddest song on earth and just tear your guts out. But he also can sing a song happy and make that believable too. His phrasing is just spectacular."

"George Jones is the world's greatest country singer," Hal Ketchum states flatly. "George Jones reaches in and takes your heart out while it's pounding and shows it to you. And is kind enough to give it back."

Adds John Anderson, "I've seen him do things that I've never seen another singer even try to do. He's truly a natural, a God-gifted singer."

Jones's stormy marriage to Tammy Wynette in 1969–75 made headlines and resulted in a number of brilliant duet records. Throughout this period, Jones was a crazed, cocaine-addicted alcoholic. But producer Billy Sherrill surrounded his still-stirring vocals with beautifully crafted arrangements and made him an even bigger recording star than before. Records like 1972's "A Picture of Me (Without You)," 1974's "The Grand Tour," 1978's "Bartender's Blues," and 1980's "He Stopped Loving Her Today" showcased him at the peak of his powers.

But his rampages became ever more self-destructive. His erratic, unpre-

dictable behavior on the road earned him the unflattering nickname of "No-Show Jones." After he married his fourth wife, Nancy Sepulveda, in 1983, he began a gradual rehabilitation.

"I didn't realize what I was doing to myself," says Jones. "You're back and forth, all across the country—you're bound to get in trouble. I call it 'That Wild Life.' It'll tear you up. I can't stand no more of the stuff.

"Every time I think of drinking, I think of my sickness I went through getting over it. I had them withdrawal symptoms for about the first two years, like the doctor said I would. That's the reason I had to go back to the hospital. I thought I was dying. It scared me to death. I would just get down on the floor and just roll. It was awful."

Although they are vastly in the majority, Texans don't have a monopoly as honky-tonk performers. The Depression-era Dust Bowl migrants who settled in central California developed their rough-and-tumble country nightspots as well.

The first star act to cater to the California honky-tonk crowd was also the wildest one, The Maddox Brothers and Rose. Tooling from town to town in their fleet of matching black Cadillacs, wowing audiences with their vividly hued, eye-popping stage outfits and howling through shows with wild abandon, the family act lived up to its billing as "The Most Colorful Hillbilly Band in the Land."

The Maddox clan had migrated from Alabama in 1933. They rode the rails with the aid of hoboes and then lived in migrant labor camps in central California. Shepherded by their ambitious mother, siblings Rose, Cal, Fred, Henry, and Don got a radio show in Modesto in 1937. After the war interrupted, the band resumed its career.

"The war came along and changed a lot of things," recalled Rose Maddox (1925–1998). "Prior to the war, we just worked in honky-tonks for tips, mostly. After the war, we started getting paid for doing dances and stuff. It'd be a big barn out in the middle of nowhere and you'd think, 'How's anybody gonna be here?' That night the

116

ABOVE: *George Jones, "The Rolls Royce of Country Singers," sang "If My Heart Had Windows" in 1967.*
RIGHT: *Like many others, Faron Young lived the lifestyle he sang about—he did "Live Fast, Love Hard, Die Young."*

Faron

Young

coal-mining anthem "16 Tons" and TV's "The Ballad of Davy Crockett."

Rose Maddox's duet partner on Capitol Records in 1961–63 was Buck Owens. His sharecropper family was also part of the Dust Bowl migration westward. Born Alvis Edgar Owens Jr. in Texas in 1929, he began his music career as a honky-tonk guitarist in Phoenix, Arizona. Owens moved to Bakersfield, California, in 1951 and began playing regularly in the city's popular Blackboard club. By mid-decade he was fronting the house band.

"That was the first time I ever had a job making my living playing music and not having to have a day job," Owens recalls. "Being at the Blackboard was like being on the cutting edge of what was happening.

"On Sundays from three until seven, we'd do a jam session. And then we'd play again from nine until two at night. Wynn Stewart came in one day. He got up and sang with us and we became friends. The next Sunday or Sunday after that he brought with him this guy that was tryin' to write songs named Harlan Howard. The next thing I know, he'd gotten married to Jan Howard and they came up from L.A. to Bakersfield and stayed all night with me. Harlan and I stayed up the rest of the night on Saturday night, tryin' to write songs."

Signed to Capitol Records, Owens made his chart debut with "Second Fiddle" in 1959; then he and Howard cowrote such major early-'60s hits as "Excuse Me (I Think I've Got a Heartache)," "Above and Beyond," "Under the Influence of Love," "Foolin' Around," and "I've Got a Tiger by the Tail."

"He and I wrote songs so well and so easy," comments Owens. "I remember Harlan came down to Texas one time in about '64 and I kept seein' these signs, 'Put a tiger in your tank.' I kept after Harlan. I said, 'Let's write a song and call it "Tiger by the Tail."' I went to record about a month or two after that; and I recorded that song only for an album. It came out to be the biggest hit that I ever had.

place would be just packed to the rafters. So you had to change your style some. We got louder. We were classified as Okies, which didn't bother us.

"The *Opry* was completely different than the honky-tonk style on the West Coast. The California sound is more fun and more raunchy. Not quite so professional and after perfection as Nashville. A little bit more kickin'-ass, let's put it that way."

The flashy Maddox Brothers and Rose put on a rambunctious show, full of hijinks, humor, and honky-tonk lather. They blared Woody Guthrie's "Philadelphia Lawyer" and the risqué "Sally Let Your Bangs Hang Down" to whooping Okie audiences until 1957, after which Rose launched a successful solo career. Jonny Whiteside, whose 1997 book *Ramblin' Rose* was an homage to the band, says The Maddox Brothers and Rose "defined California's freewheeling country-music style."

Tennessee Ernie Ford (1919–1991) added a boogie-woogie beat to California's honky-tonk climate. Signed to Capitol Records in 1948, he issued a string of country-boogie hits ("Shotgun Boogie," "Smokey Mountain Boogie," "Blackberry Boogie," etc.) long before his 1955 pop breakthrough with the

ABOVE: *After the outstanding sales of his* Sixteen Tons *album, Tennessee Ernie Ford became a TV variety star.*
RIGHT: *Buck Owens migrated to Bakersfield, CA, in 1951. He made the city a country-music mecca.*

Buck Ow

ens

"We were doin' a show up in Milwaukee in about 1964. I talked Bobby Bare into closin' the show and lettin' me go to Chicago 'cause they had a two A.M. flight I could get back to California on. Now I'm drivin' along about eighty miles along this freeway about one in the morning. For some reason or other, I just thought about, 'It's sure gonna be cryin' time if I go to all this trouble and I don't make that plane.' And I just started to sing a little song there. A few days later, I just sat down and wrote it

"In those days you needed a 'throw-away' song, some song that you put on what they called a 'B-side' of a single. I put it on the back of 'Tiger by the Tail,' because I thought 'Crying Time' was a nothin' song. I did the same thing with 'Together Again,' put it on the back of 'My Heart Skips a Beat.' That shows you what I knew about music. Those are my two most famous copyrights; probably always will be."

Between 1959 and 1975 Buck Owens took nearly fifty songs into the top-ten on the country charts. In 1966 Ray Charles revived "Together Again" and "Crying Time." Kay Starr revived "Foolin' Around" in 1961. Rodney Crowell brought "Above and Beyond" into the modern era in 1989. Dwight Yoakam teamed with Buck Owens to make "Streets of Bakersfield" into a No. 1 duet in 1988. But the most famous reworking of a Buck Owens hit was done by The Beatles, who sang "Act Naturally" in 1965.

Owens became a highly successful businessman, investing heavily in real estate and radio stations. Always very television-conscious, he had his own syndicated TV show and starred for 18 years on *Hee Haw*, the most successful syndicated series of all time. He was also apparently the first country star to make music videos. Unlike most country stars of the 1960s, he recorded with his own band, The Buckaroos.

"That gave me a little different sound than the manufactured sound that comes out," he explains. "I wanted to present them. I was proud of them. It was

never just Buck Owens. It was always 'Buck Owens and The Buckaroos.' My philosophy was that AM radio was the catalyst of making me want to have all the tones be sharper, more clear. Because it was such a terrible system for playin' music: the bass would just rumble over everything. So I cut down on the bass and cut up on the high end.

"It's like a locomotive to me. It has the drive; it has the wind. It has the power of a tornado."

"On the West Coast they had a brighter, more refreshing sound," comments Harlan Howard. If you put on 'Tiger by the Tail,' it doesn't sound like it has any bass at all; but it cut through like a knife on the radio. In other words, it was a great car-radio record."

"It really has a rabid, aggressive energy to it," says Dwight Yoakam. "The edginess of how they recorded their electric-guitar sound was just like razor blades cutting through on the records."

"Everything out of Nashville is so precise," says David Frizzell. "It's 'studio' and it's perfect and it is great. But there was something about that Buckaroos sound. It was exciting. Buck Owens had the Bakersfield Sound."

The other outstanding exponent of the West Coast's honky-tonk style is Merle Haggard. Born in a railroad boxcar to a pair of Dust Bowl refugees in 1937, Haggard grew up in Bakersfield. His father died when he was nine. The troubled youngster ran away from home at age fourteen, began performing in honky-tonks a year later, and was sent to prison for burglary at age twenty. California governor Ronald Reagan pardoned Haggard in 1960.

"Wynn Stewart had a nightclub in Las Vegas," recalls Bobby Bare. "When Merle Haggard got out of prison he went to work playing bass with Wynn Stewart's band. I would go over there and hang out with them. That's where I met Merle. As a matter of fact, Wynn wrote Merle's very first record, 'Sing a Sad Song.'"

That appeared in 1963, followed by a raft of records that are regarded as country master-

Merle

pieces—"Sing Me Back Home," "Mama Tried," "Hungry Eyes," "Workin' Man Blues," "Okie from Muskogee," "Ramblin' Fever," and "Today I Started Loving You Again"—most of them composed by Haggard.

"We try to make it simple and deep at the same time," he says of his writing style. "You know, something worth talking about, a viewpoint. It's something like art."

Like Buck Owens, Merle Haggard is fiercely individualistic. He keeps Nashville at arm's length and sometimes records without heed to commerciality, notably with tribute albums to Jimmie Rodgers and Bob Wills. His band The Strangers has long been one of the most accomplished touring units in country music.

"With Merle Haggard, it's about music. It's not about the music business, it's about music," says an admiring Hal Ketchum.

"My band has always been just as much a part of my sound as I am," comments Haggard. "I've had some players in the band that were legends when they came on the band—Tiny Moore and Eldon Shamblin were legends in swing music when I hired 'em and Roy Nichols was a legend when I hired him. There's been a lot of Strangers over the years; and I think every one of them has been proud to be a Stranger. And as long as I can do it, I'll have that big band. They're all guys capable of playin' anything at the drop of the hat. We never have any sort of a format or anything. We just kind of play what we wanna play."

By the 1980s Haggard was a bona fide honky-tonk icon. As he aged, his records became ever more expressive, as hits like "I'm Always on a Mountain When I Fall" (1978), "The Way I Am" (1980), "Misery and Gin" (1980), "Big City" (1982), "Are the Good Times Really Over" (1982), and his revival of Lefty Frizzell's "That's the Way

Love Goes" (1983) so eloquently demonstrated. Clint Black is one of hundreds of young stylists who revere "The Hag."

"We worked on the road together back in '91 and did about nine months, 120 cities," Black relates. "And Merle was everything that a young artist like myself would hope that a mentor would be. He'd spend time with me. He would come by the bus, hang out, come by the dressin' room." In 1994 Black topped the charts with a song the two cowrote, "Untanglin' My Mind."

"Merle Haggard is country music in its purest, rawest form, and at its peak," says Emmylou Harris. "If you had to pick maybe one country artist, as far as a songwriter and a singer, a bandleader, a stylist, it's Merle Haggard. You can drop the needle anywhere on any record he's done over the last twenty-five or thirty years and you're gonna hear something wonderful. And you'll know that it's Merle."

"I'm a barroom musician," states Merle Haggard simply.

By the time of the 1960s ascent of The Hag, honky-tonk music had become country's most definable style. What had begun as an expression of postwar malaise in the 1940s was now thought of as "traditional" country music. Moe Bandy, Joe Stampley, Charlie Walker, Johnny Paycheck, Gene Watson, Vern Gosdin, John Conlee, Stonewall Jackson, Del Reeves, Gary Stewart, and dozens more would shepherd the style into the 1970s and 1980s. And it survives to this day in the works of Alan Jackson, George Strait, Randy Travis, Dwight Yoakam, Mark Chesnutt, Aaron Tippin, Tracy Byrd, Wade Hayes, and many others.

ABOVE: *Revered by singers and composers in all musical fields, Merle Haggard defines the term "living legend."*

Haggard

Seven

The Rise of Music City

The arrivals of Pee Wee King in 1937, Roy Acuff in 1938, Bill Monroe in 1939, and Minnie Pearl in 1940 were only the beginning. During and following World War II, *The Grand Ole Opry* embarked on an aggressive talent drive to bring the hottest names in country music to its airwaves. NBC picked up the *Opry* for weekly national broadcast in 1943, and this roughly coincides with the beginning of Nashville's climb to country-music preeminence.

During the same period of time, WLS's *National Barn Dance* was on the wane. In fact, the *Opry* "raided" the Chicago station's talent roster by bringing two of its top attractions to Nashville. In 1944 it lured folksinger Bradley Kincaid and two years later it hired Red Foley.

Foley (Clyde Julian Foley, 1910–1968) had risen to stardom at WLS as a member of The Cumberland Ridge Runners string band. By the time the *Opry* hired him, he had already achieved notoriety as a solo record maker with 1941's "Old Shep," and had launched Kentucky's *Renfro Valley Barn Dance* with another WLS fugitive, John Lair.

At the time, Roy Acuff was leaving *The Grand Ole Opry* due to a salary dispute. Foley was hired to replace him as the

LEFT: *Roy Acuff and his Smoky Mountain Boys up on the Opry stage in the War Memorial Auditorium in the early 1940s.*
ABOVE: *Folksy crooner Red Foley sold "Keepsake Albums" to his loyal radio listeners.*

George Morg[a]

styles were being showcased on the program. Honky-tonk stylists like Ernest Tubb (1942), Hank Williams (1949), and Hank Snow (1950) joined the show one by one. Comics Grandpa Jones (1946), Lonzo & Oscar (1947), The Duke of Paducah (1942), and Rod Brasfield (1944) were added to the cast.

So was George Morgan (1924–1975), a balladeer with a cry in his voice who was added to the cast's roster in 1948. Morgan introduced such country standards as "Candy Kisses" (1949), "Room Full of Roses" (1949), "Almost" (1952), and "You're the Only Good Thing" (1960).

"George Morgan was one of my idols," said Faron Young. "I came to Nashville one time and got to meet him. I got his autograph, and you know I carried that autograph with me for about twenty years."

"I'll tell you one thing about George Morgan, there was never a dull moment," says Buddy Killen. "This guy was the greatest practical joker in the world."

"I think I got my sense of humor from him," says contemporary star Lorrie Morgan, George's daughter. "My dad didn't play the 'star' thing. He was the same every time you saw him. He was good to people. His life always seemed so peaceful and so 'real.' I guess that's where I got that from, too. I don't see any reason for the star trip, and sometimes it embarrasses me when people treat me like I'm something special."

The most important of all the *Opry* headliners who rose to prominence during this era was Eddy Arnold. In 1943 he graduated from being the lead singer in Pee Wee King's Golden West Cowboys to solo stardom on the *Opry*. Arnold was a

host of the nationally broadcast "Prince Albert Show" portion of the *Opry*. Acuff returned to the show in 1947, but by then Red Foley was a radio superstar. In 1950 Foley scored a million-selling hit with "Chattanoogie Shoe Shine Boy." Discs like "Peace in the Valley," "Alabama Jubilee," and more than sixty others made him one of country's biggest hit makers of the 1940s and 1950s.

In 1954 Foley became the headliner at KWTO's *Ozark Jubilee* in Springfield, Missouri. In 1955 he became the host of *The Ozark Jubilee* show on ABC, country's first coast-to-coast TV series. He was also a regular on Fess Parker's 1962–63 ABC series *Mr. Smith Goes to Washington*.

"I got to meet Mr. Foley at the *Ozark Jubilee*," recalls Mel Tillis. "He let me sing on the *Jubilee* that night and he and I became big buddies after that for many, many, many years.

"I remember one time he came to Nashville to record. He called the office and asked if I would come over to the Anchor Motel and bring some songs. I went over there and stayed three days. Boy, out come the jug and we got to drinkin' and Red got to singin'. He did every song that I guess he knew. Boy, he could do the recitations; he could sing; and he could just make you cry. A wonderful entertainer."

Foley's folksy warmth as a vocalist made him an ideal *Opry* emcee. He presided during an era when a wide variety of

124

ABOVE: *George Morgan, standing, is pictured here at an early Nashville television broadcast.*
RIGHT: *Colonel Tom Parker managed country superstars Eddy Arnold and Hank Snow before moving on to Elvis Presley.*

Eddy Arnold

big, handsome, fair-haired man with a creamy, crooning style. Billed as "The Tennessee Plowboy," he rose to disc stardom after signing with RCA Victor Records. His sessions in the WSM studios for the label on December 4, 1944, mark the advent of modern recording in Music City. Victor had been to town in 1928 to record some of the *Opry*'s string bands, but that one-time visit did not result in establishing Nashville as a recording center.

Eddy Arnold's sessions did. "Mommy Please Stay Home With Me" and the gently yodeled "Cattle Call" emerged from them as hits. Born on a West Tennessee farm in 1918, he was now on his way to superstardom.

"The first sessions in Nashville were in a radio studio and we recorded those songs on what we called a transcription disc," Arnold recalls. "This was long before tape was ever thought of. Of course, at that time if you made a mistake or one of the musicians made a mistake, you had to do it all over again. You couldn't just do one little part, which you can today. That's the thing that I remember most about it."

Arnold's manager, Colonel Tom Parker (Andreas Van Kuijk, 1909–1997), thereafter transformed him into the hottest thing in country music. Arnold became the star of the "Ralston Purina" segment of the *Opry* and got a weekly Saturday afternoon show of his own on the national Mutual network called *Checkerboard Square Jamboree*. In 1948 Arnold became a daily radio star on the Mutual network, and a year

after that Parker arranged for him to make Hollywood movies. By the end of the decade Eddy Arnold was indisputably the No. 1 artist in country music with an estimated income of $250,000 a year.

His record sales are said to exceed sixty million. Among the dozens of early Eddy Arnold classics are "I'll Hold You in My Heart" (1947), "Molly Darling" (1948), "Anytime" (1948), "Bouquet of Roses" (1948), "Take Me in Your Arms and Hold Me" (1949), "I Really Don't Want to Know" (1954), "You Don't Know Me" (1956), and "Tennessee Stud" (1959).

When the smooth, arranged style known as the "Nashville Sound" came into vogue in the 1960s, Arnold's crooning easily adapted and he rose to even bigger stardom with "Make the World Go Away" (1965), "What's He Doing in My World" (1965), "The Tip of My Fingers" (1966), "Misty Blue" (1967), and "Then You Can Tell Me Goodbye" (1968). He was one of the early country stars to be featured on national TV via his own series in 1952, 1953, 1955, and 1956.

"God gave Eddy Arnold a gift of a voice that not many singers are fortunate enough to have," says guitarist Harold Bradley. I told him, 'Eddy, I've got some tapes from some of the old shows. If you were young and singing like that right today, you could knock Randy Travis, Vince Gill, all of 'em off the Christmas tree.' Because that voice still stands up. Eddy leaned in all kinds of directions—the country people liked him, but the people who liked pop music liked him, too. I still like to hear him. I just think he's a great singer."

The presence of hit makers like Arnold in Nashville at the *Opry* made the city more and more attractive as a recording base for the national record companies. Since both of its biggest country record sellers, Red Foley and Ernest Tubb, were in Nashville in 1945, Decca Records became the first national company to base its country recording in Tennessee's capital city.

Three engineers at WSM—George Reynolds, Carl Jenkins, and Aaron

ABOVE: *Prior to the rise of Garth Brooks, Eddy Arnold was the biggest selling country star of all time.*

Shelton—began using the station's old broadcasting studio for recording sessions, beginning with those Eddy Arnold sides in December 1944. In 1946 they opened their own Castle Studio in the downtown Tulane Hotel. Decca booked the new studio for Ernest Tubb and Red Foley. Hank Williams and others were soon using the facility.

Nashville's first million-selling tune was the pop number "Near You" of 1947. Recorded by the Francis Craig Orchestra at Castle, it was so popular that the city's first record-pressing plant was constructed to keep up with the demand for copies. Milton Berle, television's first superstar, adopted it as the theme song for his nationally telecast *Texaco Star Theater*. That same year marked the birth of Nashville's ad-jingle recording business. Pop crooner Snooky Lanson, pianist Owen Bradley, bassist George Cooper, and guitarist Harold Bradley participated in the session, which advertised Shyer's Jewelers.

In 1948 the Brown Brothers Transcription Service opened. This studio was heavily used by RCA Victor. "It was located at 4th and Union Street in Nashville over at the law offices where Andrew Jackson used to practice law," recalls engineer Glenn Snoddy. "It was an old stable. So that was my introduction to the music business in Nashville. It was a meager operation by today's standards. I think the first record that was done in that studio was a Johnnie & Jack session. I was amazed when they did twenty-two takes of a song called 'Jesus Hits Like an Atom Bomb' (1950). Of course it was right after World War II and it was a very topical subject at that time."

Johnnie & Jack were Johnnie Wright (born 1914) and Jack Anglin (1916–1963), a pair of middle Tennessee natives who'd been kicking around on the radio barn-dance circuit since the 1930s. They became brothers-in-law when Jack married Johnny's sister Louise. Johnny married Nashvillian Muriel Deason, who joined the act as "girl singer" Kitty Wells.

Anglin was drafted during World War II, which temporarily halted the singing team. By 1948 Johnnie & Jack were back in action, singing at *The Louisiana Hayride*. When they began recording in Nashville in 1949, they injected calypso and rhumba rhythms into their performances. "Poison Love" (1951), "(Oh Baby Mine) I Get So Lonely" (1954), "Down South in New Orleans" (1953), and "Ashes of Love" (1951) are among the numbers that brought them stardom on the *Opry* stage. The duo ended when Anglin was killed in a car crash en route to Patsy Cline's memorial service. Johnnie became a solo recording star, and eventually recorded duets with his "Queen of Country Music" wife.

Watchful of Nashville's growing music scene, WSM bandleader Owen Bradley (1915–1998) and his guitarist brother Harold decided to get in the ball game. They opened their Bradley Film & Recording Studio downtown in 1952, moved to Hillsboro Village in West Nashville, and then settled in 1954 in an old army Quonset hut behind a house on 16th Avenue South. It looked like an ordinary, corrugated-metal airplane hangar, but was nonetheless the first music business on what became known worldwide as "Music Row." The Sony/CBS headquarters was eventually built around this historic structure.

"We'd been recording at Castle Studios, which was in the old Tulane Hotel," reminisced Owen Bradley. "But they were gonna tear down the hotel and these WSM fellows were just kinda tired of foolin' with it. Paul Cohen, of Decca

ABOVE: *Fred Rose's discovery of singer-songwriter Hank Williams in 1946 put Acuff-Rose on the map.*

Ov

Harold Bradley

Records, had suggested we move the company's country recording to another town; and I didn't wanna move to another town. So I thought we maybe ought to find a place, put in some equipment and see if we could do it ourselves. So that's what we did. We bought a few speakers and I think a little Ampex machine or two and that was about it. A little board that you wouldn't believe. I think it cost about nine hundred dollars total to build the first Bradley studio.

"I was asked to work with Red Foley. 'Chattanoogie Shoe Shine Boy' (1950) was a thing that started out when Harry Stone, who was the manager of WSM, had an idea. We had a fellow who shined shoes named Clifford. Mr. Stone said, 'Why doesn't somebody write a song called "Boogie Woogie Shoe Shine Boy"? Why don't you write it, Owen?' I said, 'Yes sir, Mr. Stone. I'll try to do that.' He was the manager. But I really had no interest in it. Fred Rose was the one who helped get it together. We really got lucky on that one. That sold a lot of records."

Owen Bradley went on to direct the growth of Decca/MCA and build a series of landmark studios. He would produce the records of more members of the Country Music Hall of Fame than anyone else. Younger brother Harold Bradley (born 1926) became the most recorded session guitarist in history and, eventually, the president of the American Federation of Musicians union local on Music Row. That union was largely developed by George Cooper, the bassist who'd played with the Bradleys on the first Nashville jingle.

One by one the record companies began opening branch offices to capitalize on Nashville's emerging studio scene. Capitol Records sent a talent scout in 1950, but the experiment fizzled. The first permanent record company office in Nashville was established by Mercury in 1952. Outposts were established in succession by RCA Victor (1955); Decca (1958), later known as MCA; Capitol (1960); Columbia (1962), later CBS, then Sony; and Warner Bros. (1972).

The *Opry*'s galaxy of stars also attracted songwriters and song publishers to Nashville, all eager to get their material on the air or on disc. In fact, the first country-music business in the city that was independent of the *Opry* was a publishing company.

During one of his *Opry* broadcasts, Acuff mentioned that he would send a booklet of his song lyrics and pictures to anyone who mailed in a quarter. Bushel baskets of coins had to be carted from the WSM studios. Then he printed up a fifty-cent songbook and made even more money.

"If you've followed my career, I think that you have to admit that I kept my eyes and ears open," said Acuff. "I watch what's going on. When I first came here, I began to realize the value of a song. I found out that some of the little simple songs that I wrote back in those days, why they'd come in here from New York and Chicago, California, and offered me $1000–$1200 for a song. I thought, 'My goodness, is a song worth that much now?' So I just kept my songs, and I wouldn't sell 'em.

"I went to Harry Stone, the manager of WSM at that time, and I said, 'Is there any way that I can get a program on the air and sell my songs?' He said, 'Well, if you want to take the chance on it, we'll sell you fifteen minutes after eight o'clock.' I think it was eighty-five dollars that it would cost me. I figured I had enough money to gamble eighty-five dollars in selling songbooks.

LEFT: *Harold Bradley, the most recorded session guitarist ever.* ABOVE: *Brother Owen Bradley founded Music Row and produced more members of the Country Music Hall of Fame than anyone else.*

Fred Rose

So I put my songbooks on the air for sale for twenty-five cents. That was on Saturday night. By Wednesday, it scared WSM so bad they hired six girls to come out and get my mail and open it and take the quarters out. It was ten thousand letters the first week, and quarters.

"That's how I accumulated enough money to start the music publishing business. When I invested $25,000 to start Acuff-Rose Publications, that was a whole lot of money back then for a young man to have. But I didn't think I'd lose it. I wasn't afraid. I had faith in the songs. A lot of people have followed in my footsteps. Everybody's got a publishing company now."

Having seen the kind of money songs could bring, in 1942 Acuff approached songwriter Fred Rose with his idea. Rose (1898–1954) had become an established writer with "Red Hot Mama," "'Deed I Do," and "Honest and Truly" to his credit since the 1920s. After falling on hard times because of alcoholism, he went to Nashville to begin life anew in 1933. During the war years he penned singing-cowboy songs in Hollywood such as the Oscar-nominated "Be Honest with Me" (sung by Gene Autry).

He returned to Nashville in 1942 and took a piano-playing job at WSM. One night at the *Opry* he watched while tears streamed down Acuff's face as he sang "Don't Make Me Go to Bed and I'll Be Good," a song about infant mortality. This incident reportedly opened Rose's eyes to the beauty of country music and unleashed a torrent of brilliant country compositions.

"Fire Ball Mail," "No One Will Ever Know," "Blue Eyes Crying in the Rain," "Waltz of the Wind," "Low and Lonely," and "Pins and Needles in My Heart" were all provided to Acuff. For Eddy Arnold, Rose wrote "Texarkana Baby" and "It's a Sin."

For Bob Wills he penned "Roly Poly." Such classics as "Faded Love and Winter Roses," "Deep Water," "Foggy River," and "We Live in Two Different Worlds" helped define Fred Rose's country style. And it is said that there are dozens of songs that he never took credit for that are actually his compositions.

With a handshake and $25,000 in seed money provided by Acuff, the two men established Acuff-Rose in late 1942. In 1946, the company signed Hank Williams, still regarded as the greatest singer-songwriter in the history of country music. During the next decade or so, the firm published Marty Robbins, Boudleaux & Felice Bryant, The Everly Brothers, Roy Orbison, The Louvin Brothers, Don Gibson, Dallas Frazier, Hank Locklin, and a raft of other "cornerstone" country tunesmiths. Redd Stewart and Pee Wee King's "Tennessee Waltz" became the company's first huge hit when it was sung by Patti Page in 1950.

Soon other publishers were cashing in on country's postwar boom. Hill & Range Songs was established in 1944 and rounded up stars such as Eddy Arnold, Hank Snow, Ernest Tubb, Red Foley, Lefty Frizzell, Hank Snow, Johnny Cash, and Elvis Presley. It was never headquartered in Nashville, although it maintained offices in the city for years.

Tree International was founded in 1951 as Nashville's second major homegrown publisher. "Heartbreak Hotel" put it on the map in 1956, followed by the signings of such stellar staff writers as Roger Miller (1958) and Harlan Howard (1959).

Webb Pierce and *Opry* house manager Jim Denny (1911–1963) founded Cedarwood Publishing in 1953. Denny signed Mel Tillis,

ABOVE: *Fred Rose, the first country songwriter nominated for an Oscar.*
RIGHT: *Jim Denny led an exodus from the Opry in the early '50s.*
OPPOSITE: *The best-selling "The Tennessee Waltz."*

Jim Denny

Tennessee Waltz

By REDD STEWART and PEE WEE KING

RECORDED BY PATTI PAGE FOR MERCURY RECORDS

featured by

PATTI
PAGE

PUBLISHED BY

Acuff-Rose PUBLICATIONS

2510 FRANKLIN ROAD
NASHVILLE 4, TENNESSEE

MADE IN U.S.A.

Frances Preston

Marijohn Wilkin, Danny Dill, Wayne Walker, John D. Loudermilk, and other songwriters. Up to now the music business in Nashville had been clustered around the WSM radio studios downtown. But Denny thought it might be a better idea to set up shop near where the stars were recording, rather than where they were broadcasting. So he put Cedarwood in a building across the street from Owen Bradley's studio. That way he could keep an eye on who was coming and going and get song tapes to them. This began the development of the Music Row neighborhood.

"When I came here there wasn't a Music Row," remembers singer-songwriter Bill Anderson, who arrived in 1958. "The music business was centered on Seventh Avenue North in downtown Nashville in the shadow of the National Life and Accident Insurance Company Building; because on the fifth floor of that building were the studios of WSM Radio. This was within walking distance of the Ryman Auditorium, where the *Opry* was staged. Those two places were really the focal points of the Nashville music business. There were maybe three or four music publishing companies in Nashville. That's all. There were probably less than a half dozen talent agencies, booking agencies that booked the acts out on the road. You could walk between the Ryman Auditorium and the WSM Studios, right down that little stretch of sidewalk on 7th Avenue North, and see everybody that was in the music business.

"If you missed them on the sidewalk, you went in the coffee shop of the Clarkston Hotel and talked to the people about what was going on in the business. I remember one of the first times I was ever in the Clarkston Coffee Shop. Porter Wagoner was in there. We were sitting and talking and in a minute this big white limousine pulls up out front pulling a trailer. Porter gets up, excuses himself, gets in the car and they take off and go on the road. It was such a simpler time then than it is now."

"What is now Music Row was actually the edge of town," said Owen Bradley. "The city limits was just a few blocks away. They rezoned the area commercial and we were the first ones to move in. Some of the people who lived here then were just tenants in the rooming houses and the neighborhood had gone down pretty bad. I know they didn't like it when musicians would pile out of the studio at two in the morning making too much noise. But pretty soon they all disappeared, because those houses were bought up by publishers and whatnot."

In 1956, Charlie Lamb launched *The Music Reporter* as the first trade publication chronicling Nashville's emerging music industry.

To handle the royalty distribution of Nashville's fledgling publishing companies, Frances Preston opened a Broadcast Music Inc. (BMI) office in 1958. The Nashville native (born 1934) rose to become president and CEO of BMI in charge of its worldwide operations. Since local banks were unsupportive of the music community in the '50s, '60s, and '70s, BMI gave loans to song publishers and songwriters to get them on their feet. Preston recalls the business climate when her tiny office opened.

"I started the office in my home and worked out of there for a year," she says. "I met people at restaurants and backstage at *The Grand Ole Opry*. My friends who were not in the music business would say, 'Why do you work with those people? Why are you working with country

ABOVE: *Frances Preston rose from a secretarial position answering Hank Williams's Opry fan mail to become the most powerful woman in the music business at BMI.*

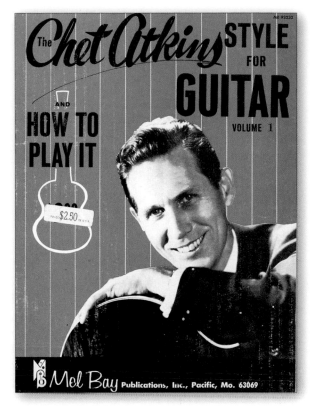

music? You could be doing so much else with your life.' I was all the time saying, 'This is going to be a very big industry.' From that one-person office at home, we're now in a nice building with about 450 employees.

"In the early days, Nashville did not really accept country music. The citizens all wanted Nashville to be known as 'The Athens of the South,' and they were very unhappy that it was being known as a country-music capital."

"I wasn't paying a damn bit of attention to the country music scene, if you get right down to it," remembers former WSM executive Irving Waugh. "My friend Jack Stapp brought me to Nashville at the latter part of 1941. I didn't know country music and didn't really have any feel for country music. As time went on, I began to pay attention to the *Opry*. It first came to my attention when I became sales manager of WSM and became aware that if an *Opry* artist such as Ernest Tubb promoted Martha White Flour, sales would pick up as far away as Pensacola, Florida. I began to appreciate the country music stars' ability to move product off the shelf. I guess that was an awakening for me."

"When I came to Nashville the music industry was looked upon by mainstream Nashville as something that they wished would go away," adds Tree publishing's president Donna Hilley. "Quite honestly, they accept us because we're putting money in their banks."

The out-of-town record companies were paying attention, however. By the mid-1950s, RCA had shifted its recording base to the Methodist Radio & Film Company's studio on McGavock Street. The first million seller recorded there was Elvis Presley's "Heartbreak Hotel." In the spring of 1957 RCA opened its Studio B on Music Row and placed Chet Atkins in charge. Following Bradley Studio and Cedarwood Publishing, this was the third building block of country music's business district and the first record-label office there.

"RCA had been recording at 1525 McGavock, which became Jim Owens TV Productions,"

Atkins recalls. "We had a little studio in there and some offices. I made a couple hits in there. But it was a bad studio. Terrible place. With all that success in the studio on McGavock Street, they were encouraged to build a better studio and move to Music Row, Studio B.

"When I first worked in Knoxville, Lowell Blanchard would introduce me as 'Chet Atkins and His Educated Guitar,' whatever that meant. 'Mr. Guitar' started after I came to Nashville. I've always just been a guitar player with a country aroma. But I've always liked all kinds of music. Classical music, folk music, I've always liked jazz, gospel, blues. I've been influenced by all that; and it helped me a lot when I was a producer, because I could borrow from all these areas."

A native East Tennessean, Atkins had originally come to Nashville as Red Foley's guitarist in 1946. Then he wandered off to other radio barn-dance jobs. He came back to town to stay as a sideman for Mother Maybelle & The Carter Sisters in 1950.

Born in 1924, Atkins had learned guitar by listening to the radio broadcasts

131

ABOVE: *Chet Atkins has taught generations how to play the guitar via instruction books and videos.*

Chet Atkins

of Merle Travis, Rhubarb Red (Les Paul), George Barnes, and others. Fred Rose recognized his talents once Atkins settled in Nashville. In addition to heading Acuff-Rose, the songwriter was the unofficial staff producer for MGM Records. He began using Atkins on recording sessions by Hank Williams, The Louvin Brothers, and others.

RCA's New York chief Steve Sholes took a shine to Atkins as well. Noting that the guitarist had a good rapport with his fellow musicians, he placed Atkins in charge of the label's recording in Nashville in 1955.

"From the beginning, even when I wasn't recording, I was telling everybody what to do," reports Atkins, "because most of these country musicians knew two chords and I knew three or four. Then when I got on the records, I'd tell people what to play."

Chet Atkins produced dozens of hit acts during his tenure as an RCA executive. Incredibly, he also found time to become the most recorded solo instrumentalist in music history. He has won more Grammy Awards than any other Nashvillian.

By the mid-1950s, a group of aggressive entrepreneurs had wrested control of the live-performance business away from the *Opry*. Hubert Long opened Nashville's

first non-*Opry* booking agency in 1953. Jim Denny left the *Opry* to open his own agency a year later and affiliated it with Cedarwood. Acuff-Rose opened a concert division. Talent bookers saw the advantage of a centrally located city from which to send out tours. These entrepreneurs gravitated to Music Row as well.

"As each building came along on Music Row, it was something new and exciting," says BMI's Frances Preston. "And each time, we thought it had reached its peak. Little did we know. When we decided that we needed an office building, we walked over the area where the Bradley Studio was and where RCA was and said, 'This is where the music business is going to be happening and we've got to be there.'"

"That was all really a slum area out there where Music Row is today," recalled Faron Young. "It had really gone downhill. People came in and started buying those big houses and remodeling and making offices in 'em. Where I built my building on Division Street, all that land was slum area. I bought it and put a big building on it. I think I had like $600,000 in it; and I sold it a few years back for $3.2 million. That's how much the real estate went up."

In 1950 a WSM DJ named David Cobb had ad-

Grand Ole

libbed an introduction to an NBC Red Foley radio show by announcing that it was coming from "Music City U.S.A." At the time, the nickname was more or less wishful thinking, but it stuck; and time proved Cobb right. The studio, publishing, and touring industries boomed side by side as the '50s progressed. Between 1950 and 1970 the number of union musicians in Nashville would triple.

The stampede of stars to the *Opry* stage continued as well. In 1952 the show welcomed Ray Price, Webb Pierce, and Johnnie & Jack. Between 1953 and 1959 Marty Robbins, The Louvin Brothers, Jean Shepard, Jim Reeves, Johnny Cash, Jimmy C. Newman, George Jones, Porter Wagoner, The Everly Brothers, Don Gibson, Skeeter Davis, Jan Howard, and Stonewall Jackson would all rise to stardom on the show.

Their electric guitars and fancy suits were a far cry from the string-band style of the early *Opry*. Significantly, founder George D. Hay left the show in 1953.

The first national notice that Nashville was emerging as country's capitol came on August 11, 1952, when *Newsweek* ran a story on the style with the headline "Country Music Is Big Business, and Nashville Its Detroit." Featuring a portrait of Roy Acuff, this was the first time country music had been on the cover of a national news magazine. The piece noted that "country" was now the preferred designation over "hillbilly," pointed out the central importance of *The Grand Ole Opry*, and stated that top Nashville stars such as Acuff, Hank Williams, Red Foley, and Pee Wee King were making $200,000 to $250,000 a year.

That same year *The Kate Smith* TV show featured *Opry* entertainers in two national broadcasts. Acuff, Mother Maybelle & The Carter Sisters, and Hank Williams entertained, and Smith pointed out to her audience that Nashville was their headquarters.

A 1955 issue of *The Reporter* noted, "As a result of this new growth and the money that has been pouring into Nashville in recent years, country music has come to be invested with new dignity and stature...an art form that not too long ago was ridiculed almost everywhere."

"We were 'writing the book' back in the early days, and didn't even know we were doing it," says former *Opry* band member, Tree executive, and songwriter Buddy Killen. "Because we did it out of our love for country music."

133

ABOVE: *These two snapshots convey the small-town excitement of a visit by a touring* Opry *troupe in the early 1950s. Nashville's central location made it a natural hub for the concert-booking business.*

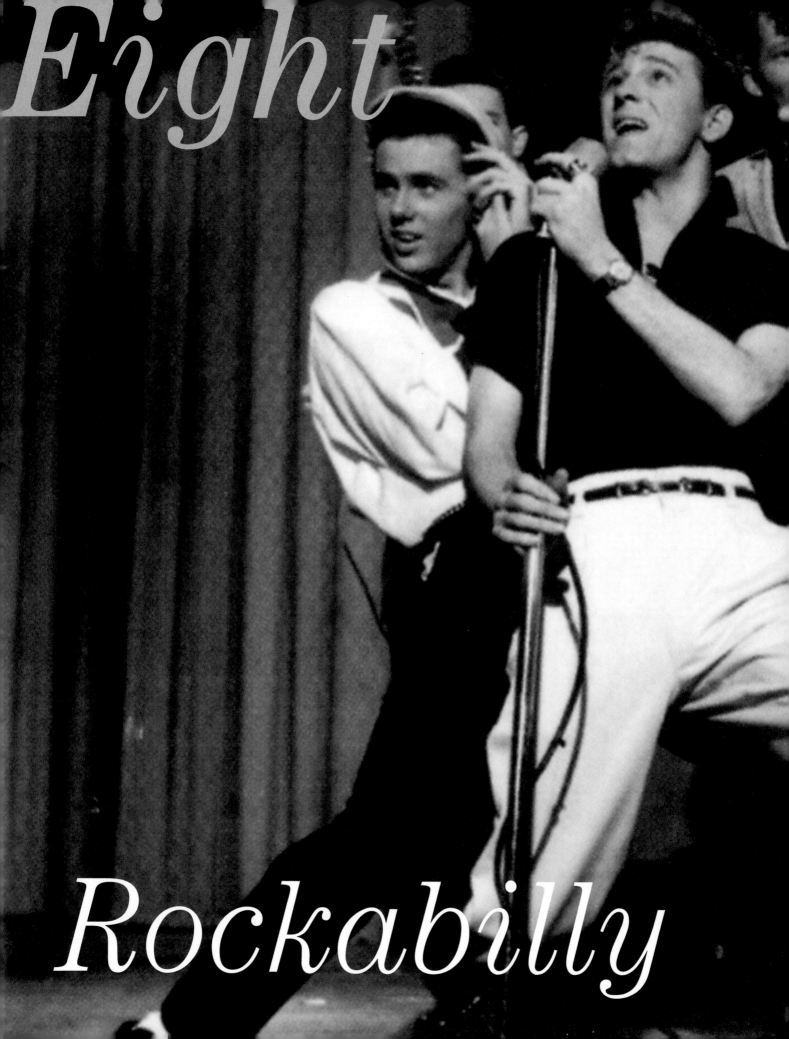

Eight

Rockabilly

The year was 1951. The setting was The Spigot, a dive bar in Philadelphia. The cowboy singer who performed there was startled by the audience reaction he got when he opened his sets with an up-tempo tune called "Rock the Joint." He'd been recording yodels and ballads with his bands The Four Aces of Western Swing and The Saddlemen since 1948 and initially started performing "Rock the Joint" as a kind of joke.

So when he was approached to record a version of Jackie Brenston's up-tempo r&b hit "Rocket 88," it didn't faze him. The resulting record opens with the sounds of a car horn blaring and a squeal of brakes. A boogie-woogie piano, a booming bass line, and a duel between the electric and steel guitars creates a dense sound under a shouted vocal.

Bill Haley (1925–1981) would claim in later years that the record's producer had his band members watch orgies in order to get them "worked up" to play in this fashion. Whatever the case, that 1951 disc marked the first instance of a hillbilly performer imitating a hard-edged "jump" blues.

"A lot of people have said in interviews, 'You did this deliberately; you were brilliant,'" Haley related. "But I didn't

135

LEFT: *Gene Vincent was one of the wildest showmen of the rockabilly era.*
ABOVE: *Bill Haley was a country bandleader in Pennsylvania when he developed rockabilly's musical mixture.*

do it deliberately. I did it out of stupidity. I just didn't realize what I was doing." According to John Swenson's 1982 biography, *Bill Haley: The Daddy of Rock and Roll*, Haley believed he "hit the music business when everything was confused."

Despite its innovation, "Rocket 88" was a stiff. Haley went back to recording conventional country music. In 1952 he and The Saddlemen recorded a tune called "Icy Heart" to cash in on Hank Williams's big hit "Cold Cold Heart." For the B-side Haley selected his old nightclub favorite "Rock the Joint." By the time he got to Nashville to promote the record, he was informed that "Rock the Joint" was the surprise hit.

This posed a problem: Black audiences were disappointed that Haley was white, and the mom-and-pop country audience wasn't all that receptive. The listening audience that was wild about "Rock the Joint" was a consumer group no one had previously addressed, teenagers.

The boots and spurs would have to go. The Saddlemen added a sax player, put on matching tuxedos, and became The Comets. They followed "Rock the Joint" with "Crazy Man Crazy" in 1953 and this led to their graduation from the local Essex label to Decca Records. Bill Haley & The Comets' first Decca release was "Rock Around the Clock." The tune created a sensation when it was featured on the soundtrack of the 1955 juvenile-delinquent film *Blackboard Jungle*. Riots erupted in theaters when the song came on the soundtrack.

Haley had touched a nerve. "Shake Rattle and Roll," "See You Later Alligator," "Don't Knock the Rock," and other hits followed in 1955–57. The countrified Haley never became a rock 'n' roll showman, but The Comets were full of acrobatic hijinks, slapstick routines, and wild abandon. The act toured the British Isles, South America, Germany, Sweden, France, Mexico, and Australia, creating audience pandemonium. But by the end of the '50s it was all over. Haley died in alcohol-soaked insanity six years before his induction into the Rock 'n' Roll Hall of Fame.

"Rocket 88," the r&b tune that

Haley had tried to ape, was originally recorded by Memphis producer Sam Phillips. Its success with postwar black listeners launched the career of its bandleader, Ike Turner, as well as that of Phillips, who formed his own label in the wake of the song's success. He called the company Sun Records. Then he went in search of the same fusion that Bill Haley had tried.

"I recall that Sam had said, several times, that he wished he could find a white singer with the soul and feeling and the kind of voice to do what was then identified as rhythm & blues songs," recalled former Sun secretary Marion Keisker. In a tale told so often that it has been burnished to a mythic sheen, a young truck driver came to the company and asked Keisker to help him make an audition disc in 1953.

She recalled that when Elvis Presley began to sing, "it seemed to me that I felt the hair on the back of my neck begin to prickle in some way. And I just snatched up a piece of tape that had been lying there and quickly threw it on the tape recorder."

In 1954 Phillips returned from a business trip to Nashville with an r&b song he'd found there. According to Keisker, "Sam said, 'I wish I could get this song recorded.' I said, 'What about the kid with the sideburns?' He said, 'Well, I don't know how to get in touch with him.' I said, 'I do.'" She called Presley. Phillips paired the young singer with guitarist Scotty Moore and bassist Bill Black, both of whom had years of country-music experience.

Presley (1935–1977) had a background that was country all the way. His stage debut was with Red Foley's "Old Shep" at age eight. Significantly, his first Sun single was a hepped-up version of Bill Monroe's "Blue Moon of Kentucky" coupled with bluesman Arthur Crudup's "That's

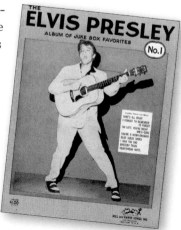

RIGHT: *Elvis Presley was still being billed as "The Hillbilly Cat" when he issued his first songbook.*

Jerry

S

Lee Lewis

All Right." Sam Phillips, born in Alabama in 1923, was fascinated with roots music, both black and white. He believed Presley's synthesis of the two belonged in country music and called the *Opry* about his discovery.

"*The Grand Ole Opry's* manager, Jim Denny, was my friend," Phillips recalls. "A lot of people didn't like Jim. He just had a mean streak in him. When I called him about Elvis, I didn't get any satisfaction on the phone about getting Elvis on *The Grand Ole Opry*. Then I went to Nashville. I said, 'Look Jim, we're not comin' to town with our red bandana in our back pocket and pullin' our wagons up around the courthouse square any-more. We need young people at *The Grand Ole Opry*, don't you think?' They said, 'We have sponsors to think about. We have tradi-tional artists on *The Grand Ole Opry*. We don't wanna insult 'em.' I said, 'This man is a *product* of *The Grand Ole Opry*.'"

"Elvis Presley worked his first show with Slim Whitman and myself at the Overton Band Shell in Memphis in August of 1954," remembers *Opry* star Billy Walker. "And I saw this phenome-non. I couldn't believe what kind of effect he had on the people. I couldn't fig-ure out what kind of music he was trying to sing. We worked on the *Louisiana Hayride* in those days, and I went back and told Horace Logan, 'Horace, this kid's got something; I don't know what it is, but he's got something.' So Horace called him up, got him to guest on the *Hayride,* and gave him a contract. I took him on a tour with me in January of 1955."

After Presley's 1954 appearance on the *Opry* led nowhere, *The Louisiana Hayride* signed him as a cast member. He remained there during the first year-and-a-half of his evolution.

"It's sort of a paradox," recalls *Hayride* boss Horace Logan. "Here is a man with incredible, unbelievable charisma. He could walk in a room absolutely unknown and everybody—men, women and children—would look at him and be drawn to him. Yet he was shy, bashful. Every time he got on stage he was nervous. He'd say, 'What do you want me to do, Mr. Logan?' I said, 'Just do what you do, Elvis.' He'd say, 'You think they like me?' I said, 'I know they like you. You just do it the way you normally do it. They'll go for it.'"

In 1955 Presley's Sun singles "Baby Let's Play House"/"I'm Left You're Right She's Gone" and "Mystery Train"/"I Forgot to Remember to Forget" became chart-topping country hits. Neither, by the way, made the national pop charts. He began to tour on country package shows with Faron Young, Mother Maybelle & The Carter Sisters, The Browns, and other mainstream country stars. None of them could follow him as a show-man. Publicized as "The Hillbilly Cat," he also appeared at barn dances in Dallas and Houston.

"Elvis was received well by most of the country artists," Logan re-calls. "Now, there were some tra-ditionalists who were turned away by Elvis. But for each one that turned away, ten turned to."

"Once we got him out on the road," says Phillips, "there was some-thing about this dude that can never be ex-plained. You find out in a hurry when you get out on the road what's hot and what ain't. Elvis Presley was hot."

"He came through with the Faron Young Show in Albuquerque, New Mexico," remembers Glen Campbell. "I'll never forget that night. He had charisma like nobody I've ever seen. I remember what he had on. He had on a light blue sport coat with a pink-and-blue...like a golf shirt now, a silky-lookin' thing. It was him and a three-piece band and they were awesome."

Colonel Tom Parker had made Eddy Arnold a country superstar in the late 1940s. By the time he saw Presley on *The Louisiana Hayride,* Parker was managing Hank

139

am Phillips

Snow. He used Snow's stardom to launch the youngster as an opening act, and then ditched Snow to manage Presley full-time in 1955. Parker negotiated RCA's purchase of Presley's Sun contract, engineered the star's incendiary early TV appearances, and eventually turned him into a Hollywood movie star.

Presley's first RCA session was held in Nashville in 1956. It resulted in the blockbuster "Heartbreak Hotel," the star's first national pop hit. He would return to Music City's recording studios many times thereafter. During the next twenty years Elvis Presley would become known as "The King of Rock 'n' Roll." What is often overlooked is his magnitude as a country star. Presley had eighteen top-ten country hits in his first four years as a recording artist. He eventually placed more than eighty-five titles on the country charts, including ten No. 1 hits. He was one of the ten most popular country acts for the decade of the '50s, and ranks first for all time in the number of hits that successfully crossed over to the pop charts. He also had one of country's longest chart careers, placing titles on the style's hit parade from 1955 to 1998.

"Country music is the thing that produced Elvis Presley," says Merle Haggard, "and we don't want to forget that. Elvis wasn't the King of Rock 'n' Roll when he started. He was a country boy, a country artist. And they can't take that away from him."

Presley's appearances on the TV shows of Tommy Dorsey, Milton Berle, and Ed Sullivan created a firestorm of interest in 1956–57. The media railed about the moral degeneration of American youth that he represented by introducing the sexuality of black music into the pop mainstream. It didn't matter: kids loved it.

"One of my good friends was a big fan," recalls K.T. Oslin. "Her father had gotten three tickets. So Noreen and Janet and I went to see Elvis at the

Coliseum in Houston. It held maybe fifteen thousand people, and that was an enormously huge crowd in those days. So it was mind blowing for that alone, to be with that many people. Then Elvis came out in white and we just went, 'Eeeeeeee!' the whole time. I was fourteen. I bought an Elvis scarf and I lost it. Wish I had it now."

"It helped that he was so good looking; and he moved so well on stage," adds Brenda Lee. "He was real unorthodox in his movements and with his singing. It was just a whole new world that opened up for all of us, teen-age girls especially."

Presley was in the midst of a 1974–77 run of top-ten country hits when he died. Few in country music can forget where they were on August 16, 1977.

"I'll never forget where I was when Elvis Presley died," says Glen Campbell. "I was pulling into Channel 5 in L.A. to do a TV show. And the guard said, 'No wonder Elvis died. He gained all that weight.' And it just hit me like a brick. I drove into a parking place and set there and cried. The first session I'd worked with Elvis was 1963 for *Viva Las Vegas*," adds the former studio guitarist. "In Vegas, we'd set up and yack all night."

"Elvis passed away on a Tuesday," recalls Ronnie McDowell. "I had been working in Nashville, rehearsing with my band, and I was driving home. I had the radio on, and they said Elvis had just passed away. I thought maybe it might be just a prank or whatever. Then I started flipping, and it was on every channel. The next day, being the world's biggest Elvis fan, I got in my Camaro and I drove a hundred miles an hour to Memphis. I wanted to see him, even if I had to see him like that. I got in line at eight o'clock that morning, and it was four abreast for maybe four miles. It was hot that day; I never will forget it. I got about fifteen or twenty feet from the gate and it was 5:30, and they shut the gates. So I never got to see him."

McDowell's tribute record "The

ABOVE: *Like nearly all the rockabilly stars Carl Perkins eventually returned to the country music of his boyhood.*

Carl Perki

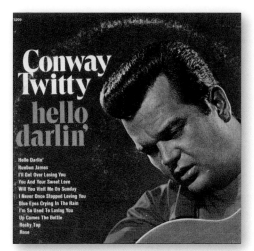

King Is Gone" sold a million and launched his country career.

"I remember when Elvis died," says Shelby Lynne. "I was outside in the yard, a dirty little kid in the country. Mama was watching *Days of Our Lives*. It cut off in the middle of it: 'Elvis Presley is dead.' This freaked me out, because the first records I ever listened to were his 45s. 'Rip It Up' was my favorite and 'Don't Be Cruel.'

"Oh, I thought I was Elvis. I used to sleep all day and stay up all night and had tinfoil on my windows. It was done with an Elvis attitude. I thought I was The King. But only The King is The King."

Records like Presley's "Mystery Train" were dubbed "rockabilly." Cleveland disc jockey Alan Freed had popularized the term "rock 'n' roll" beginning in 1954 when he titled his broadcast "Moondog Rock 'n' Roll Party." But the spare, energetic performances of country boys featuring stinging electric guitar leads and slapped upright bass got their own special designation. One explanation of the origin of the term is that Memphis rockabilly pioneers Johnny and Dorsey Burnette dubbed the music in honor of their sons, Rocky and Billy. As songwriters, the Burnette brothers provided Ricky Nelson with his 1957–59 rockabilly hits "It's Late," "Believe What You Say," and "Waitin' in School."

As illustrated by the examples of Bill Haley and Elvis Presley, the core of the rockabilly sound is the intermingling of southern black and white music traditions. It became hip for postwar white kids to tune in black-music radio stations, notably Nashville's fifty-thousand-watt powerhouse WLAC. When the blues went electric and uptempo "jump" tunes were evolving into r&b in the late 1940s, country's honky-tonk pickers were listening. They, too, were becoming electrified. Young hillbilly boys began incorporating boogie-

woogie rhythms and r&b energy into their styles. The result was the country cousin of rock 'n' roll.

"Growing up in the fifties was a wonderful thing," says Dick Clark, "because the kids had no musical prejudices. They loved everything.

"I think what happened was a complete revolution. The world prior to that had revered the old. All of a sudden, kids had their own clothes, their own music, and more importantly their own money. So everybody wanted to be youth conscious. That is when the revolution began."

"Rockabilly came about because the young country musicians started adapting this jump-type music—a little bit of gospel, a little bit of r&b, some country—and it was all kind of mixed in together," says Brenda Lee.

In the wake of Presley's stardom, dozens of other country boys made their way to the Sun Records doorstep in Memphis—Carl Mann, Billy Lee Riley, Charlie Rich, Sonny Burgess, Charlie Feathers, and Warren Smith all made exciting records in the manner of "The Hillbilly Cat." Tennessee farmboy Carl Perkins (1932–1998) heard Presley on the radio in 1954 and immediately made the pilgrimage to Memphis. A gifted guitarist and songwriter, Perkins was thrilled by the mixture of the hillbilly music and blues that was in the air.

He broke through with two top-ten country smashes in 1956, "Blue Suede Shoes"/"Honey Don't" and "Boppin' the Blues"/"Dixie Fried."

"I was floating on a cloud," Perkins recalled. "I'd had a big record. I'd had me a new Fleetwood Cadillac and we'd moved out of our three-room rented shack. Two little children was romping around and my wife got a new washing machine. I was the happiest cat in Tennessee."

141

ABOVE: *This Conway Twitty 45 r.p.m. picture sleeve dates from 1960. After re-entering the country field in 1965, Twitty sang more No. 1 records than anyone in history.*

Roy Orbiso

Louisiana's Jerry Lee Lewis (born 1935) came to Sun as well. He had traveled to Shreveport to audition for *The Louisiana Hayride* and to Nashville to audition for record labels, both without success. He arrived in Memphis in 1956 and approached Sun engineer Jack Clement with his sound.

"The girl who worked up front came back and said, 'There's this guy out here who says he can play piano like Chet Atkins,'" Clement recalls. "I said, 'Oh yeah? Well, I'll hear that. Send him on in.' So he came in. And sure enough, he played 'Wildwood Flower' on the piano and it sounded like Chet. I said, 'Do you sing? Sing something.' He sang something and I loved it. I said, 'Let's make a tape.'

"Sam Phillips was in Nashville at the time at a music convention. He came back the following Monday and I played him the tape of 'Crazy Arms.' I started the tape—the piano started playing and before it ever got to the vocal he reached over there and stopped the machine and said, 'I can sell that.' The thing was on the radio that night."

"I was ready," says Lewis, "way ahead of the game. I knew that. I never practiced. I was good. All I wanted to do was get somebody to release a record on me. Once I did get it done, I knew it was a hit."

"Hey, I don't give a doggarn whether people think I'm bragging or not," says Phillips. "Thank God I was the one that recognized these people and they didn't go unnoticed. We cut some hard records. And one of 'em was a tough-mother-honey, 'Great Balls of Fire' [1957]. But if we had nothin' else, we had fun, because by golly, it's different."

"It was pretty obvious about Jerry Lee," adds Clement. "His bass player said, 'Hey, Jerry, do that song we've been doing on the road that people like so much.' I walked into the control room. I hit 'play' and 'record' on the tape machine. Sat down. They did 'Whole Lot of Shakin' Going On' [1957] and that was it. No dry run, no nothing. One take."

The piano-pounding Lewis was the wildest showman in the Sun stable.

"One night I just filled a Coca-Cola bottle with gasoline and took it out there with me," Lewis recalls. "When I got through doing 'Great Balls of Fire,' I sprinkled some of the gasoline inside the piano and threw a match in. I never could believe a piano could burn like that, but it did."

"He was so volatile on stage that the kids were tearing their seats out of the floor in the auditorium," reports Brenda Lee.

"He came on with a leopard-skin jacket on and hair flopping around and he pounded the piano," says Dick Clark. "He stood up and kicked it. He played with his feet and his hands and his head. We were living in the world of Patti Page and Perry Como. He was a wild man."

Jerry Lee Lewis's marriage to his thirteen-year-old cousin created a scandal during his debut tour of Britain in 1958. After only three shows he returned to the United States with his career in tatters.

"The English press just made mincemeat out of him," recalls his sister and duet partner Linda Gail Lewis. "I think they were shocked about the cousin thing and the fact that she was so young. Then the other thing was that there was this little matter of his divorce wasn't final. So we had the bigamy headlines, we had the cousin head-

J

lines, and we had the child bride, all wrapped up into one."

Like many of the other rock 'n' roll pioneers, Lewis eventually returned to his country roots. His Nashville recordings of the 1960s and 1970s include such smoldering honky-tonk classics as "What's Made Milwaukee Famous," "Another Place Another Time," "She Even Woke Me up to Say Goodbye," and "Middle Age Crazy."

"I get a kick out of anything I do, if I do it right," says Lewis. "I'm livin'; I'm breathin'; I'm still rockin', brother. And I did it my way."

Mississippi's Conway Twitty (Harold Jenkins, 1933–1993) traveled to Sun Records as well. He was so profoundly influenced by Elvis Presley that he had difficulty finding his own style at first.

"On Saturday nights it was *The Grand Ole Opry*," Twitty recalled. "I had my heroes—Roy Acuff, Ernest Tubb, Eddy Arnold, Kitty Wells, and Red Foley. Then a little later came Carl Smith, Ray Price, Webb Pierce, Faron Young, and people like that. I tried to sing just like 'em. Went to Japan in the Army. The first thing I heard when I came back was Elvis Presley. That was a new kind of music—Carl Perkins's 'Blue Suede Shoes,' Bill Haley's 'Rock around the Clock.' You could just feel it grow. I headed straight for Memphis."

Because Twitty sounded so much like Presley, Sam Phillips never issued any of his Sun efforts. But another Sun act, Roy Orbison, recorded Twitty's song "Rockhouse." Twitty signed with MGM and went to Nashville to record "It's Only Make Believe" (1958), "Mona Lisa" (1959), "Danny Boy" (1959), "Lonely Blue Boy" (1960), and the rest of the tunes that made him a teen idol. Like Lewis, he returned to his country roots in the 1960s.

"He wanted to do rockabilly under the name of Conway Twitty and do country records under the name of Harold Jenkins," recalled producer Owen Bradley. "That

was the proposition that was given to me. So I talked it over with my people in New York. We decided that the only way we wanted him was if he would be country. We didn't have a hit immediately. Buck Owens was real hot at the time and we did some things sort of in that vein. Waylon Jennings brought us some songs. Harlan Howard brought us some songs. We finally found a few things that worked."

Indeed. Conway Twitty would go on to have more No. 1 country records than anyone in history and one of the genre's longest chart careers. His intensely emotional singing and passion-filled lyrics created such memorable hits as "Hello Darlin'" (1970), "Fifteen Years Ago" (1970), and "There's a Honky Tonk Angel" (1974), not to mention the sexually frank "You've Never Been This Far Before" (1973) and "Linda on My Mind" (1975).

His career continued into the 1980s and 1990s with "I'd Love to Lay You Down," "Slow Hand," "I Don't Know a Thing about Love," "That's My Job," "She's Got a Single Thing in Mind," and the like. He died on his tour bus of a stomach aneurysm while en route back to Nashville from a concert performance in 1993.

Roy Orbison (1936–1988), who'd sung Twitty's "Rockhouse" at Sun, succeeded with his own rockabilly tune "Ooby Dooby" in 1956. He, too, migrated to Nashville, becoming a pop star with his dramatic tenor performances of such '60s classics as "Only the Lonely," "Running Scared," "Crying," "Dream Baby," and "Oh Pretty Woman."

Orbison won a country-music Grammy for his 1980 duet with Emmylou Harris "That Lovin' You Feeling Again," but he didn't have a top-ten solo country hit until "You Got It," which was released after his 1988 death from a heart attack.

The member of the Sun Records roster who

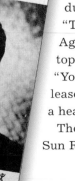

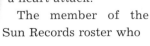

143

ABOVE: *Johnny Cash's 1958 hit song "Guess Things Happen That Way" was written by Sun Records's Jack Clement.*

Brenda Lee

most personalized the rockabilly sound was Johnny Cash.

"We didn't take Johnny Cash and say, 'We're gonna make a rocker out of you,'" says Sam Phillips. "When I heard Johnny Cash, it didn't take me long to know what we had was something potentially different. He was a story teller. And he wrote country songs like nobody else. Johnny Cash's songs were works of art.

"We did have that slap-bass feel on there. I don't know whether people remember this or not, but about the only person who was allowed to use that on *The Grand Ole Opry* back in those days was Jumpin' Bill Carlisle. But anyway, Marshall Grant could do that upright 'doghouse' bass, Luther Perkins was pickin' that one-string guitar and Johnny was kinda floggin' that flattop. And when they got that vamp goin,' I thought, "Man, this is good! This is not Burl Ives. This certainly is not Hank Snow. This is not anybody you wanna name. This is 'John R. Cash.'"

Born in Arkansas in 1932, Cash was a twenty-two-year-old appliance salesman when he arrived, literally, on Sam Phillips's doorstep. To ensure that he'd be seen, Cash went to Sun and sat on the step early in the morning, before anything was open for business.

"Sam was the first to appear," Cash recalled in his 1997 autobiography. "I stood up and introduced myself and said, 'Mr. Phillips, sir, if you listen to me you'll be glad you did.' That must have been the right thing to say. 'Well, I like to hear a boy with confidence in him,' he replied. 'Come on in.'

"I sang Hank Snow songs, a Jimmie Rodgers song, a couple of Carter Family songs, whatever else I'd taken into my repertoire from the country songs of the day. Sam kept directing me back to my own repertoire: 'What else have you written?' Though I didn't think it was any good, I told him about 'Hey Porter,' and he had me sing it for him. That did it."

The thumping "Hey Porter"/"Cry Cry Cry" became Cash's first Sun Records hit in 1955. "Folsom Prison Blues"/"So Doggone Lonesome" and "I Walk the Line"/"Get Rhythm" followed it up the charts a year later. He joined the *Opry* cast in 1956–58, signed with Columbia Records in Nashville, and then created a series of groundbreaking concept albums—1960's *Ride This Train*, 1962's *Blood Sweat and Tears*, 1964's *Bitter Tears: Ballads of the American Indian,* and 1965's *Ballads of the True West.*

His highly individual singles during this period included "Don't Take Your Guns to Town," "I Got Stripes," "Understand Your Man," "Five Feet High and Rising," and "Tennessee Flat-Top Box," all of which he wrote. Cash's rumbling baritone also immortalized Shel Silverstein's "A Boy Named Sue," Carl Perkins's "Daddy Sang Bass," Harlan Howard's "Busted," and "Ring of Fire" by Merle Kilgore and June Carter.

Johnny Cash's rough-hewn dignity and musical integrity made him country's most popular figure among the folkies of the '60s. His 1968 marriage to June Carter coincided with overcoming a long addiction to amphetamines. He became a network TV star in 1969–71 and used his program to showcase Linda Ronstadt, Bob Dylan, Joni Mitchell, Pete Seeger, Arlo Guthrie, James Taylor, and other troubadours as well as traditional country acts.

His craggy charisma only deepened in the 1970s. "What Is Truth," "Man in Black," "Sunday Morning Coming Down," "One Piece at a Time," "Oney," and the like were riveting performances, as compelling as anything he'd recorded at Sun. In the 1980s he teamed with fellow legends Willie Nelson, Kris Kristofferson, and Waylon Jennings to tour and record as The Highwaymen. In the 1990s he reinvented himself as a rock idol through a series of solo CDs with a stark, somber approach.

Cash has posted more than 130 hits on the country charts. His tally of 48 charted pop singles puts him on a par with The Rolling Stones and The Beach Boys. More of his albums are in print today, 45, than most artists ever make. He has sold in excess of fifty

145

LEFT: *Diminutive Brenda Lee stands tall as a rockabilly performer of the '50s, a pop superstar of the '60s, and a country hit maker of the '70s and '80s.*

Everly Brothers

million records and remained a successful touring attraction around the globe for thirty-eight years.

By speaking out on behalf of Native Americans, the poor, prisoners, civil-rights and antiwar crusaders, the disenfranchised, the homeless, the powerless, and the forgotten, Johnny Cash helped give country music a conscience. His principles and his courage helped to make the multimillion-selling "outlaw" phenomenon possible in Nashville.

More importantly, through five decades of singing and writing, Cash became a living icon, an international symbol of country music, and one of the entertainment world's most revered figures.

In the early days, Nashville resisted the sound being made by Memphis's upstart rockabillies. But within months of Presley's Nashville-recorded "Heartbreak Hotel," Music Row was developing its own stable of teen stylists. Gene Vincent's "Be-Bop-a-Lula," for instance, was recorded in the Bradley Studio just four months after Presley's history-making session. Vincent (1935–1971) was the rockabilly who first wore black leather, the costume of choice for rockers for generations afterward. He developed the biker image and menacing stage swagger that are still imitated today. He anticipated punk rock with his thrashing moves, leaps from amplifiers, and writhing on stage floors. He was also among the first to take the rock 'n' roll revolution overseas.

The alcohol and pill consumption that fueled his mood swings and violent outbursts was notorious. Vincent's dark, erratic behavior drove crowds wild but alienated the music business. Tormented all his life by a leg that had never healed properly following a motorcycle accident, he died of hemorrhaged stomach ulcers at age thirty-six.

"Gene Vincent was a wild man on stage," recalls George Hamilton IV. "He had a broken leg from a motorcycle accident and every time I worked with him, he'd be jumping around and bangin' his cast on the stage. He was oblivious to all the pain. He was the ultimate showman."

The rockabillies with the deepest country roots were The Everly Brothers. Ironically, the duo was one of the few rockabilly acts that failed to convert teen stardom into a sustained career on the country charts. Kentucky-bred brothers Don (born 1937) and Phil (born 1939) were child stars on their parents' radio barn-dance shows of the 1940s. In 1955 the family came to Tennessee to appear on WNOX in Knoxville. From there the teenage brothers migrated to Nashville under the sponsorship of Chet Atkins.

"I was into Little Richard, Chuck Berry, Hank Williams, Lefty Frizzell," recalls Don of those teen years. "That combination of music was what I was about. And I liked 'em equally, as well."

The team's scintillating sound debuted on the charts with the bopping "Bye Bye Love" and "Wake up Little Susie" in 1957. The latter title achieved some notoriety by being banned in Boston.

"What people really wanted was for rock 'n' roll to become a fad and just disappear and go away," comments Phil. "When Elvis would have a show, the churches would gather up tryin' to stop it. 'Wake up Little Suzie' being banned in Boston is kind of silly when you look back in retrospect. It was based on the idea that they had fallen asleep in an automobile and were out 'til a very late hour, implying God knows what. Now, forty years later, you *know* what that implies. But the song was written with an innocent idea. They actually had fallen asleep. There was no hanky panky. But it was banned, which I think helped the sales."

ABOVE: *The sublime harmonies of The Everly Brothers have inspired and influenced generations of fans.*
RIGHT: *As a singer, songwriter, and guitarist, Eddie Cochran was a "triple threat" rockabilly star.*

Cochran

Wanda Jackson

"All I Have to Do Is Dream," "Bird Dog," "Devoted to You," and "Let It Be Me" showcased the Everlys' spine-tingling twin harmonies throughout 1958–60. When the new Warner Bros. record label came courting in 1960, the duo received the music world's first million-dollar contract.

The pressure was on to deliver something major. Don's song "Cathy's Clown" was just the ticket. It was first issued in England, backed by a massive advertising campaign that coincided with the Everlys' 1960 tour there. The record shot directly to No. 1 in Britain and became The Everly Brothers' top-selling international record.

Back in the United States, "Cathy's Clown" was issued by Warners and repeated its overseas success. The single hit No. 1 and sold more than two-and-a-half million copies. It heralded a string of subsequent hit songs in 1960–62, including Phil Everly's "When Will I Be Loved," Don's "So Sad (To Watch Good Love Go Bad)," Mel Tillis's "Stick with Me Baby," Sonny Curtis's "Walk Right Back," John D. Loudermilk's "Ebony Eyes," and Carole King's "Crying in the Rain."

The Everly Brothers released 1968's *Roots* as a masterpiece LP of their career, starred in an ABC-TV variety series in 1970, and reunited with Chet Atkins for the *Pass the Chicken and Listen* album of 1972 before breaking up in 1973. During the next ten years Don and Phil both recorded fine solo efforts.

They reunited in 1983, released a trio of splendid comeback albums in 1984–88, entered the Rock 'n' Roll Hall of Fame in 1986, and continue to tour today. They became the subjects of the musical *Bye Bye Love* in Nashville in 1998.

"When I was a kid, rock 'n' roll was really hot," remembers Dolly Parton. "But we weren't really allowed to listen to a lot of that music because of the religious background, my grandpa bein' a Pentecostal holy-roller preacher. I was already bleachin' my hair and wearin' short skirts and they thought I was goin' to hell anyway. But I did love that music.

"Brenda Lee was a girl who was more my age and I related to her. She was more accepted than, say, Elvis who was shakin' his butt. They thought that was just some Satan music. But with Brenda, that was a little different. She was a young girl, so that was cute, that was acceptable. I used to just love her records, because it gave me songs that a girl could sing. I still love her records today. And I still think she's a great performer."

Brenda Lee (Brenda Mae Tarpley, born 1944) was the youngest of the rockabilly performers. Introduced by Red Foley on his *Ozark Jubilee* at age nine, the Georgia native was signed to his label, Decca, at age eleven. From the start, Lee turned in exciting rockabilly discs like "Rock the Bop," "Dum Dum," "Dynamite," "Sweet Nothin's," "One Step at a Time," and, unforgettably, "Rockin' around the Christmas Tree."

"Brenda was an amazing artist in those days," recalls Dick Clark. "She was a little bitty thing, Little Miss Dynamite. A lot of people thought she was a small adult, which wasn't true."

Lee would go on to become the world's top-selling female vocalist with such 1960s pop ballads as "I'm Sorry," "All Alone Am I," "I Want to Be Wanted," "Break It to Me Gently," and "Emotions." She recorded in German, Italian, French, Japanese, Portuguese, and Spanish. Her tour in Australia created riots. In England, she and Gene Vincent toured as "The King and Queen of Rock 'n' Roll." In Germany in 1962, The Beatles were her opening act. She urged Decca to sign them, but the label didn't listen.

She did not return to mainstream country music until the 1970s and thereafter charted with songs like "Always on My Mind," "Nobody Wins," "Big Four Poster Bed," "Tell Me What It's Like," and "Broken Trust." She collaborated with Loretta Lynn, Kitty Wells, and k.d. lang on the Grammy-nominated "Honky Tonk Angels Medley" in 1989.

Her closest rival as a female rockabilly star was Wanda Jackson. The Oklahoma native, born in 1937, was discovered by Hank Thompson and initially recorded

LEFT: *The most aggressive stylist of the female rockabilly acts was Wanda Jackson. She later became a country balladeer and a gospel performer.*

straightforward country ballads in the early 1950s. When the beautiful brunette dated Elvis Presley, he urged her to give rockabilly recording a try.

"I was at a session and I needed one more song," she relates. "I said, 'Well let's do that little thing we're opening with called "Let's Have a Party."'" It was a hit. It opened a lot of doors for me."

Her roaring performance of that tune and follow-ups such as "Fujiyama Mama" and "Man We Had a Party" are considered to be the most aggressive female rockabilly performances of all time. Jackson brushes off the controversy that her peers' music incited.

"Rock 'n' roll did take a bad rap from the older generation. But hasn't it always been that way? Young people have their music and the older generation just can't understand it. I was always a bit of a renegade or kind of a maverick, always on the cuttin' edge, it seems, in my music, my dress. I just wanted to try everything. I never had any problems with people callin' it evil music. I knew that it wasn't.

"The very first little group that I put together became The Party Timers and they had this black fellow on the piano, Big Al Downing. I can honestly say I didn't think a thing about having a black man in my band. But it was a problem for Al because in those days in Oklahoma, Texas, he couldn't go in and eat with us or with the rest of the guys in the band. So they were always bringin' him somethin' out to the car. He couldn't stay in the same motels, so they got very creative and innovative ways of gettin' Big Al in. He'd lay down in the back seat and they'd throw a blanket over him. And on our jobs, Big Al would have to stay on the bandstand while all the rest of us were out minglin' with people. But what was so neat to see was, you'd look back, and there at the bandstand would be this crowd around the piano, talkin' to Big Al."

Wanda Jackson reverted to country music with 1961's "Right or Wrong" and "In the Middle of a Heartache," but continued to showcase rockabilly in her stage

shows, even after she won a battle with alcoholism and became a born-again Christian in the 1980s.

Kentucky's The Davis Sisters might have had a run at rockabilly stardom. Their "Rock-a-Bye Boogie" of 1953 was one of the earliest records in the style by either gender. But a car crash en route home from an appearance on *The Wheeling Jamboree* killed lead singer Betty Jack Davis. Recording in the Nashville Sound style, partner Skeeter Davis would go on to solo stardom in the '60s.

Memphis and Nashville didn't corner the market on rockabilly music. The West Coast produced a number of energetic stylists, notably The Collins Kids, Ricky Nelson, Ritchie Valens, and Eddie Cochran (1938–1960). The last named was a superb electric guitarist with frantic stage energy who immortalized "Summertime Blues" in 1958.

Cochran first recorded as a member of the country duo The Cochran Brothers with future songwriting great Hank Cochran (no relation). After recording such outstanding and influential rockabilly efforts as "Cut across Shorty," "Sittin' in the Balcony," "Something Else," and "Come on Everybody," his career was cut tragically short by a fatal taxi crash during a tour of England.

Rockabilly hits came from Mississippians like Gene Simmons ("Haunted House"). Charlie Ryan waxed his original version of "Hot Rod Lincoln" in Spokane, Washington. Dale Hawkins ("Suzy-Q") hailed from Louisiana. Bobby Helms ("Jingle Bell Rock") was from Indiana. Bonnie Lou's "Daddy-O" was recorded in Cincinnati. Arkansas produced Ronnie Hawkins ("Mary Lou"). Texans were on the rockabilly bandwagon, too—like Buddy Knox ("Party Doll"), Bob Luman ("Let's Think about Living"), Bruce Channel ("Hey Baby"), Freddy Fender ("Wasted Days and Wasted Nights"), and The Big Bopper ("Chantilly Lace").

Texas was also the home of Buddy Holly (Charles Hardin Holley, 1936–1959). He and his boyhood friend Bob Montgomery entertained as "Buddy & Bob—Western and Bop" on the radio in their hometown of Lubbock while still in their teens. Like so many of their contemporaries, they sometimes added r&b elements into their developing sound. After hearing Elvis Presley, Holly stampeded to rockabilly music.

He went solo, formed a band, and came to Nashville to record in 1956. The sessions were a failure. He tried again in a studio in Clovis, New Mexico, a year later. This time he emerged with a hit record, "That'll Be the Day." Sometimes billed as Buddy Holly discs and sometimes billed as being by The Crickets, a dandy series of rockabilly singles peppered the charts in 1957–58, including "Oh Boy," "Maybe Baby," "Rave On," and the piledriving "Peggy Sue."

Buoyed by his success, Holly moved to New York and took aim at the pop mainstream with tunes like "True Love Ways," "Heart Beat," "It Doesn't Matter Anymore," and "Raining in My Heart." He also turned to record producing, notably on the debut efforts by fellow Texan Waylon Jennings. Holly had dreams of starting his own record label. In the interim, Jennings joined The Crickets as a bass player.

He recalls Holly's career advice vividly: "He said, 'Don't stay around too long. Don't wait until it starts fading away. If you leave while you're on top, they exaggerate the good.' Well, they didn't exaggerate the good—he really was that great."

Historian Colin Escott concurs. He calls Holly "the most accomplished all-around performer in early rock 'n' roll," because the West Texan wrote his songs, sang them, and was his band's lead guitarist.

Holly and his new Crickets headed to the Midwest on "The Winter Dance Party" tour in January 1959. The package show also featured Dion & The Belmonts, Ritchie Valens, and Frankie Sardo.

The bus was unheated and the midwestern winter was frigid. After freezing through trips to eleven shows in Wisconsin, Minnesota, and Iowa, Holly decided to charter a plane to the next date.

Jennings and guitarist Tommy Allsup were going to accompany him.

"But The Big Bopper was sick and wanted to take my place," recalls Jennings, who lost his seat in a coin toss. "And then Ritchie Valens wanted to get to the next date early to get some dry cleaning done and he took Tommy Allsup's place."

In one of music's most famous tragedies the plane crashed shortly after takeoff near Clear Lake, Iowa, on February 3, 1959 ("The Day the Music Died," according to Don McLean's 1971 hit "American Pie"), killing all three stars. In Britain, worship of the fallen idol was intense. Between 1959 and 1963 Holly records hit the charts sixteen times there. The Hollies named themselves in his honor, and The Beatles took their name in homage to The Crickets. The 1988 stage musical *Buddy* was a smash hit in London.

Buddy Holly's touring partners included Hank Thompson, Wanda Jackson, George Jones, Sonny James, Cowboy Copas, Hank Locklin, Faron Young, and Justin Tubb. But he never made the country charts while he was alive. In death, his songs were embraced by Mickey Gilley ("True Love Ways") and Linda Ronstadt ("That'll Be the Day"), among others. Skeeter Davis issued her Buddy Holly tribute album in 1967. Holly was inducted into the Nashville Songwriters Hall of Fame in 1994. Two years later Music Row's finest gathered in the studio to craft the all-star tribute CD *Not Fade Away: Remembering Buddy Holly.*

Rockabilly's classic era was brief. By the early 1960s the style seemed to vanish. But its devotees remain passionate, and rockabilly revival bands such as The Stray Cats have continued to form.

"To this day, if a band plays a rockabilly set, it makes people get up out of their chairs and start bopping around and tapping their feet," says pianist and producer Tony Brown.

151

ABOVE: *Buddy Holly's influence has been saluted in Nashville by Sonny Curtis, Waylon Jennings, and Skeeter Davis, among others.*

Nine

The Nashville Sound

Records were not played much on radio before the 1940s. Live music was overwhelmingly preferred by both local broadcasters and the national networks. But by the middle of World War II live music and prerecorded music were splitting radio airtime about 50/50. The concept of the radio "disc jockey," a personality who spoke between airing records, came along in the immediate postwar years.

In 1946 a change in Federal Communications Commission (FCC) regulations allowed more stations to occupy adjacent frequencies within a listening area. As a result of the more numerous stations in competition for listeners, specialized programming began to develop. For instance, the first full-time radio broadcasting aimed at blacks began in 1948.

The vinyl LP album and 45-rpm disc were introduced that year. These durable, shippable, mass-produced records made disc jockey programs even easier to create. And from the start, country record spinners thought of themselves as a distinct group.

"The Disc Jockey Convention, which was sponsored by WSM Radio, began in Nashville in 1952," recalls executive Jo Walker-Meador. "It was an effort to

153

LEFT: *Patsy Cline is regarded as the definitive Nashville Sound stylist.*
ABOVE: *Country music was the first music genre to create a Hall of Fame and museum for its greatest figures.*

bring country-music disc jockeys into Nashville to honor them and to show appreciation for promoting the *Grand Ole Opry* and playing the *Opry* artists' records."

"The second year, 1953, we organized the Country Music Disc Jockey Association, mostly to party and have fun at the old Andrew Jackson Hotel," adds former DJ Tom Perryman.

Those fun days for country broadcasters were numbered. In 1953 Todd Storz began airing a program called *Top 40* on WTIX in New Orleans. He developed the idea in Omaha at KOWH when he and the station's program director Bill Stewart were hanging out in a bar across the street from the station.

"We'd notice the waitress would be serving drinks all evening while the same songs would come up on the jukebox over and over," Stewart recalled to Philip K. Eberly in the radio-history book *Music in the Air*. "Upon cleaning up, she'd go over and put a half-dollar in the jukebox to listen to the same record she'd been listening to all evening six more times!"

The notion of frequent radio repetition of records was born. In 1955 the entire Storz broadcasting chain introduced the jukebox-inspired "top-forty" concept of radio programming on its stations in New Orleans, Omaha, Kansas City, Miami, and Minneapolis. Records played would be drawn exclusively from the forty that were top-ranked on the pop-music hit parade. This idea spread quickly throughout the United States.

At first, top-forty playlists consisted of Perry Como, Patti Page, Dinah Shore, Frank Sinatra, and the other singing stars who'd taken over from the big bands after the war. Rock 'n' roll novelties such as Bill Haley's "Rock around the Clock" or Elvis Presley's "Don't Be Cruel" were intermixed in 1955–57. They soon took over completely.

To combat competition from television and to distinguish themselves from one another, stations were developing record-spinning "formats" during this same pe-

riod. News and talk radio survived. Jazz and classical music retreated to public/educational radio stations. Dramatic programming surrendered completely to TV.

KDAV in Lubbock, Texas, became the first full-time country-music station in 1953. But as stations scrambled for top ratings, few chose to program poor-folks and adult-oriented country music full-time after 1956.

NBC dropped *The Grand Ole Opry* in 1957. WLS abandoned *The National Barn Dance* in 1960. The postwar boom of country music ended abruptly. *Opry* star Bill Anderson remembers the eye-opening transition:

"In 1954 the *Opry* had been jam-packed and the lines had been down the street and you couldn't hardly get in. They said in 1958 you could have shot a cannon off in the Ryman and you wouldn't have hit that many people. So it was a very rough time for country music. You couldn't go on stage and just sing the old plaintive country songs anymore if somebody else on the stage was rocking it up a little bit. I mean, there was just no comparison to the reaction."

"Around 1956–57, I was really out of work as far as a performer because rock 'n' roll had come in," recalls Merle Kilgore.

"I really hate to admit this now, but I hated rock 'n' roll because it killed country music," adds ex–steel guitarist Joe Talbot. "I mean, it just wiped it out. The audience liked the dance beat, the humor, the energy, the simplicity, the excitement of Elvis Presley. These people put on tremendous shows. I think that's one of the big things that caused our audience to move to rock 'n' roll, because all we had to do was stand up there and sing ten hit songs and sign autographs. These people put on a real show. That's why temporarily we lost our market to rock 'n' roll."

WYFE in New Orleans tried desperately to lure listeners back to country with an all-female DJ staff in 1959. By 1958, Long Beach's KFOX was the only full-time country broadcaster in the entire southern California region. Most stations airing country music around the clock were in small towns and rural areas.

"In 1958, the business people felt that to really promote country music they needed an industry-wide organization," says Jo Walker-Meador. "The real reason for the formation of the Country Music Association was rock 'n' roll music. Country music was suffering."

So when the Country Music Disc Jockey Association fizzled, the CMA picked up the torch. Walker-Meador, a native Tennessean born in 1924, was hired as its director. She had no experience, but the CMA was so broke that it couldn't afford to pay anyone who did.

The new organization aimed to make country respectable. In 1961 country became the first musical style to establish a Hall of Fame as a result of the CMA's efforts (the actual building opened six years later). The CMA also conducted a survey of the radio stations in America. It found to its dismay that only eighty-one stations in the land were programming country music full-time by 1961. The CMA went on a promotional blitz to convince broadcasters that the country audience was large and would spend money on products advertised on country stations. By 1969 the CMA had converted 606 stations to country—the number topped the 1,000 mark in 1975, it topped the 2,000 mark in 1982, and today more radio stations program country music than any other style.

Radio's renewed acceptance of country music wasn't due solely to CMA promotion. Part of it had to do with the Nashville Sound. Classic Nashville Sound records downplayed the twangy elements in country. The "heart" in a country song and in a country singer were retained, but the overall flavor was usually sweeter than earlier country records had been.

"A sound was created to try to improve our market position," observes former DJ Ralph Emery. "Everybody was looking for a way to cross over and go pop, to get the sales, the higher visibility. Some said they were diluting country music by doing this, and I guess they were. But they were trying to sell Nashville records to a wider audience."

"The records really sounded sophisticated, urban," comments Steve Wariner. "They started dressing them up, making them more pop," says guitarist Harold Bradley.

"My brother was hearing from New York they didn't want just 'hillbilly' sales. They wanted country to have a bigger appeal, maybe cross over into pop, to crack those all-powerful Top-40 playlists."

"We were all just trying to survive," said producer Owen Bradley. "I think we had to change," adds Chet Atkins. "I was just making records I liked. It turned out the public liked them, too."

Atkins at RCA, Bradley at Decca, Don Law at Columbia, Shelby Singleton at Mercury, and Ken Nelson at Capitol all created Nashville Sound hits. A corps of session musicians evolved who were versatile, efficient, and creative at adding just the right audio touches to these label executives' productions. Unlike studio musicians in New York or Los Angeles, the Nashville players worked without written arrangements.

These players were known as "The A-Team" and included such figures as drummer Buddy Harman, steel guitarist Pete Drake, bass players Bob Moore and Henry Strzelecki, pianists Floyd Cramer and Hargus "Pig" Robbins, vocal groups The Jordanaires and the Anita Kerr Singers, and guitarists Harold Bradley, Grady Martin, Ray Edenton, Jerry Kennedy, and Hank Garland. String and horn sections

155

ABOVE: *Jo Walker-Meador guided the development of the CMA, billed as "the world's most active trade association."*

The Jordanaires

ment was the reason they hired us over and over again. If you look at the charts, 95 percent of the songs on there, we played on."

"I've been on eighteen thousand recording sessions," says drummer Harman. "That kept me kind of busy for awhile."

"You wouldn't believe it if I showed you the dates," reports Ray Walker of The Jordanaires. "There was hardly a day we weren't recording somewhere for forty years. I can't remember not working."

Best known for backing Elvis Presley and Ricky Nelson, The Jordanaires vocal group developed the shorthand "Nashville Number System" of recording-session notation. The quartet worked four sessions a day, six days a week, for more than twenty-five years. The act also performed and recorded as a gospel quartet.

Early hits featuring elements of the Nashville Sound included Ferlin Husky's soaring pop-crossover ballad "Gone," Jim Reeves's intimately crooned "Four Walls," and Bobby Helms's lilting "Fraulein" and "You Are My Special Angel," all from 1957. But the term "Nashville Sound" didn't appear in print until 1958 when the trade publication *Music Reporter* first used it. Thereafter it became an effective catchphrase for marketing Nashville and country music.

The 1958 hits of Don Gibson are often cited as the beginning of the Nashville Sound era. And when "Oh Lonesome Me"/"I Can't Stop Loving You" crossed over to achieve success on the pop hit parade, Chet Atkins's job as a producer for RCA was ensured.

"The minute I went with RCA I said, 'I want to sign a guy I believe in, Don Gibson,'" Atkins recalls. "I knew

were generally made with players recruited from the Nashville Symphony.

"There's a certain technique to making records and you have to be able to switch," said Owen Bradley. "If you're playing it one way and somebody says, 'Could you do something else?' you need to not be offended and to think of something else to play instead of what you were playing. And that's asked of you many times. Well, these people all built little reputations for themselves individually, and it just eventually worked out that they were the 'A-Team.'"

"When we'd go into a studio, we pretty well knew as a group what to look for," recalls Moore. "We would watch who we were working with and try to make a sound for them, a particular sound they could live on. Songs make careers, so you've got to do the song to fit the artist."

"At that time, when you recorded you worked three hours in a session," recalls Ray Price. "And the rules were you had to do four songs. And I mean you better have 'em."

"We didn't have overdubbing," said Owen Bradley. "If somebody made a mistake, everyone started all over again."

"You had to play it perfectly from top to bottom," concurs Harold Bradley. "And to be able to do that at the magic mo-

ABOVE: *Between thousands of sessions as country background vocalists, The Jordanaires also recorded as a gospel quartet.*
RIGHT: *Don Gibson wrote many of the country classics he recorded during the Nashville Sound era.*

The Browns

he was a great writer. His songs would just knock me over."

"He never did try to push me during my sessions," Gibson recalls of his days working with Atkins. "He never did say, 'Well, no, I don't think you ought to do that that way or sing that way.' He just let me sing."

"He, like Owen, was a believer in letting the person exhibit themselves," concurs Ray Walker. "He'd kind of say, 'Well, you could change that right there if you'd like to.' 'What do you want me to do?' 'Well, you come up with something.' And when he'd hear it he'd say, 'Yeah, that's all right.' He was so unobtrusive. You look back now and he had a sneaky way of pulling something different out of you that you didn't know you were going to do."

"A rave review from Chet was 'not bad.'" chuckles Jimmy Dean. "That was a rave review."

The low-key Atkins approach was perfect for the retiring Gibson. Born in North Carolina in 1928, he'd been on the country-radio circuit for years when Atkins took him under his wing at RCA. Gibson had already proved himself as a writer by providing Faron Young with "Sweet Dreams" in 1956. When Gibson arrived in the studio to record his new compositions "Oh Lonesome Me" and "I Can't Stop Loving You" in 1957, he and Atkins decided to dispense with steel guitar and fiddle and to surround his expressive voice with a guitar/piano/bass/drums combo, plus background singers.

After the 1958 breakthrough Gibson joined *The Grand Ole Opry*. He went on to write such classics as "A Legend in My Time," "Blue Blue Day," and "Just One Time," and to sing such smash hits as "Sea of Heartbreak," "Funny Familiar Forgotten Feelings," "Rings of Gold" (with Dottie West), and "Woman (Sensuous Woman)" during his chart heyday, 1958–74.

The first Nashville Sound record to hit No. 1 on the pop charts was also produced by Chet Atkins. This was "The Three Bells" by The Browns in 1959. Jim Ed Brown and his sisters Bonnie and

Maxine were an Arkansas family-harmony trio that also achieved Nashville Sound success with the folk-flavored "Scarlet Ribbons" and "The Old Lamplighter" as well as lighthearted hillbilly romps such as "Looking Back to See" and "I Heard the Bluebirds Sing."

The act's lovely, one-of-a-kind sound ceased when the sisters announced they were quitting to devote time to their families in 1967. Jim Ed went on to have a successful solo career.

The Browns' repertoire was laced with folk tunes like "Shenandoah," and the folk revival had an impact on several other Nashville Sound stylists. In fact, RCA's country albums featured a logo on their jackets that read "Folk-Country." The label's roster included George Hamilton IV (1963's "Abilene"), Hank Locklin (1958's "Send Me the Pillow You Dream On"), and Porter Wagoner (1965's "Green Green Grass of Home").

Bobby Bare emphasized the connection between country and folk on such 1962–64 pop-crossover Nashville Sound hits as "Detroit City," "500 Miles Away from Home," and "Four Strong Winds." The Ohio native, born in 1935, was a regular on the country hit parade for twenty-five years thereafter. Bare's standards include "Streets of Baltimore," "Sylvia's Mother," "Dropkick Me, Jesus," and

157

on Gibson

ABOVE: *The Browns recorded a series of albums showcasing their one-of-a-kind vocal blend. They were the first Nashville Sound act to top the national pop charts.*

"Marie Laveau." In 1974 he had a major hit with his five-year-old son with "Daddy What If." The kid reemerged on the national scene in 1998–99 as the leader of the rock band Bare Jr.

The definitive male Nashville Sound vocalist was unquestionably Jim Reeves (1924–1964). His velvet baritone caressed ballad lyrics like "She'll Have to Go," "Am I Losing You," and "Welcome to My World" throughout the '60s.

"Instead of having him staying way back and sing, they moved him in to the mike and he kind of crooned," says Harold Bradley. "And it was a wonderful sound."

"Jim Reeves demanded authority," said Floyd Cramer. "He prepared totally each song that he recorded and would go into the studio knowing exactly how he wanted to sing it. He wanted everything to be done right. He was unique, very distinct, clear and precise. He was a very definite singer."

"His voice, to me, was just the ultimate," says Ronnie Milsap. "I absolutely loved Jim Reeves' music, like millions of other people who grew up listening to him. Jim Reeves was known as one of the pacesetters. I loved him so much that I wanted to do an album of his songs. The album was called *Out Where the Bright Lights Are Glowing* [1981], which is the first line of 'Four Walls.'"

Reeves was one of the first to spread the Nashville Sound to international audiences. He became a film star in South Africa, and British music fans still buy his records today.

"Chet Atkins and Jim Reeves and I went to Europe in 1964 for the very first country music show to ever play for the people," recalls Bobby Bare. "We played Frankfurt, Britain, Stockholm—and they televised all our shows and they played them back for

years. It made big stars out of all of us over there. Unfortunately, Jim Reeves was killed in a plane crash about a month after we got back in 1964, but I've been going over there ever since."

Reeves's stateside popularity was such that even after his death he continued to have huge hits. His posthumous classics include "Distant Drums" (1966), "When Two Worlds Collide" (1969), "Missing You" (1972), "Don't Let Me Cross Over" (1979, with an overdubbed Deborah Allen), and "Have You Ever Been Lonely" (1981, paired with the also deceased Patsy Cline through the wonders of studio engineering).

Jim Reeves was a native Texan who rose to fame on *The Louisiana Hayride* with the jaunty "Mexican Joe" and "Bimbo" in 1953. After arriving at the *Opry* in 1955, he shifted to his Nashville Sound crooning style.

Virtually all the established country stars shifted over to the smoother style. RCA's Eddy Arnold, for instance, became an even bigger star than he had been in the 1940s thanks to a string of huge Nashville Sound singles.

"I got to thinking, 'Well if I can just change my background a little bit, I can sing pretty much the same kind of song, but I'll reach a greater audience,'" comments Arnold. "And I tried it. And it worked. And I never looked back."

"But it created a lot of problems," says Ray Price. "My peers said I'd gone pop and wasn't singin' country music anymore. You could term it 'Nashville Sound.'" Price made the transition from honky-tonk singer to tuxedo-clad balladeer with

ABOVE: *This Bobby Bare album was issued in 1978.*
RIGHT: *This 1966 sheet music is for one of the many posthumous Jim Reeves hits.*

Skeeter Davis

records like the heavily orchestrated version of the folk song "Danny Boy" in 1967. "For the Good Times" (1970), "I Won't Mention It Again" (1971), "She's Got to Be a Saint" (1972), and the like, confirmed his newfound reputation as one of country's smoothest and most expressive stylists.

Former honky-tonker Faron Young also took to the new sound, notably with 1972's huge international hit "It's Four in the Morning." Other vocalists such as Webb Pierce, Kitty Wells, Roy Acuff, and Ernest Tubb were simply "too country" for the new uptown style.

With its "heart" songs and less aggressive approach, the Nashville Sound was a boon to country's female performers. One of the style's biggest hits was 1963's "The End of the World," a plaintive performance by Skeeter Davis (Kentucky's Mary Frances Penick, born 1931). She had originally been the harmony-singing half of The Davis Sisters, a duo with her childhood friend Betty Jack Davis.

"When we started recording 'Rock-a-Bye Boogie' [1953], everybody flipped," Davis recalls. "We were at the beginning of the rockabilly sound. We thought the studio was a friendly place where everybody just came in.

"We went to Wheeling, West Virginia, for an appearance to do 'I Forgot More Than You'll Ever Know' and they had us do 'Rock-a-Bye Boogie,' too. Nobody knew which side was going to be the hit. Everybody seemed to like both sides. We were returning from Wheeling that night so we could get home and go to church the next morning, and this man hit us head-on on that little narrow road near Cincinnati. Betty Jack was killed instantly right there."

Atkins urged Skeeter Davis to continue on RCA as a solo performer. She began hitting the charts with "answer" records in 1959–60, such as "Lost to a Geisha Girl" (an answer to Hank

Locklin's "Geisha Girl") and "(I Can't Help You) I'm Falling Too" (an answer to Locklin's "Please Help Me I'm Falling").

"When we found 'The End of the World' in 1962, Jim Reeves was there and he and Chet Atkins were going to go play golf. So Chet gave me this stack of records. When I got home and played all the songs. The stack had that 'Breaking Up Is Hard to Do' and 'I Can't Stay Mad at You.' I picked 'The End of the World' and 'I Can't Stay Mad at You' [1963], which both got up in the top-four of the pop charts. 'The End of the World' was an international No. 1 song. When I took it back to Chet, he really wasn't all that impressed with it. I said, 'You have to let me do this.'

"I was one of the opening acts on the first Rolling Stones tour. They would sing my songs with me and I was shocked that they knew them. I have worked with Aretha Franklin, Gladys Knight, and all these people. I did get flack, criticized in those days [for leaving country music]. But I am so thankful that I did those songs—'Last Date,' 'The End of the World.'"

Davis reverted to country with a spree of hits in the 1960s and 1970s. Her 1972 LP *Skeeter Sings Dolly* was the first salute to the songwriting genius of Dolly Parton. Davis was one of the few *Opry* stars to embrace the hippie movement and to speak out against the Vietnam War. In 1985 the rock band NRBQ persuaded her to return to rockabilly and backed her on the LP *She Sings, They Play*.

The advent of the Nashville Sound also boosted the career of Dottie West (1932–1991). Because of it, she won the first female country Grammy Award ever presented. The Tennessee native was eking out a living on a Cleveland, Ohio, TV show with her steel-guitarist husband Bill when she decided to crack the Nashville recording scene.

159

ABOVE: *As this LP indicates, Skeeter Davis's Nashville Sound trademark was harmonizing with herself on discs.*

Connie Smith

"I came home for vacation from Cleveland," she recalled. "In 1959 Bill and I were headed back to Cleveland, going north on Dickerson Road. I said when we got to the Starday Records building, 'Just pull right in here. I'm going in there and I hope they're gonna listen to me.' I took my guitar in there, and said, 'I really am gonna make hit records. I am gonna be a singer in Nashville. And this is the only thing I have to show you and it's a scrapbook from the TV show that I do.'

"And it worked. It's funny; looking back, I don't even think I realized how tough it might be. When you're that young, you're not afraid. I had absolutely no doubt that I could be a top singer. I was just 'goin' for it,' that's all."

After writing the 1963 Jim Reeves hit "Is This Me," West moved over to his label, RCA. Chet Atkins became her Nashville Sound shepherd.

"Dottie West was one of the most lovable people, just a terrific woman," Atkins reminisces fondly. "Jim Reeves first touted her to me. And then Buddy Killen would bring demos around of Dottie singing. So I called her. She was outside mowin' the grass, I found out later. I told her who I was and I wanted to sign her up and she didn't believe it. She thought somebody was pullin' a joke on her. Right away she came in with 'Here Comes My Baby,'" which won the first female country Grammy. Dottie West sang with immense feeling on such Nashville Sound highlights as "Would You Hold It against Me" (1966), "Paper Mansions" (1967), "Country Girl" (1968), and duets with Don Gibson, Jimmy Dean, and Jim Reeves. She went on to have an impressively long career thanks to a chart resurgence in the early 1970s with "Country Sunshine" and "Last Time I Saw Him," another in the late 1970s as the duet partner of Kenny Rogers, and then

chart-topping success in the 1980s with "A Lesson in Leavin'" and "Are You Happy Baby."

Widely loved for her open-hearted generosity to her fellow songwriters and for discovering such talents as Larry Gatlin and Steve Wariner, West died after an automobile accident on her way to an *Opry* performance in Nashville in 1991.

Perhaps the most electrifying voice of the female stylists of the period belongs to Connie Smith. Born in southern Indiana in 1941, Smith, one of fourteen children of an abusive alcoholic father, learned to pour her turbulent emotions into singing. She was a housewife when Bill Anderson discovered her at an Ohio talent contest and brought her to Nashville in 1963.

After Anderson pitched his discovery to Atkins, Smith was signed to RCA in June 1964. She recorded Anderson's "Once a Day" in July. By that fall's DJ Convention she was "The Cinderella of Country Music" with a No. 1 hit. Surrounded by throbbing rhythm guitars and tasteful steel guitar passages, her fiery delivery blazed brightly on such heartache tunes of 1965–75 as "The Hurtin's All Over," "Just One Time," "Just for What I Am," and "If It Ain't Love."

But Smith was never happy in the limelight. Family, not show business, was important to her. Except for appearances on the *Opry* she essentially dropped out of music to raise her children. Among country aficionados, however, she was never forgotten. She staged a comeback in 1998–99 with a new album on Warner Bros. Records produced by younger star Marty Stuart, whom she'd married in 1997.

Chet Atkins's counterpart at Decca Records was Owen Bradley. And it was Bradley who produced the ultimate Nashville Sound stylist, male or female. That was the immortal Patsy Cline (1932–1963). More than three decades after her

ABOVE: *Connie Smith's vocals on both country and gospel songs are filled with fire and passion.*
RIGHT: *Dottie West hit the country charts throughout the '60s and '70s, but didn't garner a No. 1 solo hit until 1980.*

West

death at age thirty she remains the voice against which all other female country singers must measure themselves.

"Yeah, she was a country singer, but more than that she was just a great singer, one of the greatest voices of our time," says admirer Kathy Mattea. "It never gets any better than when you hear a Patsy record," adds Shelby Lynne. "She can tear my heart completely out."

The Virginia native began barnstorming Nashville with performances such as "Walkin' after Midnight" and "A Poor Man's Roses" in

1957. But she did not hit her stride until Bradley began "sweetening" her sound in the 1960s.

"There's other voices around that might be on the same level as Patsy's," says her widower Charlie Dick, "but the way she did a song it was like a three-minute movie. I went in there one night when Owen was recording her and he put me out. I said, 'What's the problem?' He said, 'Well, Patsy's been crying on every one of these records, really crying, I don't want to break the mood. You stay out of here.'"

"I Fall to Pieces," featuring the

creamy harmonies of The Jordanaires, shot to No. 1 on the country charts and into the top ten on the pop charts in 1961. "Crazy," released later that year, duplicated its success. So did "She's Got You" in 1962. All three were ballads.

"At first, she didn't want any harmonies on her records," recalls Jordanaires member Ray Walker. "She was afraid four men would cover her up. When Owen told her that he wanted us on the record, she fell in love with us and we fell in love with her, right off. Patsy Cline feared ballads. She didn't like slow songs because fast ones had always been her bread and butter. But when she sang her first ballad, we knew there was something coming."

Cline's hits catapulted her into superstardom. She became the first female country artist to headline on her own tours. A product of the honky-tonks, she was tough enough to handle any male promoter, DJ, band member, fan, or foe who was put in her path.

"Patsy wasn't mean," says Jan Howard. "She was ornery and she said what she thought. In that time, I think probably she felt like she had to be, to hold her own. There wasn't anybody gonna push her around."

"She took no guff off of nobody," remembered Faron Young. "She'd get in a limousine or a bus with a bunch of guys, and somebody'd start smarting her off, she could smart you off right back. She didn't take no baloney off of nobody. And I loved her for it."

"I met her in 1956 when I was on the Jimmy Dean show in Washington D.C.," recalls George Hamilton IV. "As soon as she realized that I was shocked by four-letter words, she came out with some I'd never heard in my life. I've never heard a sailor cuss like Patsy Cline. I'd turn purple and she'd get a big laugh out of that."

The whole community, it seems, fell in love with the larger-than-life personality and big heart of Patsy Cline. Loretta Lynn, Dottie West, Barbara Mandrell, June Carter, and Brenda Lee all became close female friends.

ABOVE: *As this Patsy Cline LP jacket indicates, The Jordanaires were a big part of the Nashville Sound. They developed the "Nashville Number System" of recording-session notation.*

Greene

"Patsy got to where she would never leave our presence without kissing us all goodbye," says Ray Walker of The Jordanaires. "In 1963 we were at the *Opry* one night. She had had two bad car wrecks. She had made her appearance just a few months prior in the wheelchair, but she was walking again. Somebody at the wreck stole her full-length black mink. The insurance company had just replaced that coat. When we started to leave she came around and kissed us all. She was walking around toward the back steps of the Ryman Auditorium and I stepped to the edge of the stage and said, 'Patsy honey, be careful, we love you.' She flipped that collar up around that black hair of hers, turned around and cocked that head that sassy little way and she said, 'Honey, I've had two bad ones, the third one will be a charm or it will kill me.' Three weeks later she was dead."

En route in stormy weather from a show in Kansas City, the small plane carrying *Opry* stars Patsy Cline, Cowboy Copas, and Hawkshaw Hawkins, plus pilot Randy Hughes, crashed near Camden, Tennessee, on March 5, 1963. The country community was devastated.

"They didn't know whether to go on with the *Opry* or not after the plane crash took Patsy," Walker recalls. "Everyone got together on the stage and we made a little speech about them being gone and had a tribute to Patsy. Then we sang 'How Great Thou Art' and Roy Acuff said, 'Let's go on with the show.' Everyone went on with the show. That's what they would have wanted. Everyone did the best they could do. It was very hard."

Hawkshaw Hawkins's hits of the day included "Lonesome 7-7203," written by Justin Tubb. Cowboy Copas had scored a No. 1 hit with "Alabam'" in 1960. But it was the music of Patsy Cline that was to endure.

"Sweet Dreams," "Faded Love," and "He Called Me Baby" all became hits after her death. Her *Greatest Hits* album is the biggest-selling hits collection by any female recording artist in history and continues to be one of the top-selling albums for MCA Records, which inherited Decca's legacy. *Sweet Dreams*, the 1985 movie of her life, earned an Oscar nomination for Jessica Lange. Since then, several books and stage musicals about her have appeared.

Owen Bradley's other Nashville Sound clients at Decca included Wilma Burgess ("Misty Blue," 1966), Ernie Ashworth ("Talk Back Trembling Lips," 1963), Bill Anderson ("Still," 1963), Burl Ives ("A Little Bitty Tear," 1962), and Conway Twitty, whom Bradley launched on a country career that brought the singer more No. 1 hits than anyone else in history. When the producer suggested to Twitty that he speak, rather than sing, the opening lines to 1970's "Hello Darlin'," an instant classic was born.

Decca's Jack Greene became the first big winner when the Country Music Association introduced its awards show in 1967. He remembers it well: "It was in conjunction with the Disc Jockey Convention. 'There Goes My Everything' was a No. 1 record. I had just left Ernest Tubb's band in May of that year, and then this was in October when I won the awards. What a special night. Four awards—Song of the Year, Single, Album, and Male Vocalist."

Greene, born in Tennessee in 1930, went on to record several other notable Nashville Sound ballads, including 1967's "All the Time," 1968's "You Are My Treasure," and 1969's "Statue of a Fool." The gentle, polite, and kindly personality continues as a mainstay of *The Grand Ole Opry* to this day.

163

TOP: *Jack Greene's "There Goes My Everything" is the song that made him the first big CMA award winner.*
ABOVE: *Jeannie Seely was billed as "Miss Country Soul." She brought mini-skirts and sass to the Opry stage.*

Jeannie Seely

Greene's duet partner was native Pennsylvanian Jeannie Seely (born 1940). Known as "Miss Country Soul," Seely's big Nashville Sound hits included the torch standard "Don't Touch Me," a Grammy winner of 1966.

Although Capitol Records retained its West Coast character with releases by Buck Owens and Merle Haggard, the label's Ken Nelson also created Nashville Sound products. Capitol stars Ferlin Husky (1960's "Wings of a Dove"), Wanda Jackson (1961's "Right or Wrong"), Roy Clark (1963's "Tips of My Fingers"), and Freddie Hart (1973's "Easy Lovin'") all had major hits in the style.

Sonny James (James Hugh Loden, born in Alabama in 1929) racked up an astonishing string of twenty-five consecutive chart-topping hits for Capitol in 1964–72. He'd achieved teen stardom with "Young Love" in 1957, but the Nashville Sound recordings are what brought him an enduring career. Many of them were countrified remakes of pop tunes (Gene Pitney's "Only Love Can Break a Heart," Brook Benton's "It's Just a Matter of Time," Johnny Preston's "Running Bear," etc.). But occasionally, James introduced a lasting original song, notably 1964's "You're the Only World I Know," 1968's "Heaven Says Hello," and 1972's "When the Snow Is on the Roses." His hits continued into the late 1970s.

Even when Capitol wasn't recording in Nashville, it was issuing records with Nashville Sound production values, like Bobbie Gentry's "Ode to Billie Joe" (1967) and the many pop-crossover hits of Glen Campbell. A native of Arkansas born to a sharecropper family in 1936, Campbell initially rose to prominence in Los Angeles as a session gui-

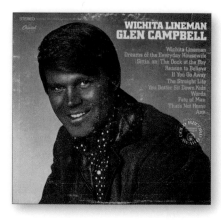

tarist. He toured as a member of The Champs ("Tequila") and The Beach Boys, and backed artists as varied as Frank Sinatra, Ricky Nelson, The Mamas and Papas, Merle Haggard, Bobby Darin, and Dean Martin in the studio.

When he began to sing, Campbell's effortless country tenor had just the right amount of "heart" for country audiences, yet enough polish to make him palatable to pop fans as well. In addition, his guitar playing was extremely sophisticated. In other words, he had the perfect Nashville Sound ingredients.

He broke through with John Hartford's rambling-boy song "Gentle on My Mind" in 1967. It has now been played on radio and TV more times than any other country song in the BMI repertoire. "By the Time I Get to Phoenix" (1967), "Dreams of the Everyday Housewife" (1968), "Wichita Lineman" (1968), and "Galveston" (1969) made him an undisputed superstar.

In 1968–72 he starred in his own network TV series. His 1969 hit "True Grit" was from the film of the same name, which starred him with the legendary John Wayne. Campbell rebounded from an early '70s lull with "Rhinestone Cowboy," "Country Boy," "Southern Nights," and other tunes in 1975–77. In the 1980s he switched to recording in Nashville and earned a dozen mainstream country hits.

Campbell's confessional autobiography *Rhinestone Cowboy* of 1994 detailed his tempestuous romance with Tanya Tucker, his long cocaine problem, and his religious conversion. Still in command of his voice and guitar prowess, he helped launch the careers of such contemporary country stars as Alan Jackson and Bryan White in the 1990s.

TOP: *Smooth-voiced Sonny James has the longest continuous streak of No. 1 records in the country field.*
ABOVE: *Glen Campbell's performance of "Wichita Lineman" made it ASCAP's No. 1 country song of the century.*

The output of Capitol's fellow independent-label upstart Mercury Records illustrates how diverse the Nashville Sound really was. Although associated with ballads, the collaborative nature of Music Row's A-Team resulted in a great many audio innovations.

"When you say 'Nashville Sound,' it should be 'Nashville Sounds,' plural," says guitarist Harold Bradley. "Because if we just had one sound, like Muscle Shoals or Memphis, we'd be out of business."

Thus, Mercury's Nashville Sound stars recorded in musical settings that were stark and folksy (Roger Miller), wacky and madcap (Ray Stevens), smooth and creamy (Leroy Van Dyke), tough and punchy (Dave Dudley), and flat-out barroom majestic (Jerry Lee Lewis).

In the wake of Patti Page's titanic success with "The Tennessee Waltz" in 1950–51, Mercury became the first label to establish a permanent Nashville address. That was in 1952. George Jones was added to the roster in 1957, but it wasn't until Shelby Singleton became head of the Music City operation in 1961 that the label became a major force in country music.

Singleton hired A-Team guitarist Jerry Kennedy to produce the label's output. Kennedy urged Mercury's Smash Records division to sign Roger Miller (1936–1992). In 1964 the producer recorded Miller with full Nashville Sound accompaniment on three songs that were to be the centerpiece of the artist's debut LP. The next day, a small group of A-Team members assembled to record the "throwaway" tracks for the rest of the album. These off-the-cuff sessions illustrate the spontaneity and creativity that were possible with Nashville Sound players.

According to Daniel Cooper's booklet for the CD collection *King of the Road*, Miller was only interested in earning enough money to move from

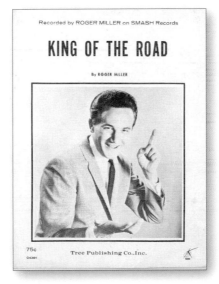

Recorded by ROGER MILLER on SMASH Records

KING OF THE ROAD

By ROGER MILLER

75¢
04381   Tree Publishing Co.,Inc.

Nashville to L.A. in 1964. He was relaxed and casual. Kennedy, pianist Pig Robbins, guitarists Ray Edenton and Harold Bradley, drummer Buddy Harman and bassist Bob Moore all fell into his mood. The seasoned pros locked into a groove when Miller began to sing "Chug-a-Lug." When Kennedy's kids heard the tape of "Dang Me" from that session, they shouted their approval. Kennedy scrapped the big-production Nashville Sound single and issued the funky "Dang Me" instead. Miller pocketed the $1,500 in session money and moved to California. By the end of the year both "Dang Me" and "Chug-a-Lug" were country/pop sensations.

The singer-songwriter had every reason to doubt their success. Miller was raised by a succession of uncles in Oklahoma. Neighbor Sheb Wooley ("The Purple People Eater") taught him guitar, bought him a fiddle, and led him to dream of a music career. After army service in Korea and Georgia (where he befriended future star Bill Anderson), Miller moved to Nashville. But a single for Mercury failed, as did two more for Decca. He was dropped by RCA despite three charting singles. Miller was writing hits for others and working as a sideman for Minnie Pearl, Ray Price, and Faron Young, but getting nowhere as an artist himself.

The Smash/Mercury sessions were his way of fluffing off his recording career. But the nifty creativity of the Nashville Sound made him a star instead. The two initial hits (plus 1964's zany "Do-Wacka-Do") were followed in 1965 by "King of the Road," "England Swings," "Kansas City Star," "Engine Engine #9," and "One Dyin' and a Buryin'," all of which charted both pop and country. "Husbands and Wives" came along in 1966, and "Walkin' in

oger Miller

ABOVE: *Witty, wacky Roger Miller strikes a pose on the sheet music of his 1965 hobo hit "King of the Road."*

the Sunshine" hit the year after that. Miller also introduced works by others, notably Bobby Russell's "Little Green Apples" (1968) and Kris Kristofferson's "Me and Bobby McGee" (1969).

He won eleven Grammy Awards in 1964–65. He starred in his own variety TV series in 1966. *Life, Time,* and the *Saturday Evening Post* (a cover story, no less) all clocked in with stories about country's new genius.

In 1974 Miller wrote the songs for the Disney cartoon *Robin Hood.* In 1982 he penned "Old Friends" and recorded it with Willie Nelson and Ray Price. Then, in 1985, *Big River* opened on Broadway with a score by Roger Miller. The retelling of the Huckleberry Finn story captured seven Tony Awards. After John Goodman left the role of "Pap," Miller played the part himself.

Miller died of throat cancer in 1992. His memorial service was held at the Ryman Auditorium, the home of the *Opry* throughout the Nashville Sound era.

Mercury label-mate Ray Stevens had a similar experience with the elusive Nashville Sound. "It's still a little mysterious as to how it happened," says Stevens (Ray Ragsdale, born in Georgia in 1939).

"'Ahab the Arab' was my first big hit. I moved to Nashville from Atlanta on January 2, 1962, and I think we cut it a couple of weeks after I got here. It was one of those things that just fell into place very quickly. I wrote the song the night before the session, in a panic, because I had my session booked and I didn't really feel I had something that was going to be a hit. We went in the studio and we cut it in about forty-five minutes. It is live. No overdubs. We took about four or five takes and that was it."

The tune launched a career that featured similar crossover novelty ditties such as "Gitarzan" (1969) and "The Streak"

(1974), as well as more thoughtful material such as "Everything Is Beautiful" (1970), "Misty" (1975), and "Mr. Businessman" (1968).

Mercury's Leroy Van Dyke was another hit maker who benefited from the pop-crossover skills of Nashville's A-Team players.

"When I started, country music, pop music and r&b music were fairly well categorized," Van Dyke recalls. "There was very little intermingling of records and songs at that time. I came out with a song in 1961 that was one of the first major 'crossovers.' The song was 'Walk on By.'" That single was named the biggest country single of all time by *Billboard* magazine in its one-hundredth-anniversary issue.

Leroy Van Dyke, a Missouri native born in 1929, sang while he was in the army during the Korean War. "I had my guitar with me in Korea and spent all my extra time in my squad tent floggin' that guitar. The colonel called me one day and said, 'We have a USO show comin' to the unit and Marilyn Monroe is the star' and wanted to know if I would open the show. I said, 'You've gotta be kiddin'!' There's thirty thousand servicemen over here that haven't seen a woman for years or months and you want me to open for Marilyn Monroe?!' Well I did and it worked all right.

I guess I was the only country act to ever open for Marilyn Monroe. And I'll have to say she was a trooper. She walked out there in a snowstorm and entertained those folks. Didn't complain about anything."

While he was in the service, Van Dyke wrote his first hit, 1957's "The Auctioneer." In the wake of Nashville Sound stardom, he starred in the 1967 movie *What Am I Bid?* and eventually became a headliner in Branson, Missouri.

Dave Dudley (David Pedruska, born 1928 in

TOP: *Ray Stevens is known as country's leading humorist.*
ABOVE: *Leroy Van Dyke bases his country career in Missouri.*
RIGHT: *Texan Jeannie C. Riley shot to stardom with "Harper Valley P.T.A." in 1968.*

Riley

DAVE DUDLEY
TRUCK DRIVIN' SON-OF-A-GUN

PolyGram Country Collection

SPEED TRAPS, WEIGHT STATIONS &
DETOUR SIGNS • QUITTIN' TIME •
JUST A FEW MORE MILES •
TWO SIX PACKS AWAY •
OPERATION X •
JACK KNIFE

WRECK OF THE OLD SLOW BINDER •
TRUCK DRIVIN' SON-OF-A-GUN •
TRUCK DRIVER'S WALTZ •
SUGARLAND, U.S.A. •
D. J. MEMPHIS JOE •
I GOT LOST

Mercury

Dave Dudley

Wisconsin) used the money he'd earned as a DJ and honky-tonk entertainer to finance his recording of the truck-driver classic "Six Days on the Road." After it became a hit, Mercury signed him in 1963. With spare, sympathetic Nashville Sound accompaniment he then scored hits with such workingman tunes as "Cowboy Boots," "Mad," "Last Day in the Mines," and "The Pool Shark."

Mercury Records also revived the career of rockabilly Jerry Lee Lewis with Nashville Sound recordings. The label's subsequent successes of the 1960s and 1970s include The Statler Brothers, Tom T. Hall, Johnny Rodriguez, and Reba McEntire.

After he left the label in 1966, Shelby Singleton formed his own entertainment complex. His Plantation Records label issued "Harper Valley P.T.A." by Jeannie C. Riley in 1968. At the recording session, "I had a funny feeling I'd never had before," wrote songwriter Tom T. Hall in his book *The Storyteller's Nashville*. "The session was on a Friday night. By Saturday afternoon local radio stations were playing the tape. Records were in the mail the following Wednesday. Before the week was out, Nashville's record-pressing plants were shipping singles of 'Harper Valley P.T.A.' to stores as fast as they could make them."

"Harper Valley P.T.A." sold six million records, won a Grammy and a CMA Award, crossed over to top the pop charts and made stars of both Jeannie C. Riley and Tom T. Hall. Both of them always credited the clever session instrumental work—especially Jerry Kennedy's stuttering dobro—as a reason for its success. Whatever the case, Jeannie C. Riley's performance inspired a 1978 movie and a 1981–82 NBC-TV series. Riley, a Texas beauty born in 1945, placed twenty more singles on the country charts in 1968–75.

The Mercury executives' experience with the A-Team's diversity was typical. Singleton thought so much of the studio musicians' abilities that he brought his label's r&b stars—Clyde McPhatter, Ruth Brown, Brook Benton, and others—to Nashville to record.

Perhaps the best illustration of the Nashville Sound's success was a series of recordings by another r&b star, Ray Charles. Born in Georgia in 1930, Charles was an established star on both pop and r&b charts when he approached his record company about making an orchestrated album of country songs.

He remembers the reaction: "They said, 'Ray, we don't feel that you should do something like that because you're gonna lose a lot of your fans.' I said, 'Well, I think I'll gain as many fans as I'll lose if I do it right.' And that was it." The resulting album was the landmark *Modern Sounds in Country & Western Music*. Released in 1962, the LP brought Don Gibson's "I Can't Stop Loving You," Ted Daffan's "Born to Lose," and Cindy Walker's "You Don't Know Me" onto the pop hit parade.

With considerably more enthusiasm, the label issued a second such collection in 1963, including hit versions of "Take These Chains from My Heart," "You Are My Sunshine," and "Your Cheating Heart." Charles continued to popularize country music on the pop hit parade with hits such as "Busted" (1963) and "Crying Time" (1965). His 1966 album *Country and Western Meets Rhythm and Blues* spawned his hit version of "Together Again." When he signed with Columbia Records in the 1980s, the label brought him to Music Row to record "Born to Love Me" (1982) and a series of hit duets with George Jones, Willie Nelson, and other country celebrities.

Columbia's initial forays with the Nashville Sound took a somewhat dif-

169

LEFT: *This album is one of several that Dave Dudley devoted to trucking songs.*

ABOVE: *In 1962 Ray Charles issued this landmark collection of orchestrated country songs.*

ferent approach than Owen Bradley did at Decca or Chet Atkins did at RCA. Columbia producer Don Law hired guitarist Grady Martin to lead his sessions and came up with what historians have called "saga songs" as vehicles for the label's vocalists. Influenced by the folk revival, these were compositions with distinct plots that were recorded with clever audio gimmicks to capture the ears of pop fans as well as country listeners.

Examples of Columbia's saga-song hits include Lefty Frizzell's "Long Black Veil" and "Saginaw Michigan" and Johnny Cash's "Five Feet High and Rising," "Don't Take Your Guns to Town," and "The Ballad of Ira Hayes."

The concept was wildly successful for the label. In 1959 "El Paso" by Marty Robbins, "Waterloo" by Stonewall Jackson, and "The Battle of New Orleans" by Johnny Horton all muscled their way to the top of top-forty playlists. In 1961 Horton's "North to Alaska" and Jimmy Dean's mining tale "Big Bad John" also became major crossover hits. "Wolverton Mountain" by Claude King was a Nashville Sound pop blockbuster in 1962.

"'Big Bad John' was a huge crossover thing," recalls Jimmy Dean. "It was the No. 1 record in 1961. They say that necessity is the mother of invention. I was on the way to Nashville from New York to record, and I had three sides, and I needed another side, 'cause we tried to go for four sides in a session in those days. I had worked in summer stock in a play called *Destry Rides Again* with a fellow named John Mento who was six-foot-five. Around the dressing room I used to call him 'Big John' when I would speak to him. And it just had a kind of powerful ring to it. So on the way to Nashville I took out a pencil and wrote 'Big Bad John.' I just put John Mento in a mine and killed him is all. Nothing to that.

"I remember distinctly when we were recording 'Big Bad John,' and Floyd Cramer said to Don Law, 'You know, Don, you don't need the piano doing that same thing the voice is doing, "baum-baum." Let me try something.' He pulled a coat rack over, tied a piece of steel on it that they used to weigh TV cameras with, put it on there with a coat hanger, got a hammer and said, 'Now put some echo on this, and let's see what happens.' It's the first and only time that Floyd Cramer ever played hammer. But it established an effect and he was permitted to utilize that creativity."

"'Big Bad John' really didn't have any tune at all," recalls Gordon Stoker of The Jordanaires. "I really think [Jordanaires member] Neal Matthews wrote, 'Big John, big John, big bad John.' Do you remember Jimmy talking on the record or us singing 'Big John, big John'? That's what the public remembers, but we don't get credit for it. Jimmy's always laughed about that. He said it made his sausage company possible."

Jimmy Dean (born 1928) was a Texan who had blazed trails as an early country TV star in the '50s. "Big Bad John" led to a string of similar discs, including 1962's "P.T. 109," which was based on President Kennedy's wartime exploits. In 1963–66 Dean starred in his own variety series on ABC, and then became a regular on *Daniel Boone* in 1967–70 on NBC. He also acted memorably in the 1971 James Bond feature *Diamonds Are Forever*. In later years his Jimmy Dean sausage company made him a wealthy man.

The inventiveness that characterized the recording of "Big Bad John" was typical of the saga-song sessions. The "thump-thump-thump" drumbeats of "Waterloo" and The Jordanaires' shouts of "hup-two-three-four" in "The Battle of New Orleans" are other illustrations of this. The latter was sung by Johnny Horton (1925–1960), one of the most electrifying of the Nashville Sound vocalists. But it took awhile for the hair-raising rasp of his urgent tenor to be heard.

The Los Angeles native had been

ABOVE: *This is the picture sleeve that accompanied Jimmy Dean's 45 r.p.m. single of "Big Bad John."*
RIGHT: *Marty Robbins, easily the finest entertainer and most versatile vocalist of the Nashville Sound era.*

Robbins

recording for five years before "Honky Tonk Man" became his first hit in 1956. A regular on *The Louisiana Hayride*, Horton scored big country hits with "I'm a One-Woman Man" (1956), "All Grown Up" (1958), and "When It's Springtime in Alaska" (1959) before his "Battle of New Orleans" saga song made him a pop star. He followed it with "Johnny Reb," "Sink the Bismarck," and the title tune of the John Wayne movie *North To Alaska*. All of them made the pop hit parade as well as the country charts.

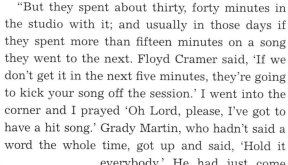

"Johnny Horton was one of the kindest, nicest and one of the smartest people I ever met," says songwriter Merle Kilgore. "When Hank Williams came back to *The Louisiana Hayride* from *The Grand Ole Opry*, he was married to Billie Jean. Billie Jean later became Mrs. Johnny Horton. Hank stopped Johnny Horton as they were walking backstage and he said [to Billie Jean], 'One of these days you're going to marry this man.' That was the most chilling thing. Johnny Horton came to me and told me what Hank Williams had just said, and I never forgot that. Of course, it actually happened."

Not only did Johnny Horton marry Hank's widow; he died after performing in the same Austin, Texas, club where Hank had performed his final show. En route back to the *Hayride*, Horton was killed in a head-on car crash.

Kilgore provided Horton with "Johnny Reb," but couldn't get the singer to record a song that became an even bigger hit—"I sang him 'Wolverton Mountain.' He said, 'Merle, that's the worst song you've ever written.' George Jones said, 'I hate mountain songs.' Tillman Franks called me and said, 'Claude King is doing a folk album. Do you have any mountain songs or anything like that?' I said, 'Do I?!' So I sung 'Wolverton Mountain.' They said, 'Hey, that's pretty good.'"

"But they spent about thirty, forty minutes in the studio with it; and usually in those days if they spent more than fifteen minutes on a song they went to the next. Floyd Cramer said, 'If we don't get it in the next five minutes, they're going to kick your song off the session.' I went into the corner and I prayed 'Oh Lord, please, I've got to have a hit song.' Grady Martin, who hadn't said a word the whole time, got up and said, 'Hold it everybody.' He had just come from the Bahamas with Burl Ives and he started, 'Here's the tempo.' Dolores Dinning of the Dinning Sisters went 'Ah-oo-hoo.' Don Law came in and said, 'That's it.' One take."

The recording sessions of Marty Robbins (Martin Robinson, 1925–1982) are fondly recalled by all who knew him. Always full of hijinks and humor, Robbins was the greatest showman of the Nashville Sound performers.

"Marty's fans could picture him being at the microphone so sincerely, tears in his eyes on those ballads," says Duane West of The Jordanaires. "He'd tease you and try to get you to laugh during the instrumental break, but when he got back to the microphone it was all serious again. He never missed a beat."

The fun and games cloaked an awesome talent. Robbins played guitar and piano effortlessly. He was equally adept with cowboy songs, rockabilly, Nashville Sound ballads, Hawaiian music, honky-tonk, saga songs, vaudeville, comedy, and contemporary pop. He was a superb songwriter. He was the consummate entertainer. He was dashingly handsome, irresistibly charming, and hilariously funny.

"I think if you went around town asking people who was the best singer we ever had around here, everybody would pretty much say, 'The rest of us are just tryin'—it's Marty Robbins,'" says Marty Stuart. "My mom told me that she named me after

172

ABOVE: *Johnny Horton was billed as "The Singing Fisherman." This LP was issued after his 1960 death in an auto accident.*

him. I said, 'Well why didn't you get a little closer and get me some of that singin' ability, too?'"

"People ask about my influence and where it started," adds Marty Roe of Diamond Rio. "Well, it has to be my name. I was named after Marty Robbins, about a year after he won the Grammy for 'El Paso.' My father was a huge fan of his. So I got tagged with that and grew up listenin' to a lot of Marty Robbins records."

What records they were. After Jimmy Dickens discovered him singing at a radio station in Arizona and brought him to Columbia Records, Robbins gave the label a major hit with 1953's "I'll Go on Alone." He helped lead the rockabilly revolution with "Maybelline" and "That's All Right" in 1955. "Singing the Blues" crossed over from country to pop in 1956, so Robbins went to New York to record an all-out pop tune, 1957's "A White Sport Coat (And a Pink Carnation)." This was also the year that he recorded his Hawaiian LP *Song of the Islands*.

The Marty Robbins cowboy classics "El Paso" and "Big Iron" both crossed over to become pop hits in 1959–60. From that point forward he was practically a force of nature on the country-music scene. When Grady Martin's amplifier broke during one of the singer's recording sessions, the resulting sound was used on 1961's "Don't Worry." This Nashville Sound innovation introduced the "fuzz tone" guitar that became popular in psychedelic rock music. The rhythmic "Devil Woman" and "Ruby Ann" were disc highlights of 1962. "Begging to You" (1963), "Ribbon of Darkness" (1965), "Tonight Carmen" (1967), and "I Walk Alone" (1968) are just a sampling of the brilliant records he released during the rest of the decade.

"Marty Robbins was very nocturnal; he could not sleep; he was restless," recalls Ralph Emery. "At night Marty would come up to my all-night radio show. We opened the phone lines and took requests. We would go on for hours, shut down the records, and he'd play and talk and sing," showcasing the vast repertoire of one of the most ver-

satile performers in history. Emery dubbed him "Old Golden Throat."

"Marty would stay with me until I signed off, which was 4:00 A.M. Once I asked him, 'When do you sleep?' He said, 'Oh, I get home, I go to bed about 6:00.' I said, 'Well when do you get up?' 'Oh, 9:00 or 10:00.' I said, 'Hey, that's only three hours or four hours.' He said, 'That's enough.'"

Robbins wrote Frankie Laine's 1969 hit "You Gave Me a Mountain," and then his own "My Woman, My Woman, My Wife," a No. 1 hit and Grammy winner of 1970. Over the years, he earned more than twenty-five BMI songwriting awards. He displayed the same consistency as a hit maker in the 1970s as he had in the 1950s and 1960s. "Walking Piece of Heaven" (1973), "Love Me" (1973), "El Paso City" (1976), and "Among My Souvenirs" (1976) are just a handful of his sixteen top-ten hits during the decade.

He starred in his own TV series and appeared in eleven motion pictures. Despite chronic heart disease he continued to race at NASCAR tracks. He survived several operations for the former and crashes at the latter.

In the summer of 1982 he returned to the country top-ten for the forty-third time with "Some Memories Just Won't Die." That October he was inducted into the Country Music Hall of Fame. Two months later Robbins was on his way back to Nashville to attend the premiere of Clint Eastwood's *Honkytonk Man*, in which he appeared and sang the title tune. Felled by chest pain, he underwent another heart operation, but never regained consciousness.

On December 11, 1982, a cold rain fell as mourners filed into the Nashville funeral home that held his body. Mink-coated Music Row women wept alongside blue-jean-clad fans. Brenda Lee sang "One Day at a Time."

"To a lot of people, Marty Robbins was bigger than life," Lee said; "and I think a lot of them thought he was bigger than death, too."

Johnny Horton

Ten

WORLD FAMOUS

Budweiser
MARKET
STREET
Tootsies
ORCHID
LOUNGE

Songwriters

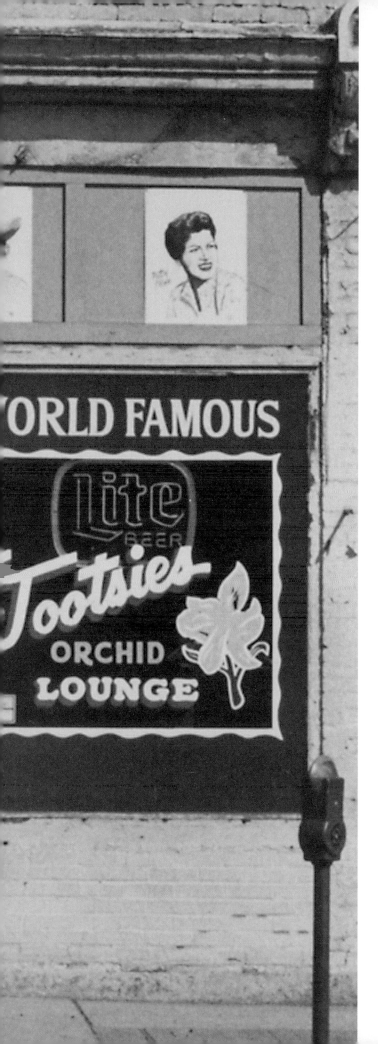

The success of the Nashville Sound did more than put country music back on its feet. It created a community that is unique in the world of show business. Threatened by rock 'n' roll, denigrated by sophisticates, and even disliked by the power structure of their capital city, country-music people "circled the wagons" and banded together.

Their working neighborhood was the run-down section of West Nashville that became known as Music Row after businesses followed the lead of Bradley Studio, Cedarwood Publishing, and RCA Records by locating music firms there. The fact that they were "ghetto-ized" in that district made them a community in a geographic sense. And the fact that they were entertainment "underdogs" drew them together socially as well.

In addition, once Music City started making money, New York and Los Angeles didn't care how and pretty much ignored the community's development. "After I made a hit I could do anything I wanted, because they didn't know what the hell I was doing," says Chet Atkins. "They had no idea. And Decca didn't know what Owen Bradley was doing. So they stayed out of our way and let us make records the way we wanted to."

LEFT: *The Nashville landmark Tootsie's Orchid Lounge was the songwriting community's "watering hole" in the 1960s.* ABOVE: *Merle Kilgore promoted one of his most famous compositions with this LP jacket.*

So a community evolved that was insulated from the pop-music world as well as from mainstream Nashville. As the booking agencies, publishers, and record labels clustered on Music Row in the 1960s, the personalities who populated them became friends as well as competitors.

"It was very much a family affair to us," comments Lynn Anderson. "Everyone on the Row kind of knew each other. Like a little small town, everybody knows who's dating whom, who's broken up with whom, what kind of car you drive, everything else. It was much more of a community feeling at that point."

"You could walk down Music Row and you could pop in any office and talk to anybody," adds Norma Jean. "There was more time, because it was a smaller business. You could go into an office and take your songs, and people would listen to you. You could go in and talk to producers and record companies. You can't do that now."

"In Nashville, country music grew on the basis of cooperation," says former music publisher Bill Denny. "The music publishers and the artists and the agencies here all kind of work together."

"If Chet got a hit, then Owen rejoiced and if Owen got a hit, Chet rejoiced," reports Harold Bradley. "Because they had the big picture—whatever was good for Nashville was really good for them. They were great friends. They never sat down to say, 'This is good for the town,' or whatever. They went and did their jobs and had a wonderful attitude toward each other and the community."

"We were competing, but we were having a lot of fun," says Bobby Bare. "Back in the '60s and early '70s, it was a closer knit place. Everybody knew where everybody was. If you wanted to find somebody, all you did was go down to Tootsie's or give her a call. She knew where everybody was."

"Tootsie's Orchid Lounge was a little beer joint," explains Charlie Dick. "Plus, there was a restaurant across the street that was open twenty-four hours a day, and that was a good meeting place, too."

"We would sit around at the old Tootsie's Orchid Lounge, and pick each other's brains about songs," recalls Billy Walker. "There were dozens of hit songs that I heard for the first time in there."

For years, songwriters such as Hank Cochran, Justin Tubb, Willie Nelson, Harlan Howard, Roger Miller, and Tom T. Hall congregated at Tootsie's, hoping to catch the ear of an *Opry* star. Singers slipped into Tootsie's through the back door for a quick beer between shows at the Ryman Auditorium, which was located across the alley. When there were no stars to pitch songs to, the songwriters sang them to each other.

The glue that stuck Music City together was songwriting. One of the mottoes of Nashville is, "It all begins with a song," because more than any other style of popular music, country emphasizes lyrics and craftsmanship. The city's everyday music business doesn't revolve around stars; it revolves around writing and publishing.

After the initial success of Nashville's founding song publishers Acuff-Rose, Tree, and Cedarwood in the 1950s, similar firms sprang up in Nashville. By 1960, the founders had been joined by Southern Music (1958), Hubert Long's Moss Rose Publications (1959), Ted Daffan's Silver Star Music, Starday Music, and Open Road Music. As the 1960s progressed, Pete Drake/Window (1961), Hall-Clement (1962), Combine (1963), Al Gallico Music (1963), and hundreds of other song businesses cemented Nashville's position as the headquarters of country songwriting.

Opry stars began forming publishing companies, and, like the others, they signed staff songwriters, to whom they paid a "draw" against

THIS OLE HOUSE

WORDS AND MUSIC BY STUART HAMBLEN

HAMBLEN MUSIC CO.
KEYS MUSIC, INC.

ABOVE: *Stuart Hamblen was one of country's songwriting pioneers. This is the sheet music for one of his many classics.*
RIGHT: *Blind Leon Payne performed in Texas during the 1940s. He composed the standard "I Love You Because."*

Leon

Vaughn Horton

future royalties. Sure-Fire (The Wilburn Brothers), Newkeys (Jimmy C. Newman), House of Cash (Johnny Cash), Glaser Publications (The Glaser Brothers), Sawgrass (Mel Tillis), Pamper (Ray Price), and Stallion (Bill Anderson) were all in place by 1969. So were Ray Baker's Blue Crest, Ken Nelson's Central Songs, Harlan Howard's Wilderness Music, 4-Star, Champion/MCA, and United Artists Music. In 1972 more than five hundred song-publishing firms were listed in Nashville's directory.

A network of support organizations arose. After BMI's Nashville inauguration and the formation of the CMA, both in 1958, came the establishment of The Recording Academy (1964), SESAC (1964), the Country Music Foundation (1964), the American Society of Composers, Authors, and Publishers (ASCAP; 1968), and the Nashville Songwriters Association (1970). With their interlocking boards of directors they provided a common ground and rallying causes for the fledgling Nashville industry. Most of them focused on songwriters' issues.

The road to Nashville and its hundreds of professional songwriters was paved in the 1930s by country pioneers like Bob Miller and Carson Robison, two of the earliest Tin Pan Alley tunesmiths who wrote specifically for hillbilly entertainers. Elsie McWilliams wrote many of the songs that her brother-in-law Jimmie Rodgers sang to fame.

Jenny Lou Carson (Lucille Overstake, 1915–1978) provided songs for The Girls of the Golden West and other fellow cast members at *The National Barn Dance* in the 1930s. Then she became even more prominent by crafting such big hits as Tex Ritter's "Jealous Heart" (1944) and Hank Snow's "Let Me Go, Lover" (1954).

In California, radio entertainer Stuart Hamblen (1908–1989) began recording his own compositions in 1929. His "Texas Plains" became the basis for Patsy Montana's 1935 hit "I Wanna Be a Cowboy's Sweetheart." Later Hamblen contributions include "This Old House," "It Is No Secret (What God Can Do)," "Open up Your Heart and Let the Sun Shine In," and "Remember Me (I'm the One Who Loves You)."

In Texas, blind songwriter Leon Payne (1917–1969) began penning hillbilly hits in the mid-'40s. "I Love You Because" (Ernest Tubb, 1950), "Things Have Gone to Pieces" (George Jones, 1965), and "Blue Side of Lonesome" (Jim Reeves, 1966) are some of the classics from Payne's pen.

In New York, songwriter Vaughn Horton (1911–1988) began specializing in hillbilly tunes when he and his brother Roy (born 1914) formed their Pinetoppers band in the late 1940s. Vaughn went on to write "Mockin' Bird Hill," "Hillbilly Fever," "Sugarfoot Rag," "Choo Choo Ch'Boogie," and "Jolly Old St. Nicholas" among others. Roy became a longtime executive with Peer-Southern Music.

Companies like Ralph Peer's Peer-Southern publishing company in New York (established 1928) and the Chicago-based M.M. Cole publishing outfit (founded 1930) administered most country copyrights in the early years. There was no Nashville, no Music Row. And if you intended to write for country's biggest stars in the 1940s, your best bet was to head to Hollywood to find the singing cowboys.

That's what Cindy Walker did. Born in central Texas in 1918, she was performing in Billy Rose's Casa de Manana club in Fort Worth by age sixteen. She also wrote its theme song. Her father was a cotton broker who had business in Los Angeles in 1939. When he suggested that Cindy and her mother accompany him, she jumped at the chance.

"Los Angeles meant music to me," she recalls. "Mama worried about packing

LEFT: *Songwriter Jenny Lou Carson adopted a cowgirl image on the cover of this songbook.*
ABOVE: *Vaughn Horton was one of the few New Yorkers to specialize in country songs.*

the right clothes while I worried about getting all my songs in one briefcase.

"We were driving down the street in Los Angeles and I saw a sign on a building that said 'Crosby Enterprises.' 'Stop the car!' I said to Papa. 'I've got a song for Bing Crosby.' 'He's not going to be in there,' said Papa. 'Well it's his office, there's going to be somebody that knows him there,' I said. Papa thought I was squirrelly."

"Foxy" is more like it. Cindy talked her way past the receptionist, brought her mother upstairs to play piano, and sang "Lone Star Trail" for Crosby's brother Larry. Bing recorded it in 1941, and Cindy landed a recording contract of her own with his label, Decca Records. Her first session for the label was with Texas Jim Lewis's band in August 1940.

The humorous "Seven Beers with the Wrong Man," her debut single, also became country's first promotional "video" when she filmed it as one of the Soundies. These were short sixteen-millimeter films collected in machines that were visual jukeboxes in clubs and taverns of the 1940s.

In 1940 Walker appeared in Gene Autry's feature *Ride, Tenderfoot, Ride*. In 1944 she had a top-ten Decca hit with "When My Blue Moon Turns to Gold Again." But she was less and less interested in her film and recording career. Instead, she pursued celebrities, pitching her tunes.

"I saw this huge white bus with Bob Wills' name painted on the side. I knew he had to be in Hollywood, so I started calling all the hotels to see where he was registered." Once again, her perseverance paid off. Within a week, Wills had recorded five of her tunes, including "Dusty Skies" and "Cherokee Maiden." He would go on to record more than fifty Cindy Walker songs, among them "Bubbles

in My Beer," "Blue Bonnet Lane," "Miss Molly," and "You're from Texas."

She added a third superstar to her conquests when she began providing songs like "Silver Spurs" and "I Was Just Walking out the Door" to Autry. Walker's lovely "Blue Canadian Rockies" became the title tune to the singing cowboy's 1952 film.

Cindy Walker had the beauty, comedic talent, dancing ability, and singing voice to have been a major star. But in 1947 she turned her back on her performing career to concentrate full-time on songwriting. By 1954 Nashville was emerging as country's capital city. She and her widowed mother moved back home to Mexia, Texas, that year. They commuted by rail to Nashville regularly to meet producers, publishers, and stars.

Walker's ability to custom-tailor songs for specific voices became legendary and is illustrated by such diverse creations as "Distant Drums" for Jim Reeves, "I Don't Care" (Webb Pierce, revived by Ricky Skaggs), "Two Glasses, Joe" (Ernest Tubb), "In the Misty Moonlight" (Jerry Wallace, revived by Dean Martin), and "Jim I Wore a Tie Today" (Eddy Arnold).

"I was at the DJ Convention in the old Andrew Jackson Hotel in Nashville when Eddy Arnold told me he had a great idea for a song called 'You Don't Know Me,' about a guy who was too shy to tell this woman he loved her. I wasn't sure I could write it, but I went back to Mexia and worked on it.

"The beginning finally came to me, 'You give your hand to me/And then you say hello/And I can hardly speak/My heart is beating so.' But I couldn't get the ending. Then I thought, 'You give your hand to me/And then you say goodbye/I watch you walk away/Beside the lucky guy.' I called Eddy and said, 'I've got it!' He said, 'Got what?' He had completely forgotten about the song."

The Bryants

ABOVE: *Boudleaux and Felice Bryant were Nashville's first full-time professional songwriters.*
RIGHT: *Texan Cindy Walker has been called "the greatest living songwriter of country music."*

Danny Dill

Wayne Walker

"You Don't Know Me" became a standard, recorded by everyone from Ray Charles to Bette Midler. Walker's "Dream Baby (How Long Must I Dream)" entered the repertoires of Roy Orbison, Glen Campbell, Lacy J. Dalton, Cher, The Marvelettes, Bruce Springsteen, and dozens of others. "My best song? I don't think I've written it yet," she says.

Harlan Howard calls Cindy Walker "the greatest living songwriter of country music." Her career arc perfectly illustrates the shift from Los Angeles and its singing cowboys to Nashville and its *Grand Ole Opry* stars as the epicenter of country music.

The first songwriters to recognize Nashville's coming importance were Boudleaux and Felice Bryant. In 1950 they became the first people to move to the city with the specific intention of writing songs for the *Opry* stars to record.

Boudleaux Bryant (1920–1987) was an itinerant fiddler from Georgia. Felice Scaduto (born 1925) was a poet and sometime radio entertainer in Milwaukee. She was the elevator operator in her town's Schroeder Hotel in the summer of 1945 when Bryant registered as a guest. A love-at-first-sight courtship ensued; they were married within weeks.

The animated, vivacious young bride became restless when her new husband settled in small-town Georgia and left her at home when he went off to play in a local dance band. To while away the hours she wrote poems. When Felice showed these to Boudleaux, a songwriting team was born. Working steadily over the next few years, they accumulated about eighty songs and began peppering song publishers with letters.

Fred Rose learned of the Bryants in 1948. He convinced Jimmy Dickens to record their "Country Boy," a top-ten hit in 1949. A year later, Rose convinced the reluctant songwriters to move to Nashville.

Dickens had subsequent success with the Bryants' "We Could" and "Hole in My Pocket." In addition to Dickens, the team connected with hot up-and-comer Carl Smith, who recorded "It's a Lovely Lovely World," "Hey Joe," and "Back up Buddy" in 1952–54. Thanks to Rose's connections Frankie Laine made "Hey Joe" a top-ten pop hit as well.

Rose wasn't the Bryants' only supporter. Chet Atkins struck up a friendship with the songwriters, which resulted in Eddy Arnold's recording a number of Bryant songs in 1953–55.

That was just the beginning. Rose and Atkins were both quite close to Nashville's rockabilly teen act The Everly Brothers. The Bryants penned "Bye Bye Love," "Wake up Little Susie," "All I Have to Do Is Dream," "Devoted to You," and other songs that propelled the Everlys to stardom. Roy Orbison recorded "Love Hurts," launching yet another Bryant standard. Buddy Holly recorded "Raining in My Heart," which also proved to be a timeless classic.

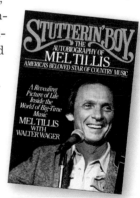

In 1968 The Osborne Brothers introduced the Bryants' "Rocky Top." Lynn Anderson revived it two years later. The University of Tennessee adopted it as its "fight song" at football games. It has now joined "The Tennessee Waltz" as an official state song.

When they moved to Nashville as songwriters, "everybody thought we were crazy," says Felice Bryant, "but we saw the far vision." In a 1980 interview with *Music City News* she added, "Nashville is like a big, old fat Momma; she just says, 'You sing, honey? Let Momma hear ya.'"

When Jim Denny and Webb Pierce opened Cedarwood Publishing in 1953 their first employee was Danny Dill. He was not only a staff songwriter; he was the office manager, song plugger, and any other

183

LEFT: *Danny Dill was Cedarwood Publishing's first employee.*
TOP: *Wayne Walker, one of Cedarwood's most active composers.*
RIGHT: *Mel Tillis bought Cedarwood, the publisher that launched his career. This is his 1984 book.*

Mel Tillis

worker the company needed. The Tennessee native, born in 1924, had been performing on the *Opry* since 1946. Dill's first songwriting success came when Carl Smith recorded his "If You Saw Her through My Eyes" in 1954. Among his later works are Lefty Frizzell's "Long Black Veil," cowritten with Marijohn Wilkin, and Bobby Bare's "Detroit City," cowritten with Mel Tillis.

A definite sign that the songwriting community was on the rise came in 1953 when BMI presented writer/publisher awards in Nashville for the first time. A year later, Cedarwood found its next big discovery when Webb Pierce recorded "More and More," written by Merle Kilgore. Born in 1934, Oklahoma native Kilgore was billed as "The Tall Texan" on Louisiana television. After Johnny Horton hit with his "Johnny Reb," Kilgore moved to Nashville in 1961. The lively raconteur's subsequent successes as a songwriter included Claude King's "Wolverton Mountain" (1962) and Johnny Cash's "Ring of Fire" (cowritten with June Carter, 1963).

Cedarwood struck again in 1956. That's when staff songwriter Wayne Walker (1925–1979) came up with "I've Got a New Heartache," recorded by Ray Price. Walker left a legacy of lasting lyrics, including 1957's "Are You Sincere" (Andy Williams), 1959's "All the Time" (Kitty Wells), and 1964's "Burning Memories" (Ray Price).

Stuttering Mel Tillis heard Music City's siren call down in Florida. Born in the Sunshine State in 1932, he arrived on Cedarwood's doorstep in 1956. "I was determined to go to Nashville," Tillis wrote in his 1984 autobiography *Stutterin' Boy*. "We checked into the Holman Motel, just outside Nashville, which was cheaper than the places in town, and we went into town every day. First we went around to the more active music publishers. There were only about three that mattered in those days."

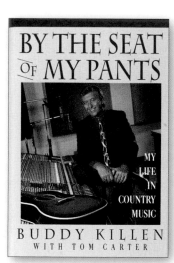

He auditioned at Tree and Acuff-Rose, but was turned down. Mae Boren Axton, the cowriter of Elvis Presley's "Heartbreak Hotel," used her connections to get Tillis an interview with Jim Denny at Cedarwood. Co-owner Webb Pierce recorded a string of Tillis tunes, including "I Ain't Never," "Tupelo County Jail," and "No Love Have I" in 1957–59. Tillis moved to Nashville in 1957 and was soon providing songs to other stars as well, including Bobby Bare ("Detroit City"), Brenda Lee ("Emotions"), Waylon Jennings ("Mental Revenge"), and Kenny Rogers & The First Edition ("Ruby Don't Take Your Love to Town").

Tillis translated his songwriting renown into a highly successful career as a singer in the 1970s. Between 1969 and 1985 he racked up thirty-five top-ten hits. Named country's Entertainer of the Year in 1976, he turned his stuttering into a comedic gimmick and became a regular in Burt Reynolds's movies. Daughter Pam Tillis became a country star in the '90s.

In the days when he was struggling for recognition, Tillis took jobs as a sideman for others. When he joined Minnie Pearl's band, the comic asked him if he knew a fiddler. Tillis recommended the Andrew Jackson Hotel's bellhop, Roger Miller. Tree executive Buddy Killen (born in Alabama, 1932) aided Miller as well. Killen was playing the pinball machine in Tootsie's Orchid Lounge (then known as "Mom's") in 1957 when a nervous young man panhandled him for $5. During the conversation, the youngster mentioned that he was a songwriter. Killen auditioned him the next day and signed the young Miller to Tree.

Prior to achieving singing stardom, Roger Miller provided songs to such Nashville stars as George Jones ("Tall Tall Trees," 1957) and Ray Price ("Invitation To the Blues," 1958). As a bass player at the *Opry*, Killen forged strong artist connections. Through his song plugging, Miller's

184

ABOVE: *Music Row pioneer Buddy Killen published his memoirs in 1994. He was a key figure in the careers of such stars as Roger Miller, Dottie West, Joe Tex, and Bill Anderson.*

"Half a Mind" got to Ernest Tubb (1958) and "Billy Bayou" was recorded by Jim Reeves (1959). The future standards "Husbands and Wives" and "When Two Worlds Collide" also date from this period.

Miller's cowriter on "When Two Worlds Collide" was his close friend Bill Anderson. The two were enthusiastic country fans who attended hillbilly shows together in Georgia. While Miller was bothering Killen in a Nashville bar, Anderson was working as a disc jockey in Commerce, Georgia. Born in 1937, he was only nineteen when he wrote "City Lights" on the roof of his small residence hotel there.

"My dad said later that he knew I had the imagination to be a great songwriter if I could look at Commerce and write about 'a Great White Way,'" commented Anderson in his 1989 autobiography *Whispering Bill*. "It was more like two or three traffic lights, and even they didn't work all the time. But those few words opened the doors to the world of country music for his son."

Ray Price's version of "City Lights" hit No. 1 on the country charts in the fall of 1958. On the strength of that, Bill Anderson moved to Nashville. Since then, he has earned more than fifty songwriting citations from BMI.

"Saginaw Michigan" (Lefty Frizzell, 1964), "Once a Day" (Connie Smith, 1964), "Cold Hard Facts of Life" (Porter Wagoner, 1967), and others made Anderson one of the most important country composers of the 1960s. "The Lord Knows I'm Drinkin'" (Cal Smith, 1973), "Slippin' Away" (Jean Shepard, 1973), and "I May Never Get to Heaven" (Conway Twitty, 1979) confirmed his status in the 1970s.

With his distinctive "Whisperin' Bill" singing style, Anderson also became a highly successful recording artist. He joined the *Opry* cast and wrote more than thirty top-ten hits for himself as a Decca/MCA Records act of 1958–82, including "Still," "Po' Folks," "8 x 10," and "I Love You Drops." But in the go-go '80s, Bill Anderson was deemed "square" and out of date by Music Row's "countrypolitan" producers and singers. In the 1990s he staged one of the most remarkable comebacks in Nashville songwriting history. Anderson's creative rebirth began when Steve Wariner revived his song "The Tips of My Fingers" in 1992. Since then, Anderson has been writing for some of the hottest young artists in country music, including Vince Gill (1995's "Which Bridge to Cross"), Bryan White (1997's "One Small Miracle"), and Mark Wills (1999's "Wish You Were Here").

"I love my life," reflects Bill Anderson. "I feel very blessed to have had a long career and to still be active. In a way, I still feel like the nineteen-year-old kid that wrote 'City Lights.' This may sound corny, but I have still not lost that sense of awe and wonder about this whole thing. When I got into songwriting, I wanted to do it for my life's work. I just plunged into it with the idea of being in it forever. It's a dream job."

In retrospect, 1958 was a watershed year in the development of the Nashville songwriting community. For it not only marked the dawn of Bill Anderson's songwriting career; it was also the year that a flurry of prominent composers made the pilgrimage to Music City, notably Ted Harris ("Paper Roses"), Jerry Chesnut ("It's Four in the Morning," "T-R-O-U-B-L-E"), and Marijohn Wilkin. It was the year that Ray Price and Hal Smith formed Pamper Music and that Peer Music opened a Nashville office. It marked the formation of the CMA. It was the year that BMI made the commitment to its emerging industry by opening its Nashville office. And in 1958, "Pick Me up on Your Way Down" became the first hit song for Harlan Howard.

"I came from being a schoolteacher making $125 a month, so I was used to living on nothing," says Marijohn Wilkin. Unlike the others, she declined to live on advances against her future royalties. "Every songwriter in town was in debt up to their necks to their publisher. I wasn't made that way." Also unlike the others, Wilkin could read and write music.

Bill

Marijohn Wilkin

She picked up her living expenses by drafting the written sheet music ("lead sheets") for Cedarwood's writers. Plus she recorded song demonstration tapes ("demos") at $10 a session, did the company's clerical work for $50 a week, and formed the Marijohn Singers as a studio backup vocal group.

Wilkin, a Texas native born in 1920, arrived in Nashville after serving a stint with Red Foley's troupe at *The Ozark Jubilee*. She initially worked in a piano bar called The Voo-Doo Room in Nashville's Printer's Alley nightclub district. After signing with Cedarwood, she and staff writer John D. Loudermilk cowrote "Waterloo," which became a pop-crossover hit in 1959 for Stonewall Jackson. With Wayne Walker, she cowrote "Cut across Shorty," a rockabilly number for Eddie Cochran and a country hit for Carl Smith. With Dill, she cowrote "Long Black Veil," one of Lefty Frizzell's most memorable hits.

"Every writer has to write for someone," Wilkin wrote in her 1978 autobiography *Lord, Let Me Leave a Song*. "During the years at Cedarwood, we wrote for Jim Denny. He had a fourth-grade education and a gravelly voice that could scare you to death—but more than these he had a heart as big as anyone could have."

When Denny died in 1963, she formed her own publishing company, Buckhorn Music. Son Bucky Wilkin instantly put the firm on the map by writing and recording (as "Ronny & The Daytonas") the hot-rod rock 'n' roll hit "G.T.O." (1964). By this time, Marijohn Wilkin was mixing booze and pills. She was spared from a fatal overdose during Thanksgiving weekend in 1964 by an unexpected visit from Red Foley and Mel Tillis. She attempted suicide with a gun the following Easter.

Despite her troubles, she signed a number of talented songwriters to Buckhorn. One of Marijohn Wilkin's discoveries was Kris Kristofferson. In 1970 she returned from a vacation in Europe to find that Ray Price had turned one of Kristofferson's Buckhorn songs into the smash hit "For the Good Times." After Wilkin became sober and underwent an intense religious conversion, she and Kristofferson cowrote the inspirational "One Day at a Time." It became an international phenomenon in 1980.

Wilkin's "Waterloo" cowriter John D. Loudermilk followed her to Music City in 1959. Like her (and Bill Anderson), Loudermilk was college-educated. Born in North Carolina in 1934, he was just out of school when he provided George Hamilton IV with the teen ballad "A Rose and a Baby Ruth" in 1955.

"Sad Movies" (Sue Thompson), "Talk Back Trembling Lips" (Ernie Ashworth), "Tobacco Road" (The Nashville Teens), "Break My Mind" (George Hamilton IV), "Then You Can Tell Me Goodbye" (Eddy Arnold), and "Abilene" (George Hamilton IV) are among the highlights of Loudermilk's catalog. He had more success on the pop charts than any other Nashville writer of his generation.

Realizing what Cindy Walker had realized five years earlier, the West Coast publishing company Pamper Music relocated to Nashville in 1959. When it did, it introduced the town to one of the most unforgettable of the many colorful country songwriting personalities. Hank Cochran, known as "Hanktum," is regarded by his peers as the best song plugger of them all.

Born in 1935, Cochran spent part of his childhood in a Memphis orphanage. By age ten he'd had enough. He ran away, and that ended his formal schooling. He worked his way west as a manual laborer. In New Mexico, he picked up the guitar after being inspired by the records of Hank Williams. In Los Angeles he teamed up with Eddie Cochran (no relation) as The Cochran Brothers.

Back on his own, he was signed by the new Pamper firm as a fifty-dollar-a-week staff songwriter in 1958.

187

LEFT: *"Whispering" Bill Anderson's durable songwriting career stretches from 1958 to the present day.*
ABOVE: *Marijohn Wilkin discovered Kris Kristofferson and cowrote "One Day at a Time" with him.*

Anderson

Cochran arrived in Nashville during the hard-partying 1959 Disc Jockey Convention, ready for action. He took a room at Mom Upchurch's boarding house in East Nashville (also the home, at one time or another, of Carl Smith, Jimmy Dickens, Grandpa Jones, Stonewall Jackson, Mother Maybelle & The Carter Sisters, Johnny Paycheck, Faron Young, and a host of session musicians, touring band members, bookers, and promoters). Cochran began hanging out at Tootsie's to rub shoulders with his fellow starving songwriters as well as to catch the ears of thirsty *Opry* stars.

Within days of his arrival, he got one of his songs recorded; and one by one the stars of the day fell under the spell of his wit, charm, and talent. Patsy Cline sang "I Fall to Pieces." Eddy Arnold and Ray Price both had hits with "Make the World Go Away." Burl Ives won a Grammy with Cochran's "Funny Way of Laughing" and also recorded his "Little Bitty Tear." Jeannie Seely, who was married to Cochran from 1969 to 1979, won her Grammy with his "Don't Touch Me."

George Jones ("You Comb Her Hair"), Jim Reeves ("I'd Fight the World"), and Ray Price ("Don't You Ever Get Tired of Hurting Me") introduced more Cochran classics in the 1960s. In the following decade

the songwriter's successes included "It's Not Love (But It's Not Bad)," sung by Merle Haggard, and "She's Got You," sung by Loretta Lynn.

In the 1980s George Strait scored with Cochran's cowritten "The Chair" and "Ocean Front Property." Mickey Gilley ("That's All That Matters to Me") and Ronnie Milsap ("Don't You Ever Get Tired of Hurting Me") dipped into his catalog for chart-topping singles. A fruitful collaboration with Vern Gosdin yielded "Set 'Em Up Joe," "Who You Gonna Blame It on This Time," and other hits in the late '80s and early '90s.

Cochran has taken many fellow writers under his wings over the years, including Dean Dillon, Clinton Gregory, and Willie Nelson. The first of his protégés was Harlan Howard.

"I've always wanted to be a songwriter," says Howard, "and I knew I wanted to do it all my life. Cindy Walker is probably my biggest songwriting hero. I want to be like that, a whole life devoted to songwriting."

His Kentucky parents separated when he was a boy in Detroit, and the troubled youngster found solace in the sounds of *The Grand Ole Opry* on the radio. Howard was such a huge Ernest Tubb fan that he hitchhiked to Nashville and hid in the Ryman Auditorium until showtime in order to see his idol in person. Born in 1929, he migrated to California after his military service, working in a factory while penning songs on the side.

Howard's first success came in 1958 when Charlie Walker recorded "Pick Me up on Your Way Down." Ray Price liked what he heard and telephoned the songwriter to ask for a song for himself. Price's resulting recording of "Heartaches by the Number" hit the top of the country charts in 1959, and a version of the song by Guy Mitchell became a No. 1 pop hit.

"I was still working at a printing company factory in L.A.," Howard recalls. "I had success, but I had no money. It takes a long time to get the money after you have a hit. I didn't even have a tape recorder."

Hank Cochran had befriended Howard before

ABOVE: *North Carolina's John D. Loudermilk grins from the jacket of a 1971 album of original tunes.*

Glenn Sutton

Another regular Sutton client was Jerry Lee Lewis, to whom he provided "What's Made Milwaukee Famous," "To Make Love Sweeter for You," and "She Still Comes Around (To Love What's Left of Me)." During Sutton's heyday George Jones, Stonewall Jackson, David Houston, and dozens of other stars were on the charts with his tunes.

His fellow 1964 Nashville immigrants arrived with diverse résumés from many different points on the compass. Floridian Bobby Braddock (born 1940) came as the piano player in Marty Robbins's band. He soon demonstrated that he was an agile tunesmith by cowriting "He Stopped Loving Her Today," "D-I-V-O-R-C-E," "Time Marches On," "Golden Ring," and dozens of other classics.

Dolly Parton arrived from East Tennessee on the day after her high school graduation in 1964. Red Lane (Hollis Rudolph DeLaughter, born 1939) was a Louisiana native who was brought to Tree Publishing by Justin Tubb. Lane proved to be a true individualist at the company. He lives in an earthbound airplane anchored in the countryside outside Nashville. And his unique catalog includes such distinctive lyrics as John Conlee's "Miss Emily's Picture," Tammy Wynette's "Til I Get It Right," Dottie West's "Country Girl," and Merle Haggard's "My Own Kind of Hat."

Sonny Throckmorton (born 1941) was the son of a Pentecostal preacher who'd settled in Texas. Steel guitarist Pete Drake sponsored his 1964 move to Music City. But the songwriter struggled for years before anyone took an interest in his songs. He was fired by Tree Publishing for coming up hitless and went back to Texas. Songwriters Curly Putman and Dave Kirby persuaded him to return to the company in 1975, and within a year Throckmorton had 150 recordings of his songs.

"Middle Age Crazy," "Last Cheater's Waltz," "I Wish I Was Eighteen Again," "The Way I Am," "If We're Not Back in Love by Monday," "Why Not Me," and others made Throckmorton the hottest writer in town in 1976–85.

Tom T. Hall arrived on Music Row on New Year's Day, 1964, with forty-six dollars and a guitar. He recalls, "Songwriting was more a calling than a profession. When I got to Nashville, it was a folk art. Now it's an industry." Thanks to Jimmy C. Newman's 1963 hit with Hall's "D.J. For a Day," Newkeys Music put him under contract. "When I first started, I had the old American work ethic. I would write songs from nine to five, five days a week. On Friday I would turn in my reel-to-reel tape and all my lyrics typed up; and I would get my fifty dollars. I'd earned my pay. Then I'd walk down to Tootsie's and drink beer." Within months of his arrival, Dave Dudley was on the charts with Hall's "Mad" and Newman encored with "Artificial Rose." Loretta Lynn, Johnny Cash, Faron Young, George Jones, Waylon Jennings, and dozens of others subsequently recorded his creations.

Born in 1936, Tom T. Hall frequently used his Kentucky boyhood experiences to inspire songs. In 1967 singer Margie Singleton asked him to write her a song in the manner of Bobbie Gentry's big hit "Ode to Billie Joe." Hall delved into his memories and came up with "Harper Valley P.T.A.," a song of small-town hypocrisy. But Singleton was out on tour when the song was finished, so Hall pitched it to other acts. In the summer of 1968 Jeannie C. Riley recorded it in Columbia's studio.

Its subsequent No. 1 success put Hall at the forefront of the Nashville songwriting ranks. By the 1990s he was so revered that "alternate country" acts

191

ABOVE: *Madcap Glenn Sutton once appeared at a black-tie Music Row banquet dressed as Batman.*

Bobby Braddock

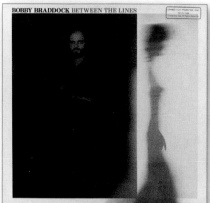

recorded a tribute album to him, he became the subject of an award-winning CD boxed set, and Alan Jackson turned his song "Little Bitty" into a chart topping hit. That was just the latest in a long string of memorable versions of his works.

Bobby Bare turned Hall's "Margie's at the Lincoln Park Inn" into a chart-topping hit in 1969. Guitar wizard Leo Kottke covered "Pamela Brown." Gram Parsons and Emmylou Harris sang "I Can't Dance." George Kent issued "Mama Bake a Pie" as a 1970 single. "That's How I Got to Memphis" has been recorded by singers ranging from Bobby Bare (1970) to Deryl Dodd (1998).

Hall landed a recording contract at Mercury Records in 1967. His voice isn't impressive for its power or range. But his phrasing is perfectly tuned to his direct, to-the-point lyrics. Hall's performances took more than fifty singles up the popularity charts of 1967–87 and more than twenty of those became top-ten hits.

Tom T. Hall is known in Nashville as "The Storyteller." As he progressed as a singer-songwriter, he devised a particular method for gathering new inspiration—"I am not a judge; I am a witness," Hall says. "That's what I think my role in life is. I like to watch and see and relate these stories. I like to travel; I am a good listener; and I am fascinated with people." So he gets in his car and goes. He wanders through small southern towns, soaking up atmosphere, eating in cafes, meeting ordinary citizens, and listening to the way people talk and what they talk about.

"One time I hitchhiked to Chicago and back. It was a big adventure. I love that sort of thing."

His 1970 album was called *I Witness Life*. He described his wanderings in the title of his 1971 collection, *In Search*

of a Song. A season spent beach-combing in 1985 yielded *Song in a Seashell*.

As one of the greatest singer-songwriters in Nashville's illustrious history, Tom T. Hall gave us "(Old Dogs, Children and) Watermelon Wine," "I Love," "The Year That Clayton Delaney Died," and dozens of other earthy masterpieces.

"You know, I didn't know what I was doing when I wrote those songs," he comments. "Didn't have any idea. I didn't know that I was being 'journalistic.' The songs were done instinctively. They just rolled off my head." Their creator calls them simply tales of "ordinary people doing extraordinary things."

Along with his contemporaries Dolly Parton and Kris Kristofferson, Hall illustrates the evolution of country songwriting from a simple folk art to a truly poetic expression. Kristofferson was the one who probably did the most to elevate the Nashville songwriter from anonymity to stardom.

Born in 1936, Kristofferson was just shy of his thirteenth birthday when a radio event captured his attention in Texas. He heard the tumultuous reception that Hank Williams got encoring six times with "Lovesick Blues" on *The Grand Ole Opry*. It fired his imagination. His father was a U.S. Air Force major general. Kristofferson became a Rhodes Scholar and then an army helicopter pilot. But the lure of Nashville was too exciting to ignore.

He was two weeks away from beginning his career teaching English literature at West Point in 1965 when he brought his song lyrics to Music Row instead. To the dismay of his family, Kristofferson fell into the "starving bohemian" culture of the country songwriters, tending bar at a Music Row tavern, working as a janitor at Columbia Studios, and soaking up everything about the country-music business that he could.

ABOVE: *This collection of Bobby Braddock songs was issued in 1979.*

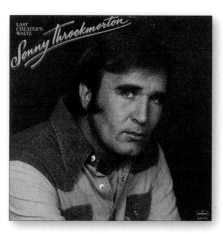

"I came to Nashville because I was moved by country performers and country writing—Hank Williams," he recalls. "So I went there to learn my trade. I'd sent my songs to Nashville while I was in the Army. You know that everybody who writes a song is convinced that it's better than anything they hear on the radio. I promise you that mine weren't.

"Nashville is a writer's town. There were three or four years when I wasn't getting anything recorded. So I was singing to a bunch of other songwriters, sort of an 'underground' of writers, and got a lot of encouragement from that."

Songwriter/publisher Marijohn Wilkin became a benefactor. Johnny Cash encouraged him. Songwriter Mickey Newbury ("Sweet Memories") was another early supporter. Still, there were several lean years for the aspiring tunesmith. Kristofferson finally broke through in 1969 when Roger Miller recorded his song "Me and Bobby McGee." The following year Waylon Jennings ("The Taker"), Ray Price ("For the Good Times"), and Johnny Cash ("Sunday Morning Coming Down") all took Kristofferson songs to the top of the charts.

His vivid, poetic imagery and unflinchingly graphic stories became the talk of Music Row. Kristofferson's lyrics were openly sexual, and his characters were nakedly emotional. Everyone in the country community admired him deeply.

Then Janis Joplin recorded a bluesy version of "Me and Bobby McGee," and Kristofferson's popularity exploded beyond country's boundaries. Sammi Smith's version of "Help Me Make It through the Night" also became a big pop hit in 1971. Bobby Bare's treatments of "Come Sundown" and "Please Don't Tell Me How the Story Ends" (1971), Brenda Lee's hit with "Nobody Wins" (1973), The Glaser Brothers' "Loving Her Was Easier" (1981), and Bob Dylan's recording of

"They Killed Him" (1986) added further luster to Kristofferson's songwriting reputation.

He became a hit recording artist himself, with 1973's religious anthem "Why Me" and a series of duets with Rita Coolidge, his wife from 1973 to 1980. Kristofferson's movie career blossomed in 1971 when he costarred in *Cisco Pike*. Subsequent features included *Pat Garrett & Billy the Kid*, *Blume In Love*, *Semi-Tough*, and *A Star Is Born*.

He and costar Willie Nelson captured the ambiance of a writer's life in Music City with their 1984 film *Songwriter*. Both had a career resurgence in the '90s in their Highwaymen collaboration with Waylon Jennings and Johnny Cash.

"Songwriting was a craft I had to learn," comments Kristofferson. "And I've picked up the rhythms of people's speech as part of my education. Since I've been a teenager I've been working construction, gettin' out and seein' as many different ways of life as I can. Part of my education has been being a laborer, a fire fighter, a helicopter pilot, a paratrooper, and a ranger.

"I'm just blessed to be in that tiny percentage of the population who gets to do something creative as a job, to stir people's emotions."

By the late 1960s it seemed like boys and girls were getting off the Greyhound bus every week in downtown Nashville, carrying their guitars and their songs to "Momma." Whitey Shafer, Frank Dycus, and George Richey arrived in 1967.

In 1968–70 such figures as Tony Joe White ("Rainy Night in Georgia"), Joe South ("Rose Garden"), and Eddie Rabbitt ("Kentucky Rain") moved to Music City. So did future songwriting greats Jimbeau Hinson, Bob McDill, Alex Harvey, Rory Michael Bourke, Linda Hargrove, Charlie Black, Eddy Raven, Billy Joe Shaver, Dennis Morgan, and Allen Reynolds.

Guy Clark, Johnny Russell, Don

ABOVE: *Like many Nashville songwriters, Sonny Throckmorton is also a very affecting vocalist. This 1978 LP was one of his several attempts as a recording artist.*

Tom T. Hall

Cook, Freddy Weller, Larry Gatlin, Rodney Crowell, Roger Murrah, and Wayland Holyfield were members of the "Class of 1972." Long-haul trucker Max D. Barnes, computer operator Don Schlitz, and carpenter Paul Overstreet came to Nashville in 1973. Steve Earle, Kent Robbins, and Richard Leigh arrived in 1974. Songwriter John Scott Sherrill was on his way to California when his van broke down and caught fire in Nashville in 1975. So he stayed. Even Nashville natives caught the fever, notably Bobby Russell ("Honey," "Little Green Apples," "The Night the Lights Went out in Georgia") and Don Wayne ("Country Bumpkin").

The deluge of writers led to a distinct style of nightclub performance in Music City. Evenings dubbed "Writers Nights" featured a number of songwriters onstage swapping songs and stories. The first of these was held at The Exit/In near the Vanderbilt University campus in late 1971. According to Walter Carter's essay "It All Begins with a Song" in *The Encyclopedia of Country Music*, a typical Writers Night there "might include Jimmy Buffett singing a country song parody 'Why Don't We Get Drunk (And Screw),' John Hiatt singing 'Sure as I'm Sittin' Here' (before it was a pop hit by Three Dog Night), Mac Gayden playing his recent soul music hit 'She Shot a Hole in My Soul' and Rodney Crowell, newly arrived in town and taking a night off from washing dishes across the street at T.G.I. Friday's restaurant."

The Bluebird Cafe, in suburban Green Hills, was founded in 1982 specifically as a nightspot to showcase Nashville's songwriters. It pioneered a style of presentation called "Writers in the Round." This features three or four writers facing one another in a circle surrounded by the audience. Paul Overstreet, Don Schlitz, Thom Schuyler, and Fred Knobloch inaugurated Writers in the Round in 1987, which was aped a year later by Pam Tillis, Ashley Cleveland, Karen Staley, and Tricia Walker trading quips and tunes as "Women in the Round."

Such events now take place at a number of Nashville nightspots, including The Sutler, Dou-glas Corner, and Radio Cafe. The Bluebird now books Writers Nights in other cities as well.

Thom Schuyler's song "16th Avenue," a 1982 hit for Lacy J. Dalton, is now the anthem for an entire community of composers. "Momma" country music still beckons them to Nashville, year after year—Dean Dillon in 1976; Schuyler, Kye Fleming, and John Jarrard in 1977; Kix Brooks and John Prine in 1979; Mike Reid in 1980; Pat Alger in 1981; Paul Kennerley and Fred Knobloch in 1983; Vince Gill and Skip Ewing in 1984; Nanci Griffith, Alan Jackson, and Peter McCann in 1985; Garth Brooks in 1987; K.T. Oslin in 1988; Gary Burr in 1989.

"I think if you want to be a professional you're gonna have to go where the action is and learn the tricks of the trade," observes Chet Atkins. "They come here and they work in restaurants—girls and boys—and some of them make it and some don't."

"The streets of Nashville are still filled with people who come here looking for that dream," says Bill Anderson. "I imagine somewhere while we've been talking, somebody's gotten off the bus or gotten off an airplane or driven their car into Nashville and said, 'OK, here I am.'

"They're still coming here and they still sweep the dreams off the sidewalk sometimes. But a lot of them do manage to come true."

195

LEFT: *Songwriter Tom T. Hall is known as "The Storyteller."*
ABOVE: *Kris Kristofferson parlayed songwriting renown into stardom. This fan magazine featured him on its cover in 1982.*

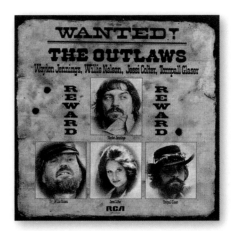

"The Nashville Sound worked against me in every way. I hated that sound. I liked things more on the edge."

The speaker is Waylon Jennings. He helped spearhead a musical revolution in Nashville in the 1970s. Along with such figures as Willie Nelson, David Allan Coe, Johnny Paycheck, and Hank Williams Jr., Jennings rebelled against the factory atmosphere of the Nashville Sound era. As a result, they were dubbed "outlaws."

"They only had one way of doing it," Jennings adds. "There was a Nashville Sound. I knew it was good for somebody, but I hated it for me."

Explains Travis Tritt, "You didn't play on your own records. Nobody was allowed to produce their own records. Nobody was allowed to choose their own band for their records. They had to come in and use the studio players."

"Nashville needed a kick in the proverbial hillbilly butt," says journalist/songwriter Hazel Smith. "And the 'outlaw' music was that kick."

The movement began when Willie Nelson left Nashville in 1971 to return to his Texas homeland. Born in 1933, he'd moved to Music City as a songwriter in 1960. "Hello Walls," "Night Life," "Family Bible," "Crazy," and "Funny How Time Slips Away" had

197

LEFT: *The Eagles were the definitive California country-rock band.*
ABOVE: Wanted: The Outlaws *became the first platinum country album after its release in 1976.*

made him one of the most respected tunesmiths in town. But recording success eluded him. His eccentric, behind-the-beat phrasing and reedy tenor were out of step with the prevailing records on country radio. So when his house burned down and his second marriage ended in divorce, he decided to hit the road.

"In Nashville at that time there was no place to play, hardly," he explains. "If you didn't play Printers Alley or *The Grand Ole Opry*, you were kind of out of luck. That's really why I started thinking about moving back to Texas, so I could play and make some money.

"I had a few too many chords to be 'traditional country' and my phrasing was a little off. It was hard to figure out exactly what to call me, what label to put on it. I'm a stylist, I guess. They say a stylist is a guy who can't sing. So maybe that's me."

He discovered the music scene in Austin, Texas, particularly a club called Armadillo World Headquarters. Nelson began performing there and found an audience for country music that Nashville didn't realize existed.

"There was a lot of activity going on with young people and country music," he recalls. "They were getting into groups like Commander Cody and Gram Parsons. The Armadillo World Headquarters in Austin was the hot thing."

Chet Flippo, then a journalist for *Rolling Stone* magazine, was one of the first to chronicle the emerging Austin scene. He remembers, "When I first met Willie there he had short hair and looked like an insurance salesman. Six months later he had a ponytail and was smoking dope at the Armadillo. And he had found his audience, this mixture of hippies and cowboys. He didn't look like a country star. He didn't act like a country star, or dress like one."

Nelson has always been "different." He is completely unmaterialistic and rolls through life as a gypsy minstrel. He was delighted to discover that his offbeat style was popular with counter-culture audiences as well as with Texas honky-tonk patrons.

"The tunes that we were putting together and the way we were playing them were being accepted pretty good," he says. "I felt like if we could record that way, that would be what the people would want to hear."

In 1973–74 he issued a pair of concept albums called *Shotgun Willie* and *Phases and Stages*. They weren't big sellers, but journalists embraced them enthusiastically as thoughtful, innovative examples of what country music could be at its best. In 1975 he crafted a dry, minimalist audio tapestry titled *Red Headed Stranger*. Recorded in a small Texas studio on a shoestring budget, Nelson felt that it captured his raw, rootsy style perfectly. Columbia Records felt otherwise.

"They thought it was 'under produced,'" he reports. Despite feeling that *Red Headed Stranger* was uncommercial, Columbia issued and promoted Nelson's vision. To everyone's surprise, his rendition of Fred Rose's "Blue Eyes Crying in the Rain" emerged from the package as a No. 1 country hit and a big pop-crossover success as well.

He issued *The Sound In Your Mind* in 1976 and scored another No. 1 with its revival of Lefty Frizzell's "If You've Got the Money (I've Got the Time)." His *The Troublemaker*, a gospel concept collection, became yet another surprise-hit LP, as did its single "Uncloudy Day." His *To Lefty from Willie* (1977) tribute LP to Frizzell also defied Music City's expectations by becoming a hit.

ABOVE: *Willie Nelson's* Red Headed Stranger *LP contained his breakthrough hit "Blue Eyes Crying in the Rain."*

Wayl

"Willie always took a lot of pride in being unpredictable," says former Columbia executive Rick Blackburn. "He called me on the phone one day and said, 'I have this great idea for making my next record. I think I'll take ten of my all-time favorite songs like "Moonlight in Vermont" and "Stardust" and "Sunny Side of the Street" and all the old standards and just record those. What do you think?' I said, 'I think you're crazy. You're a great songwriter. I think you ought to record songs that you've written. I don't know if that's going to sell or not.'

"Willie just said, 'Thank you very much,' and hung up the phone. The next thing you know, about four months later, we get his tape of the album *Stardust*. It went on to sell probably about seven million and he never lets me forget that story."

Released in 1978, *Stardust* spawned the pop standards "Georgia on My Mind," "All of Me," "Blue Skies," and "September Song" as major country hits. His 1979 output included a collaboration with pop performer Leon Russell and *Willie Nelson Sings Kristofferson*. He was also recruited for a role in Robert Redford's movie *The Electric Horseman* and sang its hit theme song "My Heroes Have Always Been Cowboys."

In 1980 Nelson starred in *Honeysuckle Rose* on the silver screen and hit No. 1 with its soundtrack songs "On the Road Again" and "Angel Flying Too Close to the Ground." He was now the biggest record seller in country music. No one questioned his musical decisions, no matter how idiosyncratic. *San Antonio Rose* (1980) was a collaboration with Ray Price that yielded a major hit with their revival of the Bob Wills chestnut "Faded Love." *Somewhere over the Rainbow* (1981) and *Without a Song* (1983) were further collections of pop standards.

"Willie Nelson is the common-man's troubadour," believes Ray Benson of Asleep at the Wheel. "He brought real class and distinction without losing the funkiness and the originality of the music."

Nelson was pushing fifty when "Always on My Mind" made him an unlikely pop idol in 1982. He recorded duet albums with Webb Pierce, Hank Snow, Roger Miller, and Merle Haggard. His LP *Half Nelson* (1985) collected collaborations with everyone from Ray Charles ("Seven Spanish Angels") to Julio Iglesias ("To All the Girls I've Loved Before"). Neil Young, Carlos Santana, George Jones, Mel Tillis, and even the late Hank Williams sang with him on the album.

Along with Neil Young, John Conlee, and John Cougar Mellencamp, Nelson spearheaded the FarmAid charity concerts to help America's failing family farms in the 1980s. Even after he reached his sixties, Willie Nelson continued to tour and record prodigiously. And he is still "different" from everyone else in his profession.

"Willie Nelson may be the most influential man of this century in country music," states Merle Haggard. "That's the way I think about him. The borders he's crossed, the way he's brought things together and his ability to always be there when somebody needs somethin'—I can't say enough about Willie Nelson. I'm a fan."

Nelson's most frequent collaborator is Waylon Jennings. If he was the "outlaw" movement's spiritual visionary, Jennings was its firebrand evangelist. Possessed of a thrilling baritone, abundant songwriting talent, and sexy/dangerous charisma, Waylon

ABOVE: *The 1975 Waylon Jennings LP* Dreaming My Dreams *is regarded as one of his masterworks as an artist.*

Jennings was the movement's lightning rod in Music City.

After narrowly missing death in Buddy Holly's plane crash, Jennings had settled in Phoenix in the 1960s as the "house act" at a club called J.D.'s. Bobby Bare heard him there and urged Chet Atkins to sign Jennings to RCA.

After moving to Music City, Jennings immediately established his image by appearing in a 1966 film titled *Nashville Rebel*. He placed more than twenty-five singles on the country charts, including a number of top-ten hits, in 1965–73, but became increasingly unhappy with the constraints placed on his music.

In frustration, he once took a gun to a recording session and threatened to blow the fingers off Music Row's A-Team players. Jennings wanted the artistic freedom to record his own songs with his own band in his own style. He was inspired to pursue this after visiting Nelson in Texas.

"He called me and said, 'Hoss, get down here. I think I've found something,'" Jennings recalls. "So I go down there and I looked out and here's all these long-haired kids. I said, 'What have you got me into?' And he said, 'Trust me.'" Nelson called again when he planned a big Fourth of July music festival in 1973 at Dripping Springs, Texas. The event became the emerging "outlaw" movement's defining moment.

"Trying to describe Dripping Springs is impossible," says Jennings. "It made Woodstock look like Sunday School."

"Every kind of person you could ever dream of was there," says performer Billy Joe Shaver. "I mean, hippies, cowboys, rednecks, Ku Klux Klan, everything."

"There'd be a little covey of hippies over there with their beards and smoking grass; and there's the cowboys with their beer," says Tompall Glaser. "Then there would be people who looked like they'd brought their picnic and their kids."

"And there was women that actually took their tops off," exclaims Hazel Smith. "And I had never seen anything like that before."

"We weren't acting like adults," says Jennings. "We were just crazy people."

Back in Nashville, he had been gradually becoming more and more of an independent maverick. His *Ladies Love Outlaws* LP of 1972 pictured him with longer hair and contained liner notes that called him "a rugged, exciting, renegade singer." Hazel Smith was talking to a North Carolina radio station in 1973 when she was asked what this new kind of country music was called. Recalling Jennings's "Ladies Love Outlaws" hit, she suggested that he, Willie Nelson, and her employer Tompall Glaser were "outlaws."

Jennings's *Honky Tonk Heroes* collection (1973) was a breakthrough in that it mixed his band members with Music Row's studio professionals and showcased the brilliant, rough-hewn songs of Billy Joe Shaver. This album and 1973's *Lonesome On'ry & Mean* were also the first Waylon Jennings albums that included tracks he produced himself.

"Willie and Waylon and some of the other artists wanted a larger say in the way their records were made," observes Nashville journalist/manager John Lomax III. "Up until then, it was pretty much the producer as dictator. The artists would come in off the road, the producer would hand them ten or twelve songs and say, 'Here's your next album. Learn them and we'll be cutting this afternoon.' If the artist didn't like it, that was too bad."

"We told the artists what to sing, how to sing it, when to sing it, what key," comments producer Billy Sherrill. "And they said, 'Yes, sir.' If you were wrong, they moved on. If you were right, you were a hero."

"Willie and Waylon felt like they knew better than perhaps the producer what their audiences wanted," adds Lomax. "The producer sat here in Nashville. Willie and Waylon were out there playing and seeing the audiences. They also wanted to use their band members on their records, which at the time was a pretty heretical notion."

Jessi Colter

The two troublemakers coproduced Jennings's 1974 LP *This Time*. Its title tune became the artist's first No. 1 hit. *The Ramblin' Man* (1974) spawned "I'm a Ramblin' Man" as his second straight chart topper. Like its three immediate predecessors, the jacket pictured a long-haired, unkempt rebel in a goatee and moustache.

"My clothes and the way I looked and everything, I never tried to make a statement," Jennings says. "I was wearin' what I liked. I liked my hair. One time Jane Pauley asked me on an interview, 'Here you are, you're makin' a lot of money—why do you wear Levi's and cowboy shirts when you could be wearin' beautiful suits and everything?' I said, ''Cause I can afford to wear whatever I want to.'"

The sound was radical, too, an edgy, propulsive, bottom-heavy blend of tense, stinging guitars under his drawling, expressive baritone. He forged it in a studio belonging to his friend Tompall Glaser. Flying in the face of the efficient Nashville Sound system, Jennings spent extra time working out exactly how he wanted each track to sound.

"There was no clock," says Glaser. "He could spend however many hours he needed up there in that studio to find himself. And that's how he became what he is."

"There was an atmosphere of freedom, where we didn't allow anyone to tell us what to do," adds Jennings. "I've always felt that was the turning point for country music. It was so simple, so ragged that it was right."

The masterpiece was 1975's *Dreaming My Dreams*. The snarling "Are You Sure Hank Done It This Way," hard-core country "Bob Wills Is Still the King," and languidly beautiful "Dreaming My Dreams with You" all emerged from the collection as major hits.

The success of Waylon Jennings's new sound and the *Red Headed Stranger* breakthrough by Willie Nelson wasn't lost on RCA executive Jerry Bradley. Recalling that Nelson and Jennings' wife Jessi Colter had previously recorded for the label,

he packaged tracks by them with performances by Jennings and Tompall Glaser together on one LP. *Wanted! The Outlaws* made hits of Glaser's "Put Another Log on the Fire," the Jennings-Colter duet "Suspicious Minds," and the Jennings-Nelson anthem "Good Hearted Woman." When the dust settled, the album's sales topped one million, making it the first Platinum Record in the history of country music. It also cemented "outlaws" as the name of the movement.

Jennings roared forward, releasing nine consecutive million-selling albums in 1976–81. "Luchenbach, Texas" (1977), "Mamas Don't Let Your Babies Grow up to Be Cowboys" (1978), "Amanda" (1979), "I Ain't Living Long Like This" (1980), and his other hits exploded on the charts. He became the narrator of the most popular television show in America, *The Dukes of Hazzard,* and sang its theme song "Good Ol' Boys" (1980).

Unfortunately, his personal life was roaring, too. As he reported in his candid 1996 autobiography *Waylon,*

ABOVE: *This 1975 album contained "I'm Not Lisa," which made Jessi Colter a star.*

John

Jennings was on drugs for twenty-one years. At his peak, he was spending a reported fifteen hundred dollars a day on cocaine. Federal drug agents arrested him during a recording session on Music Row in 1977. Even that didn't slow him down. He was drawing ten to fifteen thousand fans to shows and pulling in hundreds of thousands of dollars a week. But he was bankrupt.

"It took me eight years to find my way back from drugs," Jennings wrote. "Eight years to be able to write a song. Eight years to figure out who I was again. To get over it. Eight long years."

With wife Jessi Colter's help he won the battle. Jennings had twenty more top-ten hits in the 1980s, staged a 1990 comeback with the humorous "Wrong," recorded an album of children's music in 1993, toured and recorded with The Highwaymen, and took part in the hilariously ribald 1998 *Old Dogs* album of Shel Silverstein songs with fellow veterans Jerry Reed, Mel Tillis, and Bobby Bare.

"People said I was the one who busted the system," says a reflective Jennings. "I've always said, 'I may have had something to do with it, but I think they broke themselves trying to break me.'"

Wife Jessi Colter (Miriam Johnson, born 1947) boosted sales of *Wanted! The Outlaws* because she'd crossed over to the pop charts with "I'm Not Lisa" the previous year. The Phoenix native was previously married to twangy-guitar rock 'n' roll star Duane Eddy. But she achieved greater success as Jennings's partner, notably on the 1981 hit duets "Storms Never Last" and a medley of "Wild Side of Life" with "It Wasn't God Who Made Honky Tonk Angels."

Colter was distantly related to the Wild West outlaw whose name she adopted as her stage name. David Allan Coe actually was an "outlaw." The Ohio native (born 1939) spent virtually his entire youth incarcerated in reform schools, juve-

nile detention facilities, and prisons. He hit the streets of Nashville after his release from the Ohio State Penitentiary in 1967.

The colorful Coe was pretty hard to miss in those days. He lived in a hearse parked outside the Ryman Auditorium and donned a mask to bill himself as "The Mysterious Rhinestone Cowboy." He had 365 tattoos covering his body. He dyed his long hair wild colors. He joined The Outlaws motorcycle gang. He wore earrings and wrote a novel called *Psychopath*. He did magic tricks. He was a gifted mimic.

Although he recorded an album of prison songs shortly after his arrival in Music City, it was as a songwriter that he initially succeeded.

Penning "Souvenirs and California Memories" (Billie Jo Spears, 1972), "Would You Lay with Me (In a Field of Stone)" (Tanya Tucker, 1973), and "Take This Job and Shove It" (Johnny Paycheck, 1974) led to Coe's own recording contract and road show.

"We backed up David Allan Coe for several years," reports Danny Shirley of Confederate Railroad. "I used that as an education. I remember one bar in particular in Charleston, South Carolina. We'd just been in Daytona for Bike Week with Coe. We had our Harleys on the trailers, and we had on our Harley finest. So we walk in the first night in this cowboy club and we've all got our leather on and headbands, big rings, and fingerless leather gloves and all this stuff. All these cowboys had been sizing us up to see if they was gonna applaud, dance, or jump up on stage to knock us off. At the end of the night, they were coming up and saying, 'Man we had y'all pegged all wrong.' We were country.

"You learn to carry yourself in a certain way. This big drunk's in here; he's looking for a fight. If he looks at me, I gotta

203

LEFT: *Johnny Paycheck is one of the few musical "outlaws" who actually was one.*
ABOVE: *Like Paycheck, David Allan Coe served time in prison. This album illustrates Coe's flamboyant style.*

give him a look back that without saying anything verbally, says, 'I'll beat you up.' After all these years in those situations, I think we accomplished that attitude and look real well."

David Allan Coe's hits during the "outlaw" era included "You Never Even Called Me by My Name" (1975), "Long Haired Redneck" (1976), "The Ride" (1983), and "Mona Lisa Lost Her Smile" (1984). Away from the eyes and ears of his record label, he recorded a string of sexually explicit albums that he sold to his biker audience on tour. The always entertaining Coe became a polygamist with nine "wives" at a cave resort outside Nashville. When the "alternative-country" scene surfaced in the late 1990s, Coe braided his beard with beads and revived his recording career.

Johnny Paycheck, to whom Coe provided "Take This Job and Shove It," was another Nashville "bad boy" who wore the outlaw persona comfortably. Born Donald Lytle in Ohio in 1938, Paycheck was court-martialed in the navy in 1956 after assaulting an officer. Following two years in military prison, he headed to Nashville to work as a sideman in the honky-

tonk bands of George Jones, Porter Wagoner, Faron Young, and Ray Price.

As "Donny Young," he also began recording. His songs were recorded by Price ("Touch My Heart") and Tammy Wynette ("Apartment #9"). But after moderate success in the 1960s, Paycheck succumbed to drugs and booze. He went bankrupt, was arrested for burglary, and wound up as a street bum in Los Angeles. Record promoter Nick Hunter rehabilitated him, and Paycheck resumed recording in 1971.

He initially recorded in producer Billy Sherrill's nouveau Nashville Sound mode, scoring big hits with "She's All I Got" and "Someone to Give My Love To." But when the outlaw movement appeared, Paycheck embraced it enthusiastically with such 1976–77 fare as "11 Months and 29 Days," "I'm the Only Hell (Mama Ever Raised)," and "Take This Job and Shove It."

His hell-raising and erratic behavior continued. A paternity suit, a bad-check charge, a child-rape accusation, and federal tax problems characterized his tumultuous offstage life. Then just before Christmas in 1985 Paycheck shot a man during a barroom confrontation in Ohio. After exhausting

ABOVE: *This album introduced "The Devil Went Down to Georgia" as a Charlie Daniels Band classic.*

his appeals, he went to state prison in 1989. He emerged drug-free in 1991 and began singing again. In 1997 the prodigal son was made a member of *The Grand Ole Opry*.

"I used to say, 'I'm not an outlaw; I'm an outcast,'" says Charlie Daniels. "When it gets right down to the nitty gritty, I've just tried to be who I am. I've never followed trends or fads. I couldn't even if I tried. I can't be them; I can't be anybody but me.

"People really didn't know what to think of us. Some people thought we were rock, some thought we were country. Some people thought we were country-rock. There was really no name for it, actually."

Born in North Carolina in 1936, Daniels began his career as a bluegrass fiddler. But as a teenager he hit the road as the leader of the rock 'n' roll band The Jaguars. In 1967 he moved to Nashville to find work as a session guitarist. Among his more notable sessions were the Bob Dylan albums of 1969–70: *Nashville Skyline, New Morning,* and *Self Portrait*. Daniels broke through as a record maker, himself, with 1973's hit hippie song "Uneasy Rider." His 1975 southern-rebel anthems "Long Haired Country Boy" and "The South's Gonna Do It Again" propelled his 1975 collection *Fire on the Mountain* to Double Platinum status. That was also the recording that inspired the "Volunteer Jam." When he and his band were making it in 1974, they decided to record a couple of its tunes live to give it some extra spice.

Daniels booked Nashville's War Memorial Auditorium and went on the radio to advertise a Volunteer Jam concert, dubbed for Tennessee's nickname "The Volunteer State" and suggesting that the theme of the evening would be an improvisational "jam." Dickie Betts, The Allman Brothers, and three members of The Marshall Tucker Band hap-

pened to be in town. After The Charlie Daniels Band recorded its two live tunes, everyone piled onto the stage for a long boogie session. The musicians had so much fun they decided to do it again.

Since then there have been sixteen such events. The Volunteer Jam became the prototype of the cooperative, multiact extravaganza. It was the first major music event to fuse styles, genres, and personalities into a communal celebration. Its history includes blues, classical, gospel, folk, soul, and bluegrass performers. Supper-club crooning and *Grand Ole Opry* hoedown tunes have been equally welcomed.

"Jam daddy" Charlie Daniels became an American music icon. His huge bulk, six-foot-two-inch frame, and wide-brimmed cowboy hat form an indelible image for millions. A vast public has been attracted by his plainspoken honesty, just-folks humility, no-bull attitude, and open-hearted kindness.

When Epic Records signed him to its rock roster in New York in 1976, the $5 million contract was the largest ever given to a Nashville act up to that time. In the summer of 1979 Daniels rewarded the company's faith by delivering "The Devil Went Down to Georgia," which became a Gold single, topped both country and pop charts, won a Grammy Award, earned three Country Music Association trophies, became a cornerstone of the *Urban Cowboy* movie soundtrack, and propelled Daniels' *Million Mile Reflections* album to Triple Platinum sales levels.

"We were doing an album, and we didn't have a fiddle tune," he recalls. "We were in the studio recording, and we took a break and I got to thinking about an old poem by Steven Vincent Benet called 'The Mountain Whippoorwill.' It was about a fiddle contest, about a kid that had gotten hold of a fiddle and learned how to play the sounds of the mountains,

205

the wind in the pine trees, and that sort of thing. I don't know where that line, 'The Devil Went Down to Georgia,' came from, but it just popped in my mind. First thing you know we had a song. When it came out it was an international hit in Israel, England, France, Germany, and places where people don't even speak English."

The celebratory "In America" (1980), his Vietnam vets' anthem "Still in Saigon" (1982), the topical "American Farmer" (1985), and the romping honky-tonker "Drinkin' My Baby Goodbye" (1986) kept Daniels on the charts. But his real renown rests on his marathon concert performances, tireless media work, and brotherly-love attitude toward his fellow musicians.

"I've been playing honest music for too long to change now. Back in 1974, I decided to just be the best Charlie Daniels I can be. I must'a done something right—we're in our third generation of fans now. There's gotta be something in this music; they sure don't come to see me for my looks."

The "outlaw" who took center stage in the 1980s was Hank Williams Jr. (born 1949). Like the others, he was a veteran performer who seized control of his career and music. The son of the legendary Hank Williams, he was only three when his father died, but mother Audrey Williams raised him to be an imitator of the honky-tonk king. Williams Jr. made his stage debut singing his father's songs at age

eight, his *Grand Ole Opry* debut at age eleven, and his recording debut at age fourteen.

As he entered his twenties in the 1970s, Williams began to assert himself. Always a blues fan, he was captivated by the blues-based southern rock music of The Allman Brothers, The Marshall Tucker Band, Lynyrd Skynyrd, and the like. This influence began seeping into his increasingly rhythmic sound. In addition, he began singing more thoughtful material, notably "Pride's Not Hard to Swallow" (1972), "I'll Think of Something" (1974), "Stoned at the Jukebox" (1975), and "Living Proof" (1976).

His new direction found its first full expression on his 1975 LP *Hank Williams Jr. and Friends*. Just before its release the star was nearly killed when he fell from a mountain in Montana. He underwent extensive facial reconstructive surgery. During his recuperation he resolved to reemerge as his own man. Wearing dark glasses and a large cowboy hat to hide his scars, Hank Williams Jr. returned with a series of songs that designed a hell-raising outlaw persona.

In 1979–89 he became a titan on the charts with such belting performances as "Family Tradition," "Whiskey Bent and Hell Bound," "Dixie on My Mind," "A Country Boy Can Survive," "If the South Would'a Won," "If Heaven Ain't a Lot Like Dixie," and "Born To Boogie." These songs gave him his redneck rocker image. But during this same period he demonstrated musical subtlety by singing the witty "This Ain't Dallas" and "I'm for Love," reviving Fats Waller's "Ain't Misbehavin'," and inviting Ernest Tubb to be a guest vocalist on "Leave Them Boys Alone."

In 1989 he found a previously unissued recording by his father, overdubbed vocal harmonies, and issued "There's a Tear in My Beer" as a Grammy-winning duet. Williams's 1984 hit "All My Rowdy Friends Are Coming over Tonight" became the theme song for ABC-TV's *Monday Night Football*. And he provided the theme song for the 1990s youth explosion on the charts when he staged the 1988 recording session for "Young Country" fea-

ABOVE: *Country-rock pioneer Gram Parsons recorded only two solo albums before his untimely death. This 1973 collection was the first of these.*

Parsons

turing Steve Earle, Marty Stuart, Highway 101, T. Graham Brown, and Keith Whitley, among others.

Nicknamed "Bocephus" by his father after comic Rod Brasfield's ventriloquist dummy, Hank Williams Jr. rose to become one of country's finest showmen. In command of multiple instruments, shooting off guns onstage, pouring emotion into blues tunes, leaping from pianos, and bellowing with energy, the six-foot-four-inch entertainer commands an arena like few of his contemporaries can.

While the outlaws were stirring things up in Nashville, country experimentation was occurring elsewhere as well. The Texas scene included not only Willie Nelson and Ray Benson but such scruffy rebels as Jerry Jeff Walker, Kinky Friedman, Michael Martin Murphey, Doug Sahm, B.W. Stevenson, Ray Wylie Hubbard, and Rusty Wier.

In California, rock groups began to experiment with country instrumentation and harmonies. Bands such as Poco, Commander Cody & His Lost Planet Airmen, Buffalo Springfield, America, Firefall, Creedence Clearwater Revival, Pure Prairie League, and Rick Nelson's Stone Canyon Band were all part of the development of what became known as "country-rock."

This movement's founders were Gram Parsons (Cecil Ingram Connors, 1946–1973) and Chris Hillman (born 1944). After hearing The New Lost City Ramblers and Flatt & Scruggs on records, Hillman fell in love with bluegrass mandolin. At age fifteen the San Diego native discovered a cluster of other bluegrass enthusiasts and formed his first band, The Scottsville Squirrel Barkers. His next band was The Hillmen, featuring future Bluegrass Cardinals star Don Parmley and future

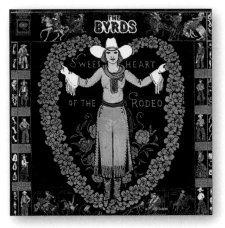

country great Vern Gosdin. With Gosdin as his protector and carrying a fake ID, the eighteen-year-old picker learned the honky-tonk ropes.

The Hillmen shared a manager with a trio of uptown folkies— David Crosby, Roger McGuinn, and Gene Clark. Hillman was recruited to play bass with them, and with the addition of drummer Michael Clarke, The Byrds shot to No. 1 in 1965 singing Bob Dylan's "Mr. Tambourine Man." At that moment, folk-rock was born.

As early as their second album The Byrds were singing country tunes such as "Satisfied Mind." Their 1968 collections *The Notorious Byrd Brothers* and, particularly, *Sweetheart of the Rodeo* are now regarded as milestones on the road to country-rock. The latter was originally recorded with the band's new member, singer-songwriter Gram Parsons.

Recalls Hillman, "I knew of him. I ran into him at some bank in Beverly Hills. David and Gene had left The Byrds and Michael wasn't being consistent, so Roger and I were looking around for new partners, and Gram came along."

Sweetheart of the Rodeo marked the first time that California rockers ventured to Nashville to record. The experience was a musical triumph but a social disaster.

"We got a guest shot on the *Opry*, but they hated us. Scared 'em to death. I think there was one person that was really nice to us that night, Skeeter Davis. But everybody else got a little nervous." DJ Ralph Emery, coincidentally Skeeter's ex-husband, greeted the band with contempt. The audience tweeted at The Byrds, mocking their name.

207

TOP: *Parsons's influence was heard in* Sweetheart of the Rodeo, *issued in 1968 by The Byrds.*
ABOVE: *Chris Hillman, standing at far right on this* Flying Burrito Brothers *LP, was Parsons's partner in The Byrds.*

Emmylou

Even future outlaw Tompall Glaser verbally attacked the group.

A year later, Parsons and Hillman founded the definitive country-rock band: "I had had enough of The Byrds. We had talked about doing some country stuff and started this group, The Flying Burrito Brothers. We were sharing a house together in the San Fernando Valley, both coming off of failed marriages and so we had a rapport. So we started writing songs like 'Sin City' and 'Wheels' and things like that. Initially it was a lot of fun. It was a great idea.

"It was maybe a little ahead of its time. I mean, we're more popular now as a group than we were back then. We would go play The Palomino in the San Fernando Valley every Monday night. And we'd get the strangest people coming in. Marlon Brando and people like that would come and watch The Flying Burrito Brothers. Then we'd get these die-hard country people that would just hoot and holler at us and get really upset because we were up there with long hair playing country music.

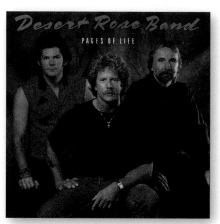

"We played the Altamont festival, and it was one of the most depressing, horrible shows we ever did. We left before the guy got killed there. But what I'm saying is we could fit into either arena. We could play the country-western clubs, like The Palomino or The Aces Club. Or we could be in the situation with The Stones at Altamont."

Parsons left the band in 1969. In 1973 he was found dead of a mixture of alcohol and heroin in a motel room in Joshua Tree, California.

"Gram was seduced by the trappings of rock 'n' roll," Hillman recalls. "That was his downfall. But some of the best stuff I've ever been around was in that era when we first got together. That was the good part of Gram, back then, the hungry, inspired kid."

Down the road, Hillman continued to make country-music history as the leader of the hit-making Desert Rose Band of 1986–94. He then reverted to bluegrass in the acclaimed Laurel Canyon Ramblers in the '90s.

In 1971, Hillman had introduced Parsons to the woman who ultimately carried on his country-rock legacy, Emmylou Harris: "The Burrito Brothers were playing at The Cellar Door in Washington, D.C. Rick Roberts, who was later in Firefall, had seen her when he was walking by this tavern, Clyde's, and he brought me down there. As I recall, she was singing folk stuff. It was just her with an acoustic guitar. She was real good. She had a presence about her. I said to Gram, 'You've got to call this girl. She's wonderful.' I finally got him to call her. And off they went."

Harris (born 1947) believes that she had no musical style until she met her mentor: "I needed to meet Gram Parsons. Really, that was what was supposed to happen to me, I think.

"He was that rock 'n' roll person that he was; that was our generation. But he understood traditional country music and could sing it. And he was the one who taught me country music."

After touring with Parsons and recording as the harmony vocalist on his two solo LPs, Harris was left devastated and stranded by his untimely death. His label offered her a solo deal. She took it and began recording *Pieces of the Sky* in 1974 as a continuation of Parsons's artistic vision. It included "Boulder To Birmingham" as her elegy to him, as well as reinterpretations of the songs of Merle Haggard, Dolly Parton, and her other country favorites.

In the summer of 1975 her remake of The Louvin Brothers' "If I Could Only Win Your Love" bolted into the country top ten. With future Desert Rose Band member Herb Pedersen singing hillbilly harmony the single was far more "coun-

ABOVE: *The Desert Rose Band's core, from left: John Jorgenson, Chris Hillman, and Herb Pedersen.*
RIGHT: *Emmylou Harris was the country-rock figure who united traditionalists and progressives.*

Harris

Linda Ronstadt

try" than most of what Nashville was producing at the time. Emmylou Harris did what had been previously unthinkable—she united hip country-rock fans and hard-line country conservatives.

Hillman says that's something he had been unable to do: "Having that rock 'n' roll background was almost a badge of 'Outsider. You aren't really one of us.' The Flying Burrito Brothers could not get on the radio, couldn't crack the country market."

"We were too rock 'n' roll for country and too country for rock 'n' roll," agrees Jim Messina, a veteran of both Poco and The Buffalo Springfield. "Back in the '60s, we could come to Nashville to perform in Buffalo Springfield and there was always a feeling like, 'Gee, isn't this a neat place?' But it was always this place that we didn't think we were really welcome."

Emmylou Harris changed all of that. Old-timers at the *Opry* cheered in 1976 when she revived Buck Owens's "Together Again," George Jones's "One of These Days," the Don Gibson/Faron Young/Patsy Cline classic "Sweet Dreams," and Kitty Wells' "Making Believe" a year later. *Elite Hotel, Luxury Liner,* and *Quarter Moon in a Ten-Cent Town* became Gold Records in 1976–78. Then she went even more hard-core country with 1979's *Blue Kentucky Girl* and her 1980 bluegrass salute *Roses In the Snow*. "Wayfaring Stranger," "Blue Kentucky Girl," "To Daddy," "Beneath Still Waters," and "Two More Bottles of Wine" continued her spree of top-ten hits in 1978–80.

Traditionalists weren't the only ones who fell under her spell. Harris took country music to pop fans and taught them to love it on its own terms. She demonstrated that country could appeal in its unvarnished state, without the trappings of the Nashville Sound, Vegas-style costuming, or Broadway-style stage presentation. She gave country back its uncompromised dignity and its pride in its heritage. She made country music hip.

"Emmylou Harris was accepted in lots of places where pure country wouldn't be," comments Buck Owens. "A lot of the young people accepted her. I don't know what kind of music they thought she sang, but she sang country music to them. She was very important."

"At that time I actually thought of Emmylou as a rocker," recalls Lacy J. Dalton. "I know now she never really was, but that was the kind of music I liked to listen to then. That's how I began to come back into the fold of country music."

Emmylou Harris reinvigorated country music in a profound way. She not only explored its roots; she added branches to the tree by introducing the works of such songwriters as Townes Van Zandt, Jesse Winchester, Delbert McClinton, and Carlene Carter. From the ranks of her superb bands Ricky Skaggs, Rodney Crowell, Pam Rose and Mary Ann Kennedy, Buddy Miller, and The Whites all graduated to their own recording careers. Singer-songwriters Vince Gill and Rosanne Cash, producer Tony Brown, and steel guitarist Hank DeVito were also part of her musical circle. Most of them migrated to Nashville after she did in 1984. Three years later she teamed with Dolly Parton and Linda Ronstadt on the landmark *Trio* album. It triumphed at the Grammy and CMA ceremonies and bore four big hits, "To Know Him Is to Love Him," "Telling Me Lies," "Those Memories," and "Wildflowers," in 1987–88. It also anticipated female collaborative efforts like the '90s Lilith Fair tours. The three superstars reunited for the equally lovely *Trio II* in 1999.

Harris became a touchstone for a generation of subsequent female stylists. She was not only the groundbreaking country-rock act; she heralded the rise of the new-traditionalism movement of the late '80s and shepherded the alternative-country movement of the '90s.

"I do best when I have a crusade," says Harris. "I think country should take pride in its roots. When I started doing this music, it never concerned me how popular it was going to be. I've always sort of done what I want to do, without thinking too much about that."

Her *Trio* partner Linda Ronstadt

LEFT: *Operetta, mariachi, folk, rock, Tin Pan Alley standards, and opera are all within Linda Ronstadt's range as a vocalist. But throughout her career she has recorded country and country-rock music.*

was another country rocker who made good. The Arizona native, born in 1946, was a folkie like Harris. But after succeeding in that arena with "Different Drum" as the lead singer of The Stone Poneys in 1967, Ronstadt embraced country-rock in the 1970s.

Her country successes of 1974–79 include such titles as "Silver Threads and Golden Needles," "I Can't Help It (If I'm Still in Love With You)" (featuring harmonies by Harris), "When Will I Be Loved," "Love Is a Rose," "The Sweetest Gift" (again featuring Harris), "Crazy," "Blue Bayou," "Poor Poor Pitiful Me," "Love Me Tender," and "I Never Will Marry." Ronstadt then left the genre to explore operetta *(The Pirates of Penzance)*, mariachi *(Canciones de Mi Padre)*, punk rock *(Mad Love)*, opera *(La Bohème)*, pop standards *(What's New)*, Afro-Cuban music *(Frenesi)*, and lullabyes *(Dedicated to the One I Love)*.

In 1999 she and Emmylou Harris released an album of duets. Ronstadt had been a major booster when Harris began her career. She also helped launch the biggest-selling country-rock act, The Eagles. After recording her *Silk Purse* album in Nashville in 1970, Ronstadt returned to California and assembled the future superstar group as her backup band.

The Eagles issued their debut LP a year later. "Take It Easy," "Peaceful Easy Feeling," and its other songs became instant successes. Between 1972 and 1977 the band scored with "Desperado," "Already Gone," "Best of My Love," "One of These Nights," "Take It to the Limit," "Tequila Sunrise," and "Lyin' Eyes." Banjo player Bernie Leadon departed at the end of 1975, and after that the group became more rock-oriented.

But a bevy of country stars saluted the group's influence with a tribute album called *Common Thread* in 1993. It won the CMA's Album of the Year Award.

"When I was with Lester Flatt's band, we played a show at Michigan State University in 1973 that changed my life," says Marty Stuart with a smile. "The open-

ing act was Gram Parsons and Emmylou Harris. Then we played and then The Eagles.

"The Eagles were out touring with an album called *Desperado*. Gram had just come from hangin' out with The Rolling Stones. He had fingernail polish on and this cockney accent, dressed up in a Nudie suit, lookin' like a rock 'n' roll star, talkin' like Rolling Stones trash and singin' George Jones songs. I thought, 'This guy's alright. He understands.' Then I saw Bernie Leadon playing banjo with The Eagles. He came to me and he says, 'Can you introduce me to Lester Flatt?' I said, 'Can you introduce me to Don Henley?' That night, I played with Gram and Emmy and I jammed with some of The Eagles."

Perhaps the high-water mark of the merger of pop/rock performers with country music was *Will the Circle Be Unbroken*, a 1972 collaboration between The Nitty Gritty Dirt Band and Nashville's finest traditional musicians. The Dirt Band had risen to fame with Jerry Jeff Walker's song "Mr. Bojangles" in 1970. When the shaggy-haired Californians arrived in Music City to record with country's veterans, they were initially viewed with a great deal of mistrust. Bill Monroe, for instance, declined to record with them. But once Maybelle Carter, Merle Travis, Doc Watson, Brother Oswald, Jimmy Martin, and, most significantly, Roy Acuff saw the band's genuine love of country music, the project had the community's blessing.

The resulting triple-disc set included "Dark as a Dungeon," "Tennessee Stud," "I Saw the Light," "Orange Blossom Special," "Wabash Cannonball," "Wildwood Flower," and thirty more old country favorites. It stunned the entire industry by selling a million, chiefly to the band's collegiate fans. Once again, it had taken "outsiders" to teach country music to respect its purest rootsy expressions.

Their country credentials ensured, The Nitty Gritty Dirt Band peppered the charts with fifteen consecutive top-ten hits in 1983–89. Members Jeff

Hanna and Jimmy Ibbotson relocated from California to Nashville. Among the long-lived group's other career highlights is its status as the first U.S. group to tour the Soviet Union (1977).

There are perhaps four lasting legacies of the outlaw and country-rock movements. First, they opened up country music to rock's vast youth market for the first time. Second, they established artists' rights of self-determination and self-production. Third, they reinvigorated country's traditions and showed that supper-club acceptability need not be the music's ultimate goal. Fourth, they put country music back in blue jeans.

"Eventually, the artists were able to gain a measure of freedom," reflects John Lomax III. "And when the records that they made started selling big, Nashville sat up and took notice. Then you saw a lot of people running around with leather jackets and fringe and beards and talking with strange words, perhaps even smoking a little pot here and there."

"There was a certain amount of drugs," acknowledges Tompall Glaser, "but not any more in our building than in the rest of town, I might add. It was the '60s and the early '70s. It was everywhere."

"We all grew beards and long hair; and we got that rebellious attitude," recollects Jack Greene. "I changed the name of my band to The Renegades. Everything changed to kind of go along with the times. It just seemed like the thing to do at that time."

"The 'outlaw' movement for me was like, 'Thank God!'" says Mark Collie. "I totally identified with Waylon Jennings and Willie Nelson. They had irreverence, which is what the youth of America has to express. It's, 'I don't give a tinker's damn what you think about the music; this is my point of view.' They call it arrogance. They call it bein' cocky. They call it bein' American. But whatever it is, they brought that back into country music; and thank God they did."

"We were just having a good time," says Bobby Bare. "And that's the way music really ought to be. That's why we got into it to start with, to get girls and have fun. Nowadays, I don't see anybody having any fun."

Points out latter-day renegade Travis Tritt, "I think that all of us out there now who have any control over our careers at all owe a debt of gratitude to the 'outlaws.'"

"There's always more than one way to do things, and that's your way," states Waylon Jennings. "And you have a right to try it at least once."

ABOVE: *The Nitty Gritty Dirt Band's collaboration with the legends of old-time country music remains a landmark recording of the 1970s.*

Twelve

Country-
politan

The 1970s and early 1980s were a period of tremendous diversity in the country sound. This was perhaps country's most experimental and innovative era. New approaches were being offered by California's country-rock acts and Nashville's outlaw movement. A new generation of honky-tonk singers came to the fore as Gene Watson, Vern Gosdin, Moe Bandy, and their peers reinvigorated hard-core country singing. Gifted singer-songwriters such as Guy Clark, Larry Gatlin, and Rodney Crowell strengthened Nashville's reputation as a song center.

The era is most often characterized by pop-oriented stylists who gave rise to the radio marketing term "countrypolitan." But performers like Kenny Rogers, Barbara Mandrell, and Crystal Gayle tell only part of the story. Ricky Skaggs and The Whites brought bluegrass influence back to the country charts. The Statler Brothers and The Oak Ridge Boys became stars with gospel quartet harmonies. Former folkies Don Williams, John Denver, and Anne Murray also found a home in country music. The era made stars of hot pickers like Jerry Reed and Roy Clark. Billie Jo Spears and Bill Anderson performed on country-disco fusion records in 1975–80.

Television marketing made novelty

215

LEFT: *Donna Fargo was one of a number of gifted singer-songwriters who emerged during the 1970s in Nashville.*
ABOVE: *The sound of "The Tennessee Swamp Fox," Tony Joe White, was introduced on this LP.*

Charley Pride

hits of veteran yodeler Slim Whitman and "One Day at a Time" newcomer Cristy Lane. It became chic to don cowboy hats, jeans, and boots and go to country nightclubs in urban centers. John Schneider and Tom Wopat graduated from TV's *Dukes of Hazzard* to become record makers, as did Mary Kay Place from *Mary Hartman, Mary Hartman* and Vicki Lawrence of *The Carol Burnett Show*. The hillbilly gag fest *Hee Haw* became the longest-running show in the history of television syndication. The trucker and CB craze resulted in a number of huge hits. Former pop acts such as B.J. Thomas, Brenda Lee, Tom Jones, and Mac Davis were all welcomed in Nashville's climate of broadened definitions and expanding opportunities.

Experimentation was everywhere. Australian folk-pop singer Olivia Newton-John was successfully marketed as a country act. Marie Osmond and Tanya Tucker were introduced as teen sensations. Football star Terry Bradford, movie star Burt Reynolds, and *Playboy* Playmate Barbe Benton made the country charts. Orion performed in a mask for the "mystique" of being the reincarnated Elvis Presley.

Asleep at the Wheel (1974), The Amazing Rhythm Aces (1975), Alabama (1980), Exile (1983), and Sawyer Brown (1984) introduced the concept of star country bands. Freddy Fender and Johnny Rodriguez became country's first Mexican American headliners. Charley Pride rose to become the genre's first black superstar.

"It was an era of wonderful exploration," states Kenny Rogers.

"The era is very difficult to categorize or characterize," comments *Billboard* magazine editor Chet Flippo. "It's like trying to nail Jello against the wall. You think you have it and then it flies off in all directions."

"Kenny Rogers was going one way; Waylon Jennings was going another," adds Charlie Daniels. "They were broadening the perimeters. Broadening the music out was a healthy thing."

The diversity was certainly an economic boon to the industry. The success in the 1960s of the Nashville Sound had brought country music's annual worth to approximately $100 million by 1970. In 1970–85 that figure would more than triple.

Country music did that by shedding its rural, haybales-and-wagon-wheels image and redefining itself as the music of Middle America. The style has always been a mirror to the lives of everyday people. When America became suburban, so did country music. Country stopped reflecting the fields and farms and marketed itself as the sound of the shopping mall and interstate highway instead.

Symbolizing country's aspirations, *The Grand Ole Opry* moved "uptown." The decaying Ryman Auditorium, its home since 1943, was located in what was then a seedy area of downtown Nashville. The show's executives decided that the *Opry* needed a new, first-class hall. They surrounded it with a $28 million musical theme park called "Opryland" that opened in suburban Nashville in 1972. Opryland's 110 landscaped acres included the new Opry House (opened in 1974), a convention hotel (1977), cable TV production facilities (1983), a $12 million showboat (1985), gardens, country-star museums, amusement rides, and stages featuring attractive, clean-cut youngsters in theatrical revues.

More than a million people went through Opryland USA's turnstiles during its first season. In 1990 the park welcomed its forty-millionth visitor. Opryland remained a highly successful enterprise until 1998, when its owners began remodeling it to become Opry Mills, a shopping attraction.

Few performers illustrate country's uptown aspirations better than Charley Pride. This son of a Mississippi sharecropper became a member of an exclusive Dallas country club thanks to country's new clout and prestige. Pride's rise is also a reflection of how much mainstream America changed during the era. Not only did he perform "low-class" hillbilly music; he was also African American. Either fact

217

LEFT: *During the uptown "countrypolitan" era, Charley Pride became the "Jackie Robinson of country music."*

would have easily barred him from a country club a generation earlier.

Born in 1938, Pride was raised listening to *Grand Ole Opry* broadcasts from Nashville. He bought his first guitar at age fourteen and began imitating his hillbilly music idols. At age sixteen he began playing baseball in the Negro American League. He spent ten years pursuing athletic stardom.

"I would go on stage in different towns," he recalls of his pitching days. "Sometimes we'd play baseball and I'd go up and sing a few songs. Peo-

ple would say, 'Pretty good. You ought to think about going into music.' I felt I could still make it in baseball." He was dropped by a minor league team in Montana. He was rejected by Gene Autry's California Angels. But his baseball dream still burned.

Back in Montana, he sang for Red Foley and Red Sovine backstage at a concert. Sovine, in particular, was gracious to the aspiring country singer. He invited him to Nashville and gave him a contact to look up.

Instead, Pride went to the New York

Mets' Florida spring-training camp in 1963. Manager Casey Stengel flatly refused to let him try out.

"My heart just sank," says Pride. "I remember saying, 'One of these days you're going to hear about me,' or something like that. I got all my bats and all the rest of my stuff and I took off. And that's when I stopped by Nashville. From the time I had gone down to the Mets and came through Nashville, my whole life changed. It sure did."

Sovine had given him the address of Cedarwood Publishing, so when Pride got off the bus in Nashville, that's where he went. Owners Jim Denny and Webb Pierce introduced him to manager Jack Johnson. He auditioned. Johnson made a tape, and then drove him back to the bus station. Johnson took the tape to producer Jack Clement, who recorded Pride singing "Snakes Crawl at Night" in 1965.

Songwriter Mel Tillis was passing by the studio and was astonished at what he heard. He went into a nearby office and stuttered, "T-T-T-There's a c-c-c-colored guy in there s-s-s-singing my song and he s-s-s-sounds just like Stonewall Jackson!" As reported in the singer's 1994 autobiography *Pride*, Clement took the tape to Chet Atkins, who signed the unusual discovery to RCA.

Atkins recalls, "We had about an hour discussion: 'Should we let the people know that he's black?' We finally decided to just put it out and if they like it and play it, fine. They can find out for themselves."

"Snakes Crawl at Night" appeared on RCA in early 1966. Pride was booked for a Detroit concert starring Merle Haggard and Buck Owens.

"We were in Detroit at Cobo Hall," recalls DJ Ralph Emery. "I could tell this crowd was wired. They were fired up to hear country music."

Pride remembers, "Ralph said, 'And now from RCA, Charley Pride!' Big applause. I came out of those shadows into those lights and it was like turning the volume down. There was silence."

"Pride sang his songs," Emery continues. "When he went off, they all loved him."

ABOVE: *Red Sovine, master of sentimental country recitation.*
RIGHT: *Jerry Reed's guitar prowess made him a favorite of both Elvis Presley and Chet Atkins. Reed also made his mark as a songwriter, singer, and movie star.*

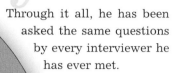

Faron Young took Charley Pride on the road. At the end of 1966 Pride scored his first top-ten hit with Jack Clement's song "Just Between You and Me." He was booked as a newcomer to round out a Texas tour with Willie Nelson, Jeannie Seely, and Stonewall Jackson in 1967.

"I made out the program and put myself down following Charley Pride," Nelson recollects. "The first night, I was halfway through my show and they were still screaming for Charley. So I knew he had something. He got out there and said either like me or don't. And they loved him."

Rex Allen showcased Charley Pride at the Arizona State Fair. Bill Anderson put him on his TV show. "Does My Ring Hurt Your Finger," "The Easy Part's Over," and a remake of Hank Williams's "Kaw-Liga" were among Pride's top-ten hits in 1967–68.

When "All I Have To Offer You Is Me" became his first No. 1 hit in 1969, he moved to a tony suburb in North Dallas. Twenty-eight more No. 1 hits in 1969–83 bought him a Texas bank, office buildings in Dallas and Nashville, a 248-acre ranch in North Texas, and the Mississippi land where his father was a sharecropper.

Charley Pride's classics of the 1970s include "Is Anybody Goin' to San Antone" (1970), "Kiss an Angel Good Morning" (1971), and "We Could" (1974), and he remained a fixture on the country charts until 1989. He joined the cast of *The Grand Ole Opry* in 1993.

Through it all, he has been asked the same questions by every interviewer he has ever met.

"I had to answer all those and still do. You know, 'How come you look like us and sound like them?' 'How come you look like them and sound like us?' Some people would say, 'We're glad to have you in our music.' I said, 'But it's my music, too.'"

Indeed it is. The banjo originated in Africa. Black string bands were common in the nineteenth-century South. Taylor's Kentucky Boys (1927) was led by black fiddler Jim Booker. The Dallas String Band, Tennessee Nighthawks, Memphis Jug Band, and Mississippi Sheiks (1930's "Sitting On Top of the World") were all African American ensembles. The black "Harmonica Wizard" Deford Bailey starred on the *Opry* in 1926–40. Jimmie Davis's accompanist in the 1930s was black guitarist Oscar Woods. Herb Jeffries was a black singing cowboy in the movies.

And although Pride was the only one who became a superstar, he was part of a generation of black country stylists in the post-civil-rights era. Linda Martel became the first black female to guest on the *Opry*. Otis Williams formed The Midnight Cowboys as modern country's first black band. Ruby Falls placed nine singles on the charts in 1975–79. O.B. McClinton billed himself as "The Chocolate Cowboy" and had fifteen chart records in 1972–87. Big Al Downing was in Wanda Jackson's rockabilly band in the 1960s, and then placed several singles in the top twenty in 1978–80.

ABOVE: *Roy Clark is best known as a humorist on TV's* Hee Haw, *but he is also notable as a top-notch instrumentalist.*

Stoney Edwards's fifteen chart records of the 1970s and 1980s were honky-tonk masterpieces. The Pointer Sisters won a 1974 Grammy for their country tune "Fairytale." Ray Charles placed thirteen singles on the country hit parade in the 1980s. Dobie Gray ("That's One to Grow On"), Anita Pointer ("Too Many Times," with Earl Thomas Conley), Aaron Neville ("I Fall to Pieces," with Trisha Yearwood), and Cleve Francis ("Love Light") have all achieved prominence since then.

Charley Pride's booster Red Sovine (Woodrow Wilson Sovine, 1918–1980) enjoyed the biggest hit of his career during the countrypolitan era. The

also led to a series of wildly successful Burt Reynolds movies.

Jerry Reed's 1977 smash "East Bound and Down" was from Burt's box-office smash *Smokey and the Bandit.* Born in Atlanta in 1937, Jerry Reed Hubbard "paid his dues" for years before achieving countrypolitan stardom. He was performing in his native Georgia by his early teens and was signed to Capitol Records at age seventeen. No hits ensued.

Atlanta music mogul Bill Lowery encouraged him to write songs. In 1962 Brenda Lee made Reed's "That's All You Gotta Do" a pop hit and he moved to Nashville. Porter Wagoner's "Misery

record was "Teddy Bear" (1976), a result of the craze for citizen-band (CB) radios. A master of the sentimental recitation and a specialist in trucker material, Sovine had already had success with "Giddyup Go" (1965) and "Phantom 309" (1967). But the CB phenomenon made him more famous than ever before. Sovine died just four years after his "Teddy Bear" comeback when he had a heart attack while driving his car in Nashville. His son Roger became the head of the Nashville office of BMI.

"Convoy" by C.W. McCall (1975), "White Knight" by Cledus Maggard (1976), and "The Bull and the Beaver" by Merle Haggard and Leona Williams (1978) were a few of the many other hit records spawned by the CB craze. It

Loves Company" (1962), Johnny Cash's "A Thing Called Love" (1972), and Elvis Presley's "Guitar Man" and "U.S. Male" (both 1968) are among his other songwriting successes. He played guitar on the Presley records and also found work as a session musician for Bobby Bare and others.

RCA's Chet Atkins was particularly fond of Reed's syncopated, complex guitar picking. He brought him to the label in 1964, but Reed didn't take off as a record maker until he crafted a series of discs that showcased his instrumental prowess as well as his gruff, manic southern vocal delivery. "Amos Moses" (1970) and "When You're Hot, You're Hot" (1971) proved to be sizable pop as well as country hits.

Atkins and Reed won a Grammy

221

ABOVE: *From left are albums representing the works of Texas tunesmiths Guy Clark, Rodney Crowell, and Larry Gatlin.*

Freddie Hart

for their dazzling guitar work on the 1970 LP *Me and Jerry*. But it was Reed's wisecracking antics on Glen Campbell's network TV show that brought him to the silver screen. Reynolds cast him in 1974's *W.W. and The Dixie Dance Kings*, which led to a string of similar wild-man roles. Reed rebounded on the charts with "She Got the Goldmine (I Got the Shaft)" and "The Bird" in 1982. He returned to the silver screen in the 1999 comedy hit *The Waterboy*. To this day, electric guitarists strive to emulate Reed's "The Claw," and his highly individualistic albums of the 1970s are still prized by collectors.

Like Reed, instrumental wizard Roy Clark parlayed his skills as a humorist and singer into a multimedia career. Born in Virginia in 1933, he honed his guitar and banjo skills on regional TV in the early 1950s. In 1960 he was recruited by Wanda Jackson for her band The Partytimers and as her opening act. Capitol Records signed him as a solo performer in 1962 and issued *The Lightning Fingers of Roy Clark* as his LP debut.

Steady chart success didn't come until he was signed by Dot Records. "Yesterday When I Was Young" (1969), "I Never Picked Cotton" (1970), "Come Live With Me" (1973), "Honeymoon Feelin'" (1974), and "If I Had To Do It All Over Again" (1976) made him a countrypolitan radio favorite. Manager Jim Halsey promoted Clark as an all-around entertainer. Thus, Clark was one of the first country musicians to perform with symphony orchestras. He led the first country troupe to tour the Soviet Union. He was

the first country star to guest-host on *The Tonight Show*.

And of course there was TV's *Hee Haw*, on which Roy Clark hosted, sang, and did comedy skits for twenty-five years, 1969–1994. He was one of the first big stars to shift his base of operations to a theater in Branson, Missouri (1983). Clark became an *Opry* cast member in 1987 and continues to dazzle audiences with his fleet fingers, genial jokes, and tenor vocals.

The stardom attained by Reed and Clark as a result of their instrumental skills illustrated country's ongoing commitment to craftsmanship. So did the ascents of a number of superb songwriters who became top recording artists in that era.

Clark's Dot Records label-mate was Donna Fargo (Yvonne Vaughn, born 1940). Raised in the mountains of North Carolina, Fargo's first profession was teaching English in the suburbs of Los Angeles. Former rock 'n' roll performer Stan Silver taught her to play guitar, produced her records, became her manager, and married her.

In 1971 Dot Records picked up her self-composed "Happiest Girl in the Whole U.S.A." for national distribution. By the end of the following year the tune had cleaned up at every awards show in sight and made her an overnight star. "Funny Face" was her second straight million seller. Fargo compositions such as "Superman," "You Were Always There," and "I've Loved You All the Way" led to $6 million in record sales in the 1970s.

She was diagnosed with multiple sclerosis in 1978. Brushing off self-

TOP: *Freddie Hart became a star in the 1970s with LPs like this.*
ABOVE: *Earl Thomas Conley on the cover of* Country Song Roundup. *He had five No. 1 hits on one LP.*
RIGHT: *Anne Murray is the subject of a Nova Scotia museum.*

Anne Murray

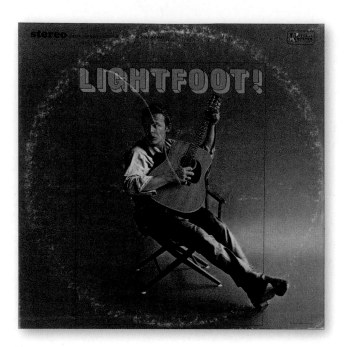

pity over the incurable, degenerative nerve disease, she continued to work at her craft. She kept the disease at bay throughout the '80s and marketed a series of inspirational greeting cards in the '90s.

"Don't pity me," she says. "In dealing with any kind of illness or crisis, you try to learn from it. I think that's what our obligation is, to have a deeper awareness. I've always tried to take anything negative and turn it around into something positive. The songwriter has a great responsibility because people are influenced so much by music."

Several of the most poetic of the singer-songwriters of the era were Texans. Guy Clark, born in 1941, was their spiritual leader. He was the first to arrive, unpacking in Nashville in 1971. Clark's country-folk albums for the RCA, Warner Bros., Asylum, and Sugar Hill labels during the next twenty-five years introduced such finely crafted songs as "Desperados Waiting For a Train," "Texas 1947," "Heartbroke," and "L.A. Freeway."

Such Texans as Townes Van Zandt ("If I Needed You"), Steve Earle ("Guitar Town"), and K.T. Oslin ("80s Ladies") eventually followed his lead to Music

City. Clark's closest collaborator was Houston native Rodney Crowell, who arrived in Nashville in 1972. Born in 1950, Crowell was involved in music from childhood. He played drums in his father's honky-tonk band, then graduated to guitar.

He was a member of Emmylou Harris's band in 1975–77 and contributed a number of songs to her albums of that period. He began recording his own LPs in 1977, but initially they served mainly as song suppliers to others. Waylon Jennings ("I Ain't Living Long Like This"), Crystal Gayle ("Til I Gain Control Again"), The Oak Ridge Boys ("Leaving Louisiana in the Broad Daylight"), and Bob Seger ("Shame on the Moon") all had hits with Crowell's tunes.

Crowell finally became a hit maker himself after signing with Columbia Records. Seven straight top-ten hits followed in 1988–90. "After All This Time" won the Grammy Award as Country Song of the Year in 1989. Following his 1992 divorce from singer-songwriter Rosanne Cash, Crowell reemphasized his career as a record producer. And once again, his albums provided hits for others, notably Alan Jackson ("Song for the Life") and Tim McGraw ("Please Remember Me").

TOP: *This was one of the first U.S. albums by Canadian troubadour Gordon Lightfoot.*
ABOVE: *Alabama's Jeanne Pruett kept the traditional country sound alive during the countrypolitan era.*

Williams

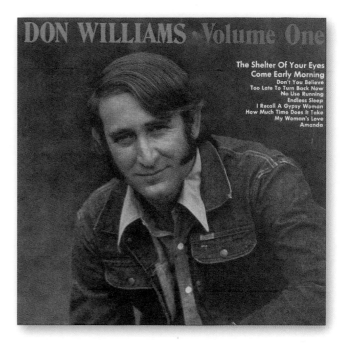

Although a native Texan, Larry Gatlin wasn't part of the hippie Clark/Crowell circle. His early musical training was in his family's gospel quartet with sister LaDonna and brothers Rudy and Steve. Born in 1948, Gatlin was onstage at age six and on Abilene TV before he reached his teens. After college, Gatlin joined the gospel group The Imperials. The act met Dottie West while both were entertaining in Las Vegas in 1972. Gatlin sent the star a tape of his songs. She sent him a plane ticket to Nashville.

Larry Gatlin's hearty tenor and his two brothers' flawless harmonies, combined with his undeniable songwriting talent, led to a stream of countrypolitan hits that included "Broken Lady" and "All the Gold in California" in 1975–79. Success continued in the 1980s with hits like "Houston" and "She Used to Be Somebody's Baby."

The singer-songwriter admitted that he had a cocaine and alcohol problem in 1984 and sought treatment. In 1992 Gatlin announced that the brothers were quitting the road. Following their "Adios Tour" and CD, Larry Gatlin took the lead in Broadway's *The Will Rogers Follies* in 1993.

Singer-songwriter Freddie Hart (Frederick Segrest, born 1926) walked the roughest road to Music City. One of fifteen siblings, he ran away from home in Alabama when he was seven. His parents enlisted their rebellious son in a Civilian Conservation Corps work crew during the Depression. He faked his age and joined the marines in 1942. Hart saw action in Guam, Iwo Jima, and Okinawa during World War II. Still in his teens and back in civilian life, he worked as a cotton picker, sawmill worker, pipeline layer, and dishwasher.

Hart first came to Nashville in 1949 and found work carrying road gear for Hank Williams. In 1953–56 Hart was a regular on the *Town Hall Party* country TV show in California. His song "Loose Talk" was recorded by Carl Smith (1955), and then by Buck Owens & Rose Maddox (1961). Porter Wagoner had a hit with Hart's "Skid Row Joe" in 1966. But Hart's own recordings in the 1950s and 1960s went nowhere. He finally broke through with

"Easy Loving" in 1971. During the next six years Freddie Hart sang fifteen top-ten hits.

Like most of the other writer-artists of the era, Jeanne Pruett initially penned songs for others. Born in Alabama in 1937, she moved to Nashville in 1956. Marty Robbins had a hit with her song "Love Me" in 1972. Her own hits of 1971–80 included the self-composed "Back to Back," "A Poor Man's Woman," and "Hold to My Unchanging Love." She rewrote steelworker John Volinkaty's "Satin Sheets," but did not take a composer credit. In 1972 it became the *Opry* star's signature song.

Ohio-bred Earl Thomas Conley (born 1941) initially provided his songs to Conway Twitty ("This Time I've Hurt Her More Than She Loves Me"), Mel Street ("Smokey Mountain Memories"), and others. A Nashvillian since 1973 and a record maker since 1975, Conley didn't graduate to recording stardom until 1980. During the next ten years he had eighteen No. 1 records on the *Billboard* charts, including his compositions "Fire and Smoke," "Don't Make It Easy for Me," and "Angel in Disguise."

Folk artist Gordon Lightfoot (born 1938) tasted success as a songwriter for Nashville's artists before he, too, was embraced as a record maker by the expansive climate

225

ABOVE: *Don Williams hasn't always worn his trademark rumpled cowboy hat. The Texan let his hair and sideburns show on the cover of his debut LP in 1973. Bobby Bare wrote its liner notes.*

Olivia Newton-John

of the countrypolitan era. The handsome Canadian was the source of "Ribbon of Darkness," a hit for both Marty Robbins and Connie Smith. In 1966 his "Early Morning Rain" was sung by George Hamilton IV and "For Lovin' Me" was on the charts for Waylon Jennings. So when Lightfoot had his own pop hits "Sundown," "Carefree Highway," and "Wreck of the Edmund Fitzgerald" in 1974–77, they were also played on country radio.

His fellow Canadian Anne Murray was somewhat surprised to find herself labeled a "country" artist. Born in Nova Scotia in 1945, the folksinging Murray was a physical education instructor who became a cast member of Canada's hootenanny TV series *Sing Along Jubilee* in 1966. Her lustrous alto led to a recording contract in 1968, and her impeccable song taste did the rest. "Snowbird" made her a star in 1970.

"'Snowbird' was a bigger pop hit than it was a country hit," Murray recalls. "But it was definitely both. It was a crossover hit. I had no sense of who I was or what I was. So I got the label of being 'country' very early."

Her pop-country style was perfect for the times. "Danny's Song," "You Needed Me," "Love Song," and remakes of George Jones's "He Thinks I Still Care" and The Everly Brothers' "Walk Right Back" became major country hits in 1972–79; and most fared equally well on the pop hit parade. In 1980 she sang the love theme for the movie *Urban Cowboy*, "Could I Have This Dance," and thereafter her records were played almost exclusively by country stations.

"A Little Good News," "Blessed Are the Believers," and others carried her disc stardom through the early 1980s. And even when she adopted an electronic pop sound for "Time Don't

Run out on Me" and "Now and Forever," country continued to embrace her. To date she has sold more than twenty million records and earned four Grammy Awards.

Texan Don Williams (born 1939) earned his folk credentials as a member of The Pozo Seco Singers. But when the act disbanded, Williams returned to Texas to work in his father-in-law's furniture store.

Publisher-producer Jack Clement liked the warm-coffee texture of Williams's baritone as well as his songwriting skills. He convinced him to move to Nashville in 1973. Issued on Clement's tiny JMI Records label, *Don Williams Vol. 1* supplied "Amanda" as a hit for Waylon Jennings. But it also contained Williams's song "The Shelter of Your Eyes" and Bob McDill's "Come Early Morning," both of which became top-twenty hits for the singer.

Don Williams Vol. II, also on JMI, contained "We Should Be Together," which became a top-ten hit in 1974. At this point, Williams was signed by Dot Records. The sound remained the same, a gentle, loping, sing-along style with catchy choruses and softly crooned verses. Williams's soothing delivery brought him more than fifty major country hits.

In 1974, "I Wouldn't Want to Live If You Didn't Love Me" became the first Don Williams No. 1 hit. "Tulsa Time" hit the top of the country charts in 1978 and was then turned into a pop hit by Eric Clapton. McDill's literate "Good Ole Boys Like Me" (1980) is generally regarded as Don Williams's masterpiece single. Year after year, song after song, Williams was a model of musical consistency.

He is a model of consistency in his personal life as well. A devoted hus-

LEFT: *Olivia Newton-John, promoted as a country star in the 1970s, recorded her "comeback" CD in Nashville in 1998.*
ABOVE: *John Denver showed his love of the outdoors in "Take Me Home Country Roads" and "Rocky Mountain High."*

band and father, Williams has a spotless reputation of moral uprightness and soft-spoken decency. He has worn the same rumpled cowboy hat onstage and in photos for twenty-five years.

John Denver (Henry John Deutschendorf Jr., 1943–1997) was another folkie who fared extremely well in the countrypolitan years. This son of an air force officer dropped out of college in Texas to join the folk scene in California. During stints in the groups The Back Porch Majority and The Chad Mitchell Trio he began to write songs. His "Leaving on a Jet Plane" was recorded by the country duo The Kendalls in 1970.

Denver embarked on his solo career in 1969, but his first three albums were not successful. In 1971 his cowritten "Take Me Home Country Roads" became a Gold Record and made him a pop star. Denver bought a home in the Colorado Rockies and issued "Sunshine on My Shoulders" as a second blockbuster in 1974.

In 1974–75 "Annie's Song," "Back Home Again," "Thank God I'm a Country Boy," and other John Denver singles all became major hits on both country and pop radio. Olivia Newton-John provided ethereal backing vocals on 1976's "Fly Away." Emmylou Harris was his duet partner on 1983's "Wild Montana Skies."

Denver's sunny tenor voice, wholesome image, and cheerful disposition made him a popular media figure. He starred in a *Rocky Mountain Christmas* TV special that was viewed by thirty million fans, hosted the 1979

Grammy Awards, and starred with George Burns in the 1977 movie comedy *Oh God*. He also worked on behalf of various environmental and humanitarian causes. Denver was just fifty-three when the plane he was piloting crashed into Monterey Bay in California in 1997.

His harmony singer on "Fly Away" was accepted on country radio around the same time. Olivia Newton-John initially recorded as a folkie. British-born (1948) and raised in Australia, Newton-John knew virtually nothing about country music when her singles were promoted to the genre's radio stations in 1973–76.

"My producers said they were releasing it 'country,' and I didn't even know what they were talking about," she confessed. Nonetheless, "Let Me Be There," "I Honestly Love You," "Have You Never Been Mellow," "Please Mr. Please," and other singles became top-ten hits.

She costarred with John Travolta in the 1978 teen movie musical *Grease*. Her love ballad from it, "Hopelessly Devoted to You," charted both pop and country, but the two stars' rocking duet "You're the One That I Want" was programmed only by pop stations. Newton-John then moved full-time to pop with the harder-rocking "Physical" and "Xanadu." She survived breast cancer in 1992–93, was divorced in 1995, and returned to Nashville to record the CD *Back With a Heart* in 1998.

The fact that she and John Denver were embraced by country radio was a matter of considerable controversy in Nashville. When

ABOVE: *From the top are Charlie Rich, Bobby Goldsboro, and Mac Davis, all pictured on the albums that defined their country-pop success.*

Dan Seals

Newton-John won the Country Music Association's Female Vocalist of the Year Award in 1974, the town's traditional, established country performers were furious. When Denver was named the Country Entertainer of the Year in 1975, presenter Charlie Rich burned the envelope on camera. A number of stars formed an alternative organization to the CMA that they called the Association of Country Entertainers (ACE). George Jones and Tammy Wynette hosted the ACE's organizational meeting at their house after the CMA Awards show in 1974.

ACE's activists included Jim Ed Brown, Bill Anderson, Hank Snow, Barbara Mandrell, Porter Wagoner, Grandpa Jones, Jimmy Dickens, Johnny Paycheck, Jean Shepard, and Justin Tubb. For them, Denver and Newton-John illustrated how far country had drifted from its heritage. The stated purpose of ACE was "to preserve the identity of country music as a separate and distinct form of entertainment."

ACE, which expired in 1981, could have looked no further than its own membership ranks to find performers who threatened "the identity of country music." Barbara Mandrell's pop-flavored records of the period were less "country" than John Denver's. Envelope burner Charlie Rich was performing orchestrated ballads, and had come to country after his "Lonely Weekends" (1960) and "Mohair Sam" (1965) pop career faded.

At heart a jazz pianist, Arkansas native Charlie Rich (1932–1995) had tried everything from the bluesy "Who Will the Next Fool Be" to the rocking "Big Boss Man" during his largely fruitless career in pop. Producer Billy Sherrill signed him to Epic Records in 1967, but the team came up empty-handed for the next five years.

In 1972–73 Rich found country success with "I Take It on Home" and "Behind Closed Doors." These ballads were followed by the lushly arranged "The Most Beautiful Girl," which topped both pop and country playlists. Continuing to mine an easy-listening vein were "A Very Special Love Song," "Rollin' With the Flow,"

and his many other hits of 1974–77. Epic dubbed the handsome, white-haired performer "The Silver Fox."

But Rich was a troubled man with a longtime alcohol problem. He disappeared from the country charts in 1982 and lived in Memphis in semi-retirement for nearly a decade before staging an impressive comeback with *Pictures and Paintings*. Containing blues, country, jazz, and pop elements, this was a CD that finally showcased Rich's diversity. Sadly, he died of a blood clot before recording a follow-up.

229

TOP: *Dan Seals, who experienced success on both pop and country charts, is pictured on the jacket of his 1984 LP.*
ABOVE: *Theatergoers in Manhattan read of Gary Morris's country background in their* Les Miserables *playbills in 1988.*

T. G. S

Lynn Anderson (1970's "Rose Garden"), Glen Campbell (1975's "Rhinestone Cowboy"), and Crystal Gayle (1977's "Don't It Make My Brown Eyes Blue") also crafted singles that were as much "pop" as "country." Debby Boone's ballad "You Light Up My Life" was imported to the country charts from the pop hit parade in 1977. "Angel of the Morning," "Queen of Hearts," "The Sweetest Thing," and Break It to Me Gently"—Juice Newton's singles of 1981–82—were shared by both playlists as well.

The lines between the two musical fields were also blurred when southern pop performers reinvented themselves as country stars. Bobby Goldsboro, a Floridian (born 1941), was the prototype. His sentimental "Honey" (1968) and "Watching Scotty Grow" (1971) were equally big in country and pop. So when the pop hits dried up, Goldsboro donned a cowboy hat and rebounded in country with "Goodbye Marie" in 1980.

Mac Davis, a West Texan (born 1942), enjoyed big pop hits like "Baby Don't Get Hooked On Me" and "Stop and Smell the Roses" in 1972–74. These made the lower reaches of the country charts. After starring in his own TV variety series in 1974–76 and acting in films such as 1979's *North Dallas Forty*, Davis emerged with five top-ten country hits in 1980–81: "It's Hard to Be Humble," "Let's Keep It That Way," "Texas in My Rearview

Mirror," "Hooked on Music," and "You're My Bestest Friend."

As a songwriter, Davis is also responsible for "Something's Burning" (Kenny Rogers & The First Edition), "Watching Scotty Grow" (Bobby Goldsboro), and Elvis Presley's "In the Ghetto" (also a hit for Dolly Parton).

Texas native Dan Seals (born 1948) was "England Dan" in the 1970s pop duo England Dan & John Ford Coley. After "I'd Really Love to See You Tonight" and the rest of the act's 1976–80 hits ended, Seals became a solo country star with a dozen No. 1 hits, including "Bop," "Everything That Glitters," and "Addicted."

Louisiana's Tony Joe White (born 1943) had big pop hits with "Polk Salad Annie" (1969) and "Rainy Night in Georgia" (1970) before he, too, attempted a countrypolitan career. Although he was arguably the most "southern" of these figures, White's country airplay in 1980–84 was minimal. However, he remains a strong songwriting presence in Music City.

"The transition from pop into country for us was no problem," says David Bellamy of the Florida duo The Bellamy Brothers. "It was more of a problem for the people around us, our management, record companies. Everyone told us, 'Those cowboy songs are dead. You don't want to do country.' But we felt we were always country. Conway Twitty took us out on the road with him and had a little faith in us."

TOP: *After singing "Raindrops Keep Falling on My Head," B.J. Thomas had success in the gospel and country fields.*
ABOVE: *The Bellamy Brothers are Howard, left, and David. They crafted records for country's dance clubs in the '90s.*

Lee

eppard

At the time, 1979, The Bellamy Brothers were known mainly as the performers of the pop smash "Let Your Love Flow" (1976). While on the road with Twitty they began singing a ditty called "If I Said You Have a Beautiful Body Would You Hold It Against Me." Said Twitty, "Boys, that's gonna be a hit." It was the first of twenty-five top-ten smashes for the Bellamys in 1979–90. After that they designed a number of catchy, rhythmic records aimed at country dance clubs.

One of the most agile vocalists in any field of music, Oklahoma native B.J. Thomas (born 1942) was a ten-year veteran of the pop charts before he found countrypolitan success. Ironically, his first pop hit was a version of Hank Williams's "I'm So Lonesome I Could Cry" (1966) that never made the country charts.

Thomas rocked out on his 1968 hits "The Eyes of a New York Woman" and "Hooked on a Feeling," and then sang the Oscar-winning theme for *Butch Cassidy and the Sundance Kid*, "Raindrops Keep Falling on My Head" (1969). But his stardom coincided with a titanic level of drug abuse. After a dramatic "born-again" conversion, he became a pioneer in the emerging contemporary-Christian field of the 1970s.

He hated the hypocrisy of the gospel business, so he turned to country music in 1975 with the gigantic hit "(Hey Won't You Play) Another Somebody Done Somebody Wrong Song." In 1983–84 he found renewed country success with "New Looks from an Old Lover," "Two Car Garage," and other singles. During his country tenure he also introduced songs that became classics for others, notably "The Wind beneath My

Wings" (Gary Morris, Bette Midler), "I Just Can't Help Believing" (Elvis Presley), and "Here You Come Again" (Dolly Parton).

B.J. Thomas reentered the pop arena as the 1980s waned. He sang the theme to TV's hit series *Growing Pains*, "As Long as We've Got Each Other," and a duet version with Dusty Springfield became an adult-contemporary hit in 1989.

"I don't think I'm a great singer," says the humble performer. "But if you want to hear somebody who believes what they're singing, then I'm one of those guys. That probably is my gift."

Nashville was creating country stars who could have slipped between genres just as easily. California-bred former gospel singer Dave Rowland (born 1942) formed a glitzy act with two women (personnel shifted frequently) whom he billed as "Sugar." Dave & Sugar initially worked as Charley Pride's backup singers and then recorded for his label, RCA. The trio's pop-country sound resulted in ten consecutive top-ten hits in 1976–79.

A light, pop-country approach was also favored by T.G. Sheppard (Bill Browder, born 1942). He succeeded by recording highly commercial radio tunes and using his skills as a promoter. His thirty top-ten hits of 1974–87 include "Devil in the Bottle," "Last Cheater's Waltz," and "Finally." The jaunty "I Loved 'Em Every One" crossed over to the pop top forty in 1981.

Former Las Vegas lounge singer Lee Greenwood made a name for himself in Republican Party circles as the singer of the 1984 flag-waving anthem "God Bless the U.S.A." Born in California in 1942, Green-

231

Greenwood

TOP: *T.G. Sheppard's initials supposedly stand for "The Good."*
CENTER: *For many years the Statler Brothers staged a big festival on the Fourth of July, as reflected in their logo.*
ABOVE: *Lee Greenwood's hit was central to his autobiography.*

Kenny Rog

wood had a 1981–92 hit streak that also included "Dixie Road" and "It Turns Me Inside Out." His booming, patriotic ballad was heavily used in the presidential campaigns of Ronald Reagan and George Bush.

Gary Morris, on the other hand, owes his career to his involvement with Democrat Jimmy Carter. Morris is a Texan with a tenor voice so powerful that he could have sung opera. And he did, in fact, translate his country stardom into operatic roles in *Les Misérables* (1988) and *La Bohème* (1984) on Broadway. Born in 1948, the burly college football star entertained on the campaign trail with Carter in 1976. He was discovered by Nashville's talent scouts after performing at the presidential inaugural festivities in Washington. Morris signed with Warner Bros. Records and unleashed a string of big-voiced hits that included 1983's "The Love She Found in Me" and "The Wind beneath My Wings."

"I think 'The Wind beneath My Wings' has been recorded now maybe three hundred times," says the singer. "I knew it was a wonderful song with a great message. But it was an incredible battle for Warner Bros. Records to get the record played on country radio. Some of my friends said, 'Are you trying to kill your career? You'll never have any success if they hear this.' Because it wasn't exciting.

It was just a very simple reading of a very wonderful piece of material."

"A lot of people started thinking that we made records on purpose to cross over to the pop charts, which was completely not true," said Eddie Rabbitt (1941–1998). "I just made the music I made. Back then a 'crossover record' was when one of my country records would start to get played on a rock 'n' roll radio station. I was lucky that way with 'Drivin' My Life Away' and 'I Love a Rainy Night.' That's all."

One of the most distinctive of all the countrypolitan acts, Rabbitt arrived in Music City from New Jersey in 1968. He wrote the prophetic "Working My Way up from the Bottom" his first night in town, and it was recorded by Roy Drusky. Elvis Presley's recording of Rabbitt's "Kentucky Rain" and Ronnie Milsap's recording of his "Pure Love" also established him as a songwriter to be reckoned with.

That he was also a performer of consequence became evident after Rabbitt got his recording contract in 1974. His echoey, rockabilly-influenced productions, multilayered vocal harmonies, feath-

TOP: *Eddie Rabbitt's 1981 LP contained many hits.*
CENTER: *The tour book from an Oak Ridge Boys concert stop.*
ABOVE: *Vern Gosdin is billed as "The Voice."*
RIGHT: *Kenny Rogers on the sheet music of his love ballad.*

Love The World Away

By BOB MORRISON and JOHNNY WILSON

Recorded by KENNY ROGERS on UNITED ARTISTS Records

From The Original Motion Picture Soundtrack
"URBAN COWBOY"
Released on Elektra/Asylum Records

$1.95

SOUTHERN NIGHTS MUSIC
Nashville, Tennessee

Distributed by

Mel Street

ery tenor voice, and impossibly catchy tunes made his singles instantly recognizable. No one, then or now, sounded like Eddie Rabbitt.

Rabbitt had thirty-two consecutive top-ten hits in 1976–88. He died of lung cancer in early 1998 and was posthumously inducted into the Nashville Songwriters Hall of Fame later that year.

The Oak Ridge Boys enjoyed some pop fame, too. In 1981–82 the quartet's peppy, catchy "Elvira" and "Bobbie Sue" bubbled up the charts and became million sellers. The act's roots go back to 1945 and the Tennessee city of Oak Ridge, the home of the atom bomb. Cashing in on that notoriety, "The Oak Ridge Quartet" began singing on the *Opry* in 1946. Dozens of members came and went during the next two decades.

In 1973 the group's personnel stabilized with lead singer Duane Allen, tenor Joe Bonsall, baritone William Lee Golden, and bass Richard Sterban. Four years later the Oaks switched from gospel to country with "Y'All Come Back Saloon." They developed a flashy, high-energy stage show with four distinct performing images, including Golden's striking "mountain-man" look. Between 1977 and 1986 the act had twenty-five top-ten country hits.

Golden was ousted from the act in 1987. Oaks band member Steve Sanders replaced him and sang on nine top-ten hits in 1987–91. Golden returned in 1996.

Sanders died of a self-inflicted gunshot two years later.

The Oaks' rivals were The Statler Brothers. Formed as the gospel quartet The Kingsmen in Virginia in 1961, the act took its "Statler" name from a box of tissues in a hotel room. The Statler Brothers joined the Johnny Cash road show in 1964. A year later they created a pop and country smash with the wry novelty "Flowers on the Wall." But members Harold Reid (bass), Don Reid (lead), Phil Balsley (baritone), and Lew DeWitt (tenor) had trouble having consistent hits until they joined Mercury Records in 1970. Unlike the Oaks, the Statlers never tried to seem "modern." Always wearing matching suits, the four specialized in straight-ahead country lyrics like "I'll Go to My Grave Loving You" (1975) and "You'll Be Back (Every Night in My Dreams)" (1982). Another trademark was unabashed nostalgia for "the good old days," exemplified by "Do You Remember These" and "Class of '57."

DeWitt left the group for health reasons in 1981 and was replaced by tenor Jimmy Fortune. He turned out to be a prolific writer of the group's hits of the '80s. The Statler Brothers aimed their TNN cable TV variety series of the '90s at older viewers and scored a big rating success.

ABOVE: *West Virginia's Mel Street died too young to take his place alongside the great honky-tonk vocalists of his era.*
RIGHT: *Gary Stewart was a honky-tonk "wild child" with the songs on this 1975 LP, the biggest of his career.*

By far the biggest star of all the countrypolitan performers was Kenny Rogers. Indeed, for a time in the late 1970s and early 1980s, he was arguably the biggest star in music, period.

"I've always felt that I was a country singer who was blessed with a lot of other musical influences," says Rogers. Born in 1938 in Houston, he began his career as a pop singer in a 1956 band called The Scholars. He played bass in the jazz group The Bobby Doyle Trio. He joined The New Christy Minstrels during the folk-revival era. Sprouting long hair and donning mod clothes, he next led The First Edition.

The group scored big pop hits with the "psychedelic" "Just Dropped In" in 1968 and with Mel Tillis's crippled-veteran saga "Ruby Don't Take Your Love to Town" in 1969. Kenny Rogers & The First Edition landed their own syndicated TV series in 1971, but the act broke up four years later. In 1976, a nearly broke Kenny Rogers limped into Nashville in search of a song that might jump-start a solo career in country music.

"Every now and then you stumble into a song that you just can't figure out why no one else had found it, because it's so obvious to you," he reminisces. "The second time I sang, 'You picked a

fine time to leave me, Lucille,' everybody in the audience was singing it.

"When we recorded that song, we knew it was going to be a big country record. I don't think there was any question in our mind that it was going to be a country home run. But no one in that room dreamed it would have the international success it had."

With its dirt-farmer country lyric and instantly memorable chorus, "Lucille" became a phenomenon of 1977. Thereafter, Rogers seemed to have an infallible ear for songs. Four more smashes, including two duets with Dottie West, in 1978 paved the way for a second "career record."

"With 'The Gambler,' I realized that we had stumbled into something really wonderful. The lyric was a philosophy, a way of life. And everybody applies it to things they do on a daily basis. Life is a gamble and how you treat that gamble is how well you survive."

The romantic, lushly produced "She Believes in Me" and "You Decorated My Life" became major pop-crossover records in 1979. Traditionalists groused that Rogers was too slick for country music.

"Music is communication," he replies. "If you want to communicate with a few people then you get them together in a

235

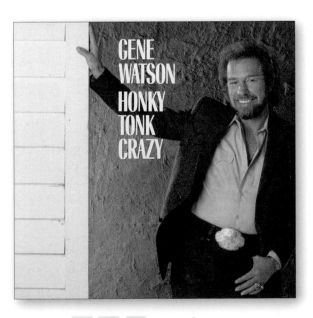

TOP: *Joe Stampley's 1978 LP was titled after one of his finest honky-tonk performances.*
ABOVE: *The peerless Gene Watson, one of contemporary country's finest vocalists, on the jacket of his 1987 collection.*

room. But if you want to talk to a lot, you have to go a different route.

"You may lose some people on the bottom end who are purists, but you gain a larger piece of the pie by bringing people in who never thought they could appreciate country music."

He became a genial "people's idol," relaxed and convivial in concert and self-deprecatingly humorous in his business relationships. The country story song "Coward of the County" and r&b star Lionel Richie's "Lady" both became chart-topping Gold Records in 1980.

"My life just exploded, and I just ran with it as best I could," he says. His pop reign ended around 1985, but Rogers continued to be a presence on the country charts until 1992. He starred in a number of highly rated made-for-TV movies and garnered widespread respect as a photographer. In 1999 he staged a country comeback with the boyhood baseball homily "The Greatest," which proved he still has an ear for a great song.

Pop-country sylists notwithstanding, even country traditionalists had plenty to choose from during this eclectic era. In 1981 Ricky Skaggs revived Flatt & Scruggs's bluegrass oldie "Don't Get Above Your Raisin'," and the *Opry*'s family trio The Whites revived Hank Locklin's "Send Me the Pillow You Dream On." Figures such as George Jones, Johnny Paycheck, Waylon Jennings, Merle Haggard, Loretta Lynn, and Willie Nelson were having the biggest hits of their careers.

We think of the era in terms of its high-profile pop-crossover acts. But it was also a time when a generation of performers took honky-tonk music to new emotional levels. Such expressive singers as The Kendalls (1977's "Heaven's Just a Sin Away"), David Frizzell

(1982's "I'm Gonna Hire a Wino to Decorate Our Home"), and John Anderson (1981's "I'm Just an Old Chunk of Coal") were big on the country charts.

West Virginia's Mel Street (King Malachi Street, 1933–1978) "kept it country" on the 1972 honky-tonkers "Borrowed Angel" and "Lovin' on Back Streets." But after a comeback hit with 1978's "If I Had a Cheating Heart," he shot himself to death on his forty-fifth birthday.

Gary Stewart, born in Kentucky in 1945, displayed hair-raising honky-tonk conviction on such 1974–80 hits as "Drinkin' Thing," "She's Acting Single (I'm Drinkin' Doubles)," and "Whiskey Trip." His live shows combined the frothing-at-the-mouth theatrics of a Jerry Lee Lewis with the blazing-guitar attack of The Allman Brothers. And his crazed, bacchanalian lifestyle was vintage honky-tonk and then some.

Kentucky-bred mortician John Conlee (born 1946) moaned exquisitely on his hits of 1978–88. Conlee's aching performances included the down-and-out "Backside of Thirty" and the blue-collar lyrics "Common Man," "Busted," "Working Man," and "Nothing behind You, Nothing in Sight." One of the most underrated stylists of the era, he displayed a consistent ability to find classic country themes in insightful, contemporary lyrics. Conlee continues to sing his signature hit, 1978's "Rose Colored Glasses," on the *Opry* stage today.

Mississippi-born and Texas-raised Moe Bandy (born 1944) delivered drinking songs with a twang that echoed the classic honky-tonk stylists. He sang "I Just Started Hatin' Cheatin' Songs Today," "Hank Williams You Wrote My Life," "Barstool Montain," and the like, in 1974–80. Bandy's career was lengthened when he teamed up with another

ABOVE: *The cover of John Conlee's tour book pictures him wearing his trademark "Rose Colored Glasses."*

John Conle

honky-tonker for a series of hit duets. That was Louisiana's Joe Stampley (born 1943). After a career as the lead singer of The Uniques ("All These Things"), Stampley found a niche in country music with such tunes as the trucker favorite "Roll on, Big Mama" (1975) and the barroom anthem "Red Wine and Blue Memories" (1978). The light-hearted "Moe and Joe" duets included "Just Good Ole Boys" (1979) and the Boy George pop parody "Where's the Dress" (1984).

When you mention "classic country" to people who came of age during the 1975–85 period, you are almost as likely to hear the names "Vern Gosdin" and "Gene Watson" as you are "George Jones." For these stylists are among the few who can stand alongside Lefty and Hank as masters of honky-tonk singing.

In the world of country music there is only one Man in Black, only one Coal Miner's Daughter, only one Bocephus, and only one star called "The Voice." With his effortless bent-note phrasing, high pangs of heartache, softly yearning sighs, sharp shards of emotion, and deep baritone dips, Vern Gosdin is a country "singer's singer." He has thrilled audiences for more than thirty years with his expressive performances, poignant songwriting, and down-home personal authenticity. Hits such as "Today My World Slipped Away," "Way Down Deep," "Set 'Em up Joe" and the Grammy Award–nominated "Chiseled in Stone" have made Gosdin one of the most revered vocalists of modern country music. One of nine brothers and sisters raised in poverty on an Alabama farm, Gosdin (born 1934) formed a duo with brother Rex, traveled to California, and joined the bluegrass band The Hillmen (which included future Rock 'n' Roll Hall of Fame Byrds member Chris Hillman). A single called "Hangin' On" introduced The Gosdin Brothers to national country radio in 1967. Vern Gosdin came back into the limelight with a string of solo hits in 1976–80. Then he hit even bigger in the 1980s.

Gene Watson was born in Texas in 1943. The ninth-grade dropout became an auto-body re-

pairman who sang on weekends. "I'm not real good at accepting compliments," he says. "The good Lord gave me this voice. I never did go looking for music. Music found me."

A widening circle of admirers in the Houston area led to records for regional labels. In 1975 his "Love in the Hot Afternoon" was picked up for national distribution by Capitol Records, which ignited a string of more than twenty top-ten hits. "Fourteen Carat Mind" (1981), "One Sided Conversation" (1978), "Should I Come Home" (1979), and the rest of his performances pierced the hearts of country-music lovers. His breathtaking remake of the Jimmy Dickens tune "Farewell Party" was, astonishingly, recorded in one take in the studio.

Watson is revered for his sobbing vocal sustains and his ability to wring every drop of emotion out of a lyric. With the tiniest vocal inflection, he can turn a word into an essay of pain. In his furry lower register, he is as intimate as a lover.

"I can't read a note of music," he says. "I don't rehearse. I don't practice. I don't warm up. I just sing. And I'll always be singing, even if it's just for my own personal entertainment. I feel each song."

237

ABOVE: *Moe Bandy's album jackets of the countrypolitan era made it plain that he was not aiming for pop-crossover success. He was a honky-tonker and proud of it.*

Thirteen

Country and the Movies

At the dawn of the 1970s, Mickey Gilley (born 1936) was a journeyman honky-tonk performer who'd given up any dreams of national stardom to become the "house act" at his own nightclub in suburban Houston. The cousin of Jerry Lee Lewis and evangelist Jimmy Swaggart had performed and recorded throughout the '50s and '60s with so little success that he was often forced to work construction jobs to make ends meet.

"In 1971 I met a gentleman by the name of Sherwood Cryer," Gilley remembers. "He wanted me to take a look at a club. I had passed this club on many different occasions. I said, 'You need to take a dozer and wipe it off, start over.' He said, 'I can fix it.' He cleaned it up to make it look halfway decent, to where we could play music in it.

"Playin' those old bars, I knew my way around a little bit at the pool table. So I kept askin' for a pool table in the bar. He put one in and I never got a chance to play pool, because there was always people on it. He saw what was goin' on, so he added a second one, then a third one, then a fourth one. The first thing I knew, the perimeter of the club was just filled up with games. He put

239

LEFT: *Country-music star Dolly Parton starred in* 9 to 5 *with Lily Tomlin and Jane Fonda.*
ABOVE: *Among the dozens of products marketed as a result of the* Urban Cowboy *movie phenomenon was Gilley's Beer.*

A CLASSIC COUNTRY MUSICAL

STARRING
MINNIE PEARL
FERLIN HUSKY
DEL REEVES

FEATURING
GEORGE JONES
LORETTA LYNN
BILL ANDERSON
SKEETER DAVIS
RAY PRICE
ROY DRUSKY
HUGH X. LEWIS
WILLIS BROS.

Forty Acre Feud

COME SEE THE
SMOKEY MOUNTAIN
JAMBOREE

"A COUNTRY MUSIC TREASURE!"

some billboards up: 'If you wanna go dancin', dance at Gilley's,' or 'You know you'll have fun at Gilley's.' People would call up and say, 'Are you open?' He'd say, 'We doze, but we never close.' Just little things, you know, to keep on people's minds.

"About six months into the operation of the club, I had this furniture company call me and ask me if I would do a television show for 'em. So me and Johnny Lee got the thing movin' pretty good. The show began to attract the people into the nightclub. I think it was the middle class and the people that enjoyed goin' out and dancin', havin' a good time. When we first started Gilley's, it was really a fun place to go.

"We have one of the most successful rodeos there in Houston. Cryer got the idea of puttin' a mechanical bull in the club. I thought that was a mistake at first. It turned out to be a blessing in disguise. It's a rodeo trainin' device and I felt like people were gonna get hurt on it. But you get some guy that has one or two drinks, and think they get nine-foot tall and bulletproof; and they wanna impress a girl and they get on that thing."

With its punching bags, pinball machines, forty pool tables, a strong-arm machine, and the mechanical bull, Gilley's became a Houston party mecca. And when its star started having national countrypolitan hits, business boomed even more. Gilley's first hit was a 1974 remake of George Morgan's "Roomful of Roses." The woman who operated the jukeboxes in Gilley's wanted him to do a version of "She Called Me Baby," which was popularized by Charlie Rich that year. She offered to pay for the session and to press three hundred copies of the single.

"So I grabbed the Gilley's house band and went into the studio," recalls the singer. "We needed a back side for the single, so off the top of my head I said, 'Why don't we record this old song "Roomful of Roses?"' I showed 'em how I was gonna do it on a piano, then said, 'No, wait a minute. I don't wanna do this. It's gonna sound like Jerry Lee Lewis.' The guy that played bass said, 'Who cares? Who's gonna hear it? It's gonna be on the back side, isn't it?' I got some of the lyrics wrong. I thought the steel guitar was out of tune. It had too much echo on it and was too loud. But it didn't make any difference. It just had that little magic touch."

The "throwaway" recording was the first of thirty-five top-ten hits for Mickey Gilley. In 1974–86 he topped the charts with "Don't the Girls All Get Prettier at Closing Time," "A Headache Tomorrow," "Tears of the Lonely," and several honky-tonk remakes of pop oldies and country classics. The club expanded to forty-eight thousand square feet. Gilley's t-shirts, Gilley's panties, a Gilley's brand of beer, Gilley's fans, Gilley's Coke bottles, and abundant other merchandise was created. The club became *the* place to perform for all country entertainers. It had its own weekly national radio show in 1977–89. In 1978 journalist Aaron Latham's curiosity was piqued by the club, its patrons, and its mechanical bull. He published "The Ballad of the Urban Cowboy: America's Search For True Grit" in the September 1978 issue of *Esquire* magazine.

"When I read the article, I was a little upset with it because I said he was makin' fun of country music," comments Gilley. "We were on our way out to California to do an interview, and Mr. Cryer said, 'Now look. I know you don't like the article that Aaron Latham wrote, but we may get a movie out of it; and there's a chance John Travolta would be the lead player.' After that point on, I never said anything except, 'Hey, "The Ballad of the Urban Cowboy" is a tremendous piece.'

"They could have just as easily called the movie *Country Night Fever* as they did *Urban Cowboy*," observes Gilley regarding John Travolta's transition from *Saturday Night Fever* to Texas two-stepping. "Basically, that's what it was. He went from doing disco to doing the hoedown."

241

RIGHT: Forty Acre Feud *was marketed during the 1950s heyday of country "exploitation" flicks. The Ernest Tubb Record Shop still sells a video of this vintage B-movie.*

The *Urban Cowboy* soundtrack, which included Gilley's "Stand By Me," Johnny Lee's pop-crossover hit "Lookin' for Love," Charlie Daniels's "The Devil Went down to Georgia," Kenny Rogers's "Love the World Away," Anne Murray's "Could I Have This Dance," and other popular numbers, "introduced people to what country's really all about," says Gilley. "All these young acts that are in the business now, the *Urban Cowboy* had somethin' to do with bringin' all these people along. Because we got a bigger audience. I think that opened the doors for a lot of people."

Released in 1980, *Urban Cowboy* was a box-office smash. Its soundtrack sold more than a million copies. Its inspiration became the most famous night-club in the world. Imitation Gilley's clubs sprouted in cities throughout the United States. Boots, jeans, and cowboy hats became fash-ion statements.

"I think the big thing about *Urban Cowboy* was that it was an idea whose time had come," observes Charlie Daniels. "That movie probably sold more cowboy hats and boots in New York City than any amount of advertising ever could have. While a lot of city people would not identify with the traditional country artists, they did identify with John Travolta. Here was a young handsome guy who had just done *Saturday Night Fever*. And he kind of le-gitimized the western way of life and music. I think country music owes John Travolta a huge debt of thanks."

The film was actually the culmination of a cinematic trend that had been building through-out the 1970s countrypolitan era. Country music has had a long relationship with the movies, but prior to the '70s it was almost always showcased in second-string "B" pictures with low budgets and skimpy production values.

During the silent era in 1904–1929 there were at least 476 movies made about hillbilly culture. J.W. Williamson's 1994 book *Southern Mountaineers in Silent Films* contains their moonshining, feud-ing, and coal-mining plot synopses. Most of these films have disappeared, but the first of them, 1904's *The Moonshiner*, still exists because it was such a huge hit with audiences.

The first hillbilly act captured on sound film was evidently harmonica player Cordelia May-berry of Blue Gap, Virginia. She and her band The Blue Ridgers cavorted for the Warner/Vitaphone cameras in 1929. Jimmie Rodgers made a short subject that year as well. Otto Gray and His Oklahoma Cowboy Band made six shorts for Film Exchange in New York in 1931.

Gene Autry (ninety films), Tex Ritter (sixty films), and Roy Rogers (ninety-one films) led the stampede of singing cow-boys in the 1930s and 1940s. Generally made by Holly-wood's "Poverty Row" studios, singing-cowboy pictures had inter-changeable plots and quickie shooting schedules. Country stars such as Bill Boyd, Ernest Tubb, Roy Acuff, LuluBelle & Scotty, Bob Wills, Foy Willing, and Spade Cooley were also re-cruited by these studios as cinema stars.

Republic Studios made hay with features built around the antics of hillbilly musical comics Judy Canova (twenty-three features) and The Weaver Brothers & Elviry (eleven features). All made sig-nificant profits for the little company by playing to rural audiences in 1938–53.

Grand Ole Opry (Republic, 1940) and *National Barn Dance* (Paramount, 1944) captured the per-formers of America's two most popular radio barn

242

ABOVE: *Singer Ferlin Husky starred in more country B-movies than anyone.*
RIGHT: *Ron Ormond was the producer, director, writer, and cameraman on many of movies he shot in Nashville in the '60s.*

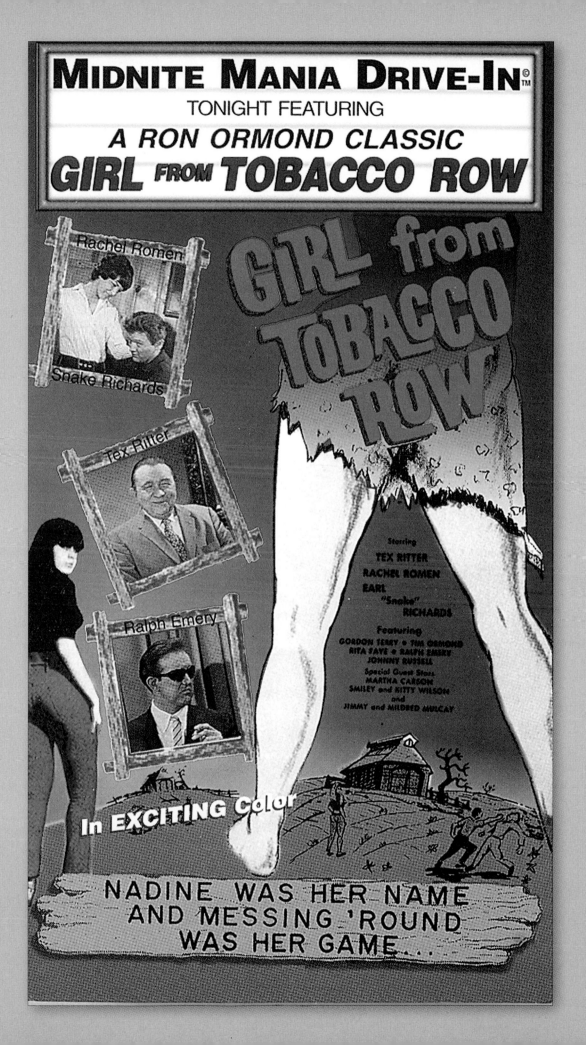

George Jones

dances. Eddy Arnold's disc success led to his starring in 1949's *Feudin' Rhythm.* Jimmie Davis became the first country star to have his life made into a movie, 1944's *Louisiana.* None of these were first-class Hollywood productions.

The enormous teen popularity of country's rockabilly acts led to a number of quickie exploitation films in the 1950s. The 1956 features *Rock Around the Clock* and *Don't Knock the Rock* ushered in this type of movie. Both featured Bill Haley & The Comets. Carl Perkins and Jerry Lee Lewis were in 1957's *Jamboree,* and the latter also sang in 1958's *High School Confidential.* Johnny Burnette was in *Rock Rock Rock* (1957); Bob Luman and David Houston were in *Carnival Rock* (1957); Ferlin Husky appeared in *Mister Rock and Roll.* Gene Vincent and his friend Eddie Cochran both appeared in 1957's *The Girl Can't Help It.* Cochran's other screen appearances include *Go Johnny Go* (1959, with Ritchie Valens) and *Untamed Youth* (1957). Vincent's other movie was 1958's *Hot Rod Gang.*

Rock It, Baby, Rock It (1957) also featured rockabilly performances, but despite its title *Rockabilly Baby* (1957) did not.

During his teen stardom, Conway Twitty was featured in the 1960 movies *Platinum High School, College Confidential,* and *Sex Kittens Go to College.* Brenda Lee appeared in 1961's *Two Little Bears.* And, of course, "The Hillbilly Cat" became a virtual factory of grade-B Hollywood flicks. Elvis Presley made twenty-nine movie musicals in 1956–69.

Several films of the same era introduced country stars as actors. *The Badge of Marshall Brennan* (1959) featured Carl Smith. David Houston had a minor part in *The Horse Soldiers* (1959). Don Gibson was in 1958's *Lost Lagoon.* Johnny Cash's thespian screen debut was 1961's *Five Minutes to Live* (also titled *Door to Door Maniac*). *Buffalo Gun* had Webb Pierce, Carl Smith, and Marty Robbins, "fightin', shootin', singin' their way to new stardom," according to its 1962 publicity. Faron Young was promoted in the

1955–56 cheapies *Hidden Guns* and *Raiders of Old California.*

"I went out to Hollywood preparing for a six-month movie," Young recalled. "Eight days later the movie was shot and in the can and ready to show it to theaters! The girl that played my girlfriend in it was a young, beautiful girl. I kept trying to get 'em to write a love scene. The director said, 'Look boy, this is a western. You don't kiss girls in western movies.' They wouldn't let me do it. This was Angie Dickinson" in one of her first film appearances.

The modern era of country-music moviemaking begins in 1958 with the release of *Country Music Holiday,* starring Ferlin Husky, June Carter, and Faron Young alongside Zsa Zsa Gabor. "Vat is thees peasant moosic?" inquires Gabor when she hears the country sound. "I like eet."

If anything, the subsequent country exploitation movies of the 1950s and 1960s were even worse than the western and rockabilly B movies had been. Several are such bombs that they are now camp classics of the so-bad-it's-good variety. Most were made ultra cheaply and were screened in secondary markets or as drive-in movie fillers. Generally fairly plotless, they mainly strung together filmed country

245

LEFT: *George Jones was one of many stars who appeared in* Country Music On Broadway *in 1964.*
ABOVE: *Grandpa Jones was featured on the lobby card, but Randy Boone was top-billed in 1966's* Country Boy.

performances. *Country Music Jubilee* of 1960 was a kind of prototype with its five-dozen country acts and minimal story line. *Sing a Song for Heaven's Sake* (1966) served the same function for gospel acts.

Country Music Caravan (later repackaged as *Country Music Carnival*), *Tennessee Jamboree*, and *Country Music on Broadway*, all from 1964, were typical of this type of film. Something called *Moonshine Mountain* was also marketed that year. So was the perfectly awful but hugely profitable Hank Williams biography *Your Cheatin' Heart*, starring the unlikely George Hamilton as the tragic honky-tonk idol.

The premise of 1966's *The Gold Guitar* was that hoodlums were trying to steal the secret of the Nashville Sound. Illustrations of just what that sound was came via performances by several stars.

"Everybody's swingin' to the sounds of Nashville when the boys from the Bowery crash the jamboree of 30 country music stars!" read the ads for *Second Fiddle to a Steel Guitar* (1965). Dottie West, Webb Pierce, Lefty Frizzell, Jimmy Dickens, and Sonny James were among those thirty performing in between the broad comedy of Arnold Stang, Huntz Hall, and Leo Gorcy.

In a similar mode was the poster for 1965's straight-to-the-drive-in feature *Forty Acre Feud:* "Lookee yonder, cousin! The Calhouns and Culpeppers are at it agin, with guns and guitars with that grand ol' country music gang singing your favorite hits!" This Ron Ormond production starred Ferlin Husky and included George Jones, Loretta Lynn, Bill Anderson, Del Reeves, and Roy Drusky. Minnie Pearl was "Ma Culpepper." Ormond was the king of Nashville's cut-rate movie moguls.

Jim Reeves
See the only movie in existence starring Jim Reeves.

Kimberley Jim

IN COLOR

A robust, action adventure, starring Jim Reeves singing as a guitar-strumming gambler from Dixie seeking his fortune in the South African diamond rush.

Prior to arriving in Music City he'd made sixty-five films, including eight cheapies per year with Lash LaRue and the same with Sunset Carson. He made his first country-music movie in 1949, *Square Dance Jubilee.*

"Ray Price has the best bedroom eyes in the business," Ormond proclaimed in *Billboard's World of Country Music* edition of 1967. "Minnie Pearl is capable of great dramatic achievements. Ralph Emery is perfect for playing the part of a hood. Roy Drusky may be a fine singer, but in movies he makes a better banker or minister. Yes, they're really actors. They have so much untapped talent it's amazing. We don't put them in movies simply because they're country singers."

Ormond was the producer, director, and part-time cameraman and actor in virtually all of his films, including *The Girl from Tobacco Row* (1966), featuring appearances by Earl Richards, Tex Ritter, Ralph Emery, Martha Carson, and Johnny Russell.

Robert Patrick was another filmmaker who specialized in country exploitation fare. *Swamp Country* (1966) had gangsters mixing with country singers Baker Knight and Rex Allen. *Hell on Wheels* (1967) was a car-race movie starring Marty Robbins that was mainly filmed at the Nashville Speedway. Connie Smith and The Stonemans portrayed themselves.

There was a type of quickie country film that mixed performances with travelogue-type footage. *Music City U.S.A.* (1966), for instance, had many songs but was held together by T. Tommy Cutrer's tour of Nashville, including stops at Ernest Tubb's record shop, Webb Pierce's home, Roy Acuff's museum, Shot Jackson's steel-guitar store, and *Record World* magazine's awards program.

ABOVE: *Jim Reeves went to South Africa to star in* Kimberley Jim. *Like many vintage country movies, it is still available on video.*

John Lair's *Renfro Valley Barn Dance* (1966) documented the old-timey charms of Kentucky's weekly rural country radio show. The posters read, "It's the biggest singin', dancin', fiddlin' show that ever burst out of Renfro Valley!" which at least was the truth. "For the first time on film!" was also perfectly accurate. Lily May Ledford, Old Joe Clark, The Farmer Sisters, Pete Stamper, Ginger Callahan, and the rest of the show's cast of the day was presented. *Country Western Hoedown* (1967) took viewers to seven barn dances—the *Opry, Renfro Valley, The Ozark Jubilee, The Midwestern Hayride* in Cincinnati, *The Old Dominion Barn Dance* in Virginia, California's *Town Hall Party,* and a briefly resuscitated *National Barn Dance* in Chicago.

The Road to Nashville (1966) showed Doodles Weaver bumbling around town trying to round up stars for a country-music movie. *From Nashville with Music* (1969) had a vacationing couple touring the town and being converted into country fans by Marty Robbins and others.

"Join the swingers with a new kind of sound!" suggested the ads for *That Tennessee Beat* (1966). "It'll turn you on!!" Minnie Pearl was an evangelist trying to get juvenile-delinquent singer Earl Richards on the straight and narrow. Merle Travis sang the title tune, and The Statler Brothers, steel guitarist Pete Drake, and The Stony Mountain Cloggers appeared.

"They found him!" trumpeted the promotion for *Here Comes That Nashville Sound* in 1971. "The Cinderella story of a country boy who was made into a superstar. But, man, could he sing!!!" Actually this was a repackaging of *Country Boy*, initially released in 1966 during the heyday of Nashville exploitation flicks. "Cinderella" was Randy Boone, who never charted. He was surrounded in this production by Sheb Wooley, Grandpa Jones, Skeeter Davis, Ray Pillow, and The Glaser Brothers. "Country music is the Now Sound," the producers proclaimed, adding that this feature had "all the greats of Nashville tumbled together in the pea-pickin'est country musical comedy ever to gyrate out of the South."

Actually it was Ferlin Husky and not Randy Boone who became the king of country's B-movie kingdom. In addition to starring in *Mister Rock and Roll, Country Music Holiday,* and *Forty Acre Feud,* he was top-billed in 1966's *Las Vegas Hillbillies* and its 1967 follow-up *Hillbillies in a Haunted House.* In the former he rebuilds a casino with the aid of Jayne Mansfield and Mamie Van Doren. In the latter he is stranded in an old mansion that is festering with spies Basil Rathbone, Lon Chaney, and Jon Carradine. Husky was also top-billed in the 1971 feature *Swamp Girl.* Mis-

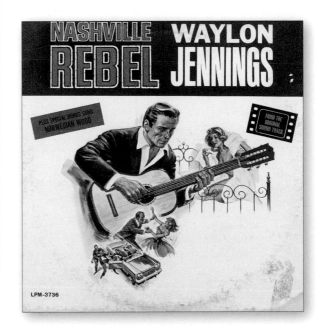

ABOVE: *Hank Williams Jr. was promoted as a movie star with this soundtrack LP for* A Time To Sing *in 1968.*
RIGHT: *Waylon Jenning's "outlaw" personna was evident as early as 1966 when this soundtrack LP appeared.*

souri native Husky (born 1927) was not only noted for hits such as "Gone," "Wings of a Dove," and "Just for You"; he had a comedic alter ego named "Simon Crum" who performed on stage and screen and had hits in his own right such as "Country Music Is Here to Stay" (1959).

Several other singers were given specialty vehicles designed to turn them into screen stars. Hank Williams Jr. was given the big buildup in MGM's *A Time to Sing* (1968). LeRoy Van Dyke got his moment in the sun in 1967's Liberty International Production *What Am I Bid?* (1967). Waylon Jennings had the title role in *Nashville Rebel* (1966), released by American International. Merle Haggard emoted in the same B studio's *Killers Three* (1968). Jim Reeves starred in the South African film *Kimberley Jim* (1965). Roy Orbison's vehicle was 1968's *Fastest Guitar Alive*. Ernie Ashworth had 1965's *The Farmer's Other Daughter*.

Johnny Cash got his own documentary, 1969's *The Man, His World, His Music*. He was also showcased in 1963's *Hootenanny Hoot*, as were Sheb Wooley and the *Opry*'s George Hamilton IV. The documentary *Festival* (1967, a.k.a. *Newport Festival*) included Cash, but even more importantly captured old-time country stars Clayton McMichen, Eck Robertson, and Cousin Emmy on film.

All-star roundups such as *Cotton Pickin' Chicken Pickers* (1967), *Travelin' Light* (1971), *The Nashville Sound* (1972), *Country Music Jamboree* (1970), *Country Music Goes to Town* (1969), and *Wild Guitar* (1962) were more typical titles from the heyday of the quickie country B flick. But as country music expanded its popularity in the 1970s, the quality of the films that showcased it began to change profoundly.

As the decade began, Glen Campbell was country's pioneer with roles in the "A" pictures *True Grit* (1969) and *Norwood* (1970). Kris Kristofferson's star-making cinematic character was a blackmailed music star in 1971's gritty *Cisco Pike*. He sang "Lovin' Her Was Easier" in the critically applauded feature. His first western was Sam Peckinpah's *Pat Garrett & Billy the Kid* of 1973, wherein he portrayed Billy. With more than thirty features, Kristofferson became the most consistent and durable screen presence of all the country stars.

Hollywood began to take country songs seriously for their dramatic value as well. The 1970 Jack Nicholson feature *Five Easy Pieces* effectively used Tammy Wynette's music throughout to comment on its plot. Similarly, director Peter Bogdanovich used the dry, spare records of Hank Williams and His Drifting Cowboys as the soundtrack for his acclaimed 1971 feature *The Last Picture Show*. The bluegrass instrumental "Dueling Banjos" emerged as a hit from the soundtrack of 1973's *Deliverance*. The Glaser Brothers did the music for the 1970 racial drama *tick...tick...tick*. Roger Miller provided the soundtrack for James Coburn's comedy western *Waterhole #3* (1967) and character voices as well as songs for Disney's animated *Robin Hood* in 1973.

In 1973 the superb *Payday* became the first serious film to explore country music itself. Starring Rip Torn, this engrossing, well-acted, and finely scripted feature took moviegoers behind the scenes, on the road with a hard-living country singer. The following year, Robert Altman's ac-

248

claimed *Nashville!* used the country-music community as a metaphor for American society. Susan Saint James promoted ex-convict Peter Fonda to country stardom in 1977's *Outlaw Blues*. The well-done 1979 TV movie *Amateur Night at the Dixie Bar and Grill* with Tanya Tucker put a small-town spin on the culture. Earl Scruggs was the focus of the 1977 documentary *Banjoman*. These efforts prefaced several even more high-profile films about country music of the 1980s.

Following his turn in *Deliverance*, Burt Reynolds embarked on a highly successful series of films with country themes. The first of these was 1973's moonshiner saga *White Lightning*, followed by 1974's *W.W. and the Dixie Dancekings*, a fetching story about a con artist promoting a country band in Music City.

Vincent Canby called the film "an unexpectedly pleasant surprise" in his *New York Times* review. "The film's supporting roles are very well cast, largely, it seems, by Nashville country music personalities who are unknown to me." They included such No. 1 hit makers as Don Williams, Mel Tillis, and Jerry Reed. Throughout the period, the *Times* indicated a similar lack of knowledge, sympathy, or understanding of the country film boom.

"*White Lightning* sold well and that is obviously the reason for taking it up again," wrote Richard Eder in his 1976 *Times* review of *Gator*, Burt Reynolds's directing debut. "There doesn't seem to be much of any other reason." The film featured Jerry Reed as the bad guy.

Reed reappeared with Reynolds in 1977's *Smokey*

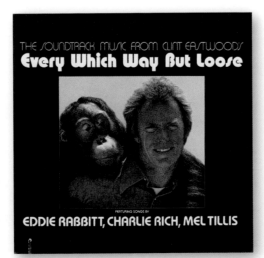

and the Bandit and scored a chart-topping country hit with its theme song "East Bound and Down." "This is a movie for audiences capable of slavering over a Pontiac Trans Am, 18-wheel tractor-trailer rigs, dismembered police cruisers and motorcycles," wrote Lawrence Van Gelder dismissively in his *New York Times* review.

Sniffed Vincent Canby in his paper's 1981 Reynolds review, "Like Hal Needham's two *Smokey* films, *The Cannonball Run* is a virtually unending series of highway gags, which begin behind the opening credits, and continue until the closing credits. . . . Because there are only a limited number of variations that can be worked out on this same old highway race, don't bother to see it unless you're already hooked on the genre."

Cannonball Run II fared no better with critics. But Janet Maslin grudgingly admitted in her *Times* review of 1984: "The fact that *Cannonball Run II* isn't much good may not prevent it from becoming this summer's best-loved, lowest-common-denominator comedy." *Smokey and the Bandit, Part 3* (1983) put Jerry Reed in the lead role.

Canby did pause to note that there was a trend occurring on the silver screen. In a 1977 "Film View" piece in *The New York Times* the critic noted, "Something curious is happening to country movies. Like country music, they are becoming a big, respectable if still largely unpublicized business." Canby reported that *Macon County Line* had earned $10 million. *Dirty Mary, Crazy Larry* brought in more than $14.5

249

ABOVE: *Several Clint Eastwood movies had country-music soundtrack albums, including 1982's* Honkytonk Man *and 1979's* Every Which Way But Loose.

Eastwood

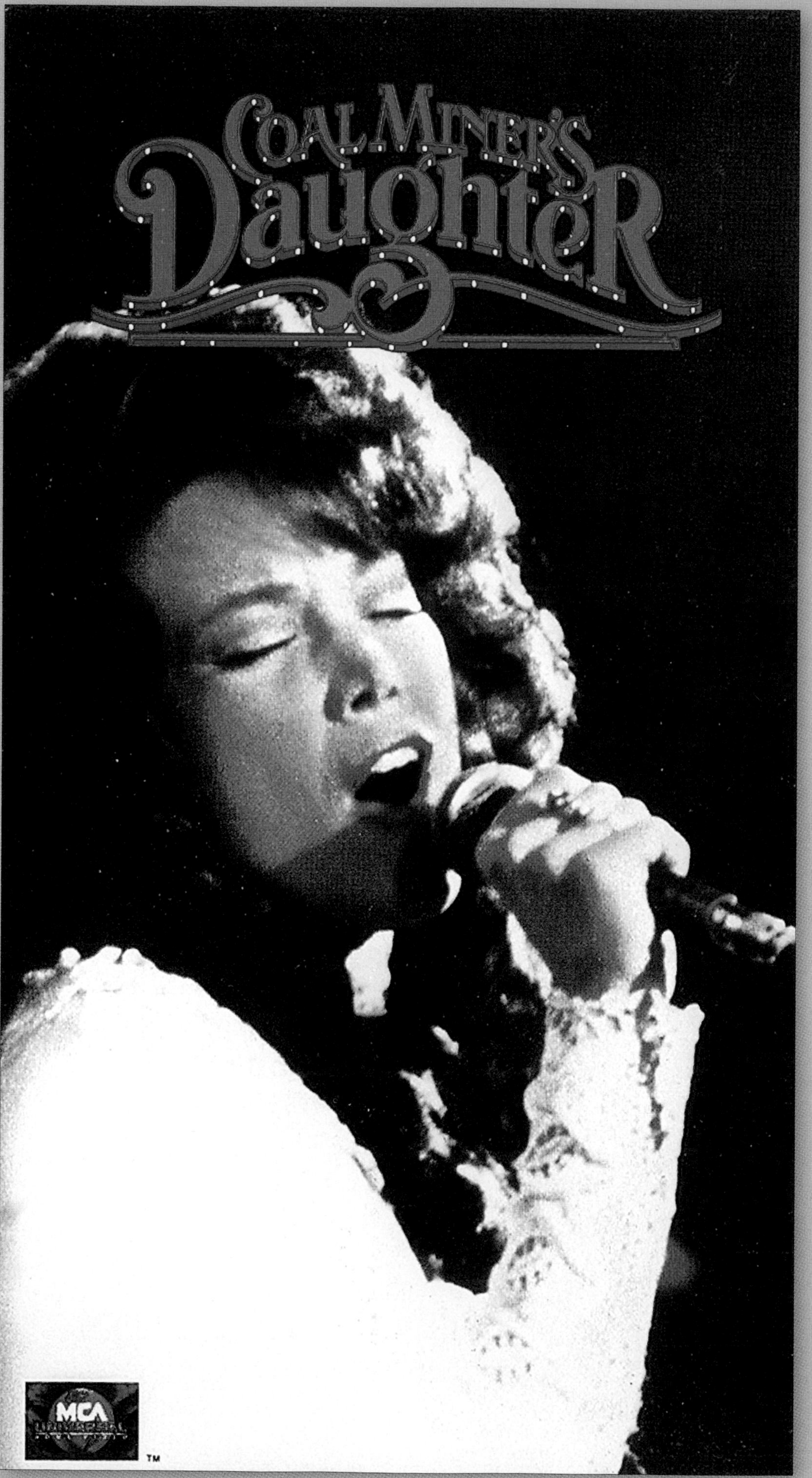
Coal Miner's
Daughter
MCA
TM

million. *Walking Tall*, the film based on Tennessee sheriff Buford T. Pusser, earned $17 million and its first sequel made $11 million. Most telling of all was that *Smokey and the Bandit* made $36 million in six months.

"What? You've never heard of *Smokey and the Bandit*? It's not the sort of movie that's talked about at cocktail parties. Country movies are supported—often exclusively—by people who live in the rural South, Southwest and Middle West.... Because a country movie is seldom three or even two years in the making, it appears to be more closely in touch with its audience than more ambitious films. The country movie aims to please and will bust a gut doing it."

Producer Walter Wood pointed out to *The New York Times* in 1983, "For the past five years, Burt Reynolds has been No. 1 at the box office, and during that period there has seldom been a good review of anything he's done." At the time, Wood was releasing Reynolds's stock-car film *Stroker Ace*, which naturally had a country-music soundtrack.

The other star who specialized in country movies was Clint Eastwood. Like Reynolds, he made films with cameos by country stars and tie-in country soundtracks.

"Clint's preference is jazz," reports soundtrack producer Snuff Garrett. "I wanted to use country acts, and he gave me a total free hand to do that. Out of the first picture, *Every Which Way But Loose* (1979), we had four No. 1 records. I remember I cut the record just before the weekend, took a copy out to Clint's office and put it on his desk. I was at home on Sunday. He called and was really happy with it.

"I wanted Mel Tillis to be in *Every Which Way But Loose*. So I met him in San Diego, played him the songs, and Tillis said, 'Hoss, I don't like either one of them songs.' I said, 'Well, these are the songs we're gonna do. You sing these two songs in the picture or you can't be in the picture.' So he said, 'Well, play 'em again.' So I played 'em again. He said, 'They sound better already.' The two songs were 'Coca Cola Cowboy' and 'Send Me down to Tucson.'" Both became No. 1 hits for Tillis.

"For years after that he said, 'The reason I had those two big songs is because of that turkey sittin' right there.' I used to kid around with Tillis a lot, impersonating him. It was fun to use a lot of influences that I respected—Merle Haggard, Marty Robbins, Johnny Gimble," all of whom appeared in Eastwood's film about country music, 1982's *Honkytonk Man*.

Janet Maslin noted in *The New York*

251

LEFT: Coal Miner's Daughter *is still available on video.*
TOP: *Jerry Reed was the star, producer, and director of* What Comes Around.
ABOVE: *Jessica Lange & Ed Harris in the film about Patsy Cline.*

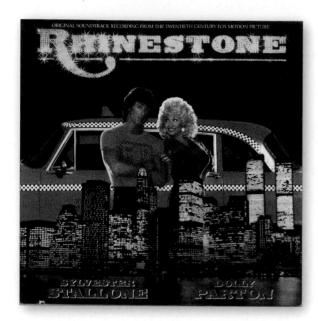

Times in 1981 that "*Any Which Way You Can* has proven to be one of the few moneymaking movies of the season. It is the sequel to *Every Which Way But Loose*, which, with 'box office in the hundreds of millions,' according to its star, is far and away the most profitable Eastwood film of all.... As a director and as an actor whose roles vary more and more, he is after a certain diversity. *Bronco Billy* (1981) was a lighthearted, witty and unexpectedly clever film." That Eastwood vehicle was about a Wild West show cowboy and again featured a star-studded country soundtrack.

Kenny Rogers was no actor, but he parlayed his pop-crossover music stardom into an occasional career in theatrical films and a wildly successful one in made-for-TV movies. Again, no one liked it but the public. The 1980 made-for-TV western *The Gambler* marked Rogers' acting debut. It drew television's largest audience when it was aired and lifted CBS to No. 1 among the networks. *The Gambler—The Adventure Continues* was offered as a sequel in 1983.

"Mr. Rogers is, of course, the very successful singer whose sagging career was revived several years ago with the recording of a song called— you guessed it—'The Gambler,'" related John J. O'Connor in his *New York Times* review. "And danged if the somewhat

corny movie didn't do mighty well in the ratings. In televisionland, that means a sequel.... Mr. Rogers is not one of your more animated actors. Getting a bit thick around the waist, he generally limits his emoting to a kind of nice-guy sincerity."

"If you've never seen anyone wear a gold chain with a sweatshirt, then by all means go see Kenny Rogers in *Six Pack*," said Janet Maslin in her *Times* review of the country star's 1982 feature film. "His singing, infrequent as it is here, comes as a happy change of pace, since his acting is much less assured. Mr. Rogers tends to overdo even the simplest gestures, stirring a bowl of chili as if he were rowing a boat, or driving a car as if he's *pretending* to drive a car. He's pleasant here, but not very natural, which is just as well; no one else in the film is any more authentic than he."

Rogers made many more TV movies—*Coward of the County*, *Wild Horses*, *The Gambler III: The Legend Continues*, *The Gambler Returns: The Luck of the Draw* (featuring the acting debut of Reba McEntire), *El Diablo*, *MacShayne: Winner Takes All*, *MacShayne: Final Role of the Dice*, *Gambler V*, and so on. None were critically applauded. Almost all of them were audience favorites.

Waylon Jennings sang his songs and was the

TOP: *Dolly Parton and Sylvester Stallone in* Rhinestone.
ABOVE: *Burt Reynolds starred in many country-themed movies.*
RIGHT: *Reynolds and Parton scored a huge home-video hit with* The Best Little Whorehouse in Texas.

Burt Reyno

MUSIC FROM THE ORIGINAL MOTION PICTURE SOUNDTRACK

With Burt and Dolly
this much fun just couldn't be legal!

THE BEST LITTLE WHOREHOUSE IN TEXAS

MCA-6112

ds

narrator/commentator throughout the 1975 moonshiner movie *Moonrunners*. "The 1958 *Thunder Road* with Robert Mitchum is a B-film classic and the best hooch-hauler ever made," wrote reviewer John Dwyer in the *Buffalo Evening News*. "*Moonrunners* shouldn't be mentioned in the same alcoholic breath." Maybe so, but the film inspired 1979–85's *The Dukes of Hazzard*, the highest-rated television series of its era. Jennings performed the same functions on it that he had in *Moonrunners*. He also sang the soundtrack to the 1975 Roy Rogers aging-cowboy film *MacIntosh & T.J.*

C.W. McCall's hit country song of the same title inspired the movie *Convoy* in 1978. Starring Kris Kristofferson as a trucker with the CB "handle" of Rubber Duck, the film received, surprise, a Canby drubbing in *The New York Times*: "The movie is a big, costly, phony exercise in myth-making, machismo, romance-of-the-open-road nonsense and incredible self indulgence," he wrote. "It takes its large cast of good actors and makes a fool of each one of them. . . . It asks us to admire the free spirit of the truckers who own their own rigs, who love their trucks as cowboys used to love their horses, and who represent—or so we are told—a vanishing breed of Americans whose backbone made this country great."

Peter Fonda and Jerry Reed's 1978 trucker film *High Ballin'* and Jan Michael Vincent's 1975 trucker movie *White Lightning*, on the other hand, got fairly good press.

Nick Nolte made his film debut opposite Don Johnson in the drag-racing *Return to Macon County* of 1975. It was the sequel to 1974's box-office smash *Macon County Line*, which featured Bobbie Gentry singing the title tune. Her song "Ode to Billie Joe" inspired a 1975 film of the same name. Country hits also inspired the plots of *Harper Valley P.T.A.* (1978), *Middle Age Crazy* (1980), *Take This Job and Shove It* (1981), *Big Bad John* (1990), and *The Night the Lights Went Out in Georgia* (1981).

All of this interaction between country culture and the cinema reached fever pitch in 1980. *Urban Cowboy*, the film that lent its name to that period in country's history, was released and became hugely popular that year. "I went back and watched that movie again not long ago," says *Billboard* magazine's Chet Flippo, "and I was appalled at how bad it is. I don't see how in the world it succeeded. And I am not speaking as a critic, but as a true Texan and a fan of country music. It was awful."

But *Urban Cowboy* wasn't country's only cinematic monument of 1980. That was also the year that Hollywood portrayed the life of Loretta Lynn in *Coal Miner's Daughter*. It was the year that Dolly Parton made her screen debut in *9 To 5* and earned an Oscar nomination for her title tune. It marked the acting debut of Willie Nelson, who was featured with Robert Redford in *Electric Horseman* in 1980.

"One of the hardest things I ever had to go through was watching my life portrayed on the screen," says Loretta Lynn. "Universal called me in Vegas and said, 'We've got the movie studio for you this afternoon at two o'clock. We're gonna bring the movie and let you see it.' This was before anybody else seen it. No one went in to see the movie but me and my husband. I thought, 'Well this is gonna be fun.' But to see it

254

on the screen completely destroyed my mind. There was things that bothered me so bad that I'd have to turn my head and hum a song while it was going on.

"They said, 'Now two days from now we're sending you to *Good Morning America* and the *Today* show, and all the TV places, to do some press on it.' Walking out of the theater, they said, 'What did you think about the movie?' I said, 'I missed the popcorn, and the movie was only about forty minutes long.' They looked at me and said, 'Loretta, the movie is two hours. What do you think about it?' And I said, 'I don't remember. I don't remember.' They took me in a studio in New York City to watch *Coal Miner's Daughter* again. Same thing happened. I couldn't remember. I know it might sound silly, but we did it the third time, and I took a notebook so I could write down what I seen that bothered me, what things that I liked and what I didn't. It bothered me so bad, 'cause it hit so close to home."

Sissy Spacek won a Best Actress Academy Award for her portrayal of Lynn, which included singing her songs. The soundtrack LP sold a million and led to a minor country career for the thespian.

"We worked a couple of months on that thing,"

recalled soundtrack producer Owen Bradley, who was also Oscar-nominated. "I don't think I really coached anybody. I just sort of listened and tried to encourage 'em. Sissy worked it out herself. I have a video on it that's priceless. I wouldn't take anything for it. It's of her learning how to be Loretta, and she's singing the songs. I had Loretta's tracks and we would play the tracks and then she would sing with 'em. It was a lot of fun. She was very easy to work with, just a real sweet person."

Dolly Parton's role opposite Lily Tomlin and Jane Fonda in *9 to 5* led to a string of movies that included musicals such as 1984's *Rhinestone* with Sylvester Stallone and 1982's *The Best Little Whorehouse in Texas* with Burt Reynolds. But she tackled nonmusical roles as well, memorably portraying a radio psychologist in *Straight Talk* (1992), a beautician in *Steel Magnolias* (1989, with Julia Roberts, Shirley MacLaine, Olympia Dukakis, Daryl Hannah, and Sally Field), and an abused woman in 1991's made-for-TV *Wild Texas Wind*. When she starred in the sentimental holiday fable *A Smokey Mountain Christmas* for ABC-TV in 1986, it garnered the network the highest TV-movie ratings it had had for two years.

The year after his screen debut,

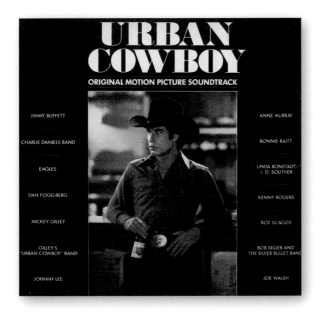

255

ABOVE: Urban Cowboy's *soundtrack LP sold millions.*
TOP: *The lesser-known* Hard Country *treated the same topic and music with more reality. It also marked the screen debut of Kim Basinger.*

Willie Nelson starred in 1982's *Honeysuckle Rose*, which was more credible than Parton's *Rhinestone* as a depiction of the country-music lifestyle. Among Nelson's many other theatrical and made-for-TV efforts are the brooding 1982 western *Barbarosa* and 1984's apt portrayal of a country composer's lot, *Songwriter*, costarring Kris Kristofferson.

"Working in film is so very boring," said Parton. "I hate to sit around and wait all the time." "Waitin' around is what I do best," countered Nelson, who waited twenty years to become an "overnight" country star. "Everything else is waitin' around, too, I've always felt."

The miniexplosion of films examining the culture of country music occurred immediately after the *Urban Cowboy/9 to 5/Electric Horseman/Coal Miner's Daughter* detonation of 1980. *Hard Country* (1981) was a somewhat grittier, and better, treatment of the same kinds of characters that *Urban Cowboy* had presented. It starred Jan Michael Vincent, introduced Kim Basinger in her first movie, had a memorable cameo by Tanya Tucker, and featured songs by Michael Martin Murphey, who also wrote its screenplay. *Heartworn Highways* (1981) was an effective country documentary. Eastwood's *Honkytonk Man* (1982) was a watchable if unsatisfying portrayal of a terminally ill, Depression-era singer trying to make it to *The Grand Ole Opry* before he dies.

The best of the lot was *Tender Mercies*. Robert Duvall's portrayal of a faded country star trying to rebuild his life earned him a Best Actor Oscar for 1983. Duvall wrote his own songs and did his own singing in the feature. He returned to country culture with 1998's *The Apostle*. Playing a rural southern evangelist, Duvall featured June Carter Cash in a strong supporting role and earned an Oscar nomination. The soundtrack album won a Grammy Award.

In the wake of *Coal Miner's Daughter* a number of biographical films on country stars appeared. Michelle Lee did a

credible job in the title role of the candid *Big Dreams & Broken Hearts: The Dottie West Story* (made for TV, 1984). Tammy Wynette's *Stand by Your Man* was a 1981 TV movie starring Annette O'Toole. Even more unlikely was Richard Thomas playing Hank Williams Jr. in the 1983 TV movie *Living Proof*. The big screen did no better, casting Gary Busey in *The Buddy Holly Story* (1978) and Dennis Quaid as Jerry Lee Lewis in *Great Balls of Fire* (1989). True fans of the rockabilly legends loathed both films.

But Hollywood redeemed itself with 1984's *Sweet Dreams*. Jessica Lange was surprisingly effective as country legend Patsy Cline and earned an Oscar nomination for her efforts.

The boom in country music, country movies, and country legends' stories led to increased demand in movies for the "heartland" country stars themselves. Like Kris Kristofferson, Jerry Reed, Dolly Parton, and Willie Nelson, Johnny Cash developed as an actor. After providing soundtrack songs for Gregory Peck's moonshiner movie *I Walk the Line* and Robert Redford's motorcycle movie *Little Fauss and Big Halsey* (both 1970), Cash resumed his acting career with 1971's *A Gunfight* (costarring Kirk Douglas), *The Gospel Road* (1973), *The Pride of Jesse Hallam* (TV, 1981),

ABOVE: *One of the more successful country soundtrack albums of the '90s was 1994's* 8 Seconds.

Murder In Coweta County (TV, 1982), and *The Baron* (TV, 1984).

"Basically what has happened is that our popularity around the world has made us legit in Hollywood," said Nashville casting director Patsy Bruce in 1984. "They see us as having built-in audience appeal, being easy to work with and acting as professionals. The worldwide popularity of country music has made us a good draw at the box office; that's why they've finally recognized us."

Hoyt Axton, Alex Harvey, Jimmy Dean (a hero in the 1971 James Bond movie *Diamonds Are Forever*), and Sheb Wooley (*Hoosiers*, 1986) all developed sideline careers as actors. Mac Davis starred in 1979's *North Dallas Forty*, 1980's *Cheaper to Keep Her,* and 1982's *The Sting II*. John Schneider's stardom on TV and on the country charts led to 1982's film drama *Eddie Macon's Run*. Barbara Mandrell made her acting debut in the 1984 TV movie *Burning Rage*.

"I don't pretend to be that good," said Mandrell. "I never fantasized about being an actress. We'll see how it goes. All I can do is the best I can. If it doesn't do well...well, I tried." She later surfaced with a recurring dramatic role on TV's *Baywatch* and quit the road in 1997 to concentrate on acting possibilities.

Mandrell's take-it-as-it-comes attitude characterized most of the country stars who turned to acting. "Some movies are fun and some aren't," commented Jerry Reed. "'Course, I'm gonna make mine fun or I'm not gonna do it. I'm not gonna get cardiac serious about playin' cowboys and Indians for anybody on earth. Somebody pitches a conniption fit because your hair's messed up? I ain't got time for that."

In 1970–85 country was all the rage on the soundtracks of such films as *The Villain, Coast to Coast, Honky Tonk Freeway, The Pursuit of D.B. Cooper,* the Grammy-winning *Follow That Bird, Southern Comfort, One from the Heart, What Comes Around* (produced, directed, and starring Jerry Reed), *Country Gold, The River Rat, Murder in Music City, Rustlers' Rhapsody,* and *Places in the Heart*. Then the "Urban Cowboy" era ended as Hollywood turned its attention away. Urbanites no longer considered it fashionable to be make-believe cowboys. Country sales nose-dived.

Even so, country music has continued to be a presence in the movies. Clint Eastwood returned to the style for the soundtracks of his films *Pink Cadillac* (1989) and *A Perfect World* (1993, costarring Kevin Costner). The 1994 rodeo movie *8 Seconds* and George Strait's portrayal of a Nashville star in 1992's *Pure Country* were strong returns to country topics. *The Thing Called Love* (1993), starring Sandra Bullock and River Phoenix (in his last role), depicted the lives of aspiring songwriters at Nashville's Bluebird Cafe. Country star K.T. Oslin portrayed the venue's owner and Trisha Yearwood, Pam Tillis, and Jo-El Sonnier were among those making cameo appearances.

Dwight Yoakam (*Sling Blade*), Reba McEntire (*Tremors*), and Randy Travis (*At Risk*) all developed film careers after achieving disc success. And such latter-day films as *Far North* (1989), *Next of Kin* (1990), *My Heroes Have Always Been Cowboys* (1991), *Honeymoon in Vegas* (1992), *The Beverly Hillbillies* (1993), *The Cowboy Way* (1994), *Chasers* (1994), *Maverick* (1994), *Traveller* (1996), *The Horse Whisperer* (1998), *Black Dog* (1998), and *Hope Floats* (1998) sported strong country-music soundtracks.

But the country industry has yet to regain the cinematic clout it had in the 1970s and early 1980s. "Urban Cowboy Goes to Boot Hill" headlined *Variety* in 1984. The national media followed with a slew of articles chronicling the downturn in country sales in the mid-1980s.

But by then the industry was already laying the foundation for the biggest renaissance in country-music history. And the cornerstone of that foundation was television.

Fourteen

Country on TV

During the downturn that followed the Urban Cowboy boom period for country music, Nashville was quietly laying the groundwork for an era that would take its stars to unprecedented levels of fame and sales. Its chief weapon in its renewed assault on American music lovers was cable television.

Variety programming withered and died on network television during the early 1980s. One by one *The Ed Sullivan Show*, *The Hollywood Palace*, *The Midnight Special,* and similar showcases fell by the wayside.

But in the late 1970s people had begun to talk about a new kind of television. Specialty channels could be distributed to households via cable instead of over the airwaves. As America became "wired" for cable, music marketers saw the potential at once. MTV was launched in August 1981. It revolutionized the world of rock by creating a new kind of teen idol, the video star.

A month later, Ted Turner became the first to see the potential for country music in cable programming when his WTBS Superstation began airing *Nashville Alive*, country's first cable series. Turner's cameras explored Music City's nightlife scene,

259

LEFT: *At its peak,* The Porter Wagoner Show *was presented in syndication to more than 100 TV markets.*
ABOVE: The Dukes of Hazzard *was America's top-rated network show in its heyday.*

including country songwriter nights and country talent contests, as well as celebrity appearances.

In the first week of March in 1983, two channels came to life in Nashville that would revolutionize the country-music world. On March 5, Country Music Television (CMT) quietly began delivering its videos, initially via satellite. Two days later, The Nashville Network (TNN) made quite a bit more noise. When the switch was thrown by Roy Acuff and Patti Page at its gala premiere, TNN was launched with the largest audience of any cable channel up to that point.

Like its pop-music counterparts MTV and VH-1, CMT is a twenty-four-hour showcase for video clips. These minimovies have completely changed the way country music is marketed.

"There were some terrible videos in the beginning," recalls CMT pioneer Stan Hitchcock with a chuckle. "It was a long battle to convince the Nashville music industry that video not only had a place, but was to become the main vehicle to drive artist development, to build a career, an image. I called meetings with all the heads of the labels and started talkin' to 'em about my belief in video. You have to understand, you were dealing with people that had a lifetime devoted to audio. And all of a sudden, here's a hillbilly comin' in talkin' to 'em about how video is gonna change their business.

"The artists were the first to believe in it. CMT was very small, very insignificant, very underfunded, but very much believed in by the small core of people. Artists started coming back to Nashville and they'd call me. I remember Waylon Jennings called and said, 'Stan, I was out in Iowa doin' a show. I was standin' there doin' autographs and somebody come up to me and instead of sayin', "Heard your latest record," they said, "Hey, I enjoyed your new video on CMT."' That's what started it. The artists started getting feedback from the audience. We were able to open up a window for a whole new generation of artists."

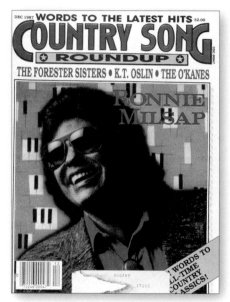

"RCA was the first to get into videos in Nashville," recalls Ronnie Milsap, "all the way back to '79 and 1980. And I was part of that. I understood it was a new marketing tool, a whole new exposure. Working with video directors on some of the earlier things really helped with getting the records out there. Everybody talks about videos today, how important they are. RCA was, to me, the smartest in getting into that before anybody in Nashville did." In 1984 Milsap became the first country star with a video on MTV, "She Loves My Car."

Blind pianist Ronnie Milsap (born 1946) was a product of the North Carolina mountains, but his vocal style was colored by rock and soul influences as well as country music. After session work with Elvis Presley in Memphis, Milsap took up residence as the house act at Roger Miller's King of the Road motor inn in East Nashville. Music Row beat a path to his door, and he eventually crossed over to the pop charts with "It Was Almost Like a Song" (1977), "Smokey Mountain Rain" (1980), "(There's) No Gettin' Over Me" (1981), "Any Day Now" (1982), and "Stranger in My House" (1983), the last three of which were all translated into the new music-video field.

Video exposure unquestionably accelerated the pace of the country-music business. Before the video era, it took years of touring for a country star to achieve name recognition. Thanks to CMT's exposure of videos, that process telescoped

ABOVE: *Although blind, Ronnie Milsap was a video pioneer. This cover story came in 1986 at the height of his fame.*

Ralph Emery

into a matter of months. As a result, records sold faster and people became stars quicker.

A second outgrowth of video exposure was that it created a completely new generation of country stars. Younger and more telegenic than their predecessors, these performers became video idols who triggered a "youthquake" among country consumers.

Third, CMT took the lead in promoting new stars. Video exposure on the channel launched the careers of such artists as Shania Twain, Dwight Yoakam, The Kentucky HeadHunters, Billy Ray Cyrus, Alison Krauss, and The Mavericks, all of whom were favorites on the channel long before their records were radio hits. As a result, record companies routinely ship clips to CMT weeks before their accompanying singles are sent to radio stations, thus preparing the marketplace for new sounds.

"The advent of CMT helped us take another giant leap forward," says MCA Records chief Bruce Hinton. "It really created a revolution in country music. A young artist could go on CMT with a video and maybe the radio station in that particular city was not ready to play this young artist, and all of a sudden they were getting requests. Once it was discovered by country radio that, yes, it was okay to play new and young artists, there became a groundswell. We had country radio go from playing 75 percent oldies and 25 percent current hits to flipflop to 75 percent current and 25 percent oldies."

"We were always, from the very beginning, a very visual act," comments Mark Miller, the leader of the band Sawyer Brown. "So we were kind of a natural for the video process. We had done a ton of TV, and the transition to video seemed real natural to us. For a lot of the more old-style country acts, it was a tougher transition. Also, I think the video process has brought a real visual aspect to a lot of people's stage shows."

"A lot of record companies did not want to do them, because it was very expensive," recalls Crystal Gayle. "But you could tell that the videos

were going to be something in the future, were really gonna take hold. They helped the audience relate to you, to get to know you a little better." Gayle outpaced most of her peers by making ten videos in 1982–85.

CMT's growth in programming these new sales tools was steady and sure. Ownership changed hands three times during the channel's first decade. But even so, it reached six million U.S. homes by 1987, fourteen million by 1991, more than thirty million by 1995, and forty-one million by 1998.

By the late 1990s CMT had been joined in the cable TV universe by several imitators. CMT is unquestionably the leader, but it does have country-video competitors, namely Great American Country (eight million homes), The Box—Country (fifteen markets), and VH-1 Country (a half-million homes).

Ralph Emery, the veteran radio DJ, became one of the first country cable stars. Born in 1933, Emery was hired by WSM as its all-night disc jockey in 1957. He turned his "graveyard shift" into a show-biz event by letting stars drop in to sing and chat whenever they felt like it, no appointments necessary. He was also a veteran of local Nashville TV, having hosted his early-morning *Ralph Emery Show* on WSMV since 1972. Emery recalls people being skeptical when he made the transition to cable television.

He recounts, "The National Life and Accident Insurance Company that owned the radio and television station sold the television station, WSMV, took the money and put it in the cable company, TNN. When the idea first began to be bandied about, there were a lot of nay sayers. I think the feeling was that country music was not a strong enough entity to produce enough revenue to support a cable system sup-

ABOVE: *Ralph Emery's cable TV renown led to a top-10 placement on the* New York Times *list of best-selling books.*

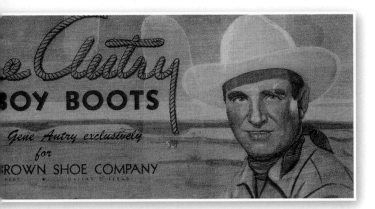

ported by commercials. I thought, 'No, no, no, you guys are way off base. There's nothing more loyal in the world than a country-music fan, and if you design a cable system just for him, believe me, he'll support it.' And he did.

"I remember I went to parties at the Tavern On The Green in New York, trying to get the New York press to support us. The interesting thing is that the launching of The Nashville Network was not on the entertainment pages of *The New York Times*. It was on the financial pages. Our PR people tried to get the *Times* to write on their entertainment pages about this new musical network, and they wouldn't do it. So finally some bright person said, 'Well, if you don't believe in country music, you believe in dollars, don't you? So let's talk about the investment, the projections. We project we're gonna lose money for the first four-and-a-half years. This is how much money we're prepared to lose, before we turn it around and start making money.' So that's how we showed up on the pages of *The New York Times* financial section."

Emery became the most famous broadcaster in country-music history, thanks to hosting TNN's flagship show, *Nashville Now,* from 1983 to 1993. He has written three best-selling volumes of his memoirs and continues to host interview specials on the channel that made him a national icon as "The Johnny Carson of Cable."

TNN was created as a country "lifestyles" channel. Following its debut in seven million U.S. households in 1983, TNN dazzled the cable industry by growing ten times that big over the next fifteen years. In 1997 it topped seventy million households—nearly all of the cable households that existed at that time.

During the same period, country sales dramatically rebounded from their post–Urban Cowboy slump. Country's revenues climbed from $460 million in 1983 to $720 million in 1990, $1 billion in 1991, and $2 billion in 1995. Television has long been viewed as the most powerful marketing tool ever invented. The fact that this sales explosion directly parallels the growth of TNN cannot be mere coincidence.

TNN has presented country music on entertainment news shows like *Today's Country,* on talk shows like *Prime Time Country* and *Nashville Now,* on history shows like *Life and Times,* on concert series like *Live at the Ryman* and *Sam's Place,* and on dance shows like *WildHorse Saloon* and *Club Dance.* On Saturday nights it presents a portion of *The Grand Ole Opry* as well as a *Backstage at the Opry* lead-in program. In addition, it has offered programming on country crafts and country cooking. Weekends are devoted to fishing, motor sports, and rodeo. Specials regularly salute country's stars.

Radio playlists shrank throughout the 1980s and 1990s. Hundreds of artists were dropped from the airwaves, particularly vintage acts, instrumentalists, bluegrass groups, folk troubadours, rockabilly bands, and experimental stylists. TNN has given all of them a forum, creating an ever broader country-music marketplace. Because it

263

LEFT: *Gene Autry's TV fame led to products such as this picture puzzle and his own line of cowboy boots.*
RIGHT: *The king of the TV merchandizers was Roy Rogers. Hundreds of products bore his likeness.*

needs to fill hours with fresh programming constantly, TNN has both extended older artists' careers and given newcomers exposure before their records get radio airplay.

Among those whose careers virtually began on TNN are Lorrie Morgan, Randy Travis, and Diamond Rio. Alan Jackson worked in its mailroom before becoming a superstar. Exposure on the channel helped create the generation of stars that includes Clint Black, Garth Brooks, Tim McGraw, Brooks & Dunn, Reba McEntire, The Judds, and Vince Gill.

"I got a call to be on *Nashville Now*," recalls singer Shelby Lynne. "The producer of the show

said, 'Shelby. I've heard a tape of yours; and we would love for you to come up in a couple weeks and do the show.' I freaked out—'This could be it!' I got laryngitis. But I got just enough voice back to do the show. And I had four record-company offers the next day."

In addition to promoting new talent, TNN has proved to be an extremely effective marketing tool for established performers. Artists such as Ray Price, Cristy Lane, Boxcar Willie, Conway Twitty, and Charley Pride sold millions of albums via TNN ads.

The channel promotes stars' concert appearances regularly and sometimes does "All Access" specials from those concerts.

Perhaps most important of all, TNN exposed the genuine likability of country artists. This genre's performers have always been known for their down-to-earth personalities. With its fan clubs, postshow "meet-and-greets," bluegrass festivals, snapshot and autograph opportunities, Fan Fair, radio-station visits, and media friendliness, country was already an intensely people-oriented art form. These qualities have been heightened by TNN exposure. TNN narrowed the distance between performers and their fans even further.

Before the cable TV era, country music's exposure on television was regular, if somewhat spotty. But country's relationship with the medium has been a long one. The identity of the first country star to appear on television is unknown. Red River Dave, Denver Darling, and Cousin Emmy all recalled appearing on experimental broadcasts in 1939. Carson Robison, Rosalie Allen, Jimmy Wakely, Cindy Walker, Spade Cooley, Merle Travis, and Tex Ritter were among the participants in the 1940–46 production of Soundies, the forerunners of today's music videos. Video jukeboxes continued to be popular in Europe, which is why Bobby Goldsboro ("Honey") and Don Williams ("Amanda") also made clips in the prevideo era.

As the first commercially available TV sets flickered to life in 1947–48, country-music faces were on them. At the time, country music was in the midst of its post–World War II boom. Jukeboxes, national radio broadcasts, songbooks, sheet music, singing-cowboy films, record sales, and live performances had brought country music a mass audience during the 1940s.

So in 1948 Pee Wee King and His Golden West Cowboys immediately went on the new TV medium in Louisville, Kentucky. In Cincinnati, *The Midwestern Hayride* began broadcasting locally on WAVE-TV that same year. Pittsburgh soon had The E-Z Time Ranch Gals, and early Philadelphia TV broadcasts featured country

ABOVE: *This 1993 book commemorated the accomplishments of* The Ozark Jubilee *as a network TV pioneer.*

singer Sally Starr. Country acts were aired live in many other communities as well.

The infant networks carried country shows, too, notably NBC's *Village Barn* (1948–50) and *Saturday Night Jamboree* (1948–49), both broadcast from New York. ABC had *Hayloft Hoedown* (1948), which originated in Philadelphia, and *ABC Barn Dance* (1949), from Chicago. In 1950 CBS launched *The Gene Autry Show*. The now-defunct Dumont network had *Windy City Jamboree* (also 1950).

In addition to Autry, country stars with their own early network TV shows included The Pickard Family (*Sunday Night at Home*, 1949, NBC), Patti Page (*Music Hall*, 1952, CBS), Pee Wee King (*Old American Barn Dance*, 1953, Dumont, and *The Pee Wee King Show*, 1955, ABC), Roy Rogers (1951–57, NBC), and Eddy Arnold (1952, CBS, and 1953, NBC).

"I did two summer replacements, one for Perry Como, over on CBS [1952], and one for Dinah Shore on NBC [1953]," recalls Arnold. *The Eddy Arnold Show* then aired as a prime-time series for a full season on ABC in 1956. "After that, *Eddy Arnold Time* was a syndicated show that we filmed in Chicago. It wasn't a great show, but it was a show."

The number of U.S. households with TV sets grew from ten thousand in 1947 to forty million in 1957. Stations sprouted in towns all over America, bringing opportunity to dozens of emerging country stars. Dottie West was broadcasting locally in Cleveland, Marty Robbins in Phoenix, Webb Pierce in Shreveport, Jim & Jesse in Tallahassee, preteen Dolly Parton in Knoxville, and the cast of Town Hall Party in Los Angeles. In 1956 *Billboard* magazine reported that there were eighty-nine local country shows airing in thirty-one different states. Scrambling for ready-made programming as TV exploded in popularity, the networks grabbed up country's biggest radio barn-dance shows, the *Midwestern Hayride* (1951–59, NBC), *National Barn Dance* (1953, Dumont), and *Grand Ole Opry* (1955–56, ABC). *The Ozark Jubilee* (1955–60, ABC) was the highest-rated and most prominent of these.

"Doing TV back then, when it was live, was very chaotic, because you never knew what was gonna happen," Brenda Lee remembers. "And of course there was no stopping; you just went right on with it and hoped for the best. But it was very honest; and I think the people recognized that. When I look back at those live shows now, I'm just astonished at some of the boo-boos we did make. But it had a lot of heart and soul.

"Red Foley discovered me, so I owe him a debt that can never be repaid. He had a show called *The Ozark Jubilee* out of Springfield, Missouri, which was the forerunner of country network television shows. A lot of us became known to the public and became household names because of him."

"Red Foley was like a father to me," concurs *Jubilee* regular Jean Shepard. "I loved this man dearly. I opened the newspaper in 1968 and it had a little thing saying, 'Singer Foley Dies.' I read it and it just broke my heart. It was just a little one-column thing, three or four paragraphs. To me, it should of been in the headlines; it should have been front page, because he was so much to country music."

Dozens of stars became *Ozark Jubilee* TV regulars, including Carl Smith, Wanda Jackson, Porter Wagoner, and Jimmy Wakely. Colleen Carroll also sang on Foley's show. Although she never attained

265

ABOVE: *As America's top-rated TV series,* The Beverly Hillbillies *spawned a slew of promotional items, including the book pictured here.*

disc stardom as a result of her 1957 TV exposure, Carroll gave birth to one who did, her son Garth Brooks.

As rock 'n' roll kicked the stuffing out of country radio in the late 1950s, country's early national TV popularity also waned. By the end of the decade only two country stars were network regulars: Tennessee Ernie Ford was a star on NBC in 1955–61 and then on ABC in 1961–65, and Jimmy Dean hosted a daytime series for CBS in 1957–59 and then prime-time series in 1957 for CBS and in 1963–66 for ABC.

"Television was a long time comin' to country music, because people didn't see country music as havin' any value," remembers Buck Owens. "They thought of all of us as havin' green teeth and two Fairlanes up on blocks out in front of the house."

Country TV pioneers Ernie Ford and Jimmy Dean faced a lot of that kind of prejudice. "They just didn't know anything about country," says Dean. "I remember once being told to 'Book Buck Owens.' Now, to book Buck Owens without his band and Don Rich singing tenor was as useless as a hog with a sidesaddle. But that's the stuff I ran into all the time. I used to be not quite as calm as I am now, and it was irritating. I fought a lot of battles."

Lynn Anderson was the token country singer on *The Lawrence Welk Show* during its 1967–68 seasons. "When I was on *The Lawrence Welk Show,* my one country song each week was the only country music on network television," she recalls. "That was it. It was the only game in town. And I truly, truly believe that that is what put me in a position to be able to have hit records like 'Rose Garden.'"

Faced with a stone wall at the networks, country music retreated to TV syndication in the 1960s. Until the rise of cable television, country music would mainly be seen on syndicated shows. These were often put on the air on weekends, next to profes-

sional wrestling and locally produced kiddie shows. And country's syndicated shows were often bought by stations in secondary markets, rather than big cities.

The trend had begun in the mid-1950s. As hundreds of new TV stations throughout the country scrambled to fill airtime when network programming wasn't available, the potential of syndicated shows wasn't lost on country's stars. Bob Atcher, Eddy Arnold, Foy Willing & The Riders of the Purple Sage, Faron Young, Jimmy Dean, and Tex Ritter were the pioneers of country TV syndication. Most of them were in a half-dozen markets or so by 1958.

Producer/director Al Gannaway visited Nashville to film in Technicolor in 1954–56. The resulting footage captured virtually all of the top *Opry* acts of the day. He continued to package these vivid performances in syndication for more than forty years under various titles.

The first of the barn dances to try TV syndication was Renfro Valley: "The *Renfro Valley* TV show was about 1956," recalls Anne Lair Henderson, the daughter of show founder John Lair. "They shot it out and around the Valley. The television series was trying to capture on film the way of life that John Lair had experienced as a boy here. There were thirteen episodes and each one had a theme. One would be maybe going on a hayride and songs that pertained to that. Part of it was shot indoors in the barn. They would have one scene talking about courting days, a couple, coming across the bridge in a horse and buggy with appropriate music and songs. There was one about molasses making. They were very natural and very good."

Following Renfro Valley's lead, the *Opry* was syndicated to twenty-five to thirty stations in 1960–63, and to twenty stations in 1965–69. The Midwestern Hayride went to thirty stations in 1966–72.

Town and Country Time, Western Ranch Party, and

LEFT: *The cartoon Hee Haw donkey "came to life" in this plush toy tucked into a denim tote.*

Hee Haw

Gannaway's *Stars of the Grand Ole Opry* were early syndicated ventures done by non-Nashville producers. Reasoning that they knew best how to market that kind of entertainment, Music City's executives began developing their own syndicated TV shows in the '60s. This launched Nashville as a television production center.

Flatt & Scruggs began syndicating their show in 1961 and were in twenty-five markets by 1965. Porter Wagoner, who also began his syndicated show in 1961, was in a hundred markets by 1970. That made him country's television king of his era.

Born in Missouri in 1927, Wagoner's local popularity led to an RCA contract in 1952. The folksy "Company's Comin'" and "A Satisfied Mind" put him on the map in 1954–55, and he joined the *Opry* in 1957. Three years later he was approached by the Chattanooga Medicine Company, the makers of Black Draught laxative, to front a TV series. He put together a troupe including trick fiddler Mac Magaha, comedian Speck Rhodes, personable banjo man Buck Trent, and "girl singer" Norma Jean.

Exposure to an estimated three million viewers per week in the 1960s made Wagoner an even bigger recording star. "Misery Loves Company," "The Cold Hard Facts of Life," "Skid Row Joe," "The Carroll County Accident," and "Green Green Grass of Home" are just a few of his '60s classics. Norma Jean left the company in 1967.

"The word got around that I was looking for a girl singer to be part of the Porter Wagoner television show," he remembers. "Dolly called and set up an appointment to come and audition. She sang a bunch of songs. I said, 'Do you know many hymns?' She said, 'Minnie Hems, who does she sew for?' She thought I was talking about a seamstress. She got the job."

Porter Wagoner and Dolly Parton took the TV show to even greater popularity and created a series of unforgettable duet records. After she left in 1974, Wagoner's show continued in syndication until 1981. In the wake of Roy Acuff's death he became the *Opry*'s unofficial ambassador.

Many stars followed the 1961 examples of Wagoner and Flatt & Scruggs. The Wilburn Brothers (begun in 1963), Arthur Smith (1963), Carl Smith (1964), Leroy Van Dyke (1965), Bobby Lord (1965), Ernest Tubb (1965), Billy Grammer (1965), Jim & Jesse (1966), The Stoneman Family (1967), Hugh X. Lewis (1968), The Oak Ridge Boys (1968), and Kitty Wells (1968) all had syndicated series during this decade.

"I think mine was about the third or fourth show of that type," recalls Bill Anderson, whose syndicated show began in 1965. "The stations would take and play the tapes Saturday afternoon or Saturday night. The station in Dallas would send the tape to the station in Houston and they'd play it the next week; so you were on different times and places in different cities.

"The thing that that television show did for Bill Anderson was it put a face with a name, put a personality with a sound. Back then it took a lot of years for people to really learn who an artist was and what an artist was all about. There weren't that many stations playing country music records. People knew 'Still' and they knew 'Po' Folks,' but a lot of people didn't know Bill Anderson. Television sped that up."

Billy Walker says TV syndication had a real impact on his career, too: "The first time I worked a concert after my *Country Carnival* television show had begun to air, we were in Norfolk, Virginia, where it was running

267

LEFT: *The most successful country TV series of all time was saluted by this lunch box bearing the likenesses of its stars, Buck Owens and Roy Clark.*

June & Johnny Cash

on TV. We worked this auditorium show in Norfolk, and they introduced Billy Walker, and gee, all of a sudden he just kind of took over the audience. I couldn't figure out why they were liking me more than they were liking anybody else, except my television show. That's the first time I really felt the power of television."

Buck Owens launched his syndicated show in 1968. He went a step further by sending out individual video clips of his performances to local stations. "In 1966 I made a video of a song called 'Sweet Rosie Jones,'" Owens reports. "I made four videos in those days [including 1969's hits 'Big in Vegas' and 'Tall Dark Stranger']. The last one was 'I Wouldn't Live in New York City If You Gave Me the Whole Damn Town' in 1970. They wanted me to change it to 'dang' and I said OK. But we went to the streets of New York and I recorded it in the street, made a video with the people. I was dressed in this outrageous costume. Not many people paid any attention to us. In New York City, they don't care what you look like. They're busy; they're on the hustle. I remember this one young black man came along and said, 'Hey, whatcha doin'?' 'Well, we're doin' television here.' And he sticks his head over the camera and says, 'Hello, L.A.!' That's New Yorkers.

"You have to remember, when I was doin' videos in the '60s, there was no place to play them. There was very little cable and the only way you could get them played on television was if the record company would buy the time. There were some people playin' records on television. One of 'em was in Atlanta. They said, 'You get us copies, we'll play 'em.' And so that's kind of what started it out. I don't know what caused me to do that. Probably just some dream of gettin' on TV, I suppose. We did it on film and then they later transferred it to tape."

By the early 1960s, television had penetrated 90 percent of American homes. Roy Rogers and Dale Evans picked up an ABC variety series in 1962. ABC was also the home of the rural sit-com *The Real McCoys* (1957–62), starring sometime country recitation artist Walter Brennan ("Old Rivers"). Roger Miller had a run on NBC in 1966. But it was CBS that became the most country-friendly of networks. Although it had few country-music shows, per se, it was the home of the wildly popular bucolic comedies *The Andy Griffith Show* (1960–68), *Gomer Pyle* (1964–70), and the No. 1–rated *The Beverly Hillbillies* (1962–71), plus its spin-offs *Petticoat Junction* (1963–70) and *Green Acres* (1965–71). All of them featured country comedy, music, and guest stars.

Hee Haw, the most musical of all the country comedy shows, was also on CBS. It went on the air in 1969 starring Buck Owens and Roy Clark. *Hee Haw* aired on CBS until 1971, and then thrived for the next twenty-five years as the most successful syndicated series in television history.

"*Hee Haw* was a real phenomenon," says latter-day cast member Phil Campbell. "My dad, Archie Campbell, was a great contributor to the show. Of course, when it premiered it was panned by almost everyone. No one thought it would last more than three weeks; and in four weeks it was the No. 1 television show in the nation."

"I went from one Stoneman family—my brothers and sisters and my heart and my soul—right into another family, called *Hee Haw*," relates banjo-playing comic Roni Stoneman. "Everybody on that show were total professionals. There was no jealousy because everybody knew their part. We were in there for one thing and that was to make a livin' and do a good job for the friends and neighbors and to have fun.

LEFT: *Johnny Cash and his wife June Carter Cash rose to unprecedented fame because of his ABC-TV network series.* ABOVE: *Cash acknowledged the show's impact with this No. 1-charting 1970 album.*

"Marjorie Main, 'Ma Kettle,' was my favorite actress when I was a little girl. I had been usin' her [raspy, braying] voice in the honky tonks in Washington, D.C. When 'the natives would get restless,' I'd say, 'Dad blame it! Set down!' and they'd start laughin' so they wouldn't fight each other. When I did the reading for *Hee Haw*, they said they wanted a skinny Marjorie Main. I said, 'You mean Ma Kettle?' And they said, 'Yes!'"

Grandpa Jones recalled that the show's genesis was in Canada. In his book *Everybody's Grandpa* he wrote, "In October 1968 I flew up to Canada to do a new television show that would feature country comedy. It was called *Hot Diggity*. I went on back to Nashville after my appearance and didn't think much more about it until a year later. Some of the people who had done *Hot Diggity* had decided to try an American show, and it was to be a summer replacement on CBS. I went home that day and told Ramona about it and said, 'Hee Haw. Who ever heard of a name like that for a show? That'll be enough to kill it right there.' But when I talked it over with Stringbean Akeman, who had also been approached, we agreed that our acts were getting a little stale and that our records weren't getting played much on the radio. Maybe a little TV exposure was what we needed. It was quite a little group that assembled in Nashville."

In addition to Clark, Owens, Akeman, Campbell, Stoneman, and Jones, the show featured Minnie Pearl, Junior Samples, Lulu Roman, The Hager Twins, Gordie Tapp, a bevy of beauties costumed like the buxom characters in the newspaper cartoon *Li'l Abner*, and guest appearances by every star in the country-music galaxy. The regulars who were veterans all became bigger stars than ever before. Grandpa Jones, for instance, did a much-imitated routine called "What's For Supper?" and

recorded a series of popular albums as a member of the *Hee Haw* gospel quartet (with Clark, Owens, and Kenny Price).

CBS also launched *The Glen Campbell Goodtime Hour* (1969–72).

"*The Glen Campbell Goodtime Hour* exposed me to the world," says Mel Tillis. "Porter Wagoner asked me to become a member of his show. I was on there for six months or so and then he fired me. The very next day I get a call from Glen Campbell." The show also made Jerry Reed into a national star and regularly showcased other talented Nashvillians. Campbell had to fight to feature each one, he says.

"I was told to cut down the country acts and get more, quote, 'stars' on the show," Campbell recalls. "I said, 'These people *are* stars, don't you understand? You live in this little world in New York. You know, there's a whole country out there. You oughta go visit it sometime. Maybe you'd have a new outlook on what you put on TV.' I said, 'You want ratings? I'll show you ratings.' I had Merle Haggard, Johnny Cash, Buck Owens, Minnie Pearl, Jerry Reed and Mel Tillis. The show was No. 1 that week. But that was the last big-rated show I had. After that, I would be singing with Fess Parker or Barbara Feldon. The next year they put on Sonny and Cher."

Critics hated CBS's country comedy and variety shows, but they were among the highest-rated series in America. Although the shows were enormously popular with viewers, advertisers perceived them as catering to older audiences; and this has been offered as one reason for their demise. Another legend has it that the wife of a high-ranking network executive despised hillbilly humor and ordered the shows axed. Despite their high ratings, the rural fun-fests—*The Beverly Hillbillies*, *Hee Haw*, *Green Acres*, and the like—were all purged from the CBS lineup in 1970–71. All are still widely shown in syndica-

Turn On To **COUNTRY** Turn On To

GENUINE

CMT

COUNTRY MUSIC TELEVISION℠

tion all over the world. Glen Campbell left the network in 1972.

Network surveys repeatedly indicated that country shows were most watched in the smaller markets of Middle America rather than the big cities. Nevertheless, some stars broke through to mass appeal thanks to TV exposure. ABC succeeded with *The Johnny Cash Show* in 1969–71. Like Glen Campbell, Johnny Cash ranked consistently in the top twenty during his network heyday.

The capstone of country's TV conquests in the '60s came in 1968 when the *Country Music Association Awards* became the first music-awards program on national television. It has remained a CBS ratings champion ever since.

Country's climb from regional art form to center stage in American pop culture continued during the next decade. A new, slicker generation of syndicated shows accompanied this progress in the 1970s. Most were produced by Nashville's Show Biz. Originally a spin-off of the Holiday Inn corporation, Show Biz was soon dubbed "the General Motors of country syndication" by *TV Guide*. The company's strong marketing efforts placed *Country Carnival*, *Marty Robbins Spotlight*, *The Country Place*, *Dolly!* and *That Good Ole Nashville Music* with many southeastern stations. Most successful of all were the Show Biz series *Pop Goes the Country* (1974–82) and *Nashville on the Road* (1975–83). The former had 140 stations at its peak and the latter was carried by 128, representing all regions of the United States.

Del Reeves, Stu Phillips, Tom T. Hall, Jim Stafford, Kenny Rogers, Ralph Emery, Rex Allen Jr., Bobby Goldsboro, Dolly Parton, and Donna Fargo all climbed on the TV syndication bandwagon at one time or another during the '70s.

On the network front, programs featuring The Everly Brothers (ABC), Jim Stafford (ABC), and Bobbie Gentry (CBS), as well as *Dean Martin Presents Music Country* (NBC), were all tried as summer-replacement shows in 1970–75. NBC offered *Music Country USA* in prime time in 1974 and *The Mac Davis*

Show in 1974–76. CBS had *Nashville 99* in its lineup throughout 1977. Crystal Gayle, John Denver, Tennessee Ernie Ford, Johnny Cash, Kenny Rogers, and Roy Clark were all stars of network specials of the '70s. ABC began carrying the Los Angeles–based *Academy of Country Music Awards* in 1974 (it has since moved to NBC and then CBS).

The highest-rated Grammy Awards telecast of all time occurred when the show broadcast from Nashville in 1973, but the accomplishment came amid much controversy. ABC was so opposed to having the Grammys in Music City that it dropped the special, which was picked up by CBS, its home ever since.

PBS began broadcasting *The Grand Ole Opry* live each spring during its fund-raising drives of 1978–81. The network was dismayed when the *Opry* decided not to continue the annual events in 1982, since they had raised more than $1 million each year they were aired. Also during the '70s, PBS launched the longest-lasting musical showcase in television history, *Austin City Limits*. Since its debut in 1976, virtually every major country act has been presented on the weekly concert series.

When variety programming on the "big three" networks died during the 1980s, exposure for all music genres suffered. Ironically, the last successful variety series was a country-music one. *Barbara Mandrell and The Mandrell Sisters* aired on NBC in 1980–82. But the star canceled her own rating triumph because of the exhausting demands of the weekly tapings. Country's other notable last-ditch network variety attempt was NBC's *Nashville Palace* of 1981–82.

CBS returned to rural humor with *The Dukes of Hazzard* (1979–85). With narration and a hit theme song (1980's "Good Ol' Boys") by Waylon Jennings and starring country singers John Schneider and Tom Wopat, it became the No. 1 show in America.

Tom Wopat played "Luke Duke" on the series. Born in 1951 and raised on a Wisconsin dairy farm, Wopat had the most musical background of the two stars, having worked in bands and in stage musicals during his youth. In the wake of the series' spectacular success he moved to Nashville and landed a country recording contract.

Wopat had moderate chart success with "Put Me Out of My Misery," "The Rock and Roll of Love," "Susannah," and a number of other titles in 1986–91. After spending a season as the host of TNN's *Prime Time Country* in 1996, he reverted to the musical stage. Wopat's credits include Broadway's *City of Angels* (1988), The Kennedy Center's *Carousel* (1986), the off-Broadway revival of *Oklahoma!* (1977), and Cy Coleman's Broadway show *I Love My Wife* (1977). Wopat was nominated for a Tony Award as the costar of the 1999 revival of *Annie Get Your Gun* with Tony winner Bernadette Peters in the title role.

John Schneider portrayed "Bo Duke" on *The Dukes of Hazzard*. Born in New York in 1959, he had mainly community-theater acting credits when he landed the role that made him a TV star. During his struggling days, Schneider had recorded an obscure pop album. When he got a recording contract as a result of his TV stardom, Schneider was initially groomed as an Elvis-type vocalist.

But after switching to Nashville recording and an MCA Records contract in 1984, he consciously lowered his voice to sound more "country." As a result, he hit his stride with nine consecutive top-ten successes, including "I've Been around Enough to Know," "Country Girls," and "What's a Memory Like You (Doing in a Love Like This)." In the 1990s Schneider reverted to acting, directing, and producing. He was particularly prominent in made-for-TV movies. In 1991 he starred on Broadway in the musical *Grand Hotel*.

As a result of the blockbuster success of *The Dukes of Hazzard*, a number of similar "country" series were launched. *Harper Valley P.T.A.* (NBC, 1981–82), *Enos* (CBS, 1980–81), and *Lobo* (NBC, 1979–81) were among these. Kenny Rogers, Johnny Cash, and Dolly Parton emerged as actors in highly rated TV movies during the decade.

Merle Haggard's "Movin' On," John Denver's "Sunshine," and Steve Wariner's "Who's the Boss" were used as themes in like-titled TV series. But apart from this exposure or on awards broadcasts, talk shows, and occasional specials, the country sound was all but silenced on networks, along with every other kind of music.

Local programming continued to be country's mainstay throughout the late 1970s and early 1980s. The CMA polled TV stations throughout the country in 1980. Of the 135 stations that responded to its questionnaire, 71.9 percent carried country shows, either local creations or syndicated productions. On a grassroots level, at least, the demand for country television seemed as healthy as ever. But following the 1981 sale of Show Biz, the production of syndicated series in Nashville declined drastically. Jim Owens Productions launched *This Week in Country Music* and *Crook & Chase* in syndication from Nashville in the mid-'80s, but by 1986 all of the other weekly syndicated country shows were gone.

And that is why the advent of cable television and the 1983 launches of CMT and TNN heralded a new beginning. Since then, TNN has become one of the ten largest cable channels in America. CMT has expanded into Europe, Asia, and Latin America and is now seen in sixty-one nations around the world.

273

ABOVE: *This video marketed Michelle Lee's insightful TV movie based on the life of country star Dottie West.*

Fifteen

Honky-Tonk Angels

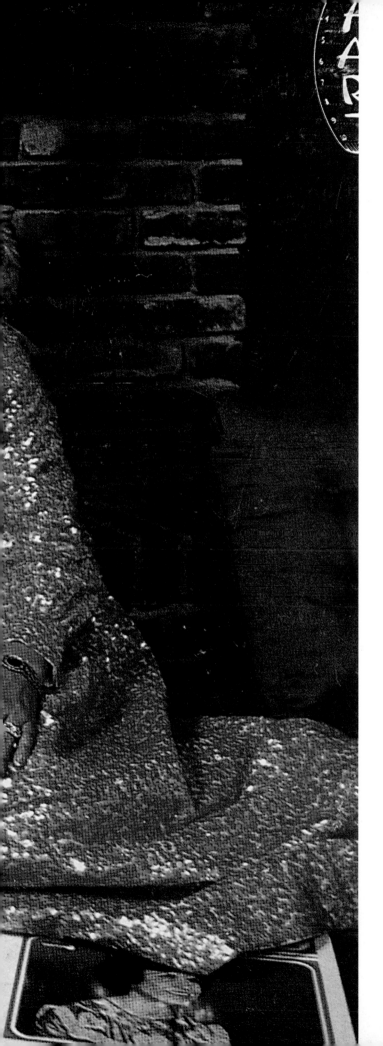

As the new millennium approached in the summer of 1999, country became the first musical style to achieve gender equality on its charts. Fully half of the style's top-forty hits were sung by women. And such figures as the eleven-million-selling Shania Twain, the six-million-selling Dixie Chicks, Faith Hill, Jo Dee Messina, Mary Chapin Carpenter, and Martina McBride were on *Billboard*'s pop/mainstream top-selling-albums chart.

This development is all the more striking since throughout its prior history country music was overwhelmingly male-dominated. The style held on to the vestiges of Victorian morality long after America's more urban musical cultures had abandoned it. Women's proper sphere was considered to be the home. Public life was discouraged and show business, in particular, was an unseemly female occupation.

So in the early years of its evolution, most women in country music were in family acts. Sara and Maybelle Carter may have been the lead voice and instrumentalist of The Carter Family, but they were chaperoned and bossed by Sara's husband A.P. None of the southern radio barn-dance shows created female stars in the 1930s.

275

LEFT: *Lynn Anderson lounges in style as a leading hit maker of the 1970s.*
ABOVE: *Brenda Lee was one of Nashville's few female teen idols.*

Loretta

Tammy Wynette

The first truly national country women stars were those promoted by Chicago's *National Barn Dance*, notably LuluBelle, Patsy Montana, and Louise Massey. In the 1940s, a large number of husband-wife acts emerged, including Wilma Lee & Stoney Cooper, Joe & Rose Lee Maphis, James & Martha Carson, Doc & Chickie Williams, Curly Fox & Texas Ruby, Bob Atcher & Bonne Blue Eyes, Daisy Mae & Old Brother Charlie, and Molly O'Day & Lynn Davis.

Perhaps not coincidentally, some of that era's biggest female singing stars left country music for pop careers, notably Patti Page, Jo Stafford, Mary Ford, and Kay Starr. Country's substyles of the '40s, bluegrass and western swing, both emphasized aggressive instrumental ability and did not welcome female performers. The only woman star at *The Grand Ole Opry* was comedian Minnie Pearl.

The development of the hard-edged honky-tonk style didn't improve women's position in country music, either. The rough cigarettes-and-whiskey atmosphere of the honky-tonk was no place for "the fairer sex." Fewer than 10 percent of the country hit records of 1945–55 featured female voices.

When Kitty Wells sang "It Wasn't God Who Made Honky Tonk Angels" in 1952, female listeners cheered their approval. The NBC radio network banned it, and Wells was forbidden to sing the outspoken tune on *The Grand Ole Opry*. But it climbed to No. 1 on the charts nonetheless, and the singer was crowned "The Queen of Country Music" thanks to her breakthrough. Goldie Hill, Jean Shepard, and The Davis Sisters also achieved chart breakthroughs in the early 1950s. But life on the road was tough even for a man. Having a stable home and children as well as a singing career was extremely difficult for women at the time.

Only Brenda Lee and Wanda Jackson emerged with national hits in the aggressive rockabilly style. With the coming of the Nashville Sound, however, it was a different story. Dottie West, Skeeter Davis, Jeannie Seely, Connie Smith, Jan Howard, and Norma Jean all emerged with hits in the 1960s as a result of the modernization of country music. So did the peerless, unforgettable Patsy Cline.

"On the tours back then, the women were just added attractions," says Cline's widower Charlie Dick. "But Patsy had worked a few shows with some of the big promoters around the country and I think they'd seen she had some drawing power. I think she helped a lot of these women go out and do it and take over."

"Patsy probably wouldn't have known what

the word 'women's lib' meant, but she was a feminist before people knew what that was," says George Hamilton IV. "This was at a time when females were sort of trotted out in their ginghams and lace and expected to brighten the proceedings, be 'window dressing' on the guys' shows. Patsy Cline would have none of that. She insisted on bein' front and center, the first woman I can remember to headline a country show."

"Back then it was more like,

277

LEFT: *Loretta Lynn is pictured here in the late 1960s when she emerged as a powerful singer-songwriter.*
ABOVE: *Tammy Wynette was an Alabama beautician before becoming a country queen.*

'You're the girl singer with the band,'" recalls Jan Howard. "There was no such thing as the Jan Howard Show, the Jean Shepard Show. You were the girl singer, that's all. That's the way it always was."

"When I first came to town, just about every show would have just one girl singer," adds Connie Smith. "You'd get so lonesome backstage, because you just wanted someone to visit with."

"There wasn't as much of a place for women in country music as there is today," says Waylon Jennings. "Women have had a rougher time than men in country music all through the years. They weren't closing acts; they couldn't have their own shows. They used to have to go get men's songs and make 'em into women's songs. Now they write for women; they didn't do that before."

"During that period of time, we were singing songs written by men," concurs Jeannie Seely. "We were singing songs from a male perspective. We were singing songs the way men wanted us to feel, whether that's the way we felt or not. Some of my early songs, it was like, 'Yeah, that's great Jeannie, but...' They didn't really want me to record them. They said, 'That's just a little bit too bold' or, 'too stark.'"

The three figures who changed female country music most profoundly were Loretta Lynn, Tammy Wynette, and Dolly Parton. Their careers, their lives, and their songs became beacons to a generation of women. Along with Patsy Cline, all three continue to be powerful influences to this day.

The first of this trio to emerge was Loretta Lynn (born 1935). The daughter of a Kentucky coal miner, Lynn was wed at age thirteen and the mother of four by age eighteen. She was a twenty-five-year-old housewife when she came to Nashville with her first record, "I'm a Honky Tonk Girl," in 1960.

"I wanted to be just like Patsy," Lynn recalls. "Bless her heart, she done everything she could to help me. Patsy was a person that said her words perfect. If you've ever listened to her singing, you'll notice that every word that she says in her songs are perfect. Right? Well, for me and Patsy to sit down and carry on a conversation, she would be laughing at everything I would say. Patsy taught me how to do a lot of my dressing. She bought a lot of my clothes for me.

"She was like my mother, my friend. It was just like a bonding that you just don't have with a lot of people.

"Take me as I am, because I couldn't change. There wasn't no way for me to change. I was having a hard enough time being me. So why should I change? Why should I change the way I say a word because somebody else wants me to?

"I wrote songs just like my Mommy wrote. I wrote about things that happened. And I was writing about things that was going on that was not talked about by other people maybe. You know, you can ask me anything. I won't tell you a lie."

Her candor and humor charmed the country-music world. Lynn's forthright "Wine Women and Song," "Blue Kentucky Girl," "Fist City," "Don't Come Home A-Drinkin'," and the like, made her a chart-topping success in 1962–69. Her strikingly original material stood up for America's housewives. "I sang it like the women lived it," she explained. By the late '60s even mainstream magazines and TV talk shows were smitten with her straight-talking, country-feminist style.

"I adore Loretta Lynn," states Gail Davies. "I

RIGHT: *East Tennessee native Dolly Parton is one of the most revered country stars in history.*
ABOVE: *She is such an icon that her image has been on coloring books, magnets, lollipops, and fashion dolls like this.*

told Loretta, 'Everyone else has conformed to get the world to accept country music. You have remained exactly the way you are, and they have come to you.' I really respect Loretta for that."

Lynn's song "Coal Miner's Daughter" topped the charts in 1970. The controversial "The Pill" and "Rated X," "Love Is the Foundation," "One's on the Way," and "You're Lookin' at Country" are among her many other hits of the '70s. In 1972 Lynn became the first woman to be named Entertainer of the Year by the Country Music Association.

Her 1960–95 fan club, headed by sisters Loudilla, Loretta, and Kay Johnson, served as the prototype for all other country-music fan organizations. Lynn and the Johnson sisters were early boosters of Nashville's "Fan Fair." Begun in 1972, it is the annual "gathering of the tribes" of the country fan clubs.

"We started Fan Fair," the star says proudly. "This is the relationship that should be in country music. The public's where it's at. They're the ones that feeds us. The best thing for all of 'em on Music Row to think while they're drivin' their Mercedes is, 'If you don't know where you come from, how are you gonna know where you're going?'"

At the fan-voted *Music City News* awards, Loretta Lynn was named the public's favorite female vocalist twelve years in a row. She also won ten Duo of the Year trophies with Conway Twitty. No other female country artist has been so showered with honors by her audience.

"I've got a room full of awards now," she says. "And as I go back and look at 'em, I know what I achieved to get each one. All you have to do is open up your life to The People. When young people ask me how I got where I'm at, I say, 'It's just absolutely hard work.' There ain't nobody gonna wave a magic wand. You pay for what success you get.

"It's very hard to be a singer and a housewife, mother and a woman. That's just too many things to be at one time. It's much easier for a man in this business."

Tammy Wynette (1942–1998) was the divorced mother of three when she arrived in Nashville in 1965. Born Virginia Wynette Pugh, she'd already picked cotton, been a barmaid, and worked as a beautician in Birmingham by then.

"She sure went through a lot of old beat-up cars and dresses with holes in them to get here," says producer Billy Sherrill, who discovered her. "So I'm sure she was pretty hungry for it. She had this beautiful, unique voice with a tear in every word. She touched people. She touched women. She was the women's spokesperson.

"I hate to say she did what she was told, but she did. And she believed in me 1000 percent. Everything I said, she did."

In 1966, "Apartment #9" became her first hit record. Wynette remembered being incredibly "green" at the recording session.

"Sherrill said, 'Now Tammy, you have to hang around and do overdubs.' I didn't know what the word meant, but it had something to do with this record, so I thought I better hang around. He brought out a little stool and set this little box on it and I could hear my voice coming through that. And I had to sing harmony along with myself with that little box, and that's how the harmony track was done. I thought, 'Oh that's how Skeeter Davis did it. I loved her records.' I just sang the only way I knew how. I told Billy, 'I am not the best, but I sure am the loudest.'"

Like her contemporary Loretta Lynn, Wynette communicated honesty and authenticity. "I learned in the very beginning that I was treated a lot better by the media if I was honest with 'em," she said. "And I feel like if you change after you've become successful, then you're defeatin' your own purpose. Because you made it by bein' the way you are. I like that intimate feelin' of bein' close to an audience. I'd rather they know that I'm just a plain human being."

Her teardrop-in-every-note delivery captivated listeners. Tammy Wynette had the longest string of No. 1 records of any woman in country history. Her performances ranged from the defiance of 1982's "Another Chance" to the trembling "D-I-V-O-R-C-E" of 1968, the feisty "Your Good Girl's Gonna Go Bad" of 1967, and the sexual "Womanhood" of 1978. Her signature song, 1968's "Stand by Your Man," is said to be the biggest-selling female country record of all time.

"I just tried to go with the times," she said. "I tried to do modern, up-to-date material. The music has changed since I came to town, so it has to have changed from Kitty Wells to me."

Wynette went through four husbands before finding happiness with songwriter George Richey. Her 1969–75 marriage to country superstar George Jones brought her classic duet records, her fourth daughter, and physical abuse.

Arsonists attacked her home; she was kidnapped and beaten; a series of abdominal operations left her in chronic physical agony; she filed for bankruptcy; she was treated for addiction to painkillers at the Betty Ford Center. Tabloids and fans were riveted to her "heroine of heartbreak" image.

Her long string of country hits ended in the late 1980s. But in 1992 Wynette and The KLF hit MTV with the international pop smash "Justified and Ancient." In '93 she teamed up with Dolly Parton and Loretta Lynn for a trio album. In '94 came a CD that paired her with Elton John, Sting, Lyle Lovett, and Smokey Robinson. A year later she reunited with Jones for a memorable duet album.

Tammy Wynette died at home in early 1998, probably of causes related to her long physical deterioration. Her memorial service in Nashville attracted fans from as far away as Kansas, New York, and California.

Parton provided the event's most emotional moment. "It's awful hard to say goodbye," she began, calling Wynette, "my little girlfriend." She performed a bit of "Didn't Hear the Thunder," a song the two cowrote, and then dedicated "Shine On" to her late friend, saying, "She shined then; she's shining now; and she'll shine forever more." People wept when Parton closed with one simple sung line, "I Will Always Love You."

East Tennessee native Dolly Parton (born 1946) had stars in her eyes from the time she was a child. With encouragement from her uncles and aunts she began singing on local TV in Knoxville at age ten. She recorded a small-label rockabilly single called "Puppy Love" at age thirteen and did a guest appearance on the *Opry*. While still in high school she recorded a 1962 single for Mercury Records.

"There was something about her," recalls song publisher Buddy Killen. "You could tell Dolly was talented even then. Even though she was so young. I signed her as a songwriter. When they would come to Nashville, her Uncle Bill would sleep in his car and Dolly would sleep in the YWCA for about a dollar a night. They would come pretty often and bring new songs for me to hear. I produced some records with her. We did a song called 'It May

281

ABOVE: *This 1977 Crystal Gayle LP contained her massive crossover hit "Don't It Make My Brown Eyes Blue."*

Barbara Mandrell

Not Kill Me but It's Sure Gonna Hurt' that she wrote."

Immediately after her high school graduation in 1964, Parton boarded a bus bound for Music City. She met Carl Dean on her first day in town and married him in 1967.

"When I came to Nashville to stay, it was kinda like goin' to Oz," she recalls. "I went hungry a lot. I walked the streets a lot. I wrote many songs talkin' about that. One of my favorites is 'Down on Music Row,' which is a song about washin' my face in the fountain at the Hall of Fame and eatin' a stale donut on the steps of RCA waitin' for the buildin's to open.

"It was a disappointment, because I thought as a dreamy eyed kid, I was just gonna graduate from high school on a Friday night, which I did in 1964, come to Nashville on Saturday mornin' and that by Monday I'd be a star, surely. Well, it was many Mondays after that. I went hungry a lot and I cried a lot, I was homesick a lot, but I had promised I wouldn't go home until I had somethin' to show for it, and I didn't.

"I know now just how fortunate I really was, because I know a lot of people that came to town about the same time I did, had more talent than I did and they never made it. So I've learned through the years that hard work is one thing, talent is another and bein' there at the right time is another. I still believe, certainly more so as I get older, that there's a great amount of luck to go along with it."

Two years after arriving in Nashville, Parton began making waves as a songwriter. Bill Phillips ("Put It Off until Tomorrow"), Skeeter Davis ("Fuel To the Flame"), and Hank Williams Jr. ("I'm in No Condition") were among the first to record her tunes.

"Porter Wagoner came to me and I said, 'Who's gonna replace Norma Jean in your show?'" remembers Chet Atkins. "And he said, 'Dolly Parton.' I said, 'Who's that?' I didn't remember having heard of her before. He says he told me, 'If she doesn't sell, I'll pay for her ses-

sion.' Anyway, I signed her up" to RCA Records in 1968.

"I remember we used to sit around that conference table when we'd have meetings and say, 'When is she gonna be the number-one singer in the world?' Then somebody'd say, 'Well, we gotta stop her from wearin' those wigs.' She's been right all of her life in what she wanted to do, you know. That was the smartest thing she could have done, 'cause it made her different. But we didn't realize it at the time."

With powerfully emotional records like "Coat of Many Colors," "Jolene," and "I Will Always Love

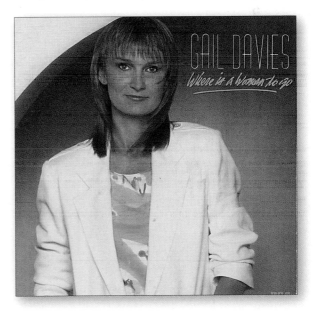

You," Parton outpaced her mentor Wagoner in 1970–74. After apprenticing as his "girl singer," she struck out on her own in 1975. By 1980 she was a multimedia phenomenon. Her empire includes song publishing, real estate, restaurants, the Dollywood theme park, a cosmetics line, a wig business, and a movie production company.

"I don't know about the other women in the business, but I think you don't have to be tough—you have to be strong," she says. "I don't have a hard heart, but I definitely have strength in the muscles around it. I think you have to take that approach. You can-

283

LEFT: *Barbara Mandrell showcased her multi-instrumental abilities on national TV in 1980–81.*
ABOVE: *After succeeding as a songwriter and singer, Gail Davies became one of Music Row's few female record producers.*

not let people walk on you or they will. You definitely have to be strong and you have to be blunt. You have to just be open and fair."

During the countrypolitan era, Dolly Parton crossed over to the pop charts with "Here You Come Again" (1977), "9 to 5" (1980), and her duet with Kenny Rogers "Islands in the Stream" (1983). Her 1987 *Trio* album with Emmylou Harris and Linda Ronstadt is regarded as one of modern country's landmark records. The three issued a best-selling follow-up in 1999. Parton's song "I Will Always Love You" achieved new notoriety as a blockbuster 1992 pop hit for Whitney Houston and as a country duet hit by Parton with Vince Gill in 1995.

Dolly Parton's bodacious figure, glitzy outfits, elaborate wigs, and flashy makeup have made her an international icon. Her rise from mountain poverty to glamour and wealth is the stuff of American legend. She describes herself as "sort of like the fairy godmother of country music."

The compelling songs and life stories of Dolly Parton, Loretta Lynn, and Tammy Wynette led to increasing interest by the media in country's female performers. *Billboard* reported in 1971 that women were recording nearly one-fourth of the popular country records of the day. *Country Music* magazine devoted an issue to female singers in 1974. *Stereo Review, Redbook,* and *Newsweek* all filed female-country stories during the next four years.

During the 1970s women doubled their share of the country marketplace from 10 to 20 percent. They sang on eighty No. 1 records during that decade, up dramatically from twelve in 1960–69 and up astronomically from just five No. 1 records in the 1950s.

On April 26, 1980, records by women on *Billboard*'s country-music chart occupied positions 1, 2, 3, 4, 5, 8, 10, and 11. This was so unprecedented that the magazine even pointed it out with a little article. Parton and Wynette were represented, as was Nashville Sound veteran Dottie West. But so was a new breed of female stylist, the glittering, gowned "show queens" of the countrypolitan era—Lynn Anderson,

Crystal Gayle, and Barbara Mandrell. Equally at home in the casinos of Las Vegas and the *Opry* house, these women did not have southern accents and recorded songs that were less identifiably "country" than their predecessors had.

Sunny, blonde Lynn Anderson had grown up in California as the equestrian-champion daughter of country songwriters Liz and Casey Anderson. Born in 1947, she was eighteen when she accompanied her parents to Music City in 1966. She was offered a recording contract at once.

"Gee, I've never felt like being a woman was any kind of burden at all," says overnight star Anderson. "I've had way too much fun. I can't say that I feel like it was more difficult for me in any way because I was a girl.

"I took a job working for a record company. They had offered me a record deal as well, thinking that this weird teenager from California who sang country music had to be some kind of an oddity, so maybe somebody would actually play her stuff."

After succeeding with "Rocky Top" and other tunes on Chart Records, she graduated to Columbia Records and scored a pop-crossover home run with 1970's "Rose Garden."

"We're sitting there with our mouths open thinking, 'How did this happen?'" she recalls. "My people had been trying to get us on the *Johnny Carson Show* for quite a long time. I had

ABOVE: *Her 1980 debut LP earned Lacy J. Dalton rave reviews in dozens of national magazines.*

Holly Dunn

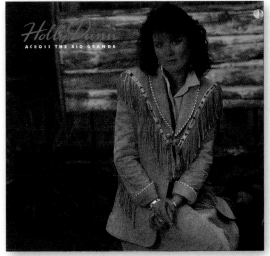

country music, but that didn't bother me. I loved it. And there were a lot of people that I call country music 'closet' fans. They loved it, but they didn't want to admit it. So they'd listen to it in privacy."

Lynn got Crystal Gayle started with a contract at her record label, Decca. But the younger sister's career didn't take off until she struck out on her own at United Artists.

Barbara Mandrell never had a big pop-crossover hit, but she became the most widely known of the show queens, thanks to weekly exposure on her own network television series. Born in Houston in 1948, Mandrell is the daughter of a country guitarist. During her childhood in southern California she learned to play steel guitar, banjo, saxophone, accordion, bass, and mandolin. Guitarist Joe Maphis got her a spot on TV's *Town Hall Party* as "The Princess of the Steel" and took the prodigy on the road. By 1962 Mandrell was touring with Johnny Cash and Patsy Cline.

She quit show business when she got married, but when she saw Dolly Parton at *The Grand Ole Opry* in 1968 Mandrell realized how much she missed the stage. She moved to Nashville and began performing in its Printers Alley nightclub district. Brenda Lee and others raved about her show, which led to a recording contract.

In 1969–72 Mandrell made her mark on the country charts with "blue-eyed-soul" remakes of r&b hits of the day. Her 1973 hit "Midnight Oil" is considered to be a female country breakthrough because of its frank sexuality. Between 1978 and 1984 Mandrell dominated the charts with seventeen top-ten hits, including "I Was Country When Country Wasn't Cool" and "Sleeping Single in a Double Bed." She achieved her most pop airplay with her 1979 rendition of Luther Ingram's r&b hit "(If Loving You Is Wrong) I Don't Want to Be Right."

Barbara Mandrell & The Mandrell Sisters showcased her as a dancer, comedian, host, and instrumentalist each week on NBC in 1980–82. Dozens of country stars got wide exposure on the show, and Mandrell also featured a gospel performance each week. It was

had four or five number-one country records. They just weren't interested. Two days later, when 'Rose Garden' was rocking up the pop charts, they called and wanted me on the show. I was the same person with the same things to say, the same clothes, the same songs as two days before it hit the pop charts. But suddenly that made me acceptable to them. I never forgot that."

"Rose Garden" and Anne Murray's "Snowbird" (also 1970) ushered in a decade of crossover stardom for country's women. Crystal Gayle's moment in the pop limelight was 1977's languid "Don't It Make My Brown Eyes Blue." Born Brenda Gail Webb in 1951, she was given her stage name by her sister, Loretta Lynn. Unlike her elder sibling, Gayle moved from the Kentucky mountains when she was a toddler. Raised in Wabash, Indiana, Gayle was as much influenced by Lesley Gore and Brenda Lee as she was by traditional country music.

Her sleek fashions, elegant long brunette hair, and soft-spoken grace were ideal for country's new uptown image. Her folkish sound and the tiny "cry" in her voice went down easily with both pop and country audiences.

"When I first started listening to country music and singing it, when I was going to school, I'd have people make fun of me. My sister was in the business and I was very proud. I took her picture to school many times. The kids were sort of laughing about

285

ABOVE: *Holly Dunn's 1988 album was marketed by Mary Tyler Moore's record label.*

Rosanne Cash

network television's last successful variety series. Wearying of the weekly production grind, she quit the show when it was attracting forty million viewers per week. Mandrell put the skills she'd learned on TV to work in her 1983 Las Vegas stage extravaganza "The Lady Is a Champ." But a year later she was severely injured in a car crash in Nashville.

After her recuperation she published her best-selling autobiography *Get To the Heart* (1990) and resumed her career. A recurring role on TV's popular *Baywatch* and a downturn in her recording popularity led Mandrell to quit touring. In 1997 she staged a farewell concert at the *Opry* House called "The Last Dance" and announced that she was going to pursue an acting career.

Not every woman of the era aspired to uptown glitz and glamour. The breakthrough of Emmylou Harris in the mid-1970s was an inspiration to many female performers.

"When I moved to Nashville in the beginning of 1976, there was a phrase being coined for country music called 'NashVegas,'" recalls Gail Davies. "Because it had lost the real guttural rawness that I loved so much about it in the '50s. I wanted to get back to that real sound. I didn't want it to sound too polished and slick. It was very difficult because songs that were hits on the charts were 'Sleeping Single in a Double Bed' and things that were very, very different from what I was. And everybody went, 'What is this? This doesn't work. She is not wearing glittery dresses. She's not wearing flashy earrings. We can't get her booked in Las Vegas.' I didn't wanna be in Las Vegas. I wanted to do raw, edgy country music."

Born Patricia Gail Dickerson in Oklahoma in 1948, Gail Davies became one of the most articulate and outspoken women of her generation. After singing fourteen top-twenty hits and writing "Someone Is Looking for Someone Like You," "Bucket to the South," and "Grandma's Song," she became one of Music Row's few female record producers.

Lacy J. Dalton (Jill Byrem, born 1946) came to Nashville from a similar background. After growing up in Pennsylvania she became a California hippie. A tape of her folksinging earned her a Columbia Records contract on Music Row in 1979. Her riveting, raspy voice attracted radio's attention immediately.

"When I got my record contract in Nashville, I was living in California," Dalton reports. "To come into Nashville from the California music scene was, for me, almost like going from color into black & white. Because there was still a lot of compromise that I needed to do to be played on country radio. In some ways, I felt like a stranger. But in other ways people were so kind to me. Pickers in the studio knew that I was nervous and I'll never forget how they took me under their wing. The thing about Southern hospitality is so real. Even though I was different, I was treated fairly and kindly."

Among her many hits of the 1980s are the anthems "Hillbilly Girl with the Blues" and "16th Avenue" and remakes of the classics "The Tennessee Waltz" and "Dream Baby."

286

TOP: *Rosanne Cash's "I Don't Know Why You Don't Want Me" on this LP earned her a Grammy Award.*
ABOVE: *Janie Fricke, the 1983 CMA Female Vocalist of the Year.*
RIGHT: *Tanya Tucker on the Opry House stage in 1982.*

Tanya Tucker

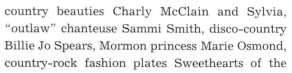

"I think women have a whole different set of problems in any business," commented singer-songwriter Holly Dunn. "I don't think it's just the music business. For the three steps we take forward there's about two we take back, sometimes. We still don't earn the money that the men do. We're still out-numbered in record sales."

Dunn was another who was inspired by the example of Emmylou Harris. Born in San Antonio in 1957, she arrived in Nashville to write songs in 1979. For six years she worked as a receptionist, studio singer, and publishing-company staff songwriter. She broke through as a record maker with "Daddy's Hands" in 1986, the first of ten top-ten hits. Holly Dunn joined the cast of *The Grand Ole Opry* in 1989. In recent years she has become a successful radio disc jockey.

Other disciples of Emmylou who had an impact on the country charts of the '80s included Carlene Carter, Juice Newton, and Rosanne Cash. The last named is the daughter of Johnny Cash, but like many of the others she was raised in California. Rosanne Cash (born 1956) made her mark with a string of records produced by Rodney Crowell, her husband from 1979 to 1992. Such 1980s hits as "Seven Year Ache" and "I Don't Know Why You Don't Want Me" showcased his punchy, country-rock productions and her liquid alto. As her songwriting became increasingly introspective and impressionistic, Cash moved from Nashville to New York, remarried, and pursued a pop-music career.

The diversity of images and musical styles available to women in the 1980s was impressive. Show queen and California country-rocker were only two of the options. Yodeler Margo Smith, blind pianist Terri Gibbs, pop-country beauties Charly McClain and Sylvia, "outlaw" chanteuse Sammi Smith, disco-country Billie Jo Spears, Mormon princess Marie Osmond, country-rock fashion plates Sweethearts of the Rodeo, and the sibling quartet The Forester Sisters were all on the country hit parade.

More than anyone else Tanya Tucker shattered the timeworn innocent-country-sweetheart stereotype. She became the field's first female star with a freely sexual image. Born in 1958 in Texas, Tucker was only thirteen when "Delta Dawn" made her an overnight sensation in 1972. As a teen she sang a number of songs with similarly "adult" lyrics. Her torrid vocals were startling; and as she progressed as a young hit maker in the '80s, she shocked conservatives with her sexy outfits, party-girl antics, sassy talk, love affairs, and out-of-wedlock children. To Music Row's surprise, fans adored the prodigal daughter.

"I don't make a conscious effort to be anything particularly different," Tucker says. "It's just, 'Hey, here I am. This is me.' I've settled down some, but I still like to rock."

Tabloid newspapers made much of her liaisons with Merle Haggard, Don Johnson, Glen Campbell, and Andy Gibb. But Tucker has recorded a consistently excellent body of work during her impressively long tenure on the charts. "San Antonio Stroll" and "Texas (When I Die)" characterized her work in the '70s. She staged a comeback in the '80s with "Strong Enough to Bend," "I'll Come Back as Another Woman," and more than a dozen other big hits. She remained in the top ten in 1997.

All three of the members of the studio backup singing group Phase II graduated to solo recording contracts. Judy Rodman and Karen Taylor-

ABOVE: *Reba McEntire's 1995 tour book reflected her stage spectacular. The concert extravaganza traveled via 12 semi-trucks, five tour buses, and a private jet.*

McEntire

Good had only moderate success, but sweet-voiced Janie Fricke ruled the country charts in 1980–86. Born in Indiana in 1947, Fricke performed both country two-steps ("Down to My Last Broken Heart") and rockers ("He's a Heartache") during her hit-making years. She developed a stage show with bouncy choreography and stylish fashions. In the '90s she became a regular on The Statler Brothers' TV show.

Between 1981 and 1989 female acts gradually moved forward, eventually occupying 25 to 35 percent of any given year's charts. By 1989 country music had become an enormous business, worth approximately $500 million. Its biggest female star mounted an eye-popping stage spectacular that traveled in multiple tractor-trailer rigs and featured special effects, multiple costume changes, illusions, dancing, massive lighting grids, video screens, and elaborate sets. Reba McEntire took female country music to an entirely new level with her emphasis on showy video productions and frankly ambitious empire building.

"I want to take charge," she said bluntly. "I'm always greedy. I want to do more. I'm very competitive, very ambitious. Who don't like to win? You show me a person who don't like to win."

She was brought up on the competitive Oklahoma rodeo circuit. Born in 1955, McEntire was raised to hoist feed sacks and ride herd just like her father and brother. The hardheaded tomboy became a barrel racer, but she was also blessed with a soaring, emotional singing voice. Cowboy singer Red Steagall discovered her and financed the Nashville recording session that earned her a contract in 1975.

Reba McEntire spent the remainder of the decade in the lower reaches of the country charts. She was styled and restyled a number of times by record executives, placed in various musical settings, and generally treated like the hick starlet that she was. When she finally began having hits in 1980–82, she used her new status to take charge.

"I've taken my career into control myself," she said. "I don't want to be a puppet anymore." Her 1984 album was titled *My Kind of Country*. It contained her remakes of classics by Ray Price, Carl Smith, Faron Young, and Connie Smith, as well as her No. 1 hits "How Blue" and "Somebody Should Leave." Her intense, highly ornamented vocal style was then spotlighted on more than twenty-five chart-busting performances of 1985–92, including "Whoever's in New England," "Fancy," and "Is There Life Out There," all of which were accompanied by her emoting in effective videos.

Her four consecutive wins as the CMA's Female Vocalist of the Year (1984–87) are unmatched by anyone. With husband Narvel Blackstock she became a show-business mogul. After a 1991 plane crash killed seven of her band members, her star rose ever higher.

"Reba McEntire is very good at zeroing in on that female audience, trying to find out what it is women wanna hear," observes Gail Davies. "And then she sings about that."

"I'm trying to sing songs for women," comments McEntire, "to say for them what they can't say for themselves. I want to be those women's friend."

289

ABOVE: *Reba was featured on the cover of every women's magazine, including this* Ladies Home Journal.

Sixteen

Young
Country

Between 1989 and 1991, the country-music business doubled, from $500 million annually to a billion. By 1995, it had doubled again, to over $2 billion. By the dawn of 1996, two-thirds of the albums on the country charts had been declared Gold, Platinum, or Multi-Platinum for their sales accomplishments.

Tabulated by the Recording Industry Association of America (RIAA), Gold Record awards are given to albums that sell in excess of five hundred thousand copies, which translates into roughly $3.5 million in gross revenues. Platinum awards are for sales above one million units, a $7 million gross. When the first RIAA Gold Record awards were made in 1958, none of them went to country artists. In 1959 only one country performer sold Gold, Tennessee Ernie Ford. In 1970 there were eight Gold-selling country artists: Johnny Cash, Charley Pride, Glen Campbell, Loretta Lynn, Tammy Wynette, Anne Murray, Ray Stevens, and Merle Haggard. A compilation of "outlaw" music became country's first Platinum LP in 1977.

Throughout the '80s, the number of Gold and Platinum awards going to country artists hovered between ten and twenty per year. By comparison, in 1994 nearly

291

LEFT: *In 1998 the Dixie Chicks took the country-music world by storm. From left are Natalie, Emily, and Martie.*
ABOVE: *Alabama. From left: Mark Herndon, Teddy Gentry, Jeff Cook, and Randy Owen on a calendar cover.*

The Judds

unusual in that, unlike rock, country did not generally promote self-contained bands.

Between 1980 and 1987 Alabama had twenty-one consecutive No. 1 records. In 1989 the Academy of Country Music named the band its Artist of the Decade. Alabama has now been on the charts longer than any other contemporary country act. And its popularity is in an upswing as the century draws to a close. *For the Record,* a compilation of forty-one No. 1 hits, was a Double Platinum sales success in 1998 and inspired a hit live cablecast from Las Vegas. The set also spawned the band's forty-second No. 1 hit. Alabama now has more chart-topping singles than any band in music history. In 1999 the group teamed up with the red-hot teen pop act 'N' Sync on the hit "God Must Have Spent a Little More Time on You."

By year's end Alabama's career sales topped sixty million records, ranking it alongside The Beatles, The Beach Boys, The Rolling Stones, and Chicago as one of the ten biggest-selling bands in the annals of popular music. Alabama has sold more concert tickets than any other country group. It has won more than 150 show-business awards.

"We've been so blessed," says Randy Owen. "I'm just a grateful ol' farm boy. I didn't start out to have No. 1 records and all this stuff with Alabama. Everybody in this band had just one goal when we started and that was to just have a job in the music business and not have to go back to factory work. Everybody in our hometown was saying, 'You guys will be back here in Fort Payne, Alabama, working in the sock mill or working on the farm, because you can't make a living playing music.' And most people don't. We are among the fortunate few."

The boys did, indeed, return to Fort Payne—not as common laborers as predicted, but as the town's most beloved citizens. Alabama's stardom paved the way for a number of other "youth-appeal" country bands, notably Exile (1983–92), Sawyer Brown (1984–present), Restless Heart (1984–98), Southern Pacific (1985–91), The Desert Rose Band (1986–94), Shenandoah (1987–present), The Kentucky HeadHunters (1989–98), and Little

seventy country artists were given RIAA Gold and Platinum plaques.

During the late '80s, Music Row's record companies had responded to the video revolution by grooming and marketing a completely new generation of country stars—attractive, suburban-looking folks who reached out to increasingly younger fans as well as to the genre's traditionally middle-aged consumers. Nashville exploded in importance in the music world as several of these young stars became the equals of the biggest acts in the pop-music world. For the first time in its history, country began to shed its inferiority complex, its underdog attitude, and its low-class stigma.

The earliest act with modern, "young-country" appeal was Alabama. Hailing from Fort Payne, Alabama, the group was composed of cousins Randy Owen and Teddy Gentry, distant cousin Jeff Cook, and drummer Mark Herndon. They'd honed their skills in a beer joint called The Bowery in Myrtle Beach, South Carolina. Some small-label singles led to an RCA recording contract in 1980. This was

TOP: *The "farewell tour" by The Judds was commemorated with this 1991 tour book.*

Kathy Mattea

Texas (1991–98). In addition to Alabama and Sawyer Brown, there are four other such bands who were hot on the charts as of 1999—Diamond Rio, The Mavericks, Ricochet, and Lonestar.

The Judds, who emerged in 1984, were a mother-daughter team who became wildly popular with young and old country fans alike. Their blend of folk, blues, and country-rock synthesized mama Naomi's love of mountain music with daughter Wynonna's infatuation with Bonnie Raitt and Emmylou Harris.

Naomi Judd (Diana Ellen Judd, born 1946) tended to dramatize and embellish the family's saga, but the general outline of the story is the following: She became pregnant in high school with Wynonna (Christine Ciminella, born 1964). Her marriage fell apart. She spent seven years in Los Angeles with daughters Wynonna and Ashley, the latter of whom later became a successful film actress. Returning to Kentucky in 1976, Naomi enlisted in nursing school and rented a mountain cottage with no TV or telephone. Wynonna turned to music to amuse herself. A two-year stint in the Bay Area included Naomi's working as an extra in *More American Graffiti.*

Mother and daughters moved to Nashville in 1979. Naomi worked as a nurse and badgered Music Row for an audition while Wynonna finished high school. Mama's unyielding faith in her daughter's abilities and dogged pursuit of opportunity led to an RCA/Curb recording contract in 1983. The freshness of The Judds' sound and the press appeal of a mother-daughter singing combination made them country's chart-topping wonders of 1984–91. Naomi tearfully announced the team's retirement because of her liver disease, and starred in a year-long farewell tour in 1991. Wynonna launched a successful solo career in 1992. The duo announced it would reunite for an

end-of-the-millennium concert in Phoenix on December 31, 1999.

The fresh approaches of acts like Alabama, Sawyer Brown, and The Judds in the mid-1980s was typical of Music Row's innovative climate during that time. In years past, country stars' careers would endure for decades. Now Nashville began patterning itself like the pop-music world by introducing new artists with more frequency. This process reached its zenith in 1986. In that year, more new stars were introduced into country's top twenty than ever before or since. Among the two-dozen breakthrough newcomers that year were Ricky Van Shelton, Keith Whitley, Kathy Mattea, Steve Earle, Dwight Yoakam, k.d. lang, Lyle Lovett, Nanci Griffith, and, most successful of all, Randy Travis.

Ricky Van Shelton (born 1952) is a native of Virginia with a supple baritone that was equally adept on rockabilly fare like "Crime of Passion" (1987) and ballads such as "I'll Leave This World Loving You" (1988).

293

TOP: *Kathea Mattea's 1994 CD featured "Walking Away a Winner."*
ABOVE: *Even pop-music magazines like* Pulse *recognized the charisma of Dwight Yoakam.*

Nanci Griffith

Kathy Mattea (born 1959), a product of the West Virginia mountains, brought a folkie sensibility to performances such as "Where've You Been" (1989) and "18 Wheels and a Dozen Roses" (1988). Kentucky-bred Dwight Yoakam (born 1956) brought an edgy, California honky-tonk attitude to hits like "Guitars, Cadillacs" (1986) and "Ain't That Lonely Yet" (1993). He also championed renewed respect for Buck Owens, with whom he duetted memorably on 1988's "Streets of Bakersfield."

Yoakam was among a number of artists who were embraced by the rock media as examples of Nashville's new hipness. Steve Earle's top-ten hits "Guitar Town" and "Goodbye's All We've Got Left" in 1986–87 were like hillbilly versions of Bruce Springsteen's blue-collar rock. The Texas-trained troubadour (born 1955) headed even more in that direction with his brilliant 1988 album *Copperhead Road*. He survived heroine addiction to become a respected Music Row producer, songwriter, record maker, and social activist of the late '90s, eventually embracing rock, folk, bluegrass, and gospel elements in his eclectic sound.

"Steve Earle really turned a lot of people on to country music who never, ever would have listened to it otherwise," believes Mary Chapin Carpenter. "It had muscle and it had attitude and it had edge."

"I feel bad about it, because I feel like I created the impression to younger artists that something really exciting was happening in Nashville," says Earle in retrospect. "And it really wasn't. It was more like a few really determined artists managed to slip through and make a little noise."

Like Earle, Lyle

Lovett and Nanci Griffith were recruited by Nashville producers from the Texas folk-music scene. As a writer Griffith was the source of Mattea's "Love at the Five and Dime," Suzy Bogguss's "Outbound Plane," and Willie Nelson's "Gulf Coast Highway." The former kindergarten teacher, born in 1954, was also the first to record the international brotherhood anthem "From a Distance."

"I had fallen in love with this song," she recalls. "And everyone at the record label said, 'There's no place for this song anywhere. I mean, this is just not "radio friendly."' Six years later, Bette Midler had the worldwide No. 1 hit with it."

Lyle Lovett (born 1956) initially appeared in the country top ten with "Cowboy Man" in 1986. Lovett soon expanded his folk-based musical palette to include horn sections, soul-gospel vocals, and other noncountry elements. Even so, he has been rewarded with three country Grammy Awards, including 1996's Best Country Album for his sublime *Road to Ensenada*.

Canada's k.d. lang was born Kathryn Dawn Lang in 1961 in Consort, Alberta. Easily the kookiest of the group, lang had a wildly physical stage show, wore a spikey crew-cut hairdo, and dressed in "retro" square-dance skirts, embroidered cowgirl blouses, and cut-off western boots. But she also had a wallop of a voice and devoutly wished to be the reincarnation of Patsy Cline. Fans as well as the Nashville industry loved her over-the-top performances, but radio shunned her records. Even without airplay *Shadowland* (1988) and *Absolute Torch and Twang* (1989) became Gold Records, and the latter won a Grammy.

294

TOP: *Nanci Griffith's LP introduced "From a Distance."*
ABOVE: *This 1996 CD won a Grammy for Lyle Lovett.*
RIGHT: *k.d. lang tried to recapture the spirit of Patsy Cline on her 1989 LP* Absolute Torch and Twang.

k.d. lang
AND THE RECLINES
ABSOLUTE
TORCH AND TWANG

1/2-25877

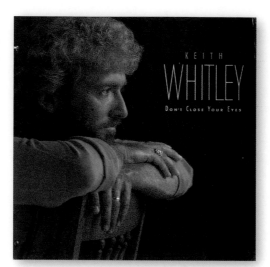

Nanci Griffith still has fond memories of the days when acts as "different" as Earle, Lovett, Yoakam, lang, and herself were promoted by country labels: "It was, 'Express yourself and be creative and don't worry about what cubbyhole you're supposed to fit in.'"

Traditionalists Keith Whitley and Randy Travis were out-of-step with the pop-country mainstream, too. Whitley's curlicued delivery harkened back to the honky-tonk stylings of Lefty Frizzell, whose Nashville grave he used to visit. Whitley (1955–1989) initially performed in Kentucky bluegrass bands. He was just fifteen when he and fellow teen Ricky Skaggs were recruited to tour with bluegrass legend Ralph Stanley. A 1978–83 stint as the lead vocalist of J.D. Crowe & The New South gave Whitley his first opportunities to record as a honky-tonk vocalist. He moved to Nashville to shoot for a major-label country contract in 1984.

In 1986 Whitley broke into the top ten with "Ten Feet Away" and "Homecoming '63." The video for the latter featured him with his new bride, singer Lorrie Morgan. His "Don't Close Your Eyes" was named the biggest country hit of 1988 by *Billboard* magazine. Its follow-up, "When You Say Nothing at All," also topped the charts. "I'm No Stranger to the Rain" was on its way to No. 1 in early 1989 when Whitley was found dead. With Morgan and manager Jack McFadden's help, he had been battling the disease of alcoholism for years. He lost his fight when he drank enough to kill himself while Morgan was on the road to promote her debut RCA album. A half-dozen posthumous hit singles, including the Whitley and Morgan duet "Til a Tear Becomes a Rose" confirmed that the country-music world had again tragically lost one of its most gifted vocalists.

North Carolinian Randy Travis (Randy Traywick, born 1959) had a similarly pure, true love for traditional country music. Of all of the members of the "Class of 1986," Travis would leave the most indelible mark.

"My dad was a huge country fan," says Travis. "He had a wonderful collection of records—Hank and Tex Ritter and all kind of different people. It's what I was exposed to, through him and my mom. It was what I grew to love and all I really cared about."

It was also what saved him. Travis was a hell-raising youngster who was constantly in trouble with local law officials. He was doing drugs and using alcohol by his midteens. A string of offenses, including burglary, were pointing him toward a jail term when Charlotte, North Carolina, nightclub manager Lib Hatcher hired him, took him in, and pointed him on the straight and narrow.

She believed so strongly in her discovery that she left her husband and moved to Nashville with Travis in 1981. She took a job managing The Nashville Palace club near Opryland. He became its short-order cook and sometime vocalist. Hatcher repeatedly hounded Music Row's executives about the singer's earthy, back-to-basics delivery. Despite the support of *Opry* stars such as Jimmy Dickens and Johnny Russell, Travis was initially rejected by the modern Music Row executives.

"I had been turned down by every label in town two or three times," Travis remembers. "They would say I was 'too country' and it doesn't sell records. Sometimes people are slow to see what is very obvious."

ABOVE: *The title tune to this Keith Whitley LP became the biggest country hit of 1988, according to* Billboard *magazine.*
RIGHT: *This issue of the aptly named* New Country *magazine saluted multi-million seller Randy Travis.*

Clint Black

Warner Bros. Records finally gave Randy Travis a try in 1985. As the year drew to a close, the label issued a single called "1982" during Christmas week. In the early weeks of the new year the single sprinted up the charts. Travis's ear-catching baritone twang, muscular physique, and square-jawed good looks made him an "overnight" sensation. "On the Other Hand," "Diggin' Up Bones," "Forever and Ever Amen," and the like, led to sales of more than thirteen million records by the end of the 1980s. He and Hatcher wed in 1990.

As of 1998, ten Randy Travis albums had been declared Gold, Platinum, or Multi-Platinum. *Always & Forever* (1987), alone, has sold more than five million copies. In the 1990s, Travis branched out into acting in movies and television dramas.

Randy Travis was dubbed the leader of Nashville's "new-traditionalist" movement. And his phenomenal breakthrough led Nashville in search of other performers who could present earthy country music in young, updated ways. More than anyone, he paved the way for the "Class of 1989."

In that year, Clint Black, Travis Tritt, Alan Jackson, and Garth Brooks all staged their chart debuts. In 1989 Vince Gill signed with MCA Records, the label that would make him a superstar. In 1989 Mary Chapin Carpenter released her first top-ten hit. These six performers heralded the dawn of the "young-country" era.

Houston-reared Clint Black

(born 1962) was the first of these artists to kick up dust. The high school dropout's debut single, "A Better Man," entered the charts in February 1989 and went straight to No. 1.

"It's wonderful when your dreams come true," he said at the time. "I've pretty much been living off nightclub gigs for the past eight or nine years. Now I find I can keep up with the bills. This is like stepping into a picture you've been looking at all your life."

A poetic songwriter, he is the only one of this group who has written all of his twenty-seven top-ten hits of 1989–99. Like the others, Black was young when his chart career began. He was twenty-seven in 1989.

Next up was Garth Brooks, then twenty-six. His "Much Too Young to Feel This Damn Old" entered the charts in March. It made the top-ten, but it was "If Tomorrow Never Comes," released in September, that made him a star. Then the former college track star, nightclub bouncer, and boot salesman issued a series of hits that made him the biggest-selling recording artist of the 1990s. Equally effective with tearjerkers ("The Dance") and rockers ("Shameless"), Brooks was gunning for a hundred million in sales by the dawn of the new millennium.

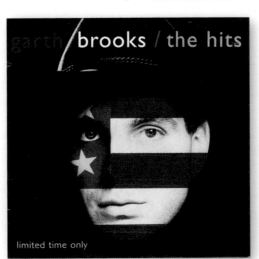

"Maybe when it's the last day of my life, I can look back and say, 'I made it through the door,'" comments Brooks somberly. "I've had very fortunate luck with the charts. A lot of people call me a 'darker' kind of guy. That's cool. I love to sink in thought. I take my music very seriously."

297

TOP: BMI Music World *concentrates on songwriting success stories, and Clint Black is certainly one of those.*
ABOVE: *Garth Brooks's 1995 collection helped drive his record sales toward the 100 million mark.*

Born in 1962, the Oklahoma native is the son of former *Ozark Jubilee* performer Colleen Carroll. But Brooks says he was as influenced by rock acts such as Kiss and Billy Joel as he was by George Jones and George Strait. In 1999 he adopted the pop-music guise of "Chris Gaines," issuing a noncountry record in advance of a film to feature that character.

The stupendous success of Garth Brooks in the early 1990s led the national media to Nashville's doorstep. Once again, the media "discovered" America's most enduring musical style. *Fortune, Entertainment Weekly, USA Today, Time* ("Country's Big Boom"), and the *New Republic* ("The Voice of America") all devoted cover stories to the young-country phenomenon. Most featured Garth Brooks as their cover boy. *People* and *USA Weekend* created special country sections. TV's *Entertainment Tonight* headquartered its music division in Nashville.

There were plenty of stories to cover. When before in the annals of country music had there been a performer with a degree in American civilization from Brown University? That was the tale of Mary Chapin Carpenter. Born in Princeton, New Jersey, in 1959, she'd been partly raised overseas, in Japan. She was working for a grant organization in Washington, D.C., and singing folk songs in the evenings when she was discovered by Columbia Records in 1987.

Her "homemade" LP *Hometown Girl* garnered favorable reviews when it was issued by the label in 1988, but was not commercially successful. Given a bigger recording budget, she crafted 1989's *State of the Heart*. She entered the charts in April

with its sprightly single "How Do." Like Brooks, she would do better on her second single, September's "Never Had It So Good," a top-ten success.

"I have to be brutally honest and say that mainstream country music is not what I grew up with," she says. "I was incredibly surprised to have country success. Still am."

That success would increase dramatically with her Cajun-flavored 1991 hit "Down at the Twist and Shout" and her three-million-selling *Come On, Come On* album of 1992. The collection spawned seven hit singles, including "Passionate Kisses," "I Feel Lucky," and "He Thinks He'll Keep Her."

The youngest member of the "Class of 1989" is Travis Tritt. The Georgia native was twenty-five when he got his recording contract and had just turned twenty-six when "Country Club" first appeared on the charts in September. His long hair, shoot-from-the-hip style, and biker image made him the inheritor of the outlaw tradition, and he cited Waylon Jennings as a major inspiration.

His label already had Randy Travis, but Travis Tritt refused to change his name. Although cowboy hats were in vogue, he refused to wear one. He was told his hair was too long and that his sound was too rocking.

"There were shouting matches," he recalls. "They didn't want me to be as rock 'n' roll as I am. Charlie Daniels gave me probably the best advice: 'Screw what the record company thinks. Find your audience and see what they want.'"

The people spoke. *Country Club* was the biggest-selling album at the

298

TOP: *Mary Chapin Carpenter's single was a chart champ.*
ABOVE: *Travis Tritt published an autobiography at age 30.*
RIGHT: *Most of the hot new country acts of the '90s, including Alan Jackson, are members of the Opry.*

OPRYLAND USA.

CELEBRATING SEVENTY YEARS OF THE
GRAND OLE OPRY
1925-1995

Opry member Alan Jackson

1990 Fan Fair and earned Tritt the first of his seven consecutive million-selling discs. By decade's end, his record sales exceeded seventeen million units, thanks to hits like 1991's "Here's a Quarter (Call Someone Who Cares)" and 1992's "Lord Have Mercy on the Working Man."

Of the group, Alan Jackson is the most "country" in background, attitude, and musical approach. Born in Georgia in 1958, he grew up poor as the son of a rural auto mechanic. Perhaps the least savvy about the ways of the music business, he carried a deep sense of humility and gratitude with him after his star began to rise in the 1990s.

"I had no earthly idea what a publisher was, or a producer, or anything," he says. "I loved music, but I didn't grow up thinking I'd ever get to do it professionally. That was another world.

"I just wanted to carry on the tradition of Real Country Music. You know that George Jones song, 'Who's Gonna Fill Their Shoes?' I don't know whether I can fill 'em, but I'd sure like to try 'em on."

His career began when his flight-attendant wife, Denise, approached Glen Campbell in an airport and asked for advice for her aspiring singer husband. The star gave her his Nashville business card, and the couple moved to Music City in 1985. Jackson took a job in the mailroom at TNN. Campbell's music publishing company got him an Arista Records contract, and Jackson's debut single, "Blue Blooded Woman," was released in October 1989. He joined his "classmates" in the top ten with "Here in the Real World" in early 1990.

Alan Jackson be-

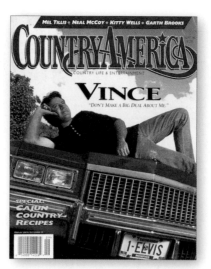

came the standard-bearer for hard-core honky-tonk music with such hits as "Don't Rock the Jukebox," "Chattahoochie," "Gone Country," "Between the Devil and Me," and "Little Man." In the summer of 1999 he celebrated his tenth anniversary with Arista when the label presented him with a plaque marking twenty-seven million in sales.

The honesty, integrity, and fundamental values that characterize Jackson's approach to his career are also hallmarks of Vince Gill. With his simple dignity, easygoing humor, unfailing generosity, and effortless graciousness, Gill would become the most beloved country star of his generation.

Born in Oklahoma in 1957, Vince Gill had been kicking around the music business for years before his big breakthrough in the 1990s. In the 1970s he performed in bluegrass bands. He then became the lead singer for the country-rock group Pure Prairie League, scoring a pop hit with "Let Me Love You Tonight" in 1980. A stint as the lead guitarist in The Cherry Bombs, the backing group for Rodney Crowell and Rosanne Cash, led Gill to move to Nashville in 1984.

He recorded three top-ten hits for RCA in 1985–87, but did not ascend to superstardom until

signing with MCA in 1989. In 1990 Vince Gill broke through with "When I Call Your Name." This tear-stained ballad set the mood for such tender-hearted performances as "I Still Believe in You," "Worlds Apart," "Pretty Little Adriana," and "Go Rest High on That Mountain." Gill is a superb electric guitarist, a skill he generally showcases on his up-tempo numbers like "Don't Let Your Love Start Slippin' Away" and "One More Last Chance."

TOP: *Vince Gill's easy-going wit and humor are captured on this magazine cover.*
ABOVE: *Marty Stuart's love of tradition made him a natural for this salute to the Country Music Hall of Fame.*

Billy Ray Cyrus

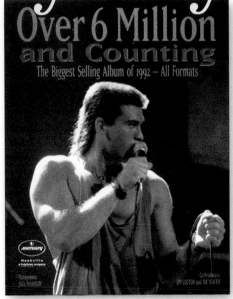

Gill's songwriting talent, instrumental abilities, and pure tenor voice made him a prolific collaborator on Music Row. He has contributed to the success of dozens of other artists' records and is enormously popular in the music community. Vince Gill has won more Grammy Awards, twelve, than any other singer in country-music history. His seventeen Country Music Association Awards are also unmatched in country's annals.

The 1989 advents of Gill, Jackson, Tritt, Brooks, Carpenter, and Black were only the beginning. A year later vocal powerhouse Joe Diffie, hard-core country Mark Chesnutt, Hank Williams disciple Aaron Tippin, "I'd Be Better Off (In a Pine Box)" singer Doug Stone, and the multitalented Marty Stuart all achieved chart breakthroughs.

Texan Mark Chesnutt (born 1963) was one of a number of Beaumont-area vocalists who would rise to prominence during the next few years. His "Too Cold at Home," "Brother Jukebox," "It Sure Is Monday," and "Bubba Shot the Jukebox" demonstrated the continuing vitality of the honky-tonk tradition.

More than any other performer of the era, Mississippian Marty Stuart (born 1958) "connected the dots" between country's heritage and its future. The charismatic mandolinist, songwriter, photographer, journalist, and industry spokesman is equally at home among bluegrass audiences and punk rockers. Stuart joined Lester Flatt's band at age thirteen, became a member of the Johnny Cash troupe in his twenties and recorded as a neo-rockabilly in the 1980s before

achieving stardom with 1990's aptly titled "Hillbilly Rock."

Paced by Garth Brooks, these 1989–90 artists created a groundswell of interest in country music. During the mid-'90s, the style gained nearly ten million new radio listeners per year; and during the same period more than five hundred U.S. stations switched to the booming country format. Communities such as Branson, Missouri; Pigeon Forge, Tennessee; and Myrtle Beach, South Carolina, built entire tourism businesses around country music. Las Vegas showrooms, European festivals, and New York nightclubs became regular stopping places on country-star tours.

Many reasons have been offered for this unprecedented upsurge. Video played a part. But recording technology did, too. Country was the first genre to convert en masse from magnetic tape to the digital recording format. It was also the first to fully embrace the compact disc. Nashville dropped the vinyl LP in 1990, just as these artists were emerging. Digital and CD technology tended to favor crisp, high-end sounds, which was a boon to acoustic instruments and vocal-oriented styles.

Around the same time, the pop/rock world apparently forgot the simple pleasures of dancing. The country industry jumped into the void by creating easy-to-learn, "line-dance" steps, building country dance clubs, and recording catchy novelty dance tunes.

"Boot Scootin' Boogie" and "Achy Breaky Heart," both issued in 1992, typified the new style of country dance records. The former was recorded by Brooks & Dunn. Comprised of singer-songwriters Kix Brooks

301

TOP: *The sales accomplishments of Billy Ray Cyrus were touted on this promotional flyer.*
ABOVE: *Texas cowboy George Strait was introduced to the world on this 1981 LP.*

John

and Ronnie Dunn, this duo initially appeared on the charts in 1991 with "Brand New Man." Neither Louisiana's Brooks (born 1955) nor Oklahoma's Dunn (born 1953) were starry-eyed kids. The former was a Music Row songwriter, and the latter was a longtime fixture of his home state's honky-tonk circuit. Both had recorded as solo acts with no success.

But as a team they built a rocking, energetic, youth-oriented "party" stage show and raked in dozens of awards. Dunn's searing tenor roared "My Maria," "Hard Workin' Man," and the like, while Brooks's raspy baritone drawled "You're Gonna Miss Me When I'm Gone," "Rock My World (Little Country Girl)," and other hits.

"Achy Breaky Heart" was sung by the extravagantly handsome Billy Ray Cyrus. Born in 1961, the Kentucky native was a ten-year "overnight success" story on Music Row. Cyrus worked his way up on the bar circuit in eastern Kentucky and West Virginia. With his tennis shoes, athletic shirts, and long hair, he was an anomaly in the cowboy-costumed 1990s. Unlike his contemporaries, he recorded with his own band, Sly Dog. His churning, rocking sound is quite distinctive, and so is the level of commitment he displays to his audience. Even by country standards, the amount of charity work he does is staggering. Because his early hits were so catchy, he became an instant favorite with children, in particular. As a result, Cyrus has held scores of dying, crippled, and infirm tots in his arms.

"I try to put on a real strong face for the kids," he says. "It is emotionally draining; you just feel weak and sad. But I've tried to make sure that I live up to my end of the deal with God. My dream was to be a successful singer, songwriter and entertainer. I prayed that my music would be heard around the world and that God would give me the vision to use my music to do good things. So I am going to see as many of these children as I can."

His debut CD, *Some Gave All,* became one of the ten biggest-selling albums of the '90s, regardless of genre. By 1994 Cyrus had sold more than thirteen million records. He suffered through an industry backlash against his peppy sound and unorthodox image before returning to the top ten with "Busy Man" in 1999.

They say that "a rising tide lifts all boats," and this was certainly true in Nashville in the early '90s. The hot newcomers created such excitement that the careers of a number of their predecessors were reignited.

Sawyer Brown, for instance, had graduated in 1984 from TV's talent contest *Star Search* to score a number of hits in the '80s. But the band's fortunes soared far higher after its revival with "The Dirt Road," "Cafe on the Corner," and "All These Years" in 1991–92.

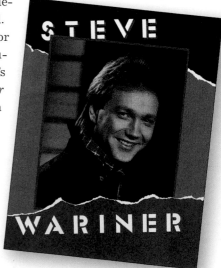

TOP: *John Michael Montgomery's CDs have sold millions.*
ABOVE: *A backstage pass for a performance by Sawyer Brown.*
RIGHT: *Steve Wariner on an early tour book.*
OPPOSITE: *John Anderson has had repeated career revivals.*

Anderson

Kellogg's

CORN
FLAKES®

K

The Original & Best®

RONNIE
DUNN

KIX
BROOKS

**BROOKS
& DUNN**

53

K. T. Oslin

Florida native and former Nashville beer-joint vocalist John Anderson (born 1954) had been considered a major force in the new-traditionalist movement of the '80s with "Swingin'" and other hits. But he, too, achieved dramatically renewed popularity in 1991–92 with "Straight Tequila Nights," "Seminole Wind," and more.

Indiana's Steve Wariner (born 1954) had logged time in the bands of Dottie West, Bob Luman, and Chet Atkins as a teen. He was a veteran of more than twenty top-ten hits when he issued "Leave Him out of This," "The Tips of My Fingers," and "A Woman Loves" in 1991–92. This trio of tunes resulted in his first Gold Record. With a career boost from Garth Brooks, Wariner rebounded again in 1998–99 with "Holes in the Floor of Heaven" and "Two Teardrops."

In addition to Cyrus, Chesnutt, Stuart, Diffie, and their peers, a number of other new performers exploded in popularity in 1991–93. The pacesetter was Kentucky's John Michael Montgomery (born 1965), who sold fifteen million records in 1993–99 thanks to hits like "I Swear" and "Sold (The Grundy County Auction Incident)." Others included Tracy Lawrence, Collin Raye,

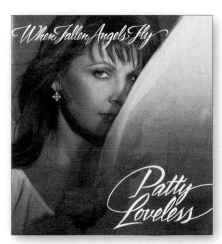

Sammy Kershaw, Clay Walker, Neal McCoy, Kenny Chesney, Toby Keith, and Tracy Byrd, all of whom ascended to million-selling status. These new-breed country stars were dubbed "hot hunks" for their heartthrob looks, or "hat acts" because they generally wore cowboy hats, whether or not they could actually ride a horse. To one degree or another, they were patterned after the originator of this trend, George Strait.

Strait (born 1952) was "the Real McCoy," raised on a two-thousand-acre ranch in Texas. He was then, and is now, simply a genuine cowboy with a genuine love of country music. That love led him to post a notice on his college bulletin board in 1975. "Country Singer Needs Band" it said. A group of students looked him up. Dubbed The Ace in the Hole Band, the combo made its debut in San Marcos, Texas, that fall. Local club owner Erv Woolsey liked what he heard.

While working as a foreman on a Texas cattle ranch, Strait recorded singles in the Lone Star State in 1976–79 and became a top regional attraction. Meanwhile, Woolsey was climbing to a vice presidency at MCA in Nashville. In 1980 the two men reunited, found a tune called "Unwound," and lobbied the label to sign the shy fellow in the cowboy hat. Strait was told to get rid of his western look. He refused.

"Unwound" became the first of George Strait's string of more than thirty-five top-ten hits in early 1981. By 1984 he was a key figure of the new-traditionalist movement. Honky-tonk lovers looked upon Strait as a savior who had rescued their music from pop-country oblivion. The awards and Gold Records were rolling in by 1985. As the '80s became the '90s, Strait basked in two consecutive wins as country's Entertainer of the Year. Newcomers like Garth Brooks, Alan Jackson, and Clint Black were

305

citing him as their inspiration, but Strait was far from finished. He graduated to movie stardom with *Pure Country* in 1992 and assembled country's largest-selling boxed CD set, *Strait out of the Box,* in 1995.

Then "Blue Clear Sky," "One Night at a Time," "Today My World Slipped Away," and others made him country's top singles artist of 1996 and 1997. Another wave of country newcomers was now citing him as a role model—Clay Walker, Tracy Byrd, Mark Wills, and others—but Strait kept outslugging every rookie on the field. He was named the CMA's Male Vocalist of the Year in 1996, 1997, and 1998. All twenty-three of his MCA albums remain in print in the new millennium. All of them are Gold, Platinum, or Multi-Platinum.

In the wake of the sales successes of the Strait-inspired hat acts, record labels scrambled to sign dozens of handsome young new traditionalists. Most of them took Strait's honky-tonk style and applied a heavy dose of backbeat to "turbo-charge" the country sound. This fit with the development of country line-dance nightclubs, the increasing flash of music videos, and the ever more physical and energetic stage shows spurred by Garth Brooks and Brooks & Dunn.

By 1997 more than twenty country stars were topping the $1 million mark in annual concert revenues. Most of them were men. For one consequence of the hat-act sales boom was that country's women lost much of the ground they'd gained during the previous three decades. In

1990, women's share of the country charts dived to 12 percent, its lowest level since the early 1960s.

Of the '80s female acts, Reba McEntire, Tanya Tucker, and Wynonna Judd retained their hit-making ways. But between 1989 and 1993 only four million-selling female stars emerged alongside the multitude of new males: Lorrie Morgan, Pam Tillis, Suzy Bogguss, and K.T. Oslin.

Oslin's success is all the more unusual in that of all the new artists, male or female, she was the only mature adult. Born Kay Toinette Oslin in 1942 and raised in Houston, she was a Broadway chorus girl and ad-jingle singer who broke through on the charts at the age of forty-five. Her torchy delivery, witty songwriting, and Patsy Cline sass captivated listeners.

"80's Ladies," released in 1987, was sung with throbbing conviction and backed with a pounding rhythm track. It made K.T. Oslin the first female songwriter in history to win Song of the Year honors at the CMA Awards. "Do Ya," "Come Next Monday," and other hits carried her into the '90s.

But after the failure of her innovative 1996 CD *My Roots Are Showing,* Oslin retired from the recording scene.

The turnaround for country's female acts began in the mid-1990s. Kentucky-bred Patty Loveless (Patricia Ramey, born 1957) led the charge. Loveless was trained in the "old school," having learned the business as a teenager backstage at the *Opry* with Dolly Parton, Porter Wagoner, and The Wilburn Brothers. She is a cousin of Loretta Lynn.

Loveless began having top-ten

TOP: *Martina McBride's* Evolution *CD sold a million and led to multiple award nominations in 1999.*
ABOVE: *The trade publication* Music Row *recognized Faith Hill's pop crossover success with this cover story.*

hits in 1988–90. But it was her resurgence in 1993–95 that put her on equal footing with the "hot hunks." "Blame It on Your Heart," "How Can I Help You Say Goodbye," "I Try to Think About Elvis," "Lonely Too Long," and her other hits of the era demonstrated an equal flair for frisky country-rockers and gutbucket country "weepers."

Georgia's Trisha Yearwood (born 1964) came to Nashville to go to music-business school at Belmont College, landed a job as a Music Row receptionist, and began singing demo tapes for songwriters. Her larger-than-life vocal talent led to a recording contract in 1991.

An admirer of Linda Ronstadt, Yearwood has a similarly powerful singing delivery. She debuted on the charts with "She's in Love with the Boy," "Wrong Side of Memphis," "Walkaway Joe," and other hits of 1991–92; began her touring career as the opening act for Garth Brooks; hit her stride as a star with 1996's "Believe Me Baby (I Lied)"; and then muscled her way to country queendom in 1997 with her pop ballad "How Do I Live" and her Garth Brooks duet "In Another's Eyes."

The electrifying soprano Martina McBride was right behind her. The Kansas farm girl (born 1966) was in awe of Connie Smith, Jeannie C. Riley, and the other women of the '60s and '70s. The spine-tingling "Independence Day" and "Wild Angels" of 1994–95 made McBride one of the most admired vocalists of her generation. When Yearwood was opening for Garth Brooks, McBride was selling t-shirts in the lobby. She succeeded Yearwood as the superstar's opening act.

"I tend to sing songs that portray women with a lot of strength and dignity and respect," says McBride. "I really believe that the music that women are making now is unique, individual. I don't sound like Trisha Yearwood's music. Trisha Yearwood's music doesn't sound like Faith Hill's. We bring a sense of ourselves to the music."

Faith Hill was next on the scene. Born in Mississippi in 1967, the blonde beauty worked in the offices of several music-industry figures, including Gary Morris and Reba McEntire. She emerged with "Wild One" as her debut hit in 1993. Hill continued to have steady success throughout the decade, but leaped to a level of stardom most of her male peers never even got near when "This Kiss" crossed over to the pop charts in 1998 and her Faith album went Triple Platinum.

Canadian Terri Clark, bluegrass star Alison Krauss, pop-country Mindy McCready, and earthy troubadour Deana Carter were among the women who rose to million-selling status in 1995–96. This surge forward for female performers was capped

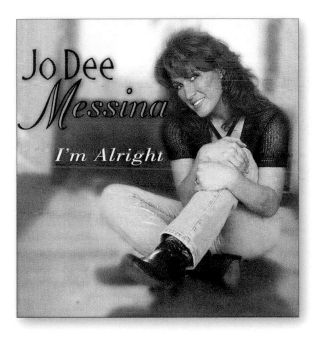

by the titanic success achieved by their "classmate" Shania Twain.

Twain, born Eileen Edwards in 1965, was adopted by her Ojibwa Indian stepfather and raised in the mining country of northern Ontario, Canada. After he and her mother were killed in a traffic accident when she was twenty-one, she raised her younger brothers on her own. Work as a vocalist at a Canadian resort led to a Nashville recording contract in 1992. Early singles were only moderately successful, but her videos attracted quite a bit of at-

307

ABOVE: *The just-folks approach of Jo Dee Messina led to multiple No. 1 hits from this CD.*

LeAnn Rimes

tention. Rock producer Robert John "Mutt" Lange saw them, telephoned her, and came to Nashville to meet her during Fan Fair 1993. They were married that December.

As songwriting collaborators, the team began turning out a series of dance-floor-ready singles that vaulted her to stardom in 1995–96. Lange's productions were multilayered sonic creations that broke new ground in country music. So did Shania Twain's image. Wearing outfits that bared her midriff, she brought a candid, wholesome sex-

iness to the field. Little girls loved her visual style and her bouncy sound.

In 1998 Twain issued the liquid ballad "You're Still the One." It crossed over to become a giant pop hit. She became the first female artist in history to have two albums selling more than eleven million copies apiece, 1995's *The Woman In Me* and 1998's *Come On Over.* She toured the globe in 1998–99, showcasing a vibrantly energetic command of the stage.

Due to her spectacular accomplishments and the arrivals of a dazzlingly diverse group of other country female performers, journalists hailed 1998 as "the year

of the woman." The male performers who had so dominated the early part of the decade now seemed to be merely carbon copies of one another. Women, on the other hand, were perceived as creating the most refreshing sounds and were viewed as the industry's new musical leaders.

As the decade—and the century—drew to a close, female performers were, indeed, providing the most diversity. The arrivals of such distinctive stylists as Lee Ann Womack, The Kinleys, Anita Cochran, SHeDAISY, and Sara Evans in 1997–99 illustrated this eloquently. The down-to-earth approach favored by Jo Dee Messina put her at the forefront. Messina dominated the charts of the late '90s with direct, female-oriented material such as "Heads Carolina Tails California," "Bye Bye," and "I'm Alright."

"There's a lot more independent women out there, taking a stronger stand for things," Messina comments. "And the music reflects that."

Raised in Massachusetts, Messina (born 1970) worked as a computer operator after she arrived in Music City in 1990. At one point her fortunes were so low that the utilities were cut off in her apartment. Despite a series of personal and professional setbacks she persevered, finally landing a recording contract in 1994 and achieving chart-topping disc stardom four years later.

Female performers also led the "teen-country" movement that emerged in the late '90s. Teenage performers such as Jessica Andrews, The Wilkinsons, Lila McCann, Alecia Elliott, and Rebecca Lynn Howard demonstrated that country could reach out to an ever younger demographic group. Some male figures were also part of this trend, notably Bryan White and South Sixty-Five.

But its biggest star was LeAnn Rimes. Born in 1982, this product of the Dallas talent-contest circuit was just thirteen when the yodel ballad "Blue" made her a star in 1996. Incredibly, she was already a seasoned stage and recording artist

ABOVE: *This CD by Lee Ann Rimes hit the charts when she was 14 years old and sold more than three million copies.*
RIGHT: *Stardom was predicted for Trisha Yearwood on this promotional flyer.*

Trisha Yea

"Move Over Boys, Here Comes a Star"

Robert Oermann, The Tennessean, June 20, 1992

CMA
AWARDS
NOMINEE

HORIZON AWARD
FEMALE VOCALIST OF THE YEAR

wood Trisha YEARWOOD

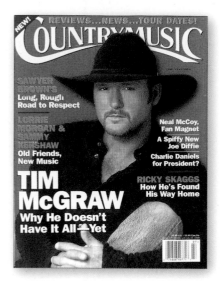

by then. Rimes won her first talent contest at age five, competed on TV's *Star Search* at age eight, and recorded her first CD at age eleven.

Propelled by singles such as "One Way Ticket," the *Blue* album sold more than three million copies. Rimes won the Best New Artist Grammy and the CMA's Horizon Award. In 1997 she crossed over to the pop charts with "How Do I Live," and in 1999 she became Elton John's duet partner.

"I think women have pretty much dominated the whole music industry over the past three or four years," says Rimes. "Right now, all kinds of music have blended together. Pop has gone country. Country has gone pop. And it's really brought a lot of people to country music."

In addition to the mass march forward of female performers, the country scene of the late '90s was characterized by the emergence of a new generation of humorists. Atlanta-bred country comic Jeff Foxworthy (born 1958) recorded the biggest-selling humor album in history, sold more than two million "redneck" funny books, and landed his own network TV series. He was soon joined by Bill Engvall, Cledus T. Judd, the fictitious "Roy D. Mercer," Tim Wilson, and a number of other comics.

The career of singer Tim McGraw grew in intensity with each year as the decade wound down. Born out of wedlock and raised in poverty in Louisiana, McGraw learned at age twelve that he was the son of

310

famed New York Mets pitcher Tug McGraw. As a teenager he was captivated by the voice of Keith Whitley. He arrived in Nashville on the day his idol died in 1989. After Tim sang for several years in the clubs, his father arranged a meeting for him with Curb Records.

Initial efforts for the label went nowhere. But Tim McGraw's 1994 collection *Not a Moment Too Soon* exploded on the charts and became the best-selling country CD of the year. The five-million-selling album contained five hit singles, including the dance club favorite "Indian Outlaw" and the tear-jerking "Don't Take the Girl." The follow-up album, *All I Want,* sold two million, again combining the rowdy ("I Like It, I Love It") with the tender ("Can't Be Really Gone"). He and touring partner Faith Hill fell in love and were married in 1996. Their award-winning 1997 duet "It's Your Love" made them "Mr. and Mrs. Country Music" in fans' eyes and helped propel his *Everywhere* CD to three million in sales. During 1995–99 Nashville continued to turn out other promising male performers, notably Ty Herndon, Jeff Carson, Wade Hayes, Trace Adkins, David Kersh, Mark Wills, and Michael Peterson. But a faction of country music emerged that rejected the "star-making machinery" of Music Row. This movement wanted to restore the grit of country's past and began to develop "alternative-country" stars. Variously described "Americana," "alt country," and "roots revival," the breakaway artists were embraced and promoted by the trade publication *Gavin* as they developed their own radio niche.

Americana's stars are an eclectic bunch. Some are exiles from the country charts, such as Emmylou Harris, Kevin Welch, Kelly Willis, Lyle Lovett, Joy Lynn White,

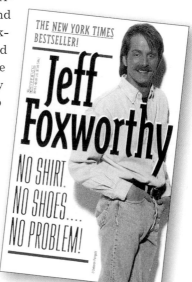

TOP: *Tim McGraw on the eve of his Entertainer of the Year nomination in 1999 as country music's cover boy.*
RIGHT: *Jeff Foxworthy's "You might be a redneck" routine led to network TV stardom and his own 1996 humor book.*

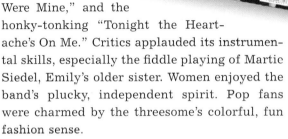

and Steve Earle. Some are established, cult-figure song poets—Lucinda Williams, Dave Olney, John Prine, Tom Russell, Jesse Winchester, and the like. Some, such as Dwight Yoakam, Mary Chapin Carpenter and The Mavericks, are mainstream country artists with Americana appeal. Bluegrass acts like Ricky Skaggs, Alison Krauss, and Laurie Lewis are embraced by the format. So are country legends who are "too old" for country radio—Waylon Jennings, Johnny Cash, Johnny Paycheck, Hank Thompson, Merle Haggard, Tom T. Hall, and others. The new field has also developed a number of artists of its own, including Dale Watson, Rosie Flores, Heather Myles, Buddy Miller, Pete Anderson, Fred Eaglesmith, and The Dead Reckoners. Most of them record for independent labels, but even Music Row's conglomerates have signed Americana talents, notably Kim Richey (Mercury), BR5-49 (Arista), Chris Knight (MCA), Jim Lauderdale (RCA), Bruce Robison (Sony), Junior Brown (Curb), and Monte Warden (Asylum).

"Alternative country is more of a rootsy kind of country," comments Asylum executive Evelyn Shriver. "And artistically speaking, it's a better kind of country music. It's the country that real music lovers embrace. And it's the kind of country that if we could ever get it on the radio, the people would absolutely love."

Dixie Chicks cooked up a musical stew that virtually everyone approved of in 1998–99. *Wide Open Spaces*, the Texas trio's major-label debut, stunned and delighted the industry by selling more than six million copies. The group was connected to the Americana movement in that lead singer Natalie Maines's father Lloyd is a producer of a number of the genre's acts

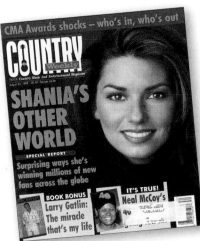

and banjo/dobro player Emily Erwin married Americana stylist Charlie Robison. Mainstream country loved Dixie Chicks because of the band's feisty songs—"I Can Love You Better," "There's Your Trouble," "You Were Mine," and the honky-tonking "Tonight the Heartache's On Me." Critics applauded its instrumental skills, especially the fiddle playing of Martic Siedel, Emily's older sister. Women enjoyed the band's plucky, independent spirit. Pop fans were charmed by the threesome's colorful, fun fashion sense.

"There's a lot more pressure on artists," says Emily Robison. "Not only do they have to put out a great album, but they have to appeal to people's eyes as well. That's fun for us. We love gettin' dressed up and bein' girls and doin' the fashion thing. But your music has to back you up. The music has to be there."

"We take pride that we're bringing back older, traditional sounding things and making it sound more modern," says Natalie Maines. That sentiment remained at the heart of country music in 1999. After a hundred years of development and a ten-year rocketship ride to unprecedented popularity, country continues to honor its traditions like no other style.

"The thing that I feel is important in country music is that we don't lose the heart of it," comments Martina McBride. "And we don't lose respect for the heritage."

Says Marty Stuart, "At the end of the day, we're hillbilly pickers. That keeps it in perspective for me. I'm a hillbilly guitar player, hillbilly mandolin player, hillbilly singer. And damn proud of it."

311

LEFT: *By the close of the '90s country was so popular it had its own weekly supermarket tabloid.*
ABOVE: *Dixie Chicks flaunt it as 1999 cover stars.*

Index

Robert K. Oermann

Dubbed "the dean of Nashville's entertainment journalists," Robert K. Oermann is a multi-media figure in Music City. As a TV personality he is seen on TNN and many other networks. He is the editor-at-large of *Country Music* magazine, is a columnist for the *Music Row* trade periodical and works as a consultant for the Hot Hits jukebox programming service. He has been scripting national radio broadcasts since 1981.

He is also a writer/producer for television whose scripts include specials for stars such as Vince Gill, Conway Twitty, Billy Ray Cyrus, and Dolly Parton, as well as regular programming for the CMT video channel. This is his sixth book. Among his prior authored works are *America's Music* (1996), *Finding Her Voice* (1993) and *The Listener's Guide To Country Music* (1983).

Oermann's honors include the Nashville Music Award (1996), a CMA Award (1988), ASCAP's Deems Taylor Award (1994) and the SESAC Journalistic Achievement Award (1983). He is a national trustee of the Recording Academy.

Born and raised in Pittsburgh, Oermann worked for his grand-mother's record shop from the age of ten. He has a degree in Fine Arts from the University of Pittsburgh and a masters in Information Studies from Syracuse. In Nashville since 1978, he was formerly Head of Technical Services at the archives of the Country Music Hall of Fame & Museum. He has one of the largest private record collections in Music City.